FROMMER'S
EasyGuide

TO
MADRID AND
BARCELONA

By
Patricia Harris and David Lyon

EasyGuides are ✦ Quick To Read ✦ Light To Carry
✦ For Expert Advice ✦ In All Price Ranges

FrommerMedia LLC

Published by
FROMMERMEDIA LLC

ISBN 978-1-62887-004-6 (paper), 978-1-62887-034-3 (e-book)

Editorial Director: Pauline Frommer
Editor: Arthur Frommer
Production Editor: Heather Wilcox
Cartographer: Elizabeth Puhl
Cover Design: Howard Grossman

For information on our other products or services, see www.frommers.com.

FrommerMedia LLC also publishes its books in a variety of electronic formats. Some content that appears in print may not be available in electronic formats.

Manufactured in the United States of America

5 4 3 2 1

CONTENTS

ABOUT THE AUTHORS

Patricia Harris and **David Lyon** drove almost every twisting mountain road in Iberia as they researched three previous Frommer's guides to Spain. But much as they enjoy the countryside, they find themselves inexorably drawn to the great cities of Madrid and Barcelona, where Spanish life and culture are writ large. Founders of HungryTravelers.com, they have a deep appreciation for the perfect codfish croqueta, an honest plate of patatas bravas, or a heap of peel-and-eat garlic shrimp—ideally consumed at an outdoor table in one of Barcelona's ancient squares or at the crowded bar in a Madrid taberna. They write about travel, food, wine, spirits, and contemporary art for journals as varied as the *Robb Report*, the *Boston Globe*, and *Westways*.

ABOUT THE FROMMER TRAVEL GUIDES

For most of the past 50 years, Frommer's has been the leading series of travel guides in North America, accounting for as many as 24% of all guidebooks sold. I think I know why.

Though we hope our books are entertaining, we nevertheless deal with travel in a serious fashion. Our guidebooks have never looked on such journeys as a mere recreation, but as a far more important human function, a time of learning and introspection, an essential part of a civilized life. We stress the culture, lifestyle, history and beliefs of the destinations we cover, and urge our readers to seek out people and new ideas as the chief rewards of travel.

We have never shied from controversy. We have, from the beginning, encouraged our authors to be intensely judgmental, critical—both pro and con—in their comments, and wholly independent. Our only clients are our readers, and we have triggered the ire of countless prominent sorts, from a tourist newspaper we called "practically worthless" (it unsuccessfully sued us) to the many rip-offs we've condemned.

And because we believe that travel should be available to everyone regardless of their incomes, we have always been cost-conscious at every level of expenditure. Though we have broadened our recommendations beyond the budget category, we insist that every lodging we include be sensibly priced. We use every form of media to assist our readers, and are particularly proud of our feisty daily website, the award-winning Frommers.com.

I have high hopes for the future of Frommer's. May these guidebooks, in all the years ahead, continue to reflect the joy of travel and the freedom that travel represents. May they always pursue a cost-conscious path, so that people of all incomes can enjoy the rewards of travel. And may they create, for both the traveler and the persons among whom we travel, a community of friends, where all human beings live in harmony and peace.

Arthur Frommer

THE BEST OF MADRID & BARCELONA

Madrid and Barcelona are the yin and yang of Iberian identity. Madrid sits on an arid high plateau in the center of the peninsula, while Barcelona clings to the Mediterranean shore. The two metropolises are great rivals in politics, sports, culture, and even language. This book brings them together to highlight two different—and equally fascinating—faces of Spain. For a trip that you will never forget, plan on seeing them both.

Although Madrid is paradoxically one of the youngest cities in Spain, it represents the culmination of the sweep of Spanish history. Felipe II moved the capital from Toledo to Madrid in 1561 just as the Spanish empire came into its own. Even today, Madrid remains the imperial heart of Spain, with the monumental architecture, royal palace, and regal art collection to prove it.

Barcelona, by contrast, is an ancient city with a mythic past. Founded by Romans, it has been a crossroads of Mediterranean cultures for 2,000 years. It rose to grandeur in the Middle Ages under the banner of the great warrior king Jaume I and became the capital of a far-flung Mediterranean empire. Nearly 8 centuries later, Barcelona's pride in its independent Catalan heritage and language remains undiminished.

Madrid retains a classicism, decorum, and sense of order befitting a national capital. With its exuberance and penchant for the fantastic, Barcelona is a leader in fashion, design, and gastronomy.

You will want to experience it all—from taking a romantic stroll along Madrid's leafy paseos to strutting down Barcelona's bustling Les Rambles. You will want to take your children to the outdoor puppet shows in Madrid's gracious Parque del Retiro and watch them marvel at the water-spitting tile lizard fountain in Antoni Gaudí's whimsical Parc Güell in Barcelona. Long after you might have gone to bed at home, you can thrill to some of the country's best live flamenco music and dance in the clubs of Madrid. On Sunday mornings in Barcelona, you can throw your backpack into the circle in front of the cathedral and join Catalans in the traditional folk dance of the sardana. In Madrid, be sure to sip sherry from an ancient wooden cask in a dark bar with hams hanging overhead. In Barcelona, celebrate the night with coupes of cava in one of the city's "champagne" bars.

Both cities are rich in detail and experiences and full of fascinating characters. You will undoubtedly make your own discoveries. This book will get you started.

MADRID'S best AUTHENTIC EXPERIENCES

o **Watching school children marvel at the portrait of the young princess in Velázquez's masterpiece "Las Meninas":** The collections of the Museo del Prado encompass nearly all the great Spanish art painted before 1900—and "Las Meninas" is one of the greatest paintings in the museum. Even Picasso felt compelled to paint an homage to this pioneering psychological portrait of the daughter of Felipe IV and her entourage. See p. 86.

o **Dunking fresh, sugar-dusted churros in thick hot chocolate at Chocolatería San Ginés:** Located in the heart of the old city, San Ginés stays open nearly around the clock, welcoming snackers from breakfast until the wee hours of the morning. See p. 77.

o **Joining Madrileño families rowing boats on the lake in Parque del Retiro:** Some families opt for the puppet shows, while others just walk around and see the flower gardens. But everyone from young families to flirty teenagers has a great time rowing around the beautiful park's shallow lake. See p. 104.

o **Trying to clap the flamenco rhythm at Casa Patas, Madrid's pioneer flamenco bar:** Some of the most famous flamenco musicians and dancers—as well as some of flamenco's brightest rising stars—perform in the intimate confines of this Andalucían bar in the Barrio de las Letras. See p. 91.

o **Seeing the response of an artistic genius to the horrors of the Spanish Civil War:** To Spaniards, history is divided between the era before and the era after the Civil War (1936–39). Picasso's "Guernica" in the Museo Nacional Centro de Arte Reina Sofía remains one of the strongest images of war ever captured in paint. See p. 88.

o **Making the rounds of the tapas bars near Plaza Santa Ana to discover each one's specialty:** Madrileños have perfected the art of tapas-hopping as a movable feast. The dense concentration of tapas bars around Plaza Santa Ana makes it possible to make an evening of it without repeating a dish. See p. 72.

o **Lining up with Spanish women to buy espadrilles at Casa Hernanz:** This venerable shop in La Latina offers no frills but does carry what seems to be Madrid's largest selection of espadrilles, all modestly priced and shelved from floor to ceiling. See p. 109.

o **Taking an evening stroll along the Paseo del Prado to see the illuminated fountains of Neptuno and Cibeles:** Sculpted in the 1780s to flank the Museo del Prado, both dramatic neoclassical fountains were relocated long ago to their respective circles on the Paseo del Prado, where evening illumination makes them seem grander than ever. See p. 106.

o **Cheering for the Real Madrid football club in a sports bar:** Madrid's top team commands a fierce loyalty among city residents from all walks of life. When a match is on, every bar in the city shows it on television. See p. 110.

o **Bargaining for a leather bag from one of the vendors at El Rastro flea market:** Madrileños and visitors alike flock to the Sunday street market that has been held in La Latina since late medieval times. Score a new pashmina, antique coins, illustrated books, out-of-print music CDs, or fashionable vintage clothes. The deals all depend on your bargaining skills. See p. 96.

MADRID'S best RESTAURANTS

- **Restaurante Sandó:** The innovative Basque menu in this new restaurant just off Gran Vía was created by legendary Spanish chefs Juan Mari and Elena Arzak. See p. 76.
- **Cervecería José Luís:** A shoeshine is part of the experience at this sleek bar-restaurante in Salamanca. See p. 80.
- **Restaurante Botín:** No visit to Madrid is complete without trying the roast suckling pig at this classic restaurant on the street below Plaza Mayor. See p. 74.
- **Alkalde:** Chef Ramón Rodríguez's creative cuisine is served at some of Salamanca's best cafe tables. See p. 79.
- **Viavélez:** Fish from Spain's northern Atlantic coast form the backbone of the Asturian menu at Paco Ron's formal restaurant and casual taberna. See p. 81.
- **Palacio de Cibeles:** Chef-owner Adolfo Muñoz brings his modernized La Manchan cuisine from Toledo to a dining room with one of the best views in Madrid. See p. 68.
- **La Huevería del Gansó:** Quirky casual restaurant in the Barrio de las Letras reinterprets the classics of Spanish bar food with duck, goose, and eggs. See p. 71.
- **Taberna del Alabardero:** This elegant tavern near the Teatro Real is a favorite of politicians, bullfighters, and literary figures who come for perfectly executed regional specialties from around the country. See p. 77.
- **El Brillante:** Best known for its fried calamari, this restaurant near the Museo Nacional Centro de Arte Reina Sofía is Madrid's quintessential Spanish fast-food experience. See p. 68.
- **Julián de Tolosa:** Some gourmets opt to sit by the big windows on Cava Baja, while others prefer the romantic downstairs seating by the wine cellar to enjoy the polished version of Basque cuisine served at this refined yet affordable steakhouse. See p. 74.

MADRID'S best HOTELS

- **Hotel Adler:** Traditional style, extraordinary service, and spacious quarters make the Adler the best luxury boutique hotel in Salamanca. See p. 64.
- **Hotel Catalonia Puerta del Sol:** Its serene hidden courtyard offers a monastery-like oasis near Plaza Santa Ana. See p. 57.
- **JC Rooms Santo Domingo:** This brand new hostel near Gran Vía combines playful contemporary style and bargain prices. See p. 61.
- **The Ritz Madrid:** Built by royal request in the early 20th century, the fully restored and updated Ritz sits amid stunning gardens a short walk from the Prado. See p. 53.
- **H10 Villa de la Reina:** Classy contemporary design at this Gran Vía boutique hotel considers the needs and tastes of female travelers. See p. 62.
- **Hotel Moderno:** This lovingly maintained and modernized family-run hotel makes a perfect base outside Puerta del Sol. See p. 57.
- **Hotel Santo Domingo:** Top-to-bottom renovation transformed a traditional hotel into contemporary luxury accommodations between Gran Vía and the Teatro Real. See p. 60.

o **Hotel Urban:** With decor featuring lots of dark wood, leather upholstery, and sumptuous fabrics, the ultra-chic Urban evokes the quiet luxury of a gentleman's club—graced by art from the owner's personal collection. See p. 57.

o **Ibis Styles Madrid Prado:** Bright, contemporary rooms are themed to the classic wine grapes of Iberia, so it's no surprise that there's a wine-tasting station in the lobby of this hotel in Barrio de Las Letras. See p. 59.

o **Hotel Ópera:** This beautifully restored hotel between the Teatro Real and Plaza del Oriente features some upper-level rooms with outdoor terraces, glassed-in Jacuzzi tubs, and skylights. See p. 60.

MADRID'S best MUSEUMS

o **Museo del Prado:** Insightful interpretative panels provide a window into the masterpieces of Spanish art. See p. 86.

o **Museo Nacional Centro de Arte Reina Sofía:** This modern and contemporary art museum captures the electric artistic movements of the 20th century with a decided emphasis on Spanish masters, such as Pablo Picasso, Joan Miró, Salvador Dalí, Juan Gris, and Antoni Tàpies. See p. 88.

o **Museo Thyssen-Bornemisza:** The two separate but complementary collections of the Baron and Baroness Thyssen-Bornemisza suggest that the couple must have had some lively dinner conversations about art through the ages. See p. 89.

o **Real Academía de Bellas Artes:** As director of the academy's art collection, Francisco de Goya arranged the galleries according to his interpretation of the progression of Spanish art. See p. 91.

o **Museo Sorolla:** The residence and studio of Spain's warmest Impressionist painter provide a glimpse of the artist at home. See p. 103.

o **Museo Naval:** This museum recalls the glory years of the Spanish galleons and the Navy's struggle for hegemony on the high seas. See p. 89.

o **Museo Lázaro Galdiano:** Often called a collection of collections, this museum chronicles the exquisite taste of a man who found beauty irresistible. See p. 103.

o **Museo Arqueológico Nacional:** The march of Iberian culture from the genius of the cave paintings of Altamira through Celtic, Roman, Visigothic, and Moorish times is captured in the art and artifacts excavated from across the country. See p. 86.

MADRID'S best HIDDEN SPACES

o **Monasterio de Las Descalzas Reales:** The blank face of the convent gives no hint of the richly painted murals, extraordinary tiles, and fine Flemish tapestries inside. See p. 97.

o **CentroCentro:** All of Madrid spreads out below the eighth floor observation deck at this new cultural center in the Palacio de Cibeles that faces the Cibeles fountain. See p. 83.

o **Museo de los Orígenes:** Legend holds that the ancient well in this palace museum belonged to Madrid's patron saint, San Isidro Labrador. See p. 95.

- **La Terraza:** Pedro Larumbe, one of Madrid's most accomplished chefs, serves casual modern cuisine on the sun roof of the ABC shopping center, with views of Salamanca on one side and old Madrid on the other. See p. 81.
- **Casa Museo Lope de Vega:** A window in the bedroom of the great dramatist-turned-priest opens onto the chapel where he would say Mass. See p. 91.
- **Ermita de San Antonio de la Florida:** Goya's tomb lies beneath a fabulous sequence of murals that he painted in this small temple on the banks of the Manzanares River. See p. 104.
- **Museo de Arte Público:** A veritable garden of abstract Spanish modern sculpture blossoms beneath the overpass linking Calle Juan Bravo to Calle Eduardo Dato. See p. 102.
- **dASSA bASSA:** One of Spain's most visible TV celebrity chefs seeks refuge in his contemporary restaurant in a former coal cellar behind Puerta de Alcalá. See p. 79.
- **Hammams Madrid Baños Arábes:** Beneath a historic water tank in La Latina, these modern baths conjure the magic of Moorish Spain. See p. 94.
- **Chapel of San Baudelio de Berlanga:** Stunning murals from an 11th-century Romanesque chapel are installed in the far corner on the lowest level of the Prado's Villanueva building. See p. 86.

MADRID'S best PARKS, PLAZAS & GARDENS

- **Puerta del Sol:** High-tech giants vie to put their stamp on this ancient plaza that has evolved as the crossroads of public transportation in Madrid. See p. 92.
- **Plaza Mayor:** The site of the Spanish Inquisition is now a favorite spot in which enjoy a cold drink at a cafe table or to buy gifts at the Christmas Market in December. See p. 95.
- **Plaza Santa Ana:** Bar-hopping and theater have gone hand-in-hand here since Lope de Vega and Calderón de la Barca first enthralled the crowds 4 centuries ago. See p. 92.
- **Real Jardín Botánico:** Orderly plantings of more than 100 species of trees and 3,000 other plants create an oasis of serenity between the Prado and the Atocha train station. See p. 90.
- **Parque del Retiro:** Once the purview of Spanish nobility, these rolling green spaces now welcome all the people of Madrid. See p. 104.
- **Jardínes de Sabatini:** Gardens at the Palacio Real merge Italian flamboyance with French horticultural rigor. See p. 99.
- **CaixaForum Madrid Vertical Garden:** The 79-foot-tall vertical garden at the Caixa-Forum helps define a pocket plaza along the Paseo del Prado. See p. 83.
- **Plaza del Oriente:** This elegant plaza and sculpture garden between the Palacio Real and Teatro Real captures the mannered grace of late-19th-century Madrid. See p. 94.
- **Plaza Dos de Mayo:** Once you have seen Goya's painting in the Prado, visit the plaza—now a neighborhood park—that honors the heroes of the uprising against Napoleon. See p. 101.

BARCELONA'S best AUTHENTIC EXPERIENCES

o **Taking an early morning stroll down Les Rambles:** The freshly washed pavement of this backbone of old Barcelona is alive in the morning with bird sellers and flower vendors. See p. 193.

o **Seeing old Barcelona through the eyes of a young Picasso at the Museu Picasso:** Picasso studied art in Barcelona and painted the city in a moody, realistic style before he began the avant-garde experimentation that defined his career. See p. 206.

o **Eating one of the famous Catalan rice dishes, *arròces*, at a beachside table:** Paella only marks the beginning of Catalan baked rice dishes. One of the most famous is *arròs negre,* made with cuttlefish or squid ink. See p. 191.

o **Enjoying the cool shade of the narrow streets as you explore the medieval quarter of the Barri Gòtic:** Organized around the cathedral, a royal palace, and several Gothic-era churches, Barcelona's warren of medieval stone streets remains a vibrant neighborhood. See p. 203.

o **Craning your neck skyward to behold the towers of the Basilica de La Sagrada Familia:** Antoni Gaudí's phantasmagoric prayer in stone, finally nearing completion, is one of the most remarkable churches designed since the heyday of Gothic cathedrals. See p. 209.

o **Shopping for food at La Boquería Sant Josep:** The largest of the city's public fresh food markets overflows with culinary riches ranging from fresh fruits and vegetables to Mediterranean fish and shellfish to herbs and spices. See p. 198.

o **Marveling at the warrior-like tiled chimneys on the roof of La Pedrera:** Generations before Darth Vader wore a hooded mask in "Star Wars," Gaudí designed the tile-covered chimneys of Casa Milà to resemble heavily armored warriors. See p. 213.

o **Hanging out at the beach at Barceloneta:** Barcelona's blue-flag beaches begin only steps from the city's old quarters. With a wealth of beachside restaurants, long stretches of soft sand, and warm Mediterranean waters, they are some of the best urban beaches in Europe. See p. 214.

o **People-watching from a cafe table in the Plaça Reial:** Everyone who visits Barcelona eventually passes through the Plaça Reial going to and from Les Rambles and the Barri Gòtic. Cafe tables provide the perfect vista from which to observe that human parade. Just keep moving around the plaza to stay in the shade. See p. 205.

o **Sipping cava from nearby Sant Sadurní d'Anoia at a "champagne" bar:** Catalan sparkling wine comes in all grades, from low-alcohol fizz to complex wines with pinpoint carbonation. Barcelonans sip the finer ones at such places as Xampú Xampany or enjoy the more casual cavas at such spots as El Xampanyet near the Museo Picasso. See p. 193 and p. 187.

BARCELONA'S best RESTAURANTS

o **La Gardunya:** Nearly hidden away at the back of La Boquería Sant Josep, this institution specialized in market cuisine before anyone invented the term. See p. 181.

o **Adagiotapas:** A rising star chef brings the creativity that won him a Michelin star for his fine-dining restaurant to a select list of creative tapas at this tiny Barri Gòtic venue. See p. 183.

○ **Roca Moo:** The world-acclaimed Roca brothers of Girona introduced their inventive Catalan cuisine to the big city in the high-style Hotel Omm in L'Eixample. See p. 191.

○ **Can Ravell:** Visitors rub elbows with the locals over classic Catalan dishes served at marble-topped butcher tables upstairs from a wine and gourmet shop. See p. 192.

○ **Suquet de l'Almirall:** Named for the famed Catalan seafood stew, this delightful Barceloneta restaurant specializes in exquisite rice and seafood dishes. See p. 194.

○ **Els Quatre Gats:** The 1890s elegance of this Art Nouveau cafe is undiminished—right down to the menus designed by a young (and presumably hungry) Picasso. See p. 182.

○ **Loidi:** Located across the street from fine-dining bastion Lasarte, Loidi serves a more affordable version of superchef Martín Berasategui's contemporary Basque cooking. See p. 190.

○ **Cal Pep:** Diners crowd the bar and spill out into the plaza as they feast on what are arguably Barcelona's best traditional tapas. See p. 181.

○ **Los Caracoles:** The eponymous snails are famous, but even more diners flock here to eat the spit-roasted chicken in a homey atmosphere. See p. 184.

○ **Òleum:** The fine-dining restaurant at the Museu Nacional d'Art de Catalunya combines an elegant setting with jaw-dropping views through gardens down to the Plaza d'Espanya. See p. 196.

BARCELONA'S best HOTELS

○ **Hostal Girona:** This good-value hostel occupies the modest upper floor of a Modernista building where L'Eixample and La Ribera neighborhoods meet. See p. 175.

○ **Citadines Aparthotel:** Recently renovated apartments offer sleek contemporary design and a full kitchen right on Les Rambles. See p. 168.

○ **Barcelona Hotel Colonial:** This new hotel with classic styling occupies a former bank in the old quarter yet is only steps from the waterfront. See p. 171.

○ **Hotel Omm:** The rooftop pool and terrace of this luxury L'Eixample hotel afford great views of the neighboring rooftop of La Pedrera. See p. 172.

○ **Hotel Neri:** This historic late-medieval palace offers tranquil luxury in the heart of the Call, Barcelona's ancient Jewish quarter. See p. 170.

○ **Ciutat Barcelona Hotel:** This modern little gem near the Museo Picasso has a pocket-size rooftop terrace with a pool just big enough to keep the kids happy. See p. 171.

○ **Hotel 54:** Snazzy Barceloneta hotel is close to the beach but removed from the noisy late-night scene. See p. 175.

○ **Casa Fuster:** It's worth the splurge to sleep in this luxurious Modernista landmark in the Gràcia neighborhood. See p. 172.

○ **Hotel Bagues:** This hotel in a former Art Nouveau jewelry store and workshop along Les Rambles captures an elegance that the street had almost forgotten. See p. 165.

○ **Petit Palace Opera Garden Ramblas:** The technology-savvy design of this hotel offers good value near many of Barcelona's top sights. See p. 171.

BARCELONA'S best MUSEUMS

o **Museu Nacional d'Art de Catalunya:** The astonishing collection of Romanesque and Gothic art proves that artists have been dreaming in Catalan since the 9th century. See p. 217.

o **Fundació Joan Miró:** Montjuïc landmark is a showcase for Miró's brilliant surrealism. See p. 216.

o **Museu Picasso:** The master's gift of more than 2,400 works includes his homage to Velázquez's "Las Meninas." See p. 206.

o **Fundació Antoní Tàpies:** Changing exhibitions reveal the audacity and playfulness of Spain's great Abstract Expressionist. See p. 210.

o **Museu del Modernisme Catalá:** This new museum lets visitors get up close to examine the craftsmanship of Modernista furniture and glass. See p. 212.

o **Casa-Museu Gaudí:** Exhibits reveal the sources of inspiration and personality of the architect and designer who changed the face of Barcelona. See p. 212.

o **Museu de Història de Catalunya:** The last standing structure of Barcelona's old port has been converted into a stunning space to tell the story of a nation within a nation. See p. 215.

o **Museu Marítim:** New exhibits and interpretations relate Spain's naval and maritime pursuits in this museum in the ancient shipyards of Barcelona. See p. 202.

BARCELONA'S best ARCHITECTURAL LANDMARKS

o **Sant Pau del Camp:** This humble medieval church and cloister exemplify a strong and simple faith. See p. 202.

o **Palau de la Musica Catalana:** Barcelona's finest concert hall is a Modernista jewel box designed by Lluis Domènech i Montaner. See p. 207.

o **La Boquería Sant Josep:** The greatest of Barcelona's fresh food markets is the city's cathedral of food. See p. 198.

o **Catedral:** One of Spain's most impressive cathedrals is an exemplar of Catalan Gothic style. See p. 203.

o **Pastelería Escribà:** This Les Rambles pastry shop and cafe is a stunning example of Parisian-style Art Nouveau design. See p. 180.

o **Gran Teatre del Liceu:** This Belle Époque opera house sparkles after a faithful 1999 reconstruction. See p. 198.

o **Basilica de La Sagrada Familia:** A masterpiece still in the making, Antoni Gaudí's greatest church should be finished by the 100th anniversary of his death in 2026. See p. 209.

o **Mirador de Colom:** The visage of great explorer Christopher Columbus has watched over the Barcelona waterfront since the 1880s. See p. 215.

o **La Pedrera:** A furnished apartment gives visitors a chance to imagine living in Gaudí's finest domestic design. See p. 213.

o *Peix:* Frank Gehry's armor-plated fish is the capstone of the sculptures along the waterfront pathways. See p. 213.

BARCELONA'S best WALKS

- **Moll de la Fusta:** Take in the historic old port along this modern pathway graced by a sculpture of a giant crayfish. See p. 213.
- **Les Rambles:** Enjoy the legendary street life along the spine of the historic old city. See p. 198.
- **Passeig Marítím de la Barceloneta:** Follow the beachside promenade from the old fisherman's village to the yacht basin at Port Olimpic. See p. 161.
- **Passeig de Gràcia:** Marvel at the Modernista architecture and suffer sticker shock in the shops along Barcelona's most elegant boulevard. See p. 221.
- **Avinguda Gaudí:** An almost continuous stream of cafes along the center of this boulevard links Gaudí's masterpiece La Sagrada Familia with Domènech i Montaner's amazing Modernista hospital complex. See p. 209 and p. 211.
- **Montjuïc:** From Font Màgica in front of the Museu Nacional d'Art de Catalunya, walk past the Olympic Stadium and into the Jardí Botanic filled with plants of the Mediterranean. See p. 215.

SUGGESTED ITINERARIES

2

This chapter is a guide to scheduling your stay in Madrid and Barcelona. In each city, we start with 1-, 2-, and 3-day itineraries to help you prioritize your time and set your pace. Even if you're normally a go-go person, you will enjoy Spain more if you find a rhythm that lets you pause on a hot afternoon at a shady cafe for a lemon granizado or a glass of cava or duck into a taberna to escape the winter chill with a glass of vermut or a quick demitasse of dark coffee. These itineraries are flexible enough to let you do that—or pop into a shop if something in the window strikes your fancy.

In addition to daily routes that emphasize must-see attractions, we have also suggested itineraries for families and others that reveal unique aspects of the cities. So that you won't miss anything, we have also included highlights from suggested side trips into the surrounding regions.

You can follow these itineraries to the letter, or you can use them as a point of departure for assembling your own personalized—even idiosyncratic—trip to Madrid and Barcelona. Think of the itineraries as modular building blocks that you can mix and match to suit your interests and the length of your trip. For example, you might want to follow up the 1-day tour of Madrid's artistic treasures with a day devoted to Madrid for fashionistas. In Barcelona, after you have spent a day enjoying the visual delights of the Modernisme masterpieces in L'Eixample, you can satisfy your taste buds with a tour of gourmet highlights. And, of course, the itineraries can be combined to create your own approach to appreciating both cities.

ICONIC MADRID IN 1, 2 & 3 DAYS

The sprawl of Madrid can seem daunting on your first visit. The trappings of a national capital are everywhere you look—the royal palace, the splendid art museums, even the leafy avenues punctuated by larger-than-life fountains of mythological figures. The plazas are broad and seemingly unrelieved by shade, yet the green parks seem to continue to the horizon. Unlike many national capitals, Madrid is just getting started at the end of the work day when the streets and cafes spring to life. However many days you plan to spend in the city, don't let one side of Madrid distract you from the others. See the art museums, but also take a walk in the park and spend an evening rubbing elbows with Spaniards at a tapas bar. If 1 day is all you can spare, start early to enjoy the genius of Spanish art, stop to smell the flowers, and revel in the outdoor life of a public square. ***Start:*** *Metro to Atocha or Banco de España.*

Day 1

1 Museo Nacional del Prado ★★★

This is one of the world's greatest art museums, but even if you are making your first visit, avoid the temptation to cram in large portions of the collection. Spend your time with just two of the greatest figures in Spanish art, Diego Velázquez (1599–1660) and Francisco de Goya (1746–1828). See p. 86.

2 Real Jardin Botánica ★

After your immersion in art, head to this adjacent garden to stroll, relax, and digest what you've seen. This gated enclosure of specimen plants is rarely crowded, and its orderly beauty captures the measured elegance of the Bourbon monarchs who founded it and whose mark is still stamped on the city. Don't leave the area without visiting the Cuesta de Moyano bookstalls. Dealers in second-hand books line this street all the way down to the traffic circle by the Atocha Metro stop. Most books are in Spanish, but the art and photo books speak a universal visual language. See p. 47.

Cross Paseo del Prado and walk 1 block north to:

3 CaixaForum ★

Here, a 24-meter-high (78-ft.) "Vertical Garden" of plants grows off the face of a wall, a more modern take on gardening.

Turn around and follow the sidewalks to the next museum. But first stop for a bite at:

4 El Brilliante 🍺

The house specialty at this popular, block-long sandwich shop is a roll filled with fried calamari.

It's literally only a few steps from it to:

5 Museo Nacional Centro de Arte Reina Sofia ★★★

This famed museum picks up chronologically where the Prado leaves off—the cusp of the 19th and 20th centuries. With galleries arranged by influence and association rather than chronology or country of origin, it's a completely different experience from the Prado. If you feel rushed or as though you've had enough art for 1 day, go directly to Room 206, which is devoted to Pablo Picasso's massive painting "Guernica," which shows the world the horrors Franco rained down on a tiny Basque village during the Spanish Civil War.

Walk 15 minutes uphill to the:

6 Plaza Santa Ana ★★

Its surrounding streets might as well be the food court of old Madrid. Until you've made an evening of strolling from bar to bar to try each establishment's specialty, you've never really had tapas. Check out the elaborate tile facade of Villa Rosa (p. 110), where a bar scene in director Pedro Almodóvar's film "High

Heels" was filmed, and be sure to visit Las Bravas (p. 72), the bar that invented the spicy sauce for fried potatoes now found all over Spain as "patatas bravas."

Round out your day by catching a performance at:

7 Casa Patas ★★

This is the bar-restaurant that led the way in the flamenco revival. Flamenco here is gutsy, passionate, and as authentic as it gets. See p. 91.

Day 2

With two of the three big art museums under your belt, you're ready to spend your second day enjoying the pomp and splendor of the city. One warning: Avoid doing this itinerary on a Wednesday, when admission to the Palacio Real and the Monasterio de las Descalzas Reales is free to all citizens of the European Union, causing long lines to form at the entrances. ***Start:*** *Metro to Ópera.*

1 Palacio Real ★★★

The kings of Spain made do with ungainly fortress residences until the original royal palace burned down in 1734, giving Felipe V the chance to build a gaudy palace to rival his Bourbon cousin's place at Versailles in France. The sheer per-fumed excess of the Gasparini Room (the dressing room of Carlos III) captures the fairy-tale vision of royalty. The Bourbon Apartments, complete with movie screening room, show the early-20th-century monarchs as more human. See p. 98.

2 Jardines de Sabatini ★★★

Those 18th-century Bourbons knew their gardens. After the crowds in the palace, these cool and tranquil gardens are a delight, however anachronistic their mani-cured hedges and neoclassical statuary might seem. See p. 99.

Across Calle Bailen is the:

3 Plaza del Oriente ★★★

This semicircular plaza combines the grace of the gardens with a certain pompos-ity of royal prerogative. That's not surprising, because Joseph Bonaparte ordered construction of the plaza when his brother Napoleon made him king of Spain (1808–13). Isabel II finished the job later in the century, erecting imposing stat-ues of Spanish royalty to bolster her own tarnished image.

Stop for lunch at:

4 Café de Oriente 🍺 ★

This delightful Belle Epoque cafe has the best outdoor tables in the city at which to see and be seen. Drinks are pricey, but it's a cheap way to pass for a diplomat, marquesa, or captain of industry. See p. 76.

5 Monasterio de las Descalzas Reales ★★

From 1559 until the Napoleonic invasion, women from noble families took the veil here, bringing their family art with them. Being surrounded by beautiful things could make a cloistered life of voluntary poverty seem a bit more attrac-tive. The convent was reactivated in the late 19th century, but most of the sisters (whom you might hear but not see) hail not from Spanish noble families but from villages in Africa and Latin America. See p. 97.

With the last "Ave" still echoing in your ears, walk to Calle San Martin and Calle Barda-
dores to the:

6 Plaza Mayor ★★★

This has been the crossroads of civic life in Madrid for centuries. Visitors and
locals shop beneath the arcades and sit at tables under umbrellas to eat and drink.
Each of the nine arched gateways to the plaza, added in 1854, leads to a different
experience of the city. Arco de Cuchilleros (arch of the knife-sharpeners) on the
southwest corner is a favorite spot for musical buskers to set up because of its
great acoustics.

Head toward that arch, as it is the gateway to the tapas bars and taverns of:

7 La Latina 🍺

Finish your day tapas-bar-hopping in this happening neighborhood.

Day 3

Madrid has an embarrassment of riches when it comes to art, and today's journey
includes a third major art museum as well as a charming artist's home and studio.
You'll also stroll the length of Madrid's grandest park and explore an elegant
neighborhood. *Start: Metro to Retiro.*

1 Parque del Retiro ★★

Sometimes called the "lungs of Madrid," this is the city's second-largest green
space (after the **Casa de Campo,** p. 104) and easily its most gracious. Originally
the grounds of a private royal retreat, it's been a fully public park since the 19th
century. Even if there's no exhibition in the grand 19th-century glass-walled
Palacio de Cristal (p. 104), it's a pleasant stroll to literally stop and smell the
roses at the Roselada garden and contemplate the sculpture "El Angel Caído," an
over-the-top depiction of Lucifer falling from heaven. More conventional sculptures of notable Spanish nobles and heroes dot the grounds.

Exit the park by the Puerta de Alcalá gate and walk a block to the magnificent fountain
at the Plaza de Cibeles, a symbol of the city. It is a short walk south on the central
promenade of the Paseo del Prado, one of the leafy boulevards built for the "mayor
king" Carlos III in the 18th century, to reach Madrid's third world-class general art
museum:

2 Museo Thyssen-Bornemisza ★★

Baron Hans Heinrich Thyssen-Bornemisza was one of the great art collectors of
the 20th century, and Madrid considered it a major feather in the civic cap when
he sold his art to Spain for a nominal sum in 1993. His Spanish-born fifth wife,
Carmen Cervera, later gave the museum *her* private collection as well, necessitat-
ing an expansion so that the works could be separate but equal. Some of the
strengths of the collections include Italian and German Gothic religious art as
well as Impressionist, post-Impressionist, and German Expressionist paintings.
See p. 89.

Next, take bus 27 north on Paseo del Prado to the Plaza Canovas del Castillo (stop
#78), and walk west on Paseo General Martínez Campos a short distance to the:

3 Museo Sorolla ★★

This is the home and studio of one of the seemingly happiest of Spanish painters,
Valencia-born Joaquín Sorolla (1863–1923). A golden light floods his

paintings—and his studio. The portrait that emerges of the artist is a man serene in his calling.

Just east of Plaza Canovas del Castillo lie the legendary shopping avenues of:

4 Salamanca ★★

This is still the most elegant neighborhood in Madrid, thanks to Belle Epoque buildings with wrought-iron balconies along broad, leafy streets. The boutiques of Spain's top fashion designers can be found on Calles Serrano, Goya, and Velázquez; and Madrid's fanciest fresh food market, **Mercado de la Paz** ★★ (p. 102), is located on Calle Ayala.

If the beautiful displays of fruits, vegetables, meats, fish, and cheese make you hungry, head to:

5 La Terraza 🍵 ★★

This is the casual restaurant of top chef Pedro Larumbe, on the upper terrace of the ABC Serrano shopping center, allowing you to enjoy great rooftop views with your bowl of gazpacho and a big salad.

MADRID & ENVIRONS FOR ART LOVERS

Any one of Madrid's big three art museums (Prado, Thyssen-Bornemisza, or Reina Sofía) would be enough of a cultural treasure for a city, but they just begin to scratch the surface of the great art on display in Madrid and its surrounding communities. This 6-day itinerary covers the major museums and lets you spend 1 day immersed in the life and works of Francisco de Goya and another day visiting in Toledo with the incomparable El Greco. It concludes with an overnight stay in the high aerie of Cuenca to contemplate late-20th-century Spanish art's flights of abstract fancy. *Start: Metro to Atocha.*

Day 1

1 Museo Nacional del Prado ★★★

Admit it: You've been champing at the bit to visit the **Prado,** so allow yourself plenty of time to be there when the museum opens. The Prado can be overrun by tour groups, so get a jump by immediately taking the elevator up one floor in the Villanueva building to get to "Las Meninas" before the crowds do. Take special note of the Goya tapestry cartoons in Salas 90–94, as you'll see the woven works at El Pardo on another day. Save the temporary exhibitions and the reassembled cloister of the San Jéronimo church, both in the modern addition, for last. See p. 86.

When you finish, walk across the Paseo del Prado to have an outdoor lunch at Las Terrazas del Thyssen in the:

2 Museo Thyssen-Bornemisza ★★★

The Prado concentrates mainly on art by Spanish artists or art once owned by the Spanish monarchy. The Thyssen-Bornemisza casts a wider net and covers a broader span of time. See p. 89.

Day 2

1 Real Academia de Bellas Artes ★★

This is your day to appreciate the multifaceted genius of Goya. You have seen some of his greatest works at the Prado, but the **Real Academia de Bellas Artes** (p. 91), just outside Puerta del Sol (Metro: Sol), gives insight into how he thought about painting, because the galleries are arranged according to his plan. Don't miss his modest little self-portrait, as if he were bewildered by his own fame.

Back at Puerta del Sol, hop a C-3 or C-4 cercanía train to the Menendez-Pelayo station and walk (about 3 min.) to:

2 Real Fábrica de Tapices ★★★

This historic factory of hand-weavers still makes tapestries for royalty, fancy hotels, and other luxury buyers. In the 18th century, many of the tapestries were woven from cartoons created by Goya. If you're lucky, one of the Goya works might even be on display. See p. 90.

Next, take bus 601 from the Moncloa station to the:

3 Palacio Real de El Pardo ★

You're guaranteed to see a number of tapestries designed by Goya and his brother-in-law here. The palace is somewhat of a historical curiosity. In addition to its notable art collection, it was a residence of Francisco Franco, and it can be jarring to think of the dictator living in such a refined setting.

When you return to the Moncloa station, take Metro Linea 6 toward Circular to Príncipe Pio. Walk along Paseo de Florida to the:

4 Ermita de San Antonio de la Florida ★

Inside is the **Panteón de Goya** ★ (p. 104), where the artist is buried beneath the frescoes that he painted on the ceiling.

Day 3

1 Toledo ★★★

Today, you are going to travel outside Madrid for a close look at another of Spain's artistic geniuses. Known even in his own day as "The Greek," or "El Greco," Doménikos Theotokópoulos (1541–1614) first came to Toledo in 1577 and stayed the rest of his life. If you follow this itinerary during 2014, the quadricentennial of his death, you may find that some of his paintings have been moved either to the Prado in Madrid or the Museo de Santa Cruz in Toledo for comprehensive El Greco retrospectives. Seeing everything Toledo offers requires spending more time, but the El Greco sites can be covered in a single long day.

Start by taking the AVE from the Atocha station to Toledo, a quick trip of 33 minutes. Once you're in the old city, head for the:

2 Museo Convento de Santo Domingo el Antiguo ★

This is the monastery church that lured the painter to Toledo in the first place. The canvases he painted are still here—and so is El Greco, who is entombed in the crypt below the church.

From Santo Domingo el Antiguo, walk to:

3 Iglesia de Santo Tomé ★★★

Here you see the master painting **"The Burial of the Count of Orgaz"** ★★★.

These two churches have only a smattering of El Greco works, but nearby is the:

4 Museo del Greco ★

This is the world's only museum devoted exclusively to the painter, so take your time here.

Then take a break at any of the outdoor cafes around the Plaza de Zocodover before moving along to the striking El Greco paintings in the:

5 Museo del Santa Cruz ★

The museum has consolidated the best of the El Grecos that once hung in now closed churches and convents, and they reflect his mature, almost hallucinatory work. If you can find time before heading back to Madrid, visit the Sacristy in the **Catedral de Toledo** ★★, which displays a complete set of El Greco portraits of the 12 apostles as well as his early masterpiece **"El Espolio" ("The Disrobing of Christ")**.

Day 4

Begin by taking the Metro to the Iglesia, Gregorio Marañón, or Rubén Darío stop and walk to:

1 Sorolla ★★

You've been traipsing after Goya and El Greco for the last few days; here you get to catch up with painter Joaquín Sorolla (1863–1923) in his house and studio, complete with family photos and other telling details.

It's hard to leave this charming environment, but when you do, walk east for about 10 minutes to the:

2 Museo Lázaro Galdiano ★★

Offering another look at an artistic lifestyle, this is the former home of astute art collector José Lázaro Galdiano; it displays his collections of paintings, crystal, ceramics, and other wonderful things that caught his eye. But, especially on the main floor, you can get a sense of how he lived in the beautiful palacio with his wife, Paula Florido.

For a lunch break, cross the street to:

3 Cerveceria José Luis ☕

Grab a slice of tortilla española at the bar—and get your shoes shined while you're there. José Luis Ruiz Soalguren believed that shiny shoes would raise your spirits and put a spring in your step, so he arranged for a shoeshine man to always be available.

From here, walk back to Paseo de la Castellana and take bus 27 to the Atocha Metro, a short block from the:

4 Museo Nacional Centro de Arte Reina Sofía ★★★

The museum keeps late hours, so you can enjoy a leisurely visit with the Spanish legends of 20th-century art from Juan Gris to Picasso to Antoní Tàpies.

Days 5 & 6

Most of the art you've been looking at for the last 4 days has been representational. Some of the best Spanish modern art from the late 20th century, however, is found in the cliff-top city of:

1 Cuenca ★★★

Because the setting, with its almost surreal landscape and Cubist old quarter, is a huge part of the experience, it would be a shame not to spend the night so that you have sufficient time to explore the vistas, back alleys, and miniature plazas of this visually fascinating village. Either the ALVIA or the AVE train from Madrid's Atocha station gets you to Cuenca in under an hour. You can save about half the cost of the fare, though, by taking the first train of the morning.

The best place to begin is at the galleries of the:

2 Fundación Antonio Saura ★★★

This museum contains not only some of the great abstract painter's own late work but his personal collection of pieces by his contemporaries. As one of the great theorists of modern Spanish painting, he lassoed many disparate styles together into a single intellectual corral.

Lest this all seem far too serious, make your next stop the:

3 Fundación Antonio Perez ★★★

Come here for art with wit and a personal sensibility that makes Salvador Dalí look like the straight man in a comedy team.

4 Museo de Arte Abstracto Espanol ★★★

Our final museum is located in one of Cuenca's famous cantilevered buildings, the so-called "Casas Colgadas," or "Hanging Houses." It somehow seems appropriate that galleries showing art on the edge should be suspended in thin air.

MADRID FOR FAMILIES

Children are the ultimate icebreakers. As you explore the city, your children will almost certainly gravitate to local kids around their own age, giving you the chance to meet parents and perhaps even learn some tips about child-friendly activities in Madrid. To get you started, we've outlined 2 full days of activities. Each features family-oriented attractions as well as general-interest museums and historic sites that have some displays or artifacts that children often find fascinating. *Start: Metro to Retiro.*

Day 1

Many local families head to **Parque del Retiro** ★★ (p. 104) on the weekends to enjoy puppet shows, listen to musicians busking for tips, and row boats on the lake. Depending on the penchant of your offspring, you can spend a half-hour or a half-day here.

Your next stop is the **Museo Naval** ★ (p. 89), about a 5-minute walk south of the Cibeles fountain on the Paseo del Prado. Security is tighter here than at most museums, so be sure to bring your passports for identification. Kids of all ages are intrigued by the large models of ships, some of which are cut away to show what the inside of a Spanish galleon really looked like.

It's an easy stroll up Paseo del Prado, retracing your steps and passing Cibeles before turning onto Calle Juan Jorge to visit the **Museo Arqueológico Nacional** ★★ (p. 86) on Calle Serrano. The Iberian peninsula was the first part of Europe to repopulate after the Ice Age and consequently has some of the oldest cultural artifacts on the continent. Children are especially fascinated by the depictions of animals in the museum's recreation of the cave paintings of Altamira.

From the Colón circle, take Bus 150 or 53 to the Sevilla stop and stroll to **Puerta del Sol** ★★ (p. 92). Here at the heart of Madrid stands a striking statue of a bear stretching to pick fruit from a strawberry tree ("madroño" in Castillian Spanish). It's a favorite backdrop for travel photos.

For a final treat for the day, walk up Calle Montera to Gran Vía to visit the **Real Madrid Tienda** (p. 110) for all manner of souvenirs from one of the world's top soccer clubs. The kids are sure to forget all about McDonald's when you take them a few doors down for Spanish-style hot dogs, burgers, grilled cheese, and milkshakes at **Nebraska** ★ (p. 79).

Day 2

Start the day by walking from the Puerta del Sol Metro stop to **Chocolatería San Ginés** ★★ (p. 77) to treat yourself (oh, and the kids too) to mugs of hot chocolate and hot churros (a kind of doughnut stick that you sprinkle with granulated sugar). This breakfast should make the little ones hyper enough to walk down Calle Mayor to visit the **Palacio Real** ★★★ (p. 98). Unless your children are budding set designers, limit your visit to the Royal Armory, which contains swords, daggers, lances, and whole suits of armor worn by Spanish royalty since the 16th century.

It's an easy walk past the Sabatini gardens on the north side of the palace to the Principe Pio station, where you can take the **Teleférico** ★ (p. 107) gondola ride for an elevated perspective on the city and a quick trip to the Casa de Campo, the green parkland below the palace. The Casa de Campo has two main attractions—an amusement park and a combination zoo/aquarium. Both are rather expensive, so you might want to decide in advance which one your family would prefer. At the **Parque de Atracciones** ★ (p. 107), admission lets you sample all the rides, from plodding ponies to whizzing roller coasters. The other option is arguably more educational: the **Zoo Aquarium de Madrid** ★ (p. 107), which is exactly what it sounds like—a display of wildlife from all over the world, a big aquarium full of fish, and a separate facility for dolphin

MADRID FOR FASHIONISTAS

Spanish women have a sense of confidence that imbues them with a style all their own. We can't say for sure that current fashion trends, such as knee-high leather riding boots and the seemingly ubiquitous flowing scarf, originated in Spain, but we did notice the trends there years before they hit the States—and Spanish women do carry them off with uncommon flair. This 1-day itinerary is a primer on Spanish style. It is, naturally, heavy on shopping, with plenty of options for those who are willing to break the bank as well as for those who love a good bargain. ***Start:*** *Metro to Moncloa or Ciudad Universitaria.*

To hone your eye and get an overview of the evolution of Spanish style, start your day at the **Museo del Traje** ★ (p. 105), or "costume" museum. Don't let the English translation trick you into thinking that this is a quaint folkloric museum—trendsetting Spanish designers, such as Cristóbal Balenciaga, are featured in the fashion galleries.

To see what's coming down the runways today, take the Metro to the Serrano stop in the upscale neighborhood of **Salamanca** (p. 102), where well-coiffed women wear beautiful shoes and are never without their designer sunglasses. Recently widened and refurbished Calle de Serrano and surrounding streets are full of fashionable boutiques of international design stars as well as the showcases of top Spanish designers, such as Agatha Ruiz de la Prada and esteemed leather manufacturer Loewe. While you are on Calle Serrano, look for one of the entrances to **ABC Serrano,** an indoor shopping center in a neoclassical former newspaper building. Custom shoes from **Gaytan** (p. 108) are available here, and the shoes, although pricey, do last forever.

But don't despair—you can also find top fashion shoes at a bargain. Take the Metro to the Chueca stop in the neighborhood of the same name. In the last decade or so, **Chueca** (p. 49) has emerged as one of the city's most appealing neighborhoods, with a youthful vibe and flourishing gay scene. Lower rents for storefronts have attracted younger designers. **Calle Augusto Figueroa** (p. 108) is known for the outlets of a number of Spanish shoe designers, such as Barrats and Farrutx. With discounts of 30 percent and higher, you may want to stock up. If you're going to need more luggage, head to the discount outlet of **Salvador Bachiller** (p. 108) near the Plaza del Chueca, where the firm's luggage, travel accessories, purses, and small leather goods are substantially reduced.

For other unique accessories, take the Metro to **Puerta del Sol** ★★ (p. 92). Over the years, we have discovered that Spanish eyeglass manufacturers have a real knack for designing handmade acetate frames that have a much more playful and warm look than the more severe styles of northern Europe.

Certain iconic Spanish apparel never goes out of style and can make a big splash back home. From Puerta del Sol, wander uphill to **Capas Seseña** (p. 109), which has been making and selling beautiful capes for men and women for more than a century. If you have the confidence to pull it off, a Seseña cape is a classic that never goes out of style. Easier on the pocketbook and perhaps less daunting to wear are the beretlike Basque wool caps sold at **La Favorita** (p. 109). You can reach the shop on Plaza Mayor by heading back down to Puerta del Sol and strolling west along Calle Mayor.

You will probably want to put down your packages for a rest at one of the cafe tables in Plaza Mayor. When you're ready to move on, exit by the archway onto Calle Toledo. In just a block or so, you will almost certainly see a line of women outside the small storefront of **Casa Hernanz** (p. 109), which specializes in hand-sewn espadrilles. Be sure you know your European shoe size before you enter.

It's only a short walk to the trendy **Mercado de San Miguel** ★★ (p. 95), a food emporium where you can enjoy a glass of wine and a few small bites. Keep your eyes peeled for photographers, who have come to favor the market for fashion shoots.

BEST OF BARCELONA

Whichever way you look, Barcelona is bound to bedazzle you. The art stretches across 12 centuries—and, for that matter, so does the architecture. The so-called old city is young and vibrant, and the so-called new city is elegant and measured. You should definitely take a stroll on jaunty Les Rambles, see Antoni Gaudí's grand Basilica de la Sagrada Familia for yourself, and spend a few hours with great paintings by Picasso. But there's much more. Sometimes a moment of quiet in an ancient church or getting lost in a tangle of medieval stone streets will bring you most in touch with the city.

If you can only spend 1 day, make the most of your time by prepurchasing tickets online at the websites of the individual attractions or at Barcelona Turisme's web shop (http://bcnshop.barcelonaturisme.com). ***Start: Metro to Sagrada Familia.***

Iconic Barcelona in 1 Day
1 Basilica de la Sagrada Familia ★★★
You've seen photographs of the cluster of its spires—the unofficial symbol of Barcelona—but until you get up close and personal with Antoni Gaudí's master-piece (p. 209), the level of carved detail, both inside and out, is impossible to imagine. The architect is buried in a tomb below the main level. He was hit by a streetcar when heading to Mass at **San Felip Neri** (p. 205) from the Sagrada Familia construction site and never saw his masterpiece in more than its rudimen-tary phases.

From the Sagrada Familia metro stop, Plaça de Catalunya is only three quick stops away. When you leave the metro, you'll be at the head of:

2 Les Rambles ★★
This is the most famous promenade in Barcelona. Stroll down the center strip to join the human parade. Keep an eye out on the left for **Cafè de L'Òpera ★** (p. 180), one of the classics among the Art Nouveau cafes on Les Rambles. It's a great place for a quick coffee or a chilling granizado on a warm day.

Just below the cafe you'll find Carrer Ferran heading off to the left into the:

3 Barri Gòtic ★★★
Spend some time just wandering through the oldest quarter of the city.

Then follow the street through Plaza Sant Jaume, flanked by huge government build-ings. On the other side of the plaza, the street name changes to Carrer Princesa. Signs will point you to the:

4 Museu Picasso ★★★
The new gallery organization, which is largely chronological, demonstrates that Picasso's genius did not spring fully formed from the head of Zeus (much as Picasso might have wanted the world to think so). Clearly he had talent even as a lad, but as an art student in Barcelona, his work was competent but derivative. Then he found his way, began to experiment, and in a few short years became Picasso. It's fun to follow the journey, even if you already know the ending.

It's only a 3-minute stroll from the Museu Picasso to one of the loveliest and most beloved churches in the city, the 14th-century Gothic:

5 Santa Maria del Mar ★★★

For such an ancient building, the restrained ornamentation of the interior seems very modern. The soaring space encourages quiet meditation. Note that the church is closed for 3 hours in the afternoon (2–5pm), so if you arrive during that time, consider waiting for it to reopen while enjoying a glass of wine at an outdoor table at the adjacent vinoteca **La Vinya del Senyor ★** (p. 187). Santa Maria is the principal church of **El Born** (p. 160), the neighborhood between the waterfront and La Ribera. Not long ago, it was a working-class neighborhood with laundry hanging off the balconies. Now its ancient buildings feature design shops and boutiques at street level and upscale apartments on the upper floors.

When you've seen enough, make your way to:

6 Cal Pepe
Time for dinner! To enjoy the experience of hanging out with the locals, try to pin down spaces at the bar that opens to Plaça de les Olles.

Day 2

It's funny that an artistic movement that began in the late 19th century should be called "Modernisme," but the Catalan version of Art Nouveau is Barcelona's signature architectural style. You have already seen one of the Modernista masterpieces (the Basilica de La Sagrada Familia), and today you can immerse yourself in Modernisme's more domestic side in L'Eixample, where the style reached its apex. Again, save yourself time and trouble by purchasing tickets to attractions online. *Start: Metro to Diagonal.*

1 Patisseries Mauri ▣ ★
Breakfast at an aristocratic Viennese tearoom sets the perfect tone for a day among the elite of L'Eixample. **Patisseries Mauri** (p. 193) dates from 1929, but the pastries themselves are timeless. In addition to beautiful sweets, the bakery serves croissants of various forms at breakfast.

Once you're sated, walk down Rambla de Catalunya to Carrer del Consell de Cent, turn left, and then left again onto:

2 Passeig de Gracia ★★★

This elegant, leafy boulevard is the main drag of Barcelona's Belle Epoque neighborhood of L'Eixample. The "extension" of the old city was built in the late 19th and early 20th centuries. Fortunately for Barcelona, this period coincided with the mature style of the leading Modernista architects.

As you stroll up Passeig de Gràcia, you'll come first to:

3 Casa Lleó Morrera ★★★

It's now private property, but look up to see the ornate arcades by Lluís Domènech i Montaner.

You can and should go into the beautiful Modernista building next door:

4 Casa Batlló ★★

Modernista architects often took inspiration from natural forms. Here Antoni Gaudí tackled no less a subject than the ocean, as you see in plaster that swirls like waves. See p. 210.

After a big dose of Modernisme, try a smaller dose of postmodernism by seeing the works of Spain's leading late-20th-century artist at the:

5 Fundació Tàpies ★★

Dedicated to the works of Antoni Tàpies, it's not a complete escape from Modernisme, though—the brick building was designed by Domènech i Montaner for the publishing company owned by his mother's family. See p. 210.

There are plenty of sidewalk cafes at which to take a lunch break before you begin your assault on the biggest rockpile of all:

6 Casa Milla ★★★

Also called **La Pedrera** ★★★ (p. 213), or "the Stone Quarry," this apartment building reflects Antoni Gaudí at the height of his design powers, and he pulled out all the stops for the building, which was to be the last of his secular commissions. It was constructed between 1906 and 1912, yet the UNESCO World Heritage site seems startlingly up to date—right down to the underground parking garage with an elevator to the residential floors. The undulating stone facade may have scandalized Barcelona with its formal daring when it was built, but La Pedrera has justly become one of the most loved buildings in the city.

After your tour, spend the remaining afternoon exploring the cross streets of L'Eixample. You'll be amazed at how many Modernista buildings line the elegant avenues. To keep the Modernista theme going, check to see whether any evening performances interest you at the **Palau de la Música Catalana** ★★★ (p. 207), Domènech i Montaner's great concert hall. If that doesn't work out, plan on having dinner at **Loidi** ★★ (p. 190), the less formal L'Eixample restaurant from Martín Berasategui, the great Basque chef who has earned a seeming galaxy of Michelin stars.

Day 3

One of the great things about Barcelona is that you don't have to leave the city to reach the mountains or to walk barefoot on a sandy Mediterranean beach. That's exactly what you will do today, as you explore the gentle heights of Montjuïc and end your day at the harbor's edge where Barcelona was born. *Start: Metro to Plaça d'Espanya.*

1 Museu Nacional d'Art de Catalunya ★★

Get your morning constitutional as you stroll uphill from Placa d'Espanya and then climb the impressive flight of stairs to the entrance of the slopes of the Parc de Montjuïc. Admission to temporary exhibitions is often free here, but it would be a shame to miss the extraordinary collection of Catalan art through the ages, especially the Romanesque murals. The museum also has a treasure-trove of 13th- through 18th-century paintings and sculptures on loan from the **Museo Thyssen-Bornemisza** in Madrid (p. 89) that helps put the works of Catalan artists into a broader European perspective. See p. 217.

Take a 7-minute stroll down Passeig de Santa Madrona to Avinguida Miramar, where you'll find:

2 Fundació Joan Miró ★★

Take a look at the building before you enter. Designed by Catalan architect Josep Lluís Sert, it's a work of art in its own right. Because the collection includes paintings, tapestries, ceramics, prints, and drawings by Miró, you can reflect on his ability to express himself in every medium. When you need a break, stop by the small cafe near the bookshop.

To complete your time on Montjuïc, walk east along Avinguda Miramar about 5 minutes to the funicular station. You can ride the funicular down to the Paral.lel metro station, where you can connect to a train to Drassanes at the:

3 Waterfront ★★

The harbor and beaches really sparkle on a sunny day, but this is a fascinating area in any weather. You have a number of options for boat tours of the harbor. The most romantic choice is a 90-minute tour aboard the sail-powered catamaran *Orsom* ★ (p. 214), which docks at the Moll de Drassanes. Depending on your timing, you might want to consider the mid-afternoon jazz cruise.

When you've returned to shore, you should still have time to walk along the Moll de la Fusta and Passeig Joan de Borbó to the:

4 Museu d'Historia de Catalunya ★★

The museum occupies a stunning multilevel space carved out of a 19th-century warehouse. Admission to temporary exhibitions is also often free at this museum, but the thoughtful permanent displays really help outsiders understand Catalan pride and identity. Don't miss the "portrait of contemporary Catalunya," with photos and quotations from chefs and other notable figures about their lives and their city.

Once you leave the museum, you can get a sense of living history by walking through the narrow streets of:

5 La Barceloneta ★★

This is the city's old fishermen's village, which has, so far, resisted wholesale gentrification. Wander at will, because it is hard to get lost; as on an island, all streets lead to the water. You might want to kick off your shoes and walk on the sand of the beaches. Eventually you'll end up on Passeig Joan de Borbó, which is lined with seafood restaurants. For dinner, the choice is yours, but you cannot go wrong at **Suquet de l'Almirall** ★★ (p. 194), where you can reflect on Catalan life and art over a bowl of the traditional Catalan seafood stew known as "suquet."

BARCELONA FOR FAMILIES

Barcelona is a great city for families. The street life alone fascinates children, and in this 2-day itinerary we recommend attractions that appeal to people of all ages. Every member of the family should return home with a memory of their own special corner of Barcelona. It's always wise not to pack too much into a single day. That's especially true if you have young ones in tow, so we've built in breaks—and some chances for kids to let off extra energy. **Start:** *Metro to Liceu or Catalunya.*

Day 1

You will almost feel like a family in a 1950s sitcom when you make a breakfast of big glasses of chocolate milk and freshly baked pastries at **Granja M. Viader** ★ (p. 181). One of Barcelona's original milk bars, it has the same nostalgic appeal for Barcelonans as old-fashioned diners have for Americans.

When you're done, head toward the harbor along **Les Rambles** ★★★ (p. 198). Walk along the center pedestrian strip so that the kids can look for street performers and check out the stalls with vendors selling birds. It's only about a 15-minute walk, and you can see your next destination, the landmark **Mirador de Colom** ★ (p. 215), by the time you're halfway there. When this monument to Christopher Columbus was dedicated in 1888, dignitaries from Spain, Italy, and the United States attended so that each country could lay claim to the great explorer. Alas, the kids won't be able to climb to the open-air observatory, because a tiny elevator was installed when the monument was constructed. It's just about big enough for a family, and you will all enjoy the harbor views when you reach the top. You can also see the tour boats that dock almost directly across the street at the Moll de Drassanes. The 40-minute harbor tour offered by **Las Golondrinas** ★ (p. 214) gives you a nice break while you take in the view of the city from the water.

From the docks, it's only a short walk out the Rambla del Mar and around the Maremagnum shopping complex to **L'Aquarium de Barcelona** ★★ (p. 214). We like the fact that this aquarium thinks locally rather than globally and concentrates on the Mediterranean. In addition to the show-stopping giant ocean tank, kids are often fascinated by some of the smaller tanks with such strange creatures as weedy sea dragons and big-bellied seahorses. Visiting between noon and 2pm gives you the best chance of hitting feeding time for the sharks, penguins, or rays.

From the aquarium, stroll along the Moll de la Fusta and under the giant sculpture of a lobster until you reach Passeig de Joan Borbó. Turn right, and in minutes you round the point of La Barceloneta and come to **Barcelona's beaches** ★★ (p. 214), where you can spend the afternoon swimming, sunning, and walking at the water's edge.

Day 2

To start the day, take the Metro to Ciutadella to walk through the gardenlike **Parc de la Ciutadella** ★ (p. 208) to the **Zoo de Barcelona** ★ (p. 208). Because it contains more than 300 species in 32 acres, you may want to plan ahead. Young children like the farm, which includes familiar barnyard animals—and a Catalan donkey, a species that was at risk of becoming extinct. The reptile house has one of the best collections of reptiles and amphibians in Europe, including dwarf crocodiles and poison dart frogs. (Make sure the kids look closely, as they'll see similar grotesqueries in stone later.)

From the zoo, walk through the streets of El Born up Via Laeitana to Carrer Princesa to reach the Museu Picasso. The neighborhood is full of gelato shops, so you can eat cones along the way. The kids will think you are brilliant when you pull out your tickets purchased online and skip the long line at the **Museu Picasso** ★★★ (p. 206). The great artist's works have a sense of vigor and immediacy that appeals to youngsters.

From the museum, the streets get even narrower and more twisting as you walk north into the **Barri Gòtic** ★★ (p. 203). If you need a short break from the crowds, step into the quiet courtyard in front of the **Museu Frederic Mares** (p. 204) for a snack in the cafe.

More than 140 images of saints wait right around the corner in the **Catedral de Barcelona** ★★ (p. 203). Your children might like to see how many they can find. The archangel Michael is one of the most widely depicted; he's usually busy slaying the devil. You can also take the elevator to the roof to check out the carved gargoyles and the views of the Barri Gòtic.

By now, your children should have gained an appreciation for the stonecarver's ability to tell stories in stone. For one more great example, walk up to Plaça de Catalunya and hop an N7 bus in the direction of Edith Llaurador-Av. Joan Garí to the **Basílica de la Sagrada Familia** ★★★ (p. 209), where you can again impress the kids with your advance-purchase tickets. But they will be even more impressed with the carved biblical scenes and fantastical animals (snails, lizards, amphibians, snakes, and reptiles serve as gargoyles) carved onto the facade. Architect Gaudí intended the bell tower to unite heaven and earth and serve as a beacon to sailors as they approached Barcelona harbor. To see whether he succeeded, ride the elevator to the tower and take in the view from every direction.

BARCELONA ART THROUGH THE AGES

Barcelona has become so linked with the extravagant architecture of Modernisme—the idiosyncratic Catalan twist on Art Nouveau—that it's easy to forget that the city has a long artistic legacy that stretches from the Middle Ages right into the 21st century. Over the course of 3 days, you can touch on a little bit from almost every era. The **Articket BCN** (p. 199) saves you money and gives you priority entrance to six museums. You can buy it at the first museum you enter or purchase it ahead of time at a Barcelona Turisme office. *Start: Metro to Plaça d'Espanya.*

Day 1

Walk up through the Font Màgica and the garden steps of the Palau Nacional to begin your art tour at the **Museu Nacional d'Art de Catalunya (MNAC)** ★★★ (p. 217). It would be easy to spend days here, wandering from one gallery to the next, but we suggest focusing on the Romanesque art of Catalunya. The region has vigorous painting and sculptural traditions, and it's hard to tell which is more powerful: the 9th- to 12th-century mural paintings rescued from crumbling mountain churches or the exquisite wooden carvings. Most powerful of all are the sculptures of Maria del Deu. The child Jesus often wears a crown and always seems serene; his mother is stoic and all-knowing, as if accepting the human tragedy and religious mystery that will unfold in the coming years.

From the front of MNAC, you can follow Passeig de Santa Madrona to Avinguda Miramar, where you'll find the other end of the chronological spectrum, the **Fundació Joan Miró** ★★ (p. 216). Miró's art was as abstract as Romanesque art was explicit. Amusement and delight are always rooted in surprise, and the wit of this quintessentially Catalan artist pops up again and again in his drawings, paintings, and especially his sculpture.

Catch the Route 55 bus from the front door of Fundació Joan Miró and ride it for about 25 minutes to Plaça de Catalunya to spend the rest of your day in the El Raval neighborhood. Having sampled modern Catalan art, try something even more recent at the **Museu d'Art Contemporani de Barcelona (MACBA)** ★ (p. 199). This great white-and-glass box designed by Richard Meier helped revitalize the north end of El Raval. The towering rooms are perfect for large-scale contemporary art—and the ramps and slopes that surround it have made the museum the largest unintended skateboard park in the city.

Whimsy is, of course, one of the watchwords of contemporary art. As you walk through El Raval, be sure to stop for a Facebook snap with **Fernando Botero's giant bronze cat, "El Gato del Raval"** ★ (p. 160), on La Rambla del Raval, a green park where wild monk parrots screech in the trees. Continue along Carrer Sant Pau to visit the oldest church in the city, **Sant Pau del Camp** ★★ (p. 202). Despite erosion from the passage of 7 centuries, the anonymous 13th-century stone carvings on the capitals of the cloister remain vigorous and vivid. The powerful Maria del Deu statue in a side chapel here is original to the church and still bears the faded colors of its 13th-century paint.

Plan on dinner in an elegant Modernista dining room designed and decorated by Lluís Domènech i Montaner, **Fonda España** ★★ (p. 177) at the Hotel España. The food here is more Basque than Catalan, as the menu is designed by multistarred Basque chef Martin Berasategui. In contrast to his other restaurants in Barcelona, Fonda serves updated traditional cuisine with such dishes as rice with prawns and clams, or roasted sea bass with a Priorat red wine sauce.

Day 2

You can linger over a breakfast of hot chocolate and churros at **Brunells** ★ (p. 185) because you don't need to get in line for the **Museu Picasso** ★★★ (p. 206)—you already bought your tickets. This charming museum of perhaps the greatest artist of the 20th century shows his origins in the student work he executed in Barcelona while still in his teens. It goes on to some of his most masterful pieces created in the 1950s—paintings illuminated with the clear blue seaside light of the French Riviera—and concludes with the brooding work of his old age, when the bull-like virility of the minotaur had deserted him.

It's about a 10-minute walk through Plaça Jaume I to **Santa Maria del Pi** ★ (p. 204). Although the huge rose window was restored in the 1950s after being destroyed by bombardments in the Spanish Civil War, it retains its original 14th-century design, showing the 24 Elders of the Apocalypse. It's a straight stroll up Les Rambles with a slight jog on Carrer Diputació to visit the **Fundació Francisco Godia** ★ (p. 211). Although the collections here include many Catalan painters of the early 20th century, the galleries of Romanesque and Gothic religious sculpture upstage the more modern work. Just 2 blocks away, great late-modern painting takes center stage at the **Fundació Antoni Tàpies** ★★ (p. 210). The museum captures the dramatic and often larger-than-life abstract art of Spain's most famous artist of the late 20th century. The cavernous galleries of the museum give the works room to breathe—indeed, you can almost hear them.

If you haven't already visited the wonderful Antoni Gaudí apartment building of **Casa Batlló** ★★ (p. 210), do it now. The oceanic design themes will make you long for the real thing, so take the Metro from Passeig de Gràcia to Drassanes and stroll the **Moll de la Fusta** (p. 213) along the waterfront, taking special note of the giant lobster sculpture by Xavier Mariscal and "Barcelona Head" by American pop artist Roy Lichtenstein. If Mariscal's work makes you hungry, dine at **Can Solé** ★★ (p. 195) and order the "cigalas." (They will be much smaller.)

Day 3

Start this day by getting to the Barcelona-Sants rail station for a 2-hour ride (more or less) to Figueres in northern Catalunya near the French border. It might seem a long way to go, but Figueres was where Salvador Dalí was born in 1904 and where he died in 1989. He was buried beneath the fly's-eye dome of his final and most bizarre creation, the **Teatre-Museu Dalí** ★★ (p. 225). Never one to be modest when a boast would do better, he claimed that this installation was the largest surreal object in the world. It is filled with his jokes, wisecracks, paintings, sculptures, and personal collections. Visiting is like unscrewing Dalí's ear to see all the gears and pulleys in his brain. You'll be back in Barcelona in time to dress for dinner at **7 Portes** (p. 194), where Dalí liked to dine. He was partial to seafood stews, so order the zarzuela with a half-lobster.

TASTES OF BARCELONA

Barcelona has come to the fore as one of Europe's great eating cities. Michelin accolades are scattered like stardust throughout the city, but even budget diners can enjoy the cooking of some of Barcelona's top chefs. A number of them have opened tapas places as creative relief valves from the pressure of running their fine-dining venues. And sometimes tried and true is even better than the cutting edge. Barcelona's gastronomic reputation was built on simple, old-fashioned places where perfect ingredients make every taste a revelation. That goes double for specialty shops, where some of the purveyors represent the third, fourth, or even fifth generation. This itinerary doesn't have to be a day-long tasting menu (unless you want it to be). Monday is not the best day for Day 1 as some shops are closed, and many wineries of Sant Sadurní d'Anoia (Day 2) close early on Fridays. *Start: Metro to Liceu.*

Day 1

All things foodie in Barcelona inevitably begin at **La Boqueria** ★★★ (p. 198), where the fruit vendors at the front of market make fresh fruit drinks on the spot. Sip a big glass of carrot-orange juice while you look around at the fruits, vegetables, meats, and fish. A rule of thumb for local restaurant dining—if you didn't see it in La Boqueria, you probably shouldn't order it.

After the market, plan on a breakfast of coffee and croissants at the beautiful Art Nouveau **Pastelería Escribà** ★★ (p. 180) right next door.

Walk off a few of those calories on your way up Les Rambles, through Plaça de Catalunya, and 3 blocks up La Rambla de Catalunya to the legendary gourmet shop **Colmado Quilez** (p. 221). The two rooms are packed from floor to high ceiling with all manner of dry and canned foods (sardines, octopus, several kinds of chickpeas, all different paprikas, saffron), and the deli cases contain treasures of cheese and charcuterie. The shop has some cook-at-home kits that include rice or pasta and a tin of other ingredients. Wow your friends and family back home by making a "fideuà negre amb sepiones" (a black-noodle paella with cuttlefish) or a "sopa de peix marisc" (a Catalan shellfish stew).

Only a block away, you can visit the first shop of the small **Cacao Sampaka** (p. 221), a chain of radically rethought chocolate in both sweet and savory forms. Albert Adrià, brother of famed chef Ferran, is one of the founders, and Sampaka's chocolates were among the first to incorporate such unusual flavors as wasabi and chile peppers.

From the nearby Passeig de Gràcia metro station, take the L4 line toward La Pau for two stops to Jaume I. Walk up Via Laietana and turn right on Avinguda Francesc Cambó to visit **Mercat Santa Caterina** ★★ (p. 206). It's a little less hectic than La Boqueria, so you can enjoy a more leisurely look at the foodstuffs. Plan on having lunch at **Cuines Santa Caterina** ★★ (p. 182), a great place to try a tempura treatment of some of those fresh market Catalan vegetables.

We hope you saved room for dessert. Walk about 5 minutes east to visit the **Museu de la Xocolata** ★ (p. 206), where the chocolate fountain and molded chocolate sculptures may give you a hankering for something sweet. Relief is in your hand; your entry ticket is a chocolate bar. When you come out, head down Carrer Comerç and turn right onto Passeig del Born. Around one side of Santa Maria del Mar, you'll find the venerable roaster **E & A Gispert** (p. 221). Just close your eyes and follow the aromas of roasting nuts and coffee beans. Meander through El Born for drinks and small plates at **Ten's Tapas** ★★ (p. 187), the creative tapas restaurant established by superchef Jordi Cruz. After a few tasty bites, you can cross Passeig de Colom and walk down Passeig Joan de Borbó to the tip of La Barceloneta for a late dinner at **Kaiku** ★★ (p. 196), where the owner and chef always seek out the most unusual items at the fish auction a few blocks away.

Day 2

Make a beeline for **Tapas 24** ★★ (p. 193), the casual and imaginative tapas restaurant from Carles Abellan. Breakfast is too early to order his famous "McFoie" burger (a hamburger topped with foie gras), but the staff makes a terrific bowl of estrellitas: fried potatoes with a broken fried egg stirred in on top (sausage optional).

You're only 2 blocks from Plaça de Catalunya, where you can catch an R4 train to the bucolic village of **Sant Sadurní d'Anoia** ★ (p. 224), where the majority of Catalunya's cava (sparkling wine) comes from. More than three dozen cellars are open for visits, so you can be casual and visit the small ones in town on a catch-as-catch-can basis, or call ahead for the full tour of the facility at Freixenet or Codorníu. Speaking of reservations, make them ahead of time so you can return to Barcelona for an evening of classic Catalan cooking beautifully prepared and lovingly served on giant marble tables upstairs at **Can Ravell** ★★★ (p. 192). Only a few options are available for each course, and they depend entirely on the season. Go with the flow for a memorable meal.

MADRID & BARCELONA IN CONTEXT

D ifferent as they are, Madrid and Barcelona are both products of a land that the rest of Europe once considered beyond the pale. One of the few things that the French and English used to agree on was that "Europe ends at the Pyrenees." In a sense, they were right, for the mountains kept Spain in splendid isolation, where it developed on its own path. It developed customs, art, architecture, and even cuisine that owed as much to Arabic North Africa as to its onetime sister provinces of the Roman Empire. Consequently, Spain does not look like, sound like, or even taste like the rest of Europe. Nowhere else is quite as rich, or quite as demanding. When you go to Spain, you must surrender to Spain.

You must accept the rhythms of daily life—so unlike the rest of Europe—and think nothing of going to dinner after 10pm and then closing down the flamenco bar after the 3am final set. You must spend the evening in a seafront promenade, walking and talking and nodding at the other walkers and talkers. You must not be bashful about elbowing your way to the bar, pointing at the tapas to order, and having your fill. For that matter, you must resolve to eat something new every day that you would otherwise spurn: blood sausage, roast suckling pig, squid in their own ink. In many places, shops and museums close in the heat of the afternoon, and you must be patient and while away the hours with lunch in a cool, shady courtyard. Do all that, and you will be ready for everything Spain will throw at you.

Rest assured, it will be a lot. The cultural renaissance that followed the 1975 death of dictator Francisco Franco continues to gather steam nearly 4 decades later. Madrid and Barcelona have emerged as major European artistic and intellectual centers and capitals of cinema, fashion, and gastronomy.

SPAIN TODAY

Seven years of international financial crises have left Spain the equivalent of "house poor." Before the collapse began in 2007, Spain had launched some of the most audacious infrastructure improvements since Europe's recovery from World War II. New roads, high-speed rail, and new and improved airports helped knit together a physically large country. Travel times were cut to a fraction of what they once were, and relatively inaccessible parts of Spain are now a short drive or train ride away. Barcelona's **El**

Prat airport opened a new Terminal 1 in 2009, at the same time redesigning the older terminals A, B, and C as Terminal 2. Plans for a third terminal await an improvement in government finances. Madrid's **Barajas** airport opened the futuristic Terminal 4, in 2006. With a satellite Terminal 4A located 1.5 miles (2.5km) from the main terminal, it is one of the largest airline terminals in the world. Air traffic between Barcelona and Madrid, once one of the busiest routes in the world, slacked off considerably after the opening of high-speed rail, which covers the distance between the two cities in just 2½ hours.

Alas, the bills for all those infrastructure upgrades came due at the same time that the credit dried up. As a result, Spain's national economy has suffered, and inflation has turned to deflation. With one-quarter of the country's workers idle, Spain's social safety net is stretched to its limits. Tourism remains the bright spot in the economy. European visitors continue to flock to Spain's beach resorts on both the Mediterranean and the Atlantic coasts, while Americans are the top visitor group to Sevilla, Madrid, and Barcelona. Spain has always been a friendly place for English speakers. Now more Spaniards than ever speak the language, often with an accent honed by American television and movies.

LOOKING BACK AT SPAIN

The majesty of Madrid and the spectacle of Barcelona both have roots in the history of Spain. Phoenicians began colonizing coastal Mediterranean Iberia around 1100 B.C., followed by the Greeks and the Carthaginians. In 218 B.C., the Romans landed and changed everything. Establishing a beachhead to battle the Carthaginians in the Second Punic War, they proceeded to lay roads across Iberia and either conquer or co-opt everyone they met along the way. The Phoenicians and Greeks had already brought wine grapes and olive trees; the Romans brought wheat, law and order, a hunger for Iberian fish paste, and an insatiable need for soldiers to fight in the Roman legions. By the time of Julius Caesar, Hispania was under Roman law and began a long period of peace and prosperity.

Tarragona, a short trip south from Barcelona, became the administrative center for eastern Hispania and retains many Roman structures to this day (p. 227). The Romans were natural architects and engineers. Throughout the country, Roman roads still form the base for many highways. **Segovia,** a short trip out of Madrid, boasts one of the greatest of the Roman aqueducts (p. 131).

When the Roman Empire crumbled in the A.D. 5th century, Iberia was first overrun by the Vandals (northern Germans who ultimately kept going south into the mountains of North Africa) and then by the Visigoths from eastern Europe. Rome had invited them to drive out the Vandals, but they decided to keep Iberia for themselves. Always a minority ruling class, the Visigoths left surprisingly few traces of their 200-year rule—mainly a few country churches in northern Spain and some of the most sophisticated gold jewelry ever fashioned, the royal jewels and crowns displayed in the **National Archaeological Museum** in Madrid (p. 86).

Centuries of Holy Wars

In A.D. 711, the game changed again. Led by the great Berber general Tariq ibn Ziyad, Moorish warriors crossed the Straits of Gibraltar and set about conquering Iberia. Within 3 years, the Moors controlled all but the far northern fringe of the peninsula, where the Basques and the Asturian Visigoths held out in their mountain lairs.

Córdoba, in southern Spain, became the capital of al-Andalus (as the Moors called Iberia) and quickly developed into the most advanced city on the continent. While northern Europe was floundering in the Dark Ages, Córdoba was a center of intellectual and scientific ferment.

By the late 11th century, powerful local kingdoms had arisen in northern Spain with the single-minded goal of restoring Christian rule to Muslim Iberia. When civil war broke out in al-Andalus, the northern Christian warriors pounced. **Alfonso VI** of Castilla seized Toldeo, Madrid, and much of central Spain in 1085; the great warlord and national hero **El Cid** won back Valencia and Catalunya (including Barcelona) in 1094. By 1214, only three major powers remained in Iberia: Castilla in the north, west, and center of Spain; Aragón in northeastern Spain; and the Moorish kingdom of Granada.

The Castilian and Aragónese bloodlines would finally meet in Spain's first power couple, **Isabel I of Castilla and León** and **Fernando II of Aragón.** They married in 1469, bringing Toledo (and nearby Madrid) and Barcelona under the same joint rule. Isabel launched the Spanish Inquisition to ferret out heretics and the Catholic kings, as the pope would dub them; made war on Granada; and drove out its last ruler in 1492. Declaring the reconquest complete, Isabel and Fernando decreed that all Muslims and Jews must either convert to Christianity or leave the country.

Later that same year, they dispatched **Christopher Columbus** to find a westward passage to the Spice Islands of Asia. In October 1492, he made landfall instead in the West Indies, laying the foundations for a far-flung empire that would bring wealth and power to Spain throughout the 16th and 17th centuries.

Imperial Spain

The grandson of Isabel and Fernando, the Habsburg king **Carlos I,** became the most powerful prince in Europe when he was crowned Holy Roman Emperor in 1519 and took the title **Carlos V.** He ruled Spain and Naples and the Holy Roman Empire and was lord of Germany, duke of Burgundy and the Netherlands, and ruler of the New World territories. His son, **Felipe II,** inherited the throne in 1556 and 5 years later moved the capital from the closed hilltop medieval city of Toledo to Madrid, where the Habsburg kings had a hunting palace.

Madrid grew quickly from dusty outpost to royal city, setting Spain on its Golden Age of arts and letters, and Madrid on its domination of the national scene. **Miguel de Cervantes** (1547–1616), a career petty bureaucrat, penned the adventures of Don Quixote and set the standard for Spanish prose. The rascal priest **Lope de Vega** (1562–1635) wrote poems and plays incessantly, redefining the Spanish theater in the company of **Calderón de la Barca** (1600–81) and **Tirso de Molina** (1579–1648).

El Greco (1541–1614) came to Toledo from Italy and brought the Italian Renaissance with him, although he could not curry favor at court and remained outside royal circles. One of his greatest works, **"The Burial of the Count of Orgaz,"** occupies a modest chapel in Toledo's **Iglesia de Santo Tomé** (p. 120). **Diego Velázquez** (1599–1660) rose to become court painter to **Felipe IV,** and the two men were bound like brothers over several decades, as Velázquez chronicled the royal family. His paintings were rarely seen in his own day and became public only when the royal art collection was installed in the **Museo del Prado** (p. 86) in the 19th century.

During the same period, Barcelona enjoyed limited political autonomy. It was a prosperous maritime center, although the relative importance of Mediterranean trade to the Spanish crown was undercut by trade with the American colonies. The Barcelona nobility and their Catalan peers, however, made one major political miscalculation: When the throne of Spain was up for grabs in the early 18th century, Barcelona backed the Habsburgs instead of the victorious Bourbons. In 1715, **Felipe V** retaliated by abolishing the autonomy of Catalunya, quashing Barcelona's influence and Catalunya's nationalist aspirations. At the same time, he launched the construction of the **Palacio Real** in Madrid (p. 98). His son **Carlos III** set about remaking the face of Madrid with the aid of Spain's principal neoclassical architect, **Ventura Rodríguez** (1717–85), who laid out the grand boulevard of the Paseo del Prado and worked with **Juan de Villanueva** (1739–1811) on the design of one of Spain's best neoclassical buildings, the Museo del Prado (p. 86).

Spain in Chaos

Napoleon Bonaparte's 1808 invasion of Spain set off 167 years of instability and political oppression. Noting that Catalunya only existed because the French monarchy had established it in the 9th century as a buffer state between the French and the Moors, Napoleon annexed the region (and the riches of Barcelona) as France's Department de Montserrat. The rest of Spain literally took to the hills to fight the French emperor in the War of Independence, finally driving his armies out in 1813. **Francisco de Goya** famously delineated the horrors of French occupation in a series of paintings now in the Prado, including scenes of French troops putting down a rebellion in Madrid.

The Catalan territory was restored to Spain, along with the Bourbon monarchy, but something in Spanish governance was irreparably broken. **Fernando VII** regained the throne but proved to be no friend of the freedom fighters and spent 2 decades putting down revolts. His arrogance and inflexibility led to the loss of Spain's most lucrative colonies in the Americas—and subsequent financial hardship for the country.

On the death of Fernando in 1833, civil war broke out between supporters of his daughter (**Isabel II**) and so-called Carlists who favored a more distant—but male—heir to the throne. Two more Carlist wars were fought, mostly in Navarra and the Basque Country, over the next 50 years, and Carlist sympathies festered into the 20th century. During this period, Spain was coming apart at the seams, and nationalist fervor ran high in many regions, especially Catalunya.

Scholars began to reestablish Catalan as a language of serious letters, and the avant-garde design style known as Art Nouveau in France and Jugendstil in Austria found native expression in Barcelona in the radical architecture of **Modernisme.** The most extreme practitioner was **Antoni Gaudí** (1852–1926), who seemed as much to grow his buildings as construct them. His masterpiece **La Sagrada Familia** (p. 209) integrates the impossibly soaring arches of High Gothic with a decorative style akin to melted candle wax. Other famous practitioners of Modernisme include **Lluís Domènech i Montaner** (1850–1923), known for the **Palau de la Música Catalana** (p. 207) in Barcelona, and **Josep Puig i Cadafalch** (1867–1956), who designed the **Codorniù bodega** in Sant Sadurní de Anoia (p. 225).

Isabel II ultimately was driven into exile in Paris, but the shaky monarchy was restored in 1874 when her son **Alfonso XII** became king. His sudden death in 1886 left his unborn son as monarch. The child was crowned **Alfonso XIII** at birth but his mother, Queen María Cristina, served as regent until 1902, and her advisors botched both the Spanish economy and its international relations. During this period, Spain lost its remaining American colonies, suffering as much from the loss of national dignity as overseas riches. Although he enjoyed immense personal popularity—he was the first Spanish celebrity king—Alfonso XIII exercised little real power. His chief legacy was to adopt the **Real Madrid** football club and to create the parador hotel system. In 1923, he allowed prime minister **Primo de Rivera** to take over the country as dictator for the next 7 years.

Civil War & the Franco Years

Primo de Rivera was overthrown, and in 1931 Spain declared the Second Republic. Initially progressive and left-wing in its politics, the new government broke into ever smaller factions. Conservative, fascist-minded parties gained ground in the elections. When a group of right-wing generals declared a coup in 1936, the Civil War began. The world took sides, with Hitler and Mussolini backing **Francisco Franco** and the Nationalist generals and most of the rest of Europe nominally backing the Republicans, also known as Loyalists or the Popular Front. Germany and Italy sent weapons and military assistance to the right, while the rest of the world sent a few volunteer brigades to the left.

Madrid, controlled by the Popular Front, held out through a brutal siege that lasted for 28 months. Eventually, the government of the Popular Front moved to Valencia for greater safety in 1936. But in the winter of 1936–37, Franco's forces slowly began to establish power, capturing the Basque country and demonstrating his ruthlessness by calling in the German Luftwaffe to destroy the Basque town of **Gernika** (Guernica in Castilian Spanish). The horror of the scene, which became the subject of one of Picasso's most famous paintings, **"Guernica"** (p. 88), repulsed the world.

At the end of the first year of war, Franco held 35 of Spain's provincial capitals, except for Madrid and Barcelona. In 1937, the Republican forces were cut in two, and Madrid was left to fend for itself. The last great offensive of the war began on December 23, 1938, with an attack by Franco's forces on Barcelona, which fell on January 26, 1939, after a campaign of 34 days. Republican forces fled to France. On March 28, some 200,000 of Franco's troops marched into Madrid, meeting no resistance. The war was over the next day, when the rest of Republican Spain surrendered. Lasting 2 years and 254 days, the war claimed one million lives. Spain lay in ruins, with Franco atop the smoking pile.

Steering Spain clear of alliances, Franco continued to rule until his death in 1975. He brought order, if not freedom, but he also isolated Spain from the rest of Europe. Only the U.S. maintained close relations, initiated in the 1950s to place air bases on Spanish soil from which bombers could reach the Soviet Union.

Democratic Spain

According to advance provisions made by Franco, **Juan Carlos de Bórbon,** the grandson of Alfonso XIII, became king when the dictator died in 1975. (Juan Carlos I remains on the throne today.) Under the terms of a 1978 constitution, Spain became a constitutional democracy with a reigning monarch who has no role as a ruler. The constitution also devolved much of the government's centralized powers to autonomous regions, addressing in part long-standing calls for self-government in Catalunya.

Franco's death was an equally momentous event for society as for politics. The initial giddiness of Spaniards was dubbed "La Movida" and symbolized an explosion of freedom that brought such iconoclasts as filmmaker **Pedro Almodóvar** to the fore. He broke into the art-house circuit with his 1988 "Women on the Verge of a Nervous Breakdown"—a wild comedy about Spanish women and their man problems—and promptly became the flag-bearer of contemporary Spanish cinema. Hallmarks of his films include neurotic but oversexed characters, unsettling mother-son relationships, and the leitmotifs of the death dance of the bullfight and the exuberant emotion of flamenco. His work is seen by critics (and many filmgoers) as defining modern Spanish sensibilities. As Almodóvar himself has observed, "I was born at a bad time for Spain, but a really good one for cinema." In the process of making films that wickedly satirize Spanish mores, Almodóvar has discovered and helped develop such major film stars as **Antonio Banderas, Penélope Cruz,** and **Javier Bardem.**

Flamenco had been suppressed under Franco but began to rise in popularity in the early 1970s just as the dictator's health declined. Young talents, such as guitarist **Paco de Lucía** and singer **Camerón de la Isla,** fed into a popular revival of the art form, and their emergence as full-fledged international stars in the early 1980s encouraged other artists to come out of the peñas (private clubs for flamenco aficionados) where they had labored—some for decades—to play the bars and clubs of Madrid and the cities of Andalucía. Today, Madrid is the epicenter of flamenco, but Sevilla, Jerez, Cádiz, and Málaga remain traditional strongholds of the essentially Andalucían music and dance.

In a similar vein, Spanish gastronomy underwent a sea change. The revolution began at a 1976 round table on gastronomy held by Madrid's new Club de Gourmets, where French chef Paul Bocuse spoke about his nouvelle cuisine and inspired Basque chefs **Pedro Subijana** and **Juan Mari Arzak** to take the same approach to Spanish food. They in turn inspired a young Catalan cook fresh out of military service named **Ferran Adrià,** who joined the staff of a tiny seasonal restaurant on the Catalan coast called **elBulli** in 1984. By 1987, he was in charge of the whole kitchen. By 1990, he had earned a second Michelin star, and by 1997, a third. In his quest for continuous reinvention of food, Adrià launched a worldwide gastronomic revolution that includes but is hardly limited to the chemistry-set pyrotechnics of molecular gastronomy.

Adrià has since closed elBulli, leaving the frontiers of gastronomy to others. It is a great time to eat in Spain. Chefs have never been held in higher regard—they have finally achieved the fame and status of rock stars and star footballers. (Two-star Michelin Barcelona/Madrid chefs **Sergi Arola** and **David Muñoz** were, in fact, a rock musician and a footballer, respectively.) And the chefs challenge each other to constantly improve. **Madrid Fusion,** held annually, is a world summit of chefs who trade information on what's hot and what's new around the globe. Often as not, the "new" comes from somewhere in Spain. Yet not all the great dining in Spain costs 150€ and up—before wine. The trickle-down of culinary aspiration reaches all the way to Spain's bars, where complex and inventive tapas, called tapas creativas, are all the rage.

In a way, Spain's coming-out parties to the world were **Expo '92** in Sevilla and the **1992 Summer Olympics** in Barcelona. The latter spurred the transformation of its host city, completely overhauling the waterfront and heralding Barcelona's reemergence on the world stage. In that same year in Madrid, the **Museo Nacional Centro de Arte de Reina Sofía** (p. 88) opened, displaying 20th-century and contemporary art in an 18th-century former hospital altered by the addition of three glass towers. Madrid's **Museo Thyssen-Bornamisza** (p. 89) also opened that year in the 18th-century Palacio Villahermosa. The acquisition of this seminal private collection of art was seen as a coup for Spain and a vote of confidence in Madrid's continued importance in the art world.

The first decade of the 21st century has ushered in many social changes. In March 2002, Spain officially abandoned its time-honored peseta and went under the euro

flamenco: KEEP AN OPEN EAR

Flamenco has undergone such a resurgence in Spain that it has again become the dominant form of popular music, finally pushing American dance pop and its Spanish imitators off the Spanish charts. Here are some musicians who have shaped the current scene and whose recordings are part of the essential flamenco collection.

PEPE HABICHUELA (B. 1944)

A product of Granada's Gypsy community, this virtuoso guitarist and band leader is known for his highly emotional style and his readiness to collaborate with other musical traditions (Indian, Arabic, and jazz).

PACO DE LUCÍA (B. 1947)

This virtuoso guitarist from Algeciras was a child prodigy who began touring at age 11 with José Greco. One of the musicians who launched the revival of flamenco, he is the acknowledged technical and stylistic master of the modern flamenco guitar.

CAMARÓN DE LA ISLA (1950–92)

A Gypsy from San Fernando (near Algeciras), Camarón vaulted from singing at bus stops to stardom at age 16, recording 10 albums with Paco de Lucía. His wrenching emotional style set a benchmark for modern flamenco singing.

CARMEN LINARES (B. 1951)

The leading female flamenco singer of her generation, her encyclopedic repertoire embraces virtually all styles and forms of flamenco. She is a popular recording and television star.

CONCHA BUIKA (B. 1972)

Born in Palma de Mallorca and raised in a Gypsy neighborhood, Buika is of sub-Saharan African descent and even worked as a Tina Turner impersonator in Las Vegas casinos. Her flamenco style blends traditional coplas (meter) with elements of jazz, soul, and pop music.

RADIO TARIFA

Controversial for their "reinvented" style of Arabic-Hispanic-Sephardic music pre-1492, this lively trio formed in the late 1990s performs fusion music as programmed by their imagined radio station on the Straits of Gibraltar. Their tunes can be heard booming from open windows all over Andalucía.

umbrella, to the consternation of many Spaniards and widespread complaints about price gouging. In what some Spaniards saw as an assault on their lifestyle—even their very identity—Spain came under increasing pressure to conform to short lunch breaks like those in other E.U. countries. What? No 3-hour siesta? It was heresy. Despite opposition, large companies began to cut lunch to 2 hours. Pro-siesta forces in Spain cited the American custom of "power naps" as a reason to retain their beloved afternoon break. Visitors should not cave to E.U. peer pressure and should continue to observe the quintessentially Spanish practice of the prolonged lunch.

In April 2005, Spain became the third European country to recognize gay marriage, after the Netherlands and Belgium. In practice, contemporary Spain is an especially attractive destination for LGBT travelers, and some resort towns, such as Sitges (p. 233) on the coast south of Barcelona, are at least as gay as they are straight during the height of the tourist season. Most major cities, including Madrid and Barcelona, have a fairly vibrant gay nightlife.

Perhaps the most radical sign that Spain had embraced Europe came in 2011, when, bowing to E.U. health policies, smoking was banned in all bars and restaurants throughout the country. Because Spaniards were among the heaviest smokers in Europe, observers predicted that the law was bound to fail. On the contrary, it is generally respected, as Spaniards have discovered how good food tastes without a side of second-hand smoke.

The smoking ban and the ongoing economic crisis have not diminished Spain's lively bar scene. Smokers simply pop out to the street for a smoke before coming back inside to eat and drink, and the crunch on personal income has meant a proliferation of the "especial de crisis" meal—a bargain plate for impecunious times.

3 WHEN TO GO

Spring and fall are ideal times to visit both Madrid and Barcelona. May and October are the best months, in terms of both weather and crowds. In summer, it's hot, hot, and hotter still, with Madrid often reaching 95°F or higher in August. Fortunately, it's a dry heat. Barcelona is appreciably cooler in the summer, but the humidity is so high that temperatures barely drop at night. The surrounding sea, however, is warm enough for swimming from late June into early October. Winter can be surprisingly delightful, especially in Madrid, where the dry cold rarely sinks below freezing at night and the sunny afternoons can reach 60°F or more. Even in Barcelona, winter days are often crisp and cold, due to the nearby mountains, but the sun is usually shining.

Much of Europe goes on vacation in August, Spaniards included. Because Barcelona is close to the beach resorts of Costa Brava, it is especially packed with tourists, but travelers also flock to Madrid. Local restaurateurs and shopkeepers also take August holidays, so be aware that you could find some places closed if you choose that month to visit.

Average Daily Temperature & Monthly Rainfall for Barcelona & Madrid

	JAN	FEB	MAR	APR	MAY	JUNE	JULY	AUG	SEPT	OCT	NOV	DEC
BARCELONA Temp. (°F)	48	49	52	55	61	68	73	73	70	63	55	50
Temp. (°C)	9	9	11	13	16	20	23	23	21	17	13	10
Rainfall (in.)	1.7	1.4	1.9	2.0	2.2	1.5	.9	1.6	3.1	3.7	2.9	2.0
MADRID Temp. (°F)	42	45	49	53	60	69	76	75	69	58	48	43
Temp. (°C)	6	7	9	12	16	21	24	24	21	14	9	6
Rainfall (in.)	1.6	1.8	1.2	1.8	1.5	1.0	.3	.4	1.1	1.5	2.3	1.7

Holidays include January 1 (New Year's Day), January 6 (Feast of the Epiphany), March 19 (Feast of St. Joseph), Good Friday, Easter Monday, May 1 (May Day), June 10 (Corpus Christi), June 29 (Feast of the Assumption), October 12 (Spain's National Day), November 1 (All Saints' Day), December 8 (Immaculate Conception), and December 25 (Christmas). In addition, Madrid celebrates the feast of San Isidro, its patron saint, on May 15, while Barcelona holds a 4-day La Mercè festival at the beginning of the last week of September in honor of patron saint Mare de Deu de la Mercè. If a holiday falls on a Thursday or Tuesday, many Spaniards take off the weekday in between to create an extra-long weekend known as a *puente,* or bridge. Be sure to book hotels well ahead of time. You can always get money from ATMs on holidays, but intercity bus service is sometimes suspended.

Events in Madrid & Barcelona

The dates given below are approximate and will help you start planning. Sometimes the exact days are not announced until 6 weeks before the actual festival. Unless otherwise noted, visit www.esmadrid.com or call ✆ **91-588-16-36** for more information on events in Madrid. For events in Barcelona, visit www.barcelonaturisme.com or call ✆ **93-285-38-34.**

JANUARY/FEBRUARY

Día de los Reyes (Three Kings Day), throughout Spain. Parades are held around the country on the eve of the Festival of the Epiphany. Various "kings" dispense candy to all the kids. January 5–6.

Gastrofestival, Madrid. While top international chefs gather for Madrid Fusion, restaurants and tapas bars offer special menus and treats. Cooking tours and demos are held; museums and galleries host food-themed films and programs. Last week of January, first week of February.

ARCO (Madrid's International Contemporary Art Fair), Madrid. One of the biggest draws on Spain's cultural calendar, this exhibit showcases the best in contemporary art from Europe, the Americas, Australia, and Asia. For more information, go to www.ifema.es or call ✆ 91-722-30-00. Dates vary, but the event usually takes place mid-February.

Madrid Carnaval. The carnival kicks off with a big parade along Paseo de la Castellana, culminating in a masked ball at the Círculo de Bellas Artes on the following night. Fancy-dress competitions last until Ash Wednesday, when the festivities end with a tear-jerking "burial of a sardine" at the Fuente de los Pajaritos in the Casa de Campo, followed by a concert in the Plaza Mayor. Just before Lent.

Barcelona Carnaval. Compared to other parts of Spain, Carnaval in Barcelona is a low-key affair. In addition to the city's main parade, stall-owners in local markets organize a competition among themselves for best costume. Just south of the city, in the seaside town of Sitges, the local gay community goes all out for Carnaval. Many Barceloneses hop the commuter rail to celebrate with them. Just before Lent.

MARCH/APRIL

Semana Santa (Holy Week), throughout Spain. From Palm Sunday until Easter Sunday, a series of processions with hooded penitents moves to the piercing wail of the saeta. Heavy floats, or pasos, bearing the image of the Virgin or Christ are carried on the penitents' shoulders. The festivities in Madrid are among the most elaborate in Spain. Not surprisingly, Catalunya has some traditions not found in the rest of Spain. The "Mona de Pascua," a whimsical chocolate and pastry cake, is traditionally given by godparents to their godchildren. On Palm Sunday, palm leaves are blessed in Gaudí's Sagrada Familia. Spaniards often take holidays on this week, and hotel prices soar to the highest of the year. Be sure to reserve in advance. Some restaurants and attractions curtail their hours. Unless you are interested in the religious spectacle, it's a good week to avoid. One week before Easter.

La Diada de Sant Jordi, Catalunya. St. George (Sant Jordi in Catalan) is the patron saint of Catalunya, and his feast day coincides with the deaths of Miguel de Cervantes and William Shakespeare. On this day, men traditionally give a single red rose to the significant women in their lives, and women give a book in return. This is one of the most colorful days in Catalunya, as thousands of rose-sellers take to the streets and bookshops set up open-air stalls along the major thoroughfares. April 23.

MAY/JUNE

Fiesta de San Isidro, Madrid. Madrileños run wild with a 10-day celebration honoring the city's patron saint. Food fairs, Castilian folkloric events, street parades, parties, music, dances, bullfights, and other festivities mark the occasion. Make hotel reservations early. Expect crowds and traffic. Mid-May.

Corpus Christi, all over Spain. A major holiday on the Spanish calendar, this event is marked by big processions in Madrid as well as in nearby cathedral cities, such as Toledo. In Catalunya, the streets of Sitges are carpeted in flowers. May or June, depending on liturgical calendar.

Suma Flamenca, Madrid. This month-long flamenco summit offers performances almost every night. Events range from intimate club performances to large-hall concerts. For information on performers and venues, see www.madrid.org/sumaflamenca. June.

Sónar, Barcelona. This international 3-day festival of advanced music and new media art has gained a reputation as one of the world's most innovative. For more information, visit http://sonar.es. Early to mid-June.

Verbena de Sant Joan, Barcelona. This traditional festival occupies all Catalans. Barcelona literally lights up, with fireworks, bonfires, and dances until dawn. The highlight of the festival is the fireworks show at Montjuïc. June 23 (eve of feast of St. John).

JULY

Veranos de la Villa, Madrid. This program presents folkloric dancing, pop music, classical music, zarzuelas, and flamenco at venues throughout the city. Open-air cinema is shown in the Parque del Retiro. The program changes every summer. Sometimes admission is charged, but these events are often free. July through August.

El Grec, Barcelona. International names in all genres of music and theater come to the city to perform in various open-air venues, including the 1929 Greek-style theater on Montjuïc.

AUGUST

Fiestas of Lavapiés and La Paloma, Madrid. These two fiestas begin with the Lavapiés on August 1 and continue through the hectic La Paloma celebration on August 15, the Day of the Virgen de la Paloma. During the fiestas, thousands of people race through the narrow streets. Apartment dwellers hurl buckets of cold water onto the crowds below to cool them off. There are children's games, floats, music, flamenco,

and zarzuelas, along with street fairs. Two weeks in early August.

SEPTEMBER

Diada de Catalunya, Barcelona. This is the most significant festival in Catalunya. It celebrates the region's autonomy from the rest of Spain, following years of repression under the dictator Franco. Demonstrations and other flag-waving events take place. The *senyera,* the flag of Catalunya, is everywhere. Not your typical tourist fare, but interesting. For more information, visit www. gencat.net or call © 93-238-80-91. September 11.

Festa de la Mercè, Barcelona. This celebration honors Mare de Deu de la Mercè, the city's patron saint, known for her compassion for animals. Beginning after dark, and after a Mass in the Igreja de la Mercè, a procession of as many as 50 "animals" (humans dressed like tigers, lions, and horses) proceeds with lots of firecrackers and sparklers to the cathedral and then on to Plaça de Sant Jaume and eventually into Les Rambles, Plaça de Catalunya, and the harborfront. Mid-September.

OCTOBER/NOVEMBER

Feria de Otoño, Madrid. Spanish and international artists participate in this cultural program, with a series of operatic, ballet, dance, music, and theatrical performances featuring companies from Strasbourg to Tokyo. This event is a premier attraction, yet tickets are reasonably priced. Make hotel reservations early. Late October to late November.

All Saints' Day, all over Spain. This public holiday is reverently celebrated, as relatives and friends lay flowers on the graves or *nichos* of the dead. Many bars in Madrid and Barcelona hold Halloween parties the night before—an imported custom that seems to be catching on. November 1.

DECEMBER

Christmas Markets, Madrid and Barcelona. More than 100 stalls set up in Plaza Mayor in Madrid to sell handicrafts, Christmas decorations, and Nativity scenes. A similar market sets up in the plaza outside Barcelona's cathedral.

VISIONS OF MADRID & BARCELONA

Spain's artistic tradition goes back around 30,000 years, if you count the magical cave paintings in the mountains above the Cantabrian coast. (Picasso himself once quipped, "After Altamira, everything is decadence.") Some of Europe's greatest masters were Spaniards or did their greatest work in Spain. Here are some not to miss—and where to see their art.

BERNAT MARTORELL (d. 1452) A painter of retables and manuscript illuminations, Martorell revolutionized Catalan painting in the second quarter of the 15th century, bringing a complexity of composition and luminous handling of color and light that drew on both the International Gothic style and Catalunya's dynamic Romanesque painting tradition. One of his greatest surviving works is the "Altarpiece of the Saints John," which is displayed in the Museu Nacional d'Art de Catalunya (p. 217).

EL GRECO (1540–1614) Crete-born Doménikos Theotokópoulos settled in Toledo in 1577 and spent the next 4 decades filling the city's churches with his singular style. His phantasmagoric color and action-filled application of paint made him an inspiration to 20th-century Expressionists. His work is found extensively throughout Toledo and in the Museo del Prado (p. 86) in Madrid.

FRANCISCO DE ZURBARÁN (1598–1664) The Spanish master of chiaroscuro concentrated on painting ascetic religious meditations for monastery walls, often using the monks as models for saints and martyrs. His forte was the struggle between passionate spirit and palpable flesh, hence his frequent rendering of St. Jeronimo. Many of his major works are in the Museo del Prado (p. 86) in Madrid.

DIEGO VELÁZQUEZ (1599–1660) Becoming Felipe IV's court painter at age 25, Velázquez created his greatest works—mostly portraits—while in the royal employ. When the paintings were later deposited in the Museo del Prado (p. 86), where they occupy several galleries, his genius was rediscovered by critics and artists. His masterpiece "Las Meninas" (1654) became one of the most influential paintings in the history of European art.

FRANCISCO DE GOYA (1746–1828) Capable of both giddy pictorialism—as in his bucolic scenes created for the tapestries hung at El Pardo (p. 105)—and harrowing, nightmare images, Goya stands with Velázquez and Picasso in the triumvirate of Spain's greatest artists. His late works painted during the French occupation carry a direct emotional force that was truly new in European art. The best of Goya's work is found in the Museo del Prado (p. 86) and in the Real Academia de Bellas Artes de San Fernando (p. 91), both in Madrid.

JOAQUÍN SOROLLA (1863–1923) Born in Valencia, Sorolla was Spain's premier painter of light and saturated color. He made a career of painting nominally representational scenes that were more about the play of light than form. Adept at portraiture as well as landscape, his most heartfelt canvases depict his native Valencian shore of churning waves, sun-modeled rocks, and innocently erotic bathers. Although some of his work can be found in the Museo del Prado (p. 86), the best selection fills the Museo Sorolla (p. 103) in Madrid.

EL clásico

Although Spain is a nominally Roman Catholic country, church attendance has fallen off from its historic highs. The true religion of most Spaniards—and particularly of residents of Barcelona and Madrid—is fútbol (soccer). It's a red-letter day on the calendar whenever Real Madrid and FC Barcelona meet. The rivalry is known simply as "El Clásico" and fills the home stadium, while tens of millions of Spaniards tune in the matches on television. Historically, Real Madrid symbolizes the hegemony of the Castilians who have ruled the country since the 15th century, while Barcelona represents the upstart rebelliousness and nationalist yearnings of Catalunya.

PABLO PICASSO (1881–1973) The quintessential artist of the 20th century did it all, inventing new styles when he had exhausted old ones. Many of his early works are housed in Barcelona's Museu Picasso (p. 206). The Museo Nacional Centro de Arte Reina Sofia (p. 88) in Madrid also displays many Picassos, most notably the iconic "Guernica."

JUAN GRIS (1887–1927) Working with a brighter palette and more mordant wit than either Picasso or Georges Braque, Gris helped pioneer Cubism. He never quit his day job drawing political satire for magazines, allowing him not to take himself too seriously. Recent reappraisals suggest that the approachable Gris influenced an entire generation of Spanish artists. The Museo Nacional Centro de Arte Reina Sofia (p. 88) in Madrid devotes a gallery to Gris and those who looked to his example.

JOAN MIRÓ (1893–1983) A poet of color and form, Miró is often categorized as a Surrealist. He did sign the Surrealist Manifesto of 1924, but his sense of form derives more from Spain's Neolithic cave paintings than the formal classicism of most Surrealism, and his lyrical celebration of color is unmatched in modern abstract art. His visionary art is best in large doses, available at the Fundació Joan Miró (p. 216) in Barcelona. Significant canvases can also be found at the Museo Nacional Centro de Arte Reina Sofia (p. 88) in Madrid.

SALVADOR DALÍ (1904–89) The clown prince of Spanish painting, Dalí defines Surrealism in popular culture. Employing a hyperrealist style to explore a world of fantasy and nightmare, he will forever be associated with limp watches. Dalí lived for a good joke, as the Teatre-Museu Dalí (p. 225) in Figueres demonstrates. Many of his works are in the Museo Nacional Centro de Arte Reina Sofia (p. 88) in Madrid.

ANTONI TÀPIES (1923–2012) Nominally an Abstract Expressionist, the mercurial painter continuously experimented with new ideas until his death. Among the first to incorporate marble dust and gravel into his compositions, he moved on to ever larger objects, including pieces of furniture. His works are characterized by boldly graphic composition and emotional immediacy. Many examples of his work are found in the Museo de Arte Abstracto Español (p. 130) and at the Fundación Antonio Pérez (p. 129) in Cuenca and in the Museo Nacional Centro de Arte Reina Sofia (p. 88) in Madrid. The best collection of his work, however, resides in the Fundació Tàpies (p. 210) in Barcelona.

MADRID & BARCELONA ON A PLATE

Although Madrileños and Barceloneses disagree about many things, they both believe that eating and drinking are the still points around which the day revolves. The famous late Spanish dinner is an accommodation for the ferocious heat of summer. In practice, Spaniards in either city eat four meals a day, sometimes supplemented by a sweet afternoon merienda (coffee break) of pastry.

Breakfast

The Spanish day starts with desayuno, a continental breakfast of coffee, hot chocolate, or tea with assorted rolls, butter, and jam. Spanish breakfast might also consist of *churros* (fried doughnut sticks) and very sweet, thick hot chocolate. Most Spaniards drink strong coffee with hot milk: either a café con leche (half coffee, half milk) or cortado (a shot of espresso "cut" with a dash of milk). If you find it too intense, ask for a café americano, which is diluted with boiling water.

Lunch

Typically the biggest meal of the day, the *almuerzo* can be as hearty as a farm-style midday "dinner" in the United States. Such lunches include three or four courses, beginning either with soup or hors d'oeuvres called entremeses. A main dish might be fish or egg, or more likely meat with vegetables. Wine is always part of the meal. Dessert is usually pastry or flan, followed by coffee. Lunch is served from 1 to 4pm, with the busiest time at 2pm.

Tapas

After work or an early evening stroll, many Spaniards visit their favorite bars to drink wine or beer and eat small plates that can range from trays of olives or a few pickled anchovies or slices of *jamón serrano* to exquisite small composed plates that mimic fancy restaurant dishes. In Madrid, the convention calls for having one drink and one tapa (or a larger plate, known as a *ración*) and then moving on to the next bar for another drink and a bite. Barceloneses don't waste time walking between establishments, instead sticking to one place and staking out their patch of bar with their elbows.

Dinner

Depending on the size of your lunch, the cena can also be a big meal with multiple courses. But if you've indulged in a big lunch and lots of tapas, it's quite acceptable to order a lighter meal—perhaps some cold cuts, sausage, a bowl of soup, or even a tortilla española (see below). Many European and American visitors skip dinner altogether in favor of more time at the tapas bars. The chic dining hour, even in rural areas, is 10 or 10:30pm, but service usually begins by 9:30pm.

Spanish Delights

Just as Spain is a tapestry of independent-minded peoples, Spanish cuisine is an amalgam of regional dishes. Certain dishes have transcended their points of origin to become national plates. Wherever you go around the country, you can always order

Once you've settled on a place for lunch or dinner, **where** you sit (or stand) will have some bearing on the final tally of your bill. Expect to pay a premium of up to 20 percent for outdoor dining. And even if you opt for eating indoors, sitting at a table will likely cost you 5 percent to 10 percent more than standing at the bar.

3

MADRID & BARCELONA IN CONTEXT — Madrid & Barcelona on a Plate

solomillo (fried pork steak), *tortilla española* (potato omelet), or *ensalada mixta* (green salad with crumbled tuna). Every place with a tourist menu will also offer paella Valenciana—generally a sticky mass of reddish rice with overcooked shrimp that bears only the vaguest resemblance to the real dish served in Valencia.

SPECIALTIES OF MADRID & ENVIRONS

A Castilian likes nothing better than to light a wood fire and roast meat over it. Segovia is famous for *cochinillo* (whole roast suckling pig), also served widely in Madrid. Drink a light red from the DO Bierzo region in northwest Castilla y León. These wines are vinted mainly from the Mencia and Garnacha Tintorera grapes. Beef-eaters should be on the lookout for *chuleta d'Ávila,* an entire rib of veal grilled like a steak. Accompany it with an aged red DOC Rioja, probably based on cabernet sauvignon and Tempranillo, or with a red DOC Priorat. The plains south of Madrid are covered with olive trees—and herds of sheep. The local cuisine has to feature cheese, in this case the famous queso Manchego. Restaurants also serve a lot of lamb and wild game, especially *perdiz* (patrtridge), *cordoniz* (quail), *conejo* (rabbit), and *venado* (venison). Bread from the local wheat is amazing, especially dabbed in olive oil from Toledo. Game and lamb are especially good with a red DO Navarra based on Granacha Tinta grapes, often blended with merlot.

SPECIALTIES OF BARCELONA & ENVIRONS

Barcelona is the hotbed of cucina de autor, where the chef is revered as if he were Picasso. If you break open your wallet and choose to dine at one of these restaurants, you might as well go whole hog and order the tasting menu with wine recommendations. But even humble Catalan food is wonderful. Suquet, a seafood stew finished with a garlic-almond paste, is sublime and complex and best accompanied by a DO Empordà white based on the Garnacha Blanca grape. In the fall, look for dishes with wild mushrooms (often surprisingly good with the drier cavas from Sant Sadurní d'Anoia) as well as wild game, which pairs nicely with Monastrell or Garnatxa reds from DO Penedès. Catalunya's rice dishes, or *arrocès,* rival those of neighboring Valencia. One of the sublime experiences of inexpensive dining in Barcelona is enjoying one of the "black rice" dishes made with squid ink. Pair with a dry cava or a tart Parellada-based white wine from DO Penedès.

Tapas in Madrid & Barcelona

Tapas bars in Madrid and Barcelona offer many of the same dishes, although pa amb tomate (grilled country bread rubbed with tomato, drizzled with olive oil, and dusted with salt) is definitely a Catalan specialty. It sounds simple, but it tastes sublime. In addition to olives, almonds, and fresh kettle-style potato chips, some of the standard tapas include the following:

Tortilla Española   Thick Spanish omelet with potato, usually served by the slice.

Pimientos rellenos   Skinless red peppers usually stuffed with tuna or cod.

Croquetas   Small fritters of thick béchamel sauce with ham, tuna, or cod.

Jamón serrano   Thin slices of air-cured mountain ham.

Jamón ibérico de bellota   Highly prized air-cured mountain ham from Iberian black pigs fed entirely on acorns; the most expensive ham in the world.

Queso manchego   Slices of the nutty sheep's-milk cheese of La Mancha.

Gambas a la plancha   Shrimp grilled in their shells, called gambas al ajillo when grilled with garlic.

Morcilla   Cooked slices of spicy blood sausage, served with bread.

Chorizo   Slices of smoked pork sausage seasoned heavily with smoked paprika.

Patatas bravas   Deep-fried potato chunks with spicy paprika aioli; invented in Madrid and available everywhere tapas are served.

Albóndigas   Meatballs, usually made with pork, served in a small casserole dish.

MADRID

4

Y ou'll never forget your first sight of Plaza Mayor. As you emerge from a shady stone portico into a vast sun-struck plaza, you are greeted by a very large and very royal equestrian statue of Felipe III. Surrounded by three-story buildings, Plaza Mayor seems the grandest imaginable stage set, where more than 200 balconies become regal box seats on the scene below. The perimeter is marked with the umbrellas of cafe tables that lure people to while away the afternoon over cold beers or strong coffees. Children race back and forth across the paving stones, flushing pigeons into flight. Travelers with backpacks lean against the plinth of the equestrian monument, eating ice cream. Plaza Mayor may be important—just look at its name, the Major Square—but more than that, it is alive.

It is Madrid in a nutshell. Spain's capital is at once *real* ("ray-AL," as the Spanish say "royal") and real (as English speakers put it). Families row on the lake in Parque del Retiro where kings once staged mock naval battles. When football club Real Madrid wins a cup or league title, the players wrap their team scarves around the elegant Cibeles fountain. People recline in the grass on the green center strips of the paseos, the boulevards built to the king's order. Dog-walkers with packs of canines strut past some of the greatest museums in the world. Tapas-hoppers make the rounds of bars beneath the sculpted visages of Spain's great playwrights. And, yes, Felipe III continues to ignore the backpackers eating ice cream beneath him.

Forever a blend of formal and casual, Madrid wants to be wooed a little before it will give itself to you. Join the Madrileños on the capital's royal stage by getting in step with the urban pace and rhythms—the hurried rush of the subway system, the clip-clop-clip-clop fast walk along Calle Arenal between Sol and Ópera, and the languid stroll of the paseos. When you put in the effort, Madrid smiles and tells you its secrets. It is, after all, the sunniest capital in Europe. The weather may be hot in summer and often chilly in winter, but the sky is the very definition of cerulean blue. As Madrileños say, *de Madrid al cielo:* from Madrid to heaven.

ESSENTIALS
Arriving

BY PLANE Madrid's international airport, **Barajas** (airport code: MAD), lies 15km (9.3 miles) east of the city center. It has four terminals that are connected by a moving sidewalk and light rail. The newest and most comfortable terminal is Terminal 4, which serves Iberia, American, British Airways, Cathay Pacific, El Al, Emirates, Finnair, LAN, Luxair, Qatar, Royal Air Maroc, Vueling, and a few additional small airlines. Terminal 1 serves Air Lingus, Aeroflot, Aerolineas Argentinas, Aeromexico, Air Canada, Air China, most Air Europa flights, Delta, Easyjet, Korean Air, Ryanair, Saudi Arabian Airlines, Transavia, Turkish Air Lines and United Airlines. Terminal 2's principal airlines include Air France, some Air Europa flights, Alitalia, Brussels Airlines, KLM, LOT, Lufthansa, SAS, Swiss and TAP Portugal. Terminal 3 is undergoing renovations. For Barajas Airport information, call ✆ **90-240-47-04,** or check www.aena.es.

Air-conditioned airport **buses** can take you from the ground floor at Terminal 4 or Level 0 at Terminals 1 and 2 to the Atocha train station a few blocks from the Prado. The fare is 5€, and you can buy tickets on the bus but only with cash. Buses leave every 10 to 15 minutes, either to or from the airport. The trip takes approximately 40 minutes.

By **taxi,** expect to pay 35€ and up, plus surcharges, for the trip to the airport and for baggage handling. If you take an unmetered limousine, make sure you negotiate the price in advance.

A **subway** connecting Barajas Airport and central Madrid provides additional ground transportation options, although it can be awkward if you have a lot of luggage and is not appreciably cheaper than the airport bus. From the airport, take line 8 to Nuevos Ministerios, where you will exit and re-enter the system and pay a second fare. The airport supplement is 3€ in addition to the usual 1.50€–2€ for travel within metropolitan Madrid.

BY TRAIN Madrid has two major railway stations: **Atocha** (Glorieta Carlos V; Metro: Atocha RENFE), for trains to and from Lisbon, Toledo, Andalucía, Basque Country, Extremadura and Barcelona, and the French frontier via Catalunya; and **Chamartín** (in the northern suburbs at Augustín de Foxá; Metro: Chamartín), for trains to and from Asturias, Cantabria, Castilla y León, the Basque Country, Aragón, Levante (Valencia), Murcia, and the French frontier via Basque Country. For information about connections from any of these stations, call **RENFE (Spanish Railways)** at ✆ **90-232-03-20** (daily 5am–11:50pm) or use the excellent multi-lingual web site **www.renfe.com**.

For tickets, go to RENFE's main office at Alcalá 44 (www.renfe.com; ✆ **90-232-03-20;** Metro: Banco de España). The office is open Monday to Friday 9:30am to 11:30pm. Frankly, it is most convenient to purchase tickets on the web site and print them out. (As of this writing, RENFE only has iOS, Android, Windows, and Blackberry apps for the commuter rail system of *cercanías;* it does not permit ticket purchases.)

BY BUS Madrid has at least 14 major bus terminals, including **Estación Sur de Autobuses,** Calle Méndez Álvaro 83 (www.estaciondeautobuses.com; ✆ **91-468-42-00;** Metro: Méndez Álvaro). Most buses pass through this large station.

BY CAR All highways within Spain radiate outward from Madrid. The following are the major highways into Madrid, with information on driving distances to the city:

Highways to Madrid

ROUTE	FROM	DISTANCE TO MADRID
N-I	Irún	507km (315 miles)
N-II	Barcelona	626km (389 miles)
N-III	Valencia	349km (217 miles)
N-IV	Cádiz	625km (388 miles)
N-V	Badajoz	409km (254 miles)
N-VI	Galicia	602km (374 miles)

Visitor Information

The most convenient **tourist office** in the heart of tourist attractions is located on Plaza Mayor 27 (Salón de Columnas de la Casa de la Panadería; ✆ **91-454-44-10;** www. esmadrid.com; Metro: Sól or Ópera); it's open daily from 9:30am to 8:30pm. In addition to personal advice and information (including providing lists of hotels and *hostales* if you specifically request them), this center has several terminals to tap into the esMadrid web site. The office also offers free downloadable audioguides in mp3 format. Ask for a street map of the next town on your itinerary, especially if you're driving.

The **Colón Tourist Center** (www.esmadrid.com) is located near the Archaeological Museum on the Paseo de Recoletos in the underground passageway beneath Plaza de Colón. It does not offer telephone service but is open for visits daily from 9:30am to 8:30pm. Like the Plaza Mayor site, it has terminals for access to esMadrid and offers special counseling for students who have come to Madrid to study Spanish. A booklet, "Learn Spanish in Madrid," gives a rundown of current talks, films, and guided tours. An overview is also available on the www.esmadrid.com web site. Similar walk-in information points with the same hours are also available at **Plaza de Cibeles** (opposite the Prado bus stop), **Plaza de Callao** on the corner with calle Preciados, and the **Paseo del Arte** next to the Museo de Reina Sofía

WEBSITES The Tourist Office of Spain (**www.spain.info**) can help you plan your trip with listings of lodging options, attractions, tour operators, and packages, plus handy tips on getting around. For the viewpoints of individual travelers, check **www. tripadvisor.com** and **www.virtualtourist.com**—but be wary, as such sites tend to highlight reviewers with personal agendas and have been known to list more positive results first for advertisers. Among the individual commercial websites touting Madrid information, **www.madridman.com** seems the most credible.

City Layout

All roads in Spain ultimately lead to Madrid, which long ago outgrew its original boundaries and continues to sprawl in all directions. But central Madrid can be navigated by its main arteries and squares.

MAIN ARTERIES & SQUARES Every new arrival ultimately stumbles onto the **Gran Vía,** which cuts a diagonal path across the city. It begins at **Plaza de España,** where you'll find the Edificio España, a 25-story 1920 skyscraper currently vacant as it is transformed into luxury residences. **Gran Vía** is lined with shops carrying a broad mix international goods, as well as some of the city's largest cinemas, many hotels, and a number of restaurants.

South of the Gran Vía lies **Puerta del Sol,** the starting point for all road distances within Spain and the central crossroads of Madrid's public transit system. The bustling square is the borderland between Madrid's oldest quarters (La Latina, Lavapiés, Las Letras) and the commercial city center. **Calle de Alcalá** begins at Sol and runs northeast for 4km (2.5 miles) through Plaza de la Independencia and the entrance to Retiro Park. Follow **Carrera de San Jerónimo** east to reach the Paseo del Prado. Follow **Calle Mayor** west to reach Plaza Mayor.

Plaza Mayor lies at the heart of Old Madrid and is an attraction in itself, with its mix of Renaissance and neoclassical architecture. The colonnaded ground level of the

papa's TOWN

plaza is filled with shops and restaurants. Pedestrians pass beneath the arches of the huge square to exit onto the narrow 16th- and 17th-century streets of the district known as La Latina, which are jammed with old-fashioned shops and many bars and taverns.

The area immediately south of Plaza Mayor—known as *barrios bajos*—is a colorful segment of La Latina with cobblestone streets lined with 16th- and 17th-century architecture. Exit Plaza Mayor through the **Arco de Cuchilleros** to Cava Baja, a street packed with markets, restaurants, and taverns. Directly west of Plaza Mayor, where Calle Mayor meets Calle Bailén, stands the **Palacio Royal** (Royal Palace).

Gran Vía ends at Calle de Alcalá, and a few hundred meters east is the grand **Plaza de Cibeles,** with its fountain to Cybele, "the mother of the gods." From Cibeles, the wide **Paseo de Recoletos** begins a short run north to Plaza de Colón. North of Colón, the long serpentine central artery of Madrid begins: **Paseo de la Castellana,** flanked by expensive shops, apartment buildings, luxury hotels, and foreign embassies.

Heading south from Cibeles is **Paseo del Prado,** where you'll find the **Museo del Prado** as well as the striking **Museo Thyssen-Bornamisza** and the **Jardín Botánico** (Botanical Garden). To the west of the garden lies **Parque del Retiro,** a magnificent park once reserved for royalty, with a restaurant, a rose garden, and two lakes. (It's best accessed from Plaza de Independencia, north of the Prado.) Paseo del Prado leads south to the Atocha railway station. Just off the roundabout is the third of Madrid's artistic triumvirate, the **Museo Nacional Centro de Arte Reina Sofía.**

STREET MAPS Arm yourself with a good map before setting out. **Falk** maps are good (www.omnimap.com/catalog/int/falk-map.htm), and are available at most newsstands and kiosks. Free maps given away by tourist offices and hotels are adequate for general orientation, but don't list the maze of small streets in Old Madrid. However, finding your way with a massive folding map is usually impractical and, frankly, makes you more vulnerable to pickpockets. The best bet is to print out a day's itinerary in advance and carry the printouts.

The Neighborhoods in Brief

Madrid unfolds in three layers. **Old Madrid** lies at the center and contains most of the attractions that travelers come to see. **Modern Madrid,** heavily rebuilt in the last half of the 20th century, envelops Old Madrid, mainly on the east and north. It mixes tony residences and shopping with office buildings and some of the more upscale business hotels. **Outer Madrid,** where the urban congestion begins to ease into the Castilian countryside, frankly holds less interest for most visitors—unless they have friends or family living there.

ART DISTRICT & PASEOS

The old city radiated from Puerta del Sol even before Habsburg kings made Madrid the capital. The hub of public transport, Sol, connects ancient and modern Madrid. Heading south and uphill from Sol is the barrio called Las Letras, because it has attracted writers for centuries. Lope de Vega, Cervantes, and even Lorca lived and worked here. It includes the Plaza Santa Ana, one of the city's best spots for tapas and nightlife.

PUERTA DEL SOL & LAS LETRAS

Madrid radiated from its eastern gate—Puerta del Sol means "Gate of the Sun"—even before Habsburg kings established their capital in the city. Today Sol is the hub of public transport, connecting ancient and modern Madrid. Sol's central location makes it easy to walk to Plaza Mayor, the Palacio Real, the art museums, Plaza Santa Ana, and the nightlife of bars in La Latina. Metro lines 1, 2, and 3 will take you anyplace else you'll want to go. Although there are some overpriced fleabag hotels in the area (not in this book!), there are also several good lodgings at fair prices. Heading south and uphill from Sol is the barrio known as Las Letras because it was home to writers from the 16th through the 20th centuries. Lope de Vega, Cervantes, and Lorca lived and worked here. Plaza Santa Ana, one of the city's best spots for tapas and nightlife, is central to Las Letras and marks the spot where the districts of Sol, Lavapiés, and La Latina all converge. It can get a little rowdy at night, but it oozes Old Madrid charm.

PLAZA MAYOR & LA LATINA

Madrid (and its visitors) party in this neighborhood. Sometimes called the "Madrid of the Asturias," it is better known as La Latina. From Plaza Mayor, the Arco de Cuchilleros leads to Cava de San Miguel, Cava Alta, and Cava Baja, all full of taverns and bars. La Latina continues downhill west to the Manzanares River. Also in this area, Muslim Madrid is centered on the Palacio de Oriente and Las Vistillas. What is now Plaza de la Paja was actually the heart of the city and its main marketplace during the medieval period. In 1617, Plaza Mayor became the hub of Madrid, and it remains a center of activity both day and night. The neighborhood around Plaza Mayor is vital and vigorous, which is a good thing when you're out partying at a bar or restaurant and a not-so-good thing when you're trying to sleep. But most lodgings are set up to seal out the racket. The bars start serving coffee on the plaza before the sun comes up, and the neighborhood has many cafes that serve inexpensive breakfasts.

ÓPERA & PALACIO REAL

Adjacent to Plaza Mayor and La Latina, this section of Madrid revolves around the Teatro Real, the Plaza de Oriente, and the Palacio Real with its parks and gardens. It forms a buffer zone between Puerta del Sol and Plaza Mayor, and the uphill, modern district around Gran Vía. Much of this neighborhood was rebuilt in the 19th century, making it more spacious and less cramped than Sol or La Latina. Several hotels are located in the vicinity of the Ópera stop on the Metro. The neighborhood's attractions, both religious and secular, are chiefly related to the monarchy.

GRAN VÍA & PLAZA DE ESPAÑA

Gran Vía was constructed in the early 20th century to be Madrid's main street. It is flanked by cinemas, department stores, and bank and corporate headquarters, although its retail offerings have definitely dimmed as the 21st century marches on. Gran Vía begins at Plaza de España, with its bronze figures of Don Quixote and his faithful squire, Sancho Panza. Hotels with a Gran Vía address seem to believe in *gran precios* (high rates) justified primarily on address rather than amenities. A certain after-dark glamour clings to Gran Vía (along with a number of less-smart creatures of the night), but walk a few steps away from the bright lights and traffic and into the adjoining neighborhoods and hotels begin to offer more value for price.

CHUECA & MALASAÑA

Chueca is a recently revitalized district north of the Gran Vía defined by the the the main streets of Hortaleza, Infantas, Barquillo, and San Lucas. It is the center of gay nightlife, with dozens of clubs, some superb restaurants, and some of the city's hippest shopping. Chueca and adjoining student-heavy Malasaña are gentrifying quickly, often offering basic and old-fashioned *hostales* on the same block with design-conscious (and,

thus, more expensive) new hotels. These neighborhoods north of Gran Vía are great for dining and clubbing but are less convenient for seeing the conventional tourist sights. Plan on riding the Metro more if you choose to stay here.

SALAMANCA, RETIRO & CHAMBERÍ

Once Madrid's city walls came down in the 1860s, the district of Salamanca to the northeast of Old Madrid became a fashionable address, and so it remains. Calle de Serrano cuts through this neighborhood and is lined with stores and boutiques. The street is also home to the U.S. Embassy. The adjacent leafy streets near Parque del Retiro and Chamberí (west of the Paseos and due north of Old Madrid) are often lumped with Salamanca because they are also upscale enclaves, though typically more residential.

GETTING AROUND
On Foot

You can walk most places in central Madrid, and it's the best way to experience the city. To save time, it's a good idea to take public transport to a neighborhood and then set off on foot to explore. Madrid was sited on the high ground to command the modest valley of the Manzanares River. The difference in elevation between popular areas of the city is fairly minor, but you will encounter uphill grades between Sol and Las Letras, and between the major art museums and Sol.

By Public Transit

Madrid has some of the most thorough and least-expensive public transit in Europe. For a full overview, check the website for **Consorcio Transportes Madrid** (www.ctm-madrid.es). This site, available in Spanish and English, has a very useful tool that recommends ways to get from one place to another using any combination of public transit and walking.

By Metro (Subway)

The Metro system (www.metromadrid.es; © **90-244-44-03**) is easy to learn and use. The fare is 1.50€ for the first five stations one-way; the price goes up 0.10€ for each additional station up to a 2€ maximum in central Madrid. (Don't expect to game the system—you have to insert your ticket to exit as well as enter the Metro.) A 10-trip **Metrobus** ticket, good on buses and Metro, costs 13€. The Metro operates from 6am to 2am (try to avoid rush hours). Twelve main Metro lines and three additional short lines to connect hub stations cover most of the city. Don't overlook using the **Circular** (which circles around the edges of Old Madrid) as a quick connector among the other lines. Be forewarned that Madrileños are very aggressive when entering and exiting the subway cars. He who hesitates is lost, so push right through. Ever wonder how they manage to stay out late at night and still put in a full day's work? Look for nappers among the lucky few who snag a seat.

By Bus

The **public buses,** marked EMT, are most useful for moving around the circular roads, or *rondas,* such as getting from Atocha to Puerta de Toledo, or for moving quickly up and down the Paseos. They run 6am to 11pm. Tickets for single bus rides are 1.50€, but few people buy just one. Buy a 10-trip Metrobus ticket (see above) or consider one of the special passes designed for tourists. If your stay is short and you have to move around the city quickly, then it can be worth your while to purchase an **Abono Transportes Turístico** for unlimited rides on Madrid's Metro and buses. The passes, which are available at Metro stations and tourist offices, are sold for 1, 2, 3, 5, and 7 days (for 8.40€, 14€, 18€, 27€, and 35€, respectively). The Abono is valid only for the ticket holder and you have to show photo ID when you buy it. Unless you'll be a heavy user of the Metro and bus systems, the **Metrobus** ticket is usually a better buy at 13€, especially since two people can share a single ticket.

Madrid City Tour is the city's hop-on, hop-off double-decker sightseeing bus. Recorded commentary is available through headphones in 14 languages, and separate narration is available for children. The buses' two routes cover most of the city's major attractions. Both start at Calle Felipe IV next to the Museo del Prado. From Nov-Feb, buses operate 10am-6pm, passing each stop about every 14 minutes. From March-Oct, they operate 9am-10pm and pass each stop every 8-9 minutes. Tickets can be purchased for 1 or 2 days. Adults pay 21€ for 1 day, 25€ for 2 days; ages 7–15 and over 65 pay 9€ for 1 day, 12€ for 2 days. Children 6 and under are free. The City Tour has the advantage of letting you get around without having to deal with public transportation. It is, however, more expensive. For more information, call ℂ **90-202-47-58** or visit www.madridcitytour.es.

By Commuter Rail

The **Cercanía** (www.renfe.com/viajeros/cercanias/index.html) train network, designed as suburban commuter rail, is also a convenient way to visit **El Escorial** (from Chamartín station), or **Alcalá de Henares** (from Atocha station). Fares on the cercanías run 1.60€ to 8.40€, depending on zone. **Note:** Cercanías are not included in the Abono Turistico or the Metrobus pass.

By Taxi

Cab fares are pretty reasonable. When you flag down a taxi, the meter should register 2.10€ 6am to 9pm or 2.20€ 9pm to 6am; for every kilometer thereafter, the fare increases between 1€ and 1.20€. A supplement is charged for trips to the railway station, the bullring, or the football stadiums. The ride to Barajas Airport carries a 5.50€ surcharge, and there is a 2.95€ supplement from railway stations and to or from Juan Carlos I Trade Fair. In addition, a 1.20€ supplement is charged on Sundays and holidays. It's customary to tip at least 10 percent of the fare. Taxis can be hailed on the street or at taxi ranks near attractions and hotels. To call a taxi, dial ℂ **91-547-82-00** or 91-405-12-13.

Tip: Be sure that the meter is turned on when you get into a taxi. Drivers prefer to estimate the cost of the ride, which will almost always cost more than the metered fare. You'll also find unmetered taxis that hire out for the day or the afternoon. They are legal, but sometimes charge exorbitant rates. To avoid them, always take a black taxi with horizontal red bands or a white one with diagonal red bands.

If you take a taxi outside the city limits, the driver is entitled to charge you twice the rate shown on the meter.

Driving

Public transit is so good that inside the city you should leave the driving to Madrileños. They're the ones who grew up watching bullfights and understand the balance of aggression and aversion necessary to navigate Madrid's nonsensical intersections.

Renting a car for excursions is another matter, as pickup points are usually at train stations or the airport, where it's easy to reach outlying highways. Citizens of non-EU countries should obtain an **International Drivers Permit** before arriving in Spain. Without one, some agencies may refuse to rent you a car. Car rentals at the airport include **Avis** (www.avis-europe.com; ✆ **91-743-88-67**), **Hertz** (www.hertz.es; ✆ **91-746-60-04**), **Europcar** (www.europcar.com; ✆ **91-743-87-58**), and **National Atesa** (www.atesa.es; ✆ **91-746-60-60**). Prices vary little among companies, so stick with whichever one dovetails with your frequent-flyer program. Most can also arrange downtown pickup and dropoff.

[FastFACTS] MADRID

Banks & ATMs You'll find a bank, or at least an ATM, wherever crowds gather in Madrid, especially in shopping districts and around major Metro stations. Most permit cash withdrawals via MC or V, and many are linked into international networks that will let you access your home bank account. Most offer a choice of language, almost always including English. Major banks include **Banco Santander, Caja Madrid,** and **BBVA.** Major overseas banks with a presence in Madrid include **Deutsche Bank** and **Citibank.** Note that most Spanish ATMs only accept 4-digit PINs, so if you have a longer PIN and want to use your card in Spain, change it at least a week before departure.

Business Hours Opening hours can be complicated in Madrid. Expect small shops and banks to open at 10a.m, close 2–5pm for lunch, and open again 5–8:30pm. Shopping centers and some international shops stay open continuously 10am–10pm.

Doctors & Dentists For a list of English-speaking doctors and dentists working in Madrid, visit the web site of the US Embassy in Madrid (see below). The PDF of the complete medical services list is available from the web site under the tab for "US Citizen Services." For dental services, you can also consult **Unidad Médica Anglo-Americana,** Conde de Arandá 1 (www.unidadmedica.com; ✆ **91-435-18-23**). Office hours are Monday to Friday

from 9am to 8pm, and Saturday 10am to 1pm. For an English-speaking doctor, contact the **U.S. Embassy,** Calle de Serrano 75 (http://spanish.madrid.usembassy.gov; ✆ **91-587-22-40**).

Drugstores For a late-night pharmacy, look in the daily newspaper under Farmacias de Guardia to learn which drugstores are open after 8pm. Another way to find one is to go to any pharmacy, which, even if closed, always posts a list of nearby pharmacies that are open late that day. Madrid has hundreds of pharmacies; one of the most central is **Farmacia de la Paloma,** Calle de Toledo 46 (✆ **91-365-34-58;** Metro: Puerta del Sol or La Latina).

Embassies If you lose your passport, fall seriously

ill, get into legal trouble, or have some other serious problem, you embassy or consulate can help. These are the Madrid addresses and contact information:

Australia: Torre Espacio, Paseo de la Castellana 259D; www.spain.embassy.gov.au; Ⓒ **91-353-66-00**

Canada: Torre Espacio, Paseo de la Castellana 259D; www.canadainternational.gc.ca; Ⓒ **91-382-84-00**

Ireland: Paseo de la Castellana 46, Ireland House; www.irlanda.es; Ⓒ **91-436-40-93**

New Zealand: Calle Pinar 7, 3rd Floor; www.nzembassy.com/spain; Ⓒ **91-523-02-26**

United Kingdom: Torre Espacio, Paseo de la Castellana 259D; Ⓒ **91-714-63-00;** www.gov.uk/government/world/organisations/british-embassy-madrid

United States: Calle Serrano 75; http://madrid.usembassy.gov; Ⓒ **91-587-22-00**

Emergencies Call Ⓒ **112** for fire, police, and ambulance services.

Hospitals & Clinics

Unidad Médica Anglo-Americana, Conde de Arandá 1 (www.unidadmedica.com; Ⓒ **91-435-18-23;** Metro: Retiro), is not a hospital but a private outpatient clinic offering specialized services. This is not an emergency clinic, although someone on the staff is always available. Unidad Medica

Anglo-Americana is open Monday to Friday 9am to 8pm, and Saturday 10am to 1pm. In a real medical emergency, call Ⓒ **112** for an ambulance.

Internet Access Most lodgings offer free Wi-Fi access, at least in public areas, if you have your own laptop, tablet, phone, or other device. Typically, bandwidth on free hotel Wi-Fi is good enough to surf the web, use email, look up maps, and sometimes even make VOIP phone calls. It is not adequate for streaming video or music. Some hotels give away basic Wi-Fi but charge for faster access. Somewhat slower free Wi-Fi access is usually available in cafes and some stores. The city government also provides free Wi-Fi at hot spots around the city and on public transit. Buses and some Metro lines also have free Wi-Fi. If you are planning to use a phone or tablet, download the GOWEX Free Wifi app for iOs from the Apple Store or for Android from the Google Play Store. With the proliferation of free hotspots, Internet cafes are vanishing—usually they are coupled with long-distance phone services in immigrant neighborhoods. Expect to pay 2€ to 4€ per hour.

Mail & Postage

Madrid's central post office is in the Palacio de Comunicaciones at Plaza de Cibeles (Ⓒ **91-523-06-94**).

Hours are Monday to Friday 8:30am to 9:30pm and Saturday 8:30am to 2pm. Sending a postcard or letter to the U.S. starts at 0.90€. To calculate the price, visit http://correos.es. You can also buy stamps at any place that sells tobacco.

Newspapers & Magazines Probably the most useful English-language publication in Madrid is not available at news kiosks. You'll have to go online to read "El País in English" (http://elpais.com/elpais/inenglish.html). The kiosks do carry "InMadrid," though the more up-to-date edition is on the web (www.inmadrid.com). The publication is geared to English speakers actually living in Madrid, but has useful information for visitors as well. The Paris-based "International New York Times" (formerly the "International Herald Tribune") is sold at most newsstands in the tourist districts, as is "USA Today," plus the European editions of "Time" and "Newsweek." "Guía del Ocio," a small magazine sold at newsstands, has entertainment listings and addresses in Spanish.

Pharmacies For a late-night pharmacy, look in the daily newspaper under Farmacias de Guardia to learn which drugstores are open after 8pm. Another way to find one is to go to any pharmacy, which, even if closed, always posts a list of nearby pharmacies that are open late that day. Madrid has hundreds of pharmacies; one of the most central is **Farmacia de la Paloma,** Calle de Toledo 46 (☎ **91-365-34-58;** Metro: Puerta del Sol or La Latina).

Police The central police station in Madrid is at Calle Leganitos, 19, next to Plaza de España. It is open daily 9am to midnight. The main phone numbers are ☎ **91-548-85-37** or ☎ **91-549-80-08.** The 24-hour number for reporting a crime is ☎ **90-210-21-12.** The Madrid City Council and the National Police have instituted a program called the **Foreign Tourist Assistance Service** (acronym in Spanish is SATE) to help tourists in filing a complaint, canceling credit cards or other documents, contacting embassies or consulates, and contacting of locating family members.

Safety As in every big, crowded city around the world, purse snatching and pickpocketing are facts of life in Madrid, especially wherever there are lots of slightly disoriented tourists paying scant attention to their belongings. Don't let down your guard and you're unlikely to be a victim.

WHERE TO STAY

Summer vacationers will be pleased to learn that Madrid hotels consider July and August to be "low" season and price their rooms accordingly. For those who prefer to travel when it is cooler, November rates are also typically low. But the economic crisis has depressed rates overall so that, for the time being, you can expect good value for your money whenever you travel.

Even in neighborhoods generally perceived as more upscale—Salamanca and the area around Ópera, for example—you can find really good lodgings to suit almost any budget. Admittedly, Chueca and Salamanca hotels put you a little farther from the main attractions, but Madrid is so spread out that no lodging will be within walking distance of everything. Select the neighborhood and lodging that suits your style and price.

If you are staying in Madrid long enough to make an apartment rental worthwhile, **Homes for Travellers** (www.homesfortravellers.com; ☎ **91-444-27-01**) has a carefully curated selection of apartments, mostly in Chueca and Malasaña, as well as near Ópera, Gran Vía, Plaza Mayor, and Puerta del Sol. Studio apartments begin around 65€ per night, while one-bedroom units start around 75€ per night. Booking is done by web site and secured by credit card deposit. Check the apartment locations carefully since some more residential neighborhoods are less convenient for sightseeing.

Arts District & Paseos

The hotels we recommend in the Arts District make visiting the big three museums easy. With the exception of the Ritz, they are all also convenient to the Atocha train station, which is also the terminus for the airport bus. It makes arriving and leaving Madrid just a little simpler.

EXPENSIVE

The Ritz ★★★ Many hotels claim to be legendary; this one actually is. When Alfonso XIII was married in 1908, he was dismayed that Madrid lacked hotels befitting his guests. He wanted a hotel that could match the Ritz in Paris or London, so he engaged César Ritz to consult on the design and lend his name. Few expenses were spared—the carpets were hand-woven, the tapestries hand-stitched at the Real Fábrica de Tapices, and all the modern amenities of 1910 were put into the rooms. The location

Madrid Hotels

Ateneo Hotel **16**

Catalonia Gran Vía
Hotel **21**

H10 Villa de la Reina **19**

HC Puerta del Sol **13**

Hostal La Macarena **10**

Hostal Persal **14**

Hostal Residencia
Don Diego **26**

Hostal Sil & Serranos **17**

Hotel Adler **26**

Hotel Cortezo **12**

Hotel De Las Letras **20**

Hotel JC Rooms
Santa Ana **15**

Hotel JC Rooms
Santo Domingo **2**

Hotel Mediodía **30**

Hotel Moderno **9**

Hotel Negresco **8**

Hotel Ópera **4**

Hotel Plaza Mayor **11**

Hotel Preciados **3**

Hotel Santo Domingo **1**

Hotel Urban **22**

HUSA Hotel
Paseo del Arte **28**

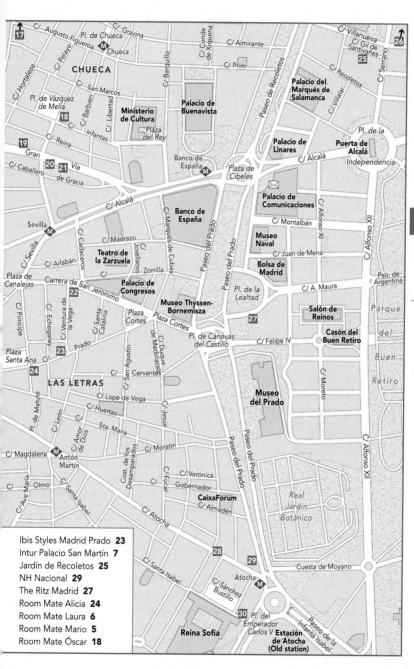

Ibis Styles Madrid Prado **23**
Intur Palacio San Martín **7**
Jardín de Recoletos **25**
NH Nacional **29**
The Ritz Madrid **27**
Room Mate Alicia **24**
Room Mate Laura **6**
Room Mate Mario **5**
Room Mate Óscar **18**

next to the Museo del Prado on the Plaza de la Lealtad with its wonderful Neptuno fountain couldn't be much more prestigious. Time could not diminish its great bones, but some of the brocade and velvet was getting a little worn when Orient Express took over management a few years ago and brought the Ritz back to being, well, The Ritz. Comfort and luxury are givens, and security for celebrity travelers is tight and professional. The Goya Restaurant here is the successor to the original established with the aid of Auguste Escoffier. You might consider staying here as a treat, but if you want to get a hint of the luxury and pampering that guests enjoy, book afternoon tea or chocolate and churros on the terrace.

Plaza de la Lealtad, 5. ℰ **800/237-1236** in the U.S. and Canada, or 91-701-67-67. www.ritz.es. 167 units. 240€–415€ double; from 418€ junior suite; from 1,180€ suite. Parking 35€. Metro: Atocha or Banco de España. **Amenities:** Restaurant; bar; concierge; exercise room; room service; sauna; spa; free Wi-Fi.

MODERATE

HUSA Hotel Paseo del Arte ★★   This large modern hotel has a spectacular location across a small plaza from the Reina Sofía, down an alley from the CaixaForum, and a 5-minute walk down Calle Atocha from Casa Patas. Because it hosts many business groups, everything is up for negotiation. Rates skyrocket when they have a conference, and drop through the floor when they don't. If you can get HUSA to throw in the buffet breakfast (otherwise a pricey 16€ per person), take the deal. It's a better buffet than the luxury hotels serve. Rooms are modestly sized, so see if you can an upgrade to one of the luxurious rooms with a private terrace. Booking through the web site gives less room for haggling, but guarantees a free room upgrade, if available, and late check out.

Calle Atocha, 123. ℰ **91-298-48-00.** www.husa.es. 260 units. 75€–140€ double; 116€–204€ terrace executive rooms. Metro: Atocha. **Amenities:** Restaurant; bar; concierge; exercise room; room service; spa; free Wi-Fi.

NH Nacional ★★   When the NH hotel chain took over this venerable railway hotel in 1997, they gutted the building and constructed a modern hotel inside the shell. The rooms are not very big, but from the wood-laminate floors to the granite sinks to the brushed stainless cabinet knobs and trim, everything is simple, robust, and modern. The desks are practical and include good task lighting and a comfortable chair. NH was one of the last chains to relent on charging for Wi-Fi, but has now made it free. There are a lot of nice little touches, like the bedside pamphlets of short stories, the abstract art on the walls, and the complimentary newspapers in several languages in the lobby. Location is great—a 5-minute walk to the Prado, the Reina Sofía, or the CaixaForum. The only shortcoming is that the Nacional hosts a lot of conferences and conventions and can get crowded when everyone needs to get out the door (or down the elevators) at precisely the same moment.

Paseo del Prado 48. ℰ **91-429-66-29.** www.nh-hotels.com. 214 units. 84€–125€ double. Parking 28€. Metro: Atocha. **Amenities:** Restaurant; bar; concierge; room service; free Wi-Fi.

INEXPENSIVE

Hotel Mediodía ★★   Built back when the Atocha train station was still called Mediodía, this is one of the rare hotels left with true single rooms as well as plenty of doubles, triple, and quadruples. The large rooms are especially handy for families. Like all older hotels, accommodations vary. Some have marble floors, while others have artificial wood parquet. Some have older porcelain fixtures in the bathrooms, others have modern tub-showers. Some guests find the variation annoying. We chalk it up to character and if we don't like the first room we're shown, we ask nicely to see another. The location is terrific—rooms on the back actually overlook the Reina Sofía (there's a perfect view from the balcony of Room 405), while rooms on the front look across the street to the Atocha train station. The "social lounge" on the ground level is a good place to entertain business associates or new travel friends.

Plaza del Emperador Carlos V, 8. ⟨ⓒ⟩ **91-530-70-08.** www.mediodiahotel.com. 173 units. 51€–65€ double; 67€–80€ triple; 77€–90€ quadruple. Metro: Atocha. **Amenities:** Snack bar; free Wi-Fi.

Puerta del Sol & Las Letras
EXPENSIVE
Hotel Urban ★★   The contemporary take on Art Deco styling makes the Urban perhaps the most sophisticated and modern-looking luxury hotel in the city, while the Puerta del Sol proximity frankly keeps the price down on some of Madrid's most comfortable rooms. The hotel was built in a former office building, and hints of that backstory linger in the soaring central atrium. The Derby owners are inveterate art collectors, and they've installed some extremely tall Papua, New Guinea, sculptures in the lobby, while gracing some of the suites with smaller South and Southeast Asian sculptures and art pieces. The large rooms feel rather like a supersized passenger cabin in a Rolls limo—all dark wood and leather, brushed metal, padded upholstery, and glass. Thorough soundproofing shuts out the outside world. The rooftop terrace has chaise lounges for catching the rays by day (then cooling off in the pool), as well as tables and stools for rooftop drinks at night.

Carrera de San Jerónimo. ⟨ⓒ⟩ **91-787-77-70.** www.derbyhotels.com. 96 units. 175€–279€ double; 203€–363€ junior suite; 295€–492€ suite. Parking 30€. Metro: Sevilla. **Amenities:** Restaurant; bar; exercise room; outdoor heated pool; free Wi-Fi.

MODERATE
HC Puerta del Sol ★★   We think that this Catalonia Hoteles property is the Goldilocks of hotels near Plaza Santa Ana—not too big, not too small, but just right. It occupies an early-20th-century building (some of the original carved woodwork is maintained in the top-floor suites) but the interior was completely rebuilt in 2011. You enter to a cool central courtyard that is a great surprise in the heart of the city. A glass roof was added so that it can be air-conditioned and the courtyard is such a serene spot that many guests hang out here to read a book and sip a drink from the discreet little bar. The modest-sized rooms have new hardwood floors, marble bathrooms, and low-key brown and gold drapes and bedspreads. Most have large windows opening either onto the courtyard or Calle Atocha.

Calle Atocha, 23. ⟨ⓒ⟩ **91-369-71-71.** www.hoteles-catalonia.com. 65€–150€ double. Metro: Vodafone Sol or Tirso de Molina. **Amenities:** Restaurant; bar; cafe; solarium; rooftop terrace; heated outdoor Jacuzzi; free Wi-Fi.

Hotel Moderno ★★   Family-owned and actively managed since it opened in 1939, the Moderno keeps reinventing itself without losing the charm that has always made it one of the nicer lodgings on Puerta del Sol. The building dates from 1857, and some of the internal structure prevents the expansion of the small rooms on the first four floors. Ask for the upper levels for a little more room to spread out. Rooms with an outdoor terrace are about an extra 30€ per night, but during times of year when you might want the windows open, they can be worth it. They have the most space as well as fabulous views of Puerta del Sol. It's a genuine pleasure to sit on your private terrace and look out at the city. A few triple and family rooms are also available.

Calle Arenal, 2. ✆ **91-531-09-00.** www.hotel-moderno.com. 97 rooms. 65€–129€ double; 110€–159€ triple. Metro: Sol. **Amenities:** Bar, concierge; free Wi-Fi.

Room Mate Alicia ★   The Room Mate hotels want to be your best friend. Each is branded with a personality and when you click on the web site you'll get a fictitious rundown as if you were reading someone's Facebook page. This approach has proved enormously successful for the group, which has five such hotels in Madrid alone. Apart from the personality marketing, the real concept behind them is affordable high design, usually accomplished by keeping some architectural elements from an older building but adding a contemporary twist. At Alicia, just outside Plaza Santa Ana, the twist is an open loft look. Some of the rooms that overlook the plaza have extremely high windows. The target audience is young travelers who stay out all night (there's breakfast until noon), but adults past party age also like Alicia for the usually affordable rates. Room pricing is very mercurial, though, and can go up and down by 50 percent from day to day. Lock in a rate in advance.

Calle del Prado, 2. ✆ **91-389-60-95.** www.room-matehotels.com. 34 units. 99€–199€ double. Metro: Vodafone Sol or Antón Martín. **Amenities:** Restaurant; babysitting; concierge; free Wi-Fi.

INEXPENSIVE

Ateneo Hotel ★★   One of the first 21st-century hotels to be shoehorned into an old building near Puerta del Sol, the Ateneo set the standard for a modest boutique lodging with its marble and stainless baths with combination tub-showers, its double-glazed windows to keep out the racket of Sol, and its comfortable, large beds in bigger than usual rooms. (During busy times they'll sometimes pass off a small room with a double bed that's otherwise rented as a single; ask for another.) Furniture tends to be comfortably upholstered, and most rooms have a spacious desk and a good desk chair. Family rooms can accommodate two adults and one or two children.

Calle Montera, 22. ✆ **91-521-20-12.** www.hotel-ateneo.com. 38 units. 80€–98€ double; 120€–156€ family room. Metro: Vodafone Sol. **Amenities:** Room service; free Wi-Fi.

Hotel Cortezo ★★   New management and a top-to-bottom renovation have given fresh vigor to this bargain hotel adjacent to the Cine Ideal and the Teatro Nuevo Apolo. Décor tends toward the gentleman's club boutique look with white linens, dark wooden headboards, and brushed stainless steel trim. Masterful photography of Madrid architectural details may inspire some of your own shots. The rooftop terrace is small but fitted with a few lounge chairs, teak strip decking, and an outdoor shower to cool off and wash off the tanning lotion. It's very popular with Scandinavian tourists. Guests are encouraged to bring their own wine to the roof for the spectacular sunsets over La Latina. Part of what makes Cortezo so welcoming is an eager and ready-to-please staff.

Calle Doctor Cortezo, 3. ✆ **91-369-01-01.** www.mediumhoteles.com. 92 units. 50€–100€ double. Parking 25€. Metro: Vodafone Sol, Tirso de Molina. **Amenities:** Breakfast buffet; bar; room service; free Wi-Fi.

Hostal Persal ★   The era of shared bathrooms has mostly vanished, even in budget hostales like this one, but sometimes architecture doesn't allow a bathroom per bedroom. Persal solved the problem neatly by linking some of the bedrooms into suites sharing a single bath. Rooms within the suite are small—honestly, almost all the doubles are cramped here—but because you get two bedrooms, they're a sensible option for families (or very friendly groups). Bathrooms can be Lilliputian, some so tiny that you'll have to turn sideways once inside to close the door. Get claustrophobic? The largest rooms are on the fourth floor. They are also the quietest, which can be an issue on this plaza that's part of the Las Letras nightlife scene.

Plaza del Angel, 12. © **91-369-46-43**. www.hostalpersal.com. 80 units. 49€–89 double; 69€–109€ triple; 89€–129€ quadruple. Metro: Tirso de Molina. **Amenities:** Restaurant; bar; cafe; concierge; free Wi-Fi.

Ibis Styles Madrid Prado ★★   Clever folks, those Ibis designers. This modest modern hotel just outside Plaza Santa Ana lacked any architectural distinction, so Ibis invented a theme that makes every room seem lively and fun. Each of the six floors is keyed to a Spanish wine region, while the individual rooms are named for a specific grape grown in that region. As you might guess, there's a lot of purple and bright green in the accents of the public areas (red and white wine grapes, naturally) while each guest room has a large, scenic mural of vineyards over the bed. This is a budget lodging, so it has no cafe or restaurant (beyond the breakfast buffet). But the lobby does have wine dispensers with a nitrogen system to ensure the wines don't fade after opening. During slow season, the hotel invites guests to free tastings in the late afternoon. At other times, you'll pay a small fee per glass.

Calle del Prado, 11. © **91-369-02-34**. www.pradohotel.com. 46 rooms. 80€–129€ double. Metro: Antón Martín. **Amenities:** Wine bar; business corner; free Wi-Fi.

JC Rooms Santa Ana ★★   With its aggressive marketing via social media, computer in each room, and eye-popping décor in fully saturated colors, it's pretty clear that the JC Rooms group is geared to a young and plugged-in clientele. This new group has reinvented the old-fashioned rooming house as limited-service hotels with great prices. Management will add one or two extra beds per room for about 15€ per night each. It makes for tight quarters, but many groups of young friends don't mind turning a hotel room into something more like a hostel dorm. It gets more interesting in the tight bathrooms with snazzy molded glass sinks and glass-partitioned shower where privacy is not an option. Rooms are themed to the autonomous regions and big cities of Spain, with wall-sized color photos to make you feel like you're there. This iteration of JC Rooms was one of the first, and the location halfway between Puerta del Sol and Plaza Santa Ana is hard to beat. Mind you, it's on the second floor (that's third floor to North Americans) so schlepping luggage is not a lot of fun.

Calle Cruz, 8, 2nd floor. © **91-531-44-03**. www.jchoteles-santaana.com. 25 rooms. 35€–82€ double. Metro: Sevilla. **Amenities:** Free central Madrid tours; free Wi-Fi.

Plaza Mayor & La Latina
INEXPENSIVE

Hostal la Macarena ★   Good looks are this hotel's strong suit, and they shouldn't be underestimated as they can affect the mood of your whole trip. Crisply maintained balconies (with geraniums) on the exterior are matched inside by simple and elegant decor in soothing honey tones. The rooms are also unusually spacious, especially this close to Plaza Mayor. If they sound too good to be true, there is a catch: The rooms are not air-conditioned. (It's the only hotel without this amenity that we recommend in Madrid.) The rooms do have very large ceiling fans and excellent insulation, so they don't get any hotter than the outside air. Still, that's pretty warm in the summer. Even the balconies are encased in glass to keep out noise and summer heat. Some larger rooms accommodate three and even four beds. Rates during July and August are about a third lower than the rates given below.

Calle Cava de San Miguel, 8. ℰ **91-365-92-21.** www.silserranos.com. 20 units. 50€–60€ double; 70€–79€ triple; 89€–99€ quadruple. Metro: Vodafone Sol or Ópera. **Amenities:** Bar; no Wi-Fi.

Hotel Plaza Mayor ★★ Bright and contemporary, this nicely located budget boutique hotel was carved out of the old Santa Cruz church in 1997, and the mass of that venerable stone building keeps the interior cool in summer and warm in winter. The downside is that some of the rooms were constructed around architectural barriers and end up quite oddly shaped—long and thin in some cases, not quite rectilinear in others. They also vary a lot in size, mostly on the small side. But they all have solid, well-made furnishings, shiny wood floors, and wall-mounted flat-screen TVs that don't take up important real estate. There's one penthouse suite, which has to be booked by email or phone. It costs 50 percent more than the standard doubles but has an outdoor patio with views across the tiled roofs of La Latina and skylights in the slanted ceiling that flood the room with light. If the penthouse is booked, opt for a "superior" room on the corner to get views of Plaza Santa Cruz, one of our favorites in Madrid's old quarters.

Calle Atocha, 2. ℰ **91-360-06-06.** www.h-plazamayor.com. 34 units. 48€–82€ double; 75€–92€ double superior. Metro: Vodafone Sol or Tirso de Molina. **Amenities:** Cafeteria; free Wi-Fi.

Ópera & Palacio Real

MODERATE

Hotel Ópera ★ Literally around the corner from the Palacio Real in one direction and from the Teatro Real in another, Hotel Ópera has a regal but modern feel. The modern-box architecture won't win any awards, but management saved its best touches for the interior. All the rooms face the exterior, which means some look out on the palace, and all are flooded with light. The décor is low-key, soft earth tones with large photos and contemporary prints to brighten the walls. Terrace rooms on the eighth floor are almost like going to another hotel They have sweeping views of the city from the terraces, glass-domed Jacuzzi tubs where you can bathe by starlight, and big skylights that make the rooms themselves bright and airy.

Cuesta de Santo Domingo, 2. ℰ **91-541-28-00.** www.hotelopera.com. 79 units. 72€–130€ double; 157€–219€ terrace rooms. Metro: Ópera. **Amenities:** Restaurant; bar; concierge; gym; room service; sauna; free Wi-Fi.

Hotel Preciados ★ This handsome Belle Époque structure maintains its original grand facade, though the interior was gutted to construct this pleasant five-story boutique hotel. Location is about as central as you can find in Madrid, edging toward Gran Vía from Puerta del Sol and up the hill from the plaza around the Teatro Real. Considerable care was taken with small touches like excellent showerheads and bedside reading lights and rooms are soothing and quiet. While some doubles are quite spacious and can accommodate an extra cot for a child, single rooms are exceptionally tiny.

Calle Preciados, 37. ℰ **91-454-44-00.** www.preciadoshotel.com. 73 units. 126€–180€ double; 190€–250€ suite. Parking 25€. Metro: Vodafone Sol, Santo Domingo, or Callao. **Amenities:** Restaurant; bar; rooftop terrace; concierge; room service; free Wi-Fi.

Hotel Santo Domingo ★★ A multi-year renovation project, completed in 2013, transformed one of the most old-fashioned lodgings in central Madrid into the epitome of casual chic. Four of the five different grades of rooms are decorated in the familiar international palette of taupes and tans with dark wood accents and pops of brilliant white in the linens and bathrooms. All have new wooden floors, completely new bathrooms, and all new furnishings. The least expensive rooms, designated "smart economy," make extensive use of lollipop color schemes to make them look bigger than they are; queen size beds eat up most of the space, but the rooms are well designed and a very good deal. In fairness, they are sold as either singles or doubles. The other doubles are much larger, stepping up in size when called standard double and getting downright spacious in the superior doubles category. There are only a few available, but the corner rooms (premium priced) are as large as a junior suite and feature two glass walls for panoramic city views. Both the bar and hotel restaurant are run by the Arzak family of San Sebastián fame. The location near Gran Vía is not an issue, thanks to good soundproofing.

Calle San Bernardo 1. ℂ **91-547-98-00.** http://hotelsantodomingo.es. 200 units. 81€–140€ smart economy; 99€–170€ double; 139€–234€ superior double; 153€–227€ corner room. Parking 30€. Metro: Santo Domingo. **Amenities:** Restaurant; bar; room service; free Wi-Fi.

Intur Palacio San Martín ★★ This elegant property served as the first American embassy in Madrid and years later was converted into a luxury hotel. That conversion in 2001 did retain some of the nicer features of this National Heritage building, including crown moldings, an anachronistic wooden elevator, and vast expanses of marble on the floors. In keeping with the late-19th-century origins, the rooms are furnished with antique reproductions in a vaguely Modernista style and feature rich carpets on the floors. Most double rooms can be fitted with an extra bed for children.

Plaza San Martín, 5. ℂ **91-701-50-00.** www.hotelpalaciosanmartin.es. 94 units. 76€–136€ double; 147€–274€ junior suite. Metro: Ópera. **Amenities:** Restaurant; bar; exercise room; room service; sauna; free Wi-Fi.

Room Mate Laura ★ Designer Tomás Alía gave this Room Mate the playful personality of a party girl with smarts. Taking a nearly impossible soaring triangular space, he hung the rooms off one side behind balconies and left a soaring lobby over the reception area. The low lighting and open railings make Laura a poor choice for travelers who have vision or balance issues, and a little questionable for those with small children. For everyone else, the rooms are a joy. They all have very high ceilings, in some cases so high that the sleeping area is tucked into an overhead loft. In typical Room Mate fashion, the furnishings are spare, contemporary Scandinavian in feel, and the showers are glass display boxes. Several rooms have hideaway cooking facilities for an extra fee. Location is great: almost equidistant from Puerta del Sol, the Teatro Real, and Gran Vía.

Travesia de Trujillos, 3. ℂ **91-701-16-70.** http://laura.room-matehotels.com. 37 units. 75€–119€ double. Metro: Ópera or Santo Domingo. **Amenities:** Concierge; free Wi-Fi.

INEXPENSIVE

JC Rooms Santo Domingo ★★ Like its sister property, JC Rooms Santa Ana (p. 59), this budget boutique hotel offers brightly decorated rooms aimed at a young clientele. The newest of the group, it opened in July 2013 in a strategic spot just off Gran Vía. The free mini-bar is restocked daily and every room has a computer with Wi-Fi. This Santo Domingo version themes its rooms to different European countries, covering many walls with gigantic photos, others with broad splashes of primary

colors. Furnishings are mostly light wood in unadorned Scandinavian style. An A
Coruña brewery restaurant is on the premises.

Cuesta de Santo Domingo, 16. ℂ **91-547-60-79.** www.jchoteles-santodomingo.com. 45 units.
59€–75€ double; 75€–86€ triple; 102€–119€ quadruple. Metro: Santo Domingo. **Amenities:** Res-
taurant-brewery; free Wi-Fi.

Room Mate Mario ★   When Tomás Alía designed this early Room Mate hotel,
his toughest task was to exorcise the youth hostel that used to occupy the building. He
pulled it off with bold graphic design. The black and white corridors lead to rooms
awash in white with bright pops of abstract color. Standard doubles, executive rooms,
and junior suites are spacious and bright, The single rooms, which may be rented for
two people used to living in intimate quarters, are the main reminder of the former
hostel. They are pretty and bright, but very tight. All rooms have a desk with Philippe
Starck lighting and a cast glass sink in the bedroom while the glass box shower serves
as a bedroom-bathroom divider.

Calle Campomanes, 4. ℂ **91-548-85-48.** http://mario.room-matehoteles.com. 54 units. 59€–116€
double. Metro: Ópera. **Amenities:** Concierge; free Wi-Fi.

Gran Vía, Chueca & Malasaña

MODERATE

H10 Villa de la Reina ★★   The brown, taupe, and tan color scheme of the décor
might seem masculine, but the huge reproduction portraits of Spanish queens in the
lobby signal that this really is the "house of the queen." Rooms are not feminine in the
soft and fluffy sense of the word, but they would do very nicely for a woman executive
in Madrid on business. The desk has to share the television, but the handsome black
and white photography of period architectural details (from buildings on Gran Vía)
gives the walls and hence the rooms considerable elegance. Marble bathrooms include
lighted magnifying makeup mirrors (equally good for men to use while shaving), and
the nice touch of a small vase with a single calla lily or similar flower stem.

Gran Vía, 22. ℂ **91-523-91-01.** www.hotelh10villadelareina.com. 74 units. 95€–210€ double;
119€–350€ junior suite. Metro: Gran Vía. **Amenities:** Restaurant; bar; room service; free Wi-Fi.

Hotel Catalonia Gran Vía ★   Location is key for this member of the Catalonia
Hoteles group, which also operates the HC Puerta del Sol (p. 57). This older hotel was
one of the first buildings constructed on Gran Vía and was designed by one of Antoni
Gaudí's teachers, Emilio Salas y Cortés. Renovated many times since its construction
in 1898, it is one of the larger hotels on the street. That footprint gave the owners the
opportunity to install a very nice seasonal rooftop pool with great views of the Cibeles
fountain. Rooms are on the small side and feature a milk chocolate and honey color
scheme with hardwood floors. Bathrooms employ a pale honey-colored marble on the
floors and walls, but the sink fixture is set in a red-brown marble that frankly looks a
little dated. Some of the upper level rooms offer outdoor terraces, and junior suites
have mini-pools.

Gran Vía, 9. ℂ **91-531-22-22.** www.hoteles-catalonia.es. 185 units. 59€–130€ double; 89€–150€
terrace room; 125€–255€ junior suite. Metro: Gran Vía. **Amenities:** Restaurant; bar; exercise room;
Jacuzzi; room service; sauna; free Wi-Fi.

Hotel De Las Letras ★★   Built for the Count of Artaza while Gran Vía was still
under construction in 1917, this former noble home was transformed into a boutique
hotel with a literary theme in 2005. It was a leader in rehabilitating Gran Vía. A few
touches remain from the count's era: the quaint polished wood and cast iron elevator,

carved details in the stone lintels, and some of the original hand-painted tiles in the lobby. As well, the bones of the noble home are still very much in evidence: large wooden-framed windows, oak hardwood floors, high ceilings, and a flood of natural light that brightens the deep, saturated wall colors. Quotations by Spanish poets, novelists, and essayists are stenciled on the walls throughout the hotel, but if you don't read Spanish, you can consider them simply fine decorative figures with a hidden semiotic meaning. Far and away the nicest rooms are the superior terrace rooms on the 5th and 6th floors. Their outdoor wood-slat terraces have panoramic views of Gran Vía in one direction, the old city in another.

Gran Vía, 11. ℰ **91-523-79-80.** www.hoteldelasletras.com. 100 units. 95€–127€ double; 135€–159€ superior terrace. Metro: Sevilla or Gran Vía. **Amenities:** Restaurant; bar; exercise room; room service; spa; free Wi-Fi.

Room Mate Óscar ★★   Perhaps Madrid's first design hotel to openly court a gay clientele (appropriately enough for Chueca), the walls in many of Óscar's rooms are silkscreened with photos of incredibly fit naked bodies (no frontal nudity) and furnished with pieces by Verner Panton and Philippe Starck. The spare and open spaces give the rooms a futuristic air, though if the price is right, spring for a deluxe room (you'll have far more space for you and your luggage). Soundproofing is excellent, both inside and out. That's a good thing, because the fictional Óscar is a party animal and so are many of his guests. You'll see them coming down for breakfast at 11:45am, secure that the buffet is still set until noon.

Plaza Vázquez de Mella, 12. ℰ **91-701-11-73.** http://oscar.room-matehotels.com. 75 units. 75€–116€ double; 125€–155€ junior suite. Metro: Gran Vía. **Amenities:** Concierge; free Wi-Fi.

INEXPENSIVE

Hotel Negresco ★★   This well-run, sweet little hotel is a remarkable deal. The rooms are fresh and beautifully maintained, but they tend to be small. Those with two single beds are actually the smallest, while rooms with a queen-size "cama matrimonial" are marginally larger and definitely more comfortable for reading in bed. (They have padded headboards.) Both configurations have a good work desk, emphasizing that the hotel is aimed at economy-minded business travelers. The location is interesting—on a small street off Gran Vía that ultimately leads into Puerta del Sol. The surroundings are surprisingly quiet. Other competing economy hotels on the street are not as nice but have helped drive prices down. There's a flower shop nearby, so if you're staying for a while, brighten the room with a bouquet. At theses prices, you can easily afford the treat. There's a snack-bar room with vending machines and an espresso maker just off reception on the ground level.

Calle Mesonero Romanos, 12. ℰ **91-523-86-10.** www.hotel-aquaria-negresco-madrid.com. 20 units. 45€–65€ double. Metro: Callao. **Amenities:** Business center; free Wi-Fi in public areas; Wi-Fi available in rooms.

Hostal Sil & Serranos ★   Under the same ownership as the Hostal La Macarena (p. 59), this hostal is decorated in a low-key, rather old-fashioned style, but every room is large by Spanish standards, and they all have air conditioning (something the Macarena lacks). Most have brand-new marble and tile baths, usually with tub showers rather than shower stalls, and simple but functional furniture. Corner room 203 has two separate balconies overlooking different streets. A solo traveler should ask for Room 311, which is tiny but has a romantic view of Malasaña's red-tiled rooftops. For families or groups, several rooms are set up for three or four people and some fourth-floor units have a second small bedroom. Location is the shortcoming here, as you'll probably take the Metro everywhere you go, but the low cost makes that a little easier to take.

Calle Fuencarral, 95, 2nd floor. ℂ **91-448-89-72.** www.silserranos.com. 29 units. 40€ single; 53€ double; 71€ triple; 90€ quadruple. Metro: Tribunal or Bilbao. **Amenities:** Free Wi-Fi.

Salamanca, Retiro & Chamberí
EXPENSIVE

Hotel Adler ★★★   This utterly beautiful hotel rescued an architecturally distinct late-19th-century building from an ignominious fate as a parking garage. All that was left of the original was the carved limestone facade, but the boutique hotel constructed inside that shell is perhaps more glamorous than the original structure. All the rooms have soaring ceilings, and many are equipped with decorative marble fireplaces. Plush carpeting underfoot coordinates with upholstered furniture. While décor varies from room to room, many have canopy or four-poster beds—or beds set into alcoves framed by columns. The designer bathrooms are some of the best we have seen in any hotel, and include contemporary marble shower areas as well as deep free-standing soaking tubs. The hotel has no meeting rooms, and hence deals almost entirely with guests on vacation. There's a definite Old World grace about the hotel—front desk staff wear frock coats, for example—yet it is comfortable, low-key, and extremely warm and inviting.

Calle Velázquez, 33. ℂ **866/376-7831** in the U.S. and Canada, or 91-426-32-20. www.adlermadrid. com. 44 units. 193€–275€ double; from 325€ junior suite. Parking 30€. Metro: Velázquez. **Amenities:** Restaurant; bar; bikes; concierge; room service; Wi-Fi available.

MODERATE

Jardín de Recoletos ★   This contemporary apartment-hotel is just a few blocks north of the Puerta de Alcalá and not far from the Paseo de Recoletos. It is within convenient walking distance of the Parque del Retiro and some of the better boutique shopping of Salamanca. A modern building erected in 1999, it aspires to the grand post-modernism of that period with its vast expanse of marble floor in the lobby and stained glass in the atrium. The rooms reel in the ambition to offer traditional styling, space, and comfort—and an adequate kitchenette that is perfect for preparing breakfast or a late night snack if you're too tired to go out. Some suites also feature a large outdoor terrace.

Calle Gil de Santivañes, 6. ℂ **91-781-16-40.** www.vphoteles.com. 43 units. 119€–169€ double; 149€–215€ suite. Parking 24€. Metro: Serrano or Recoleto. **Amenities:** Restaurant; room service; free Wi-Fi.

INEXPENSIVE

Hostal Residencia Don Diego ★   The hotel equivalent of buying the least expensive house in an exclusive neighborhood, this fifth floor hostal offers bargain comfort in otherwise pricey Salamanca. The décor is simple and modern with hardwood floors, blond wood bedside tables and desk with contemporary brushed stainless pulls, and white walls embellished with lots of mirrors and contemporary art prints. Bathrooms are modern and most units have bidets and full soaking tubs, though the few singles have shower stalls. The reception area, which has a number of comfy leather couches, doubles as a morning breakfast lounge and as a sitting lounge the rest of the day.

Calle de Velázquez, 45. ℂ **91-435-07-60.** www.hostaldondiego.com. 58 units. 57€–81€ double; 85€–105€ triple. Metro: Velázquez or Serrano. **Amenities:** Free Wi-Fi in lounge.

WHERE TO EAT

Madrid is a terrific city for eating because it has many long-standing gastronomic traditions, the most developed tapas bar scene in the world, and access to everything the country has to offer. If you like regional Spanish food, you'll find good examples here in the capital. If you like Spanish seafood, you're in good company with all the Madrileños. Fresh fish and shellfish are trucked or flown in from the coast daily. Although Madrid has roughly twice the population of Barcelona, it does not have nearly the number of Michelin-starred restaurants nor the intense foodie culture. That said, you can get an exquisite, cutting-edge meal from some of the country's leading chefs—just not from as many of them. Madrid, however, excels at more casual dining. Once you get past the idea that you must have dinner at a "restaurant," you'll discover you can eat very well indeed at a more casual "bar-restaurante" or a "cafe-bar." Indeed, given the ongoing financial troubles in Spain, casual dining spots are flourishing.

Arts District & Paseos

EXPENSIVE

Gran Café de Gijón ★ SPANISH/CONTINENTAL   A throwback to a more civilized era when Madrid's literati flocked here for heated discussions of world affairs over coffee and brandy, the Gijón attracts older Madrileños who like to remember a quieter time—and a lot of tourists happy for a break from the go-go modern city. This is really three establishments in one: the outdoor terrace where people like to observe the parade up the paseo; the street-level cafe, where the windows swing open to let in the breezes; and the downstairs formal dining room with expensive Continental food served at beautifully appointed tables. Adjacent to the upstairs cafe is a stand-up bar—the cheapest (non)seat in the house. It's a great spot to pause on a summer day for black coffee with ice cream (a blanco y negro) or a mixed drink.

Paseo de Recoletos, 21. © **91-521-54-25.** www.cafegijon.com. Reservations required for restaurant. Main courses 20€–34€; fixed-price menu 32€–75€. Daily 7:30am–2am. Metro: Banco de España.

Horcher ★ CONTINENTAL   You'll pay handsomely to dine at this avatar of old-fashioned grace and haute cuisine, but you'll never forget the experience. The restaurant launched more than a century ago in Berlin and the proprietors, reading the writing on the wall, relocated to "neutral" Spain in 1943. The restaurant is a magnificent period piece; not only are the dishes from another era, so is the impeccable and knowledgeable service. Start with specialties like smoked eel with radish sauce, an individual cheese soufflé, or lobster bisque before moving on to typical formal dishes like roast pigeon in Perigord truffle sauce, or a simple brochette of red prawns and scallops. Wild boar, duck, and venison abound on the fall menu.

Calle Alfonso XII, 6. © **91-522-07-31.** www.restaurantehorcher.com. Reservations required. Jackets and ties required for men. Main courses 32eu]–42€. Mon–Fri 1:30–4pm and 8:30pm–midnight; Sat 8:30pm–midnight. Metro: Retiro.

Viridiana ★★ SPANISH   If you like food with wit and panache, you'll love chef Abraham García, who blogs about food twice a week in the online edition of "El Mundo." He named the restaurant after the 1961 Luis Buñuel film classic and happens to be a film buff as well as a self-taught, idiosyncratic chef. (Stills from Buñuel films line the walls.) The look is almost bistro-casual, but the food is creatively prepared, imaginative, and delicious. Ask for fish and you're likely to get a composed plate like

Madrid Restaurants

Alkalde **50**
Alquezar **18**
Antigua Casa
  Ángel Sierra **30**
Asador Real **7**
Babel Restaurante
  B&B **29**
Bazaar
  Restaurant **28**
Bocaito **26**

Café de
  Oriente **5**
Casa Labra **10**
Casa Lucio **17**
Casa Marta **6**
Cervecería
  José Luis **33**

Cervecería
  La Fábrica **46**
Cervecería
  Plaza Mayor **12**
Chocolatería
  San Ginés **9**
dASSA bASSA **35**

El Brillante **49**
El Espejo **31**
El Ñeru **8**
Estado Puro **45**
Gran Café
  de Gijón **34**
Green & More **44**

Harina **36**
Horcher **38**
Iroco **51**
Julián de
  Tolosa **14**
La Biotika **47**
La Bola Taberna **3**

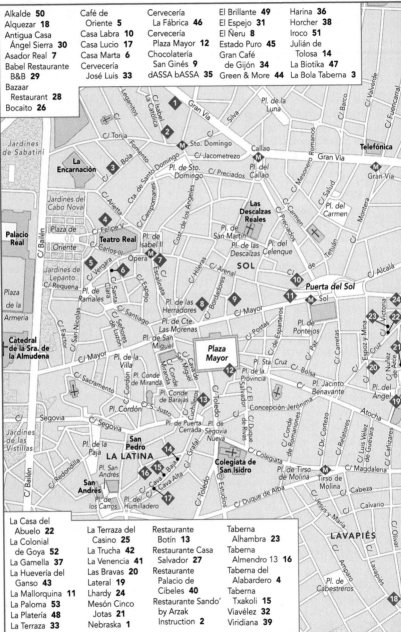

La Casa del
  Abuelo **22**
La Colonial
  de Goya **52**
La Gamella **37**
La Huevería del
  Ganso **43**
La Mallorquina **11**
La Paloma **53**
La Platería **48**
La Terraza **33**

La Terraza del
  Casino **25**
La Trucha **42**
La Venencia **41**
Las Bravas **20**
Lateral **19**
Lhardy **24**
Mesón Cinco
  Jotas **21**
Nebraska **1**

Restaurante
  Botín **13**
Restaurante Casa
  Salvador **27**
Restaurante
  Palacio de
  Cibeles **40**
Restaurante Sando'
  by Arzak
  Instruction **2**

Taberna
  Alhambra **23**
Taberna
  Almendro 13 **16**
Taberna del
  Alabardero **4**
Taberna
  Txakoli **15**
Viavélez **32**
Viridiana **39**

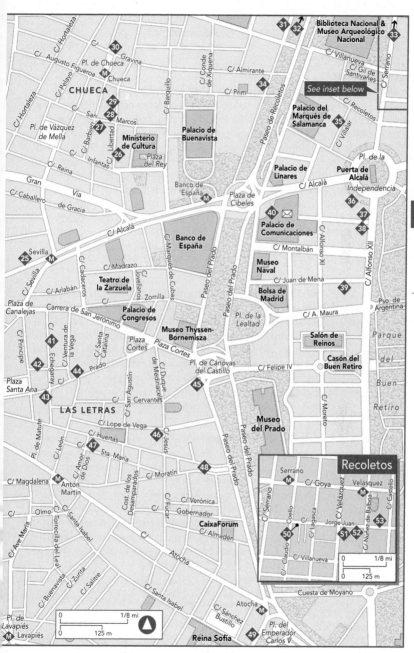

grilled butterfish with baby peas, roasted sweet potato, and an almond-garlic sauce. For meat, he might sauté a pork sirloin and serve it with Sicilian dried tomatoes, spring onions, and spiral pasta.

Calle Juan de Mena, 14. ℂ **91-531-10-39.** www.restauranteviridiana.com. Reservations recommended. Main courses 30€–37€. Mon–Sat 1:30–4pm and 8:30pm–midnight. Closed Easter week. Metro: Banco de España.

MODERATE

Café Restaurante El Espejo ★ CONTINENTAL   The name means "mirror," and El Espejo looks back to an era before World War I when people still ate prawns with special forks. Opened in 1978, El Espejo is a dead ringer for an Art Nouveau cafe-restaurant, with its dark wood paneling, glittering chandeliers, and tiles depicting Rossini-esque maidens with flowers entwined in their hair. The neighborhood is upscale Recoletos, and El Espejo reflects that genteel sensibility. If you enjoy food cooked the way Auguste Escoffier codified it, there are good bargains to be had on the set menus. Among the classics offered are roasted whole bream with a roasted red pepper cream sauce and veal cutlet in mustard sauce. If you're craving something more definitively Spanish, the oxtail braised in red wine (rabo de toro) is appropriately dark and unctuous. Desserts are plain; have a sweet sherry instead.

Paseo de Recoletos, 31. ℂ **91-308-23-47.** www.restauranteelespejo.com. Reservations suggested. Main courses 14€–22€; fixed-price menus 27€–41€. Daily 1–4pm and 9pm–midnight. Metro: Colón.

La Gamella ★ AMERICAN   This restaurant embodies a certain strain of Spanish culture that has a lifelong crush on New York City. In fact, it offers a bargain "New York Brunch" on Sundays, and plays up its Caesar salads, American style burgers, and grilled sirloin with chimichurri sauce. It even brags about putting a few drops of Jack Daniels into the steak tartare. The American theme continues with the fish—one of the most popular dishes on the menu is the plate of fish tacos with mango salsa. The result is simple but excellent food that requires more appetite than analysis.

Calle Alfonso XII, 4. ℂ **91-532-45-09.** www.lagamella.com. Reservations required. Main courses 18€–23€; fixed-price menu 28€. Mon–Fri 1:30–4pm; Mon–Sat 9pm–midnight. Closed 4 days around Easter. Metro: Retiro.

Restaurante Palacio de Cibeles ★★ SPANISH   Adolfo Muñoz, the inventive chef who brought Toldeo literally out of the dark ages for dining, opened this gourmet restaurant on the sixth floor of CentroCentro in early 2012. When the weather's appropriate, he also serves a bar menu on the terrace with deals like a burger, fries, and drink for 11€. But Madrileño gourmets flock to the elegant indoor dining room (which also has a spectacular view) for Muñoz's creative twists on La Manchan classics, like partridge two ways with two wines (stewed with tempranillo red wine sauce and roasted with sherry sauce) or roast leg of lamb with mountain herbs and pisto Manchego—a Spanish version of ratatouille with roasted tomatoes, eggplant, and squash seasoned with sherry vinegar.

Plaza de Cibeles, 1. ℂ **91-523-14-54.** www.adolfo-palaciodecibeles.com. Reservations required. Main courses 23€–32€; terrasse midday menu 15€. Daily 1–4pm; Mon–Sat 10pm–midnight. Metro: Banco de España.

INEXPENSIVE

El Brillante ★★ SPANISH   There are both Burger King and McDonald's franchises near the Reina Sofia, but Spaniards snub them in favor of the equally fast but more varied sandwiches at El Brillante. The finger-sized 4-inch mini-bocadillos make a terrific snack, while the 10-inch super bocatas really are a meal. You can get everything from sliced pork with roasted peppers to an omelet sandwich, but El Brillante is acclaimed for its fried calamari rolls. Tables are few and far between, but there's a certain style to eating while standing at the stainless steel bars, letting your spent napkins float to the floor, just as the Spaniards do. Taking half a city block, El Brillante has a door on the Carlos V roundabout and another on the plaza in front of the Reina Sofía.

Calle Atocha, 122. ℂ **91-468-05-48.** Sandwiches 3€–9€. Daily 6:30am–midnight or later. No credit cards. Metro: Atocha.

Estado Puro ★★ SPANISH   Chef Paco Roncero was one of the first of Spain's new wave chefs to decide that tapas were the purest expression of Spanish gastronomy, so he collaborated with the NH hotel chain to launch this post-modern tapas bar right on the plaza with the Neptune fountain. His most famous tapa is his deconstructed tortilla española (a layered dish of liquid egg and liquefied potato that, when quaffed from a cordial glass, tastes just like the original). Other dishes depart less from tradition but show a clever mind at work—spiced bread with a slice of foie gras and a sweet wine reduction, for example, or tempura-fried asparagus with romesco sauce. It's all in good fun, and there's a nice selection of wines by the glass to accompany the dishes.

Hotel NH Paseo del Prado, Plaza Cánovas del Castillo, 4. ℂ **91-330-24-00.** http://tapasenestado-puro.com. Tapas 5€–11€. Daily noon–midnight. Metro: Banco de España.

La Platería Bar Museo ★ SPANISH   Perhaps the ultimate in quality casual dining near the Prado, the aptly named "Silverware Bar" has good and simple food to go with its draft beer and decent selection of wine by the glass. Generous plates tend to emphasize the classics—like a hamburger smothered with caramelized onions, melted cheese, and (if you wish) slices of sausage. Speaking of sausage—the fat links of *butifarra,* a Catalan sausage, are often offered with a large plate of ratatouille. The house fish specialty is *pulpo gallego*—boiled octopus served over boiled potatoes and heavily seasoned with smoky Spanish paprika and a sharp Spanish olive oil. Most diners elect to eat at outdoor cafe tables, but the bar does have a small dining room if the weather gets cold or wet.

Calle Moratin, 49. ℂ **91-429-17-22.** Main courses 9€–14€. Daily 7:30am–midnight. Metro: Atocha.

Puerta del Sol & Las Letras
EXPENSIVE

Lhardy ★ CONTINENTAL   If you like the Palacio Real (p. 98), you might very well love dining upstairs in a formal Isabelline dining room at Lhardy. Madrid's elite has been coming here since Lhardy opened in 1839, but most people passing on the street have no idea that the formal dining rooms exist. That's because Lhardy runs a carriage-trade deli on the first floor along with a stand-up bar where you can enjoy little sandwiches, assorted tapas, and ham and cod croquetas. (Think of it as a tapas bar for lawyers and doctors.)

Carrera de San Jerónimo, 8. ℂ **91-521-33-85.** www.lhardy.com. Reservations recommended in the upstairs dining room. Main dishes 28€–39€. Deli service daily 9:30am–3pm; Mon–Sat 5–9:30pm. Restaurant service Mon 1–3:30pm; Tues–Sat 1–3:30pm and 8:30–11pm. Closed Aug. Metro: Vodafone Sol.

La Terraza del Casino ★★★ SPANISH   Super chef Paco Roncero runs this exquisite bastion of contemporary cuisine with Ferran Adrià, the elBulli master of innovation, looking over his shoulder as an advisor. The restaurant holds down the top floor of the over-the-top Baroque gentleman's club called the Casino, and if that makes you think of waiters in white tuxedo jackets and other luxe touches of a dining room for Madrid's elite, you're on the right track. But for all the elegant trappings (the outdoor terrace has a sweeping view of the Madrid city lights), Roncero's cooking is smart, fresh, seasonal, and completely devoid of gimmicks. Techniques are very au courant—he poaches skate in olive oil, for example, and serves it with a kind of pistou of parsley, garlic, and almonds. It's actually a variant of an old dish the Spanish aristocracy brought back from Italy when they used to rule large parts of it. He turns the rustic Asturian *fabada* (pork and beans) into an elegant bean veloute served with a bowl of al dente green favas drizzled with a sharp Picual olive oil.

Calle Alcalá, 15. ✆ **91-532-12-75.** www.casinodemadrid.es. Main courses 32€–45€. Mon–Fri 1:30–4pm; Mon–Sat 9–11:45pm. Closed Aug. Metro: Sevilla or Vodafone Sol.

MODERATE

Green & More ★★ SPANISH   Subtitled "La Huerta de Tudela" after the restaurant's farm in the Ebro valley in Navarre, this venture from Tudela native son Ricardo Gil is a rarity in Madrid: a restaurant where vegetables are accorded the respect usually reserved for the rarest caviar or most prime meat. Gil has a passion for veggies, and his tasting menu is a nine-course tour de force where meat serves as a seasoning rather than the main plate. Typical dishes might be a roll of Swiss chard stuffed with mushrooms and ham served with a little hollandaise, or a potato confit strudel seasoned with ham hock. More than half the a la carte menu consists of vegetable dishes, and even the fish and meat plates tend to be accompanied by roasted vegetables or smothered in vegetables. As Gil writes on the menu, "In our house, the vegetable is the queen."

Calle Prado, 15. ✆ **91-420-44-18.** www.greenandmore.es. Main courses 12€–24€; 9-course vegetable tasting menu 44€. Daily 1:30–4pm; Mon–Sat 8:30–11:30pm. Metro: Antón Martín.

El Ñeru ★ ASTURIAN   You have to push your way through a packed tapas scene in the bar to get to the back stairs that lead to an underground warren of elegantly tiled rooms. The cuisine of "The Nest" is Asturian, a regional favorite with Madrileños, and it's reflected in the fish-intensive menu, including the Asturian classic of hake braised in cider. You don't have to be a fish-lover to eat Asturian, though. El Ñeru makes a hearty *fabada Asturiana* of large white beans stewed with ham and sausage, and, for the more adventurous, a stew of tripe and garbanzo beans. A Madrid friend swears that the restaurant also makes the city's best *arroz con leche,* a creamy rice pudding with a caramelized top. Bread service includes a great spread of butter blended with Cabrales blue cheese, and the meal ends with a complimentary thimble of a yellow-green digestive liqueur.

Calle Bordadores, 5. ✆ **91-541-11-40.** www.restauranteelneru.com. Main dishes 12€–22€. Tues–Sun 1:30–4:30pm and 8:30–11pm. Metro: Vodafone Sol or Opera.

INEXPENSIVE

La Biotika ★ VEGETARIAN   Vegetarianism is a foreign concept to most Spaniards, whose idea of a vegetable is the garnish that comes with a fried pork steak. But travelers trying to stay meatless are not reduced to living on salad and tortilla española. Biotika is the longest standing vegetarian and macrobiotic restaurant in Madrid. It's located on the east side of Plaza Santa Ana, and the neo-Sixties Art Nouveau stylings

Madrid's summer gastronomic festival means great bargains during the last 2 weeks of July. Roughly two dozen restaurants in Salamanca and in the central old city (Sol, Las Letras, La Latina, and near Ópera) offer multi-course special menus with beer or water for 25€. At the same time, about 50 bars and taverns participate in the **Ruta de la Tapa.** Each establishment offers a different signature tapa and a beer for 3€. Free shuttle buses take tapas-hoppers between the old city and Salamanca. For more information, see www.esmadrid.com and search for GastroMad.

of what's basically a cafeteria can be endearing. Soups and heavy whole-grain breads are made daily on the premises and the big crisp salads tend to be good and filling. Biotika's signature "meatball without meat" consists of vegetables rolled into a ball and browned. You can also always order sautéed tofu with the vegetable of the moment, with or without brown rice.

Calle Amor de Dios, 3. ✆ **91-429-07-80.** www.labiotika.es. 3-course menus with dessert and beverage 11€–17€. Mon–Sat 10am–11:30pm; Sun 10am–3pm. Metro: Antón Martín.

Casa Labra ★★ SPANISH   Neither the passage of time nor the enmity of the Franco government could kill this classic eatery just off Puerta del Sol. Founded in 1860, Casa Labra remains unrepentantly old-fashioned with its polished dark wood and blue-and-white tiles, looking just as it did when it was a popular gathering spot for Franco's Republican enemies during the Civil War. The specialty of the house is bacalao (salt cod), the fish that's been the foundation of Spanish cuisine at least since the first restaurants opened in Madrid in the 19th century. Stop in the taberna (really, the bar) for bite-sized tapas of fried fresh cod or a small plate of bacalao croquetas. The dining room menu runs the gamut of cod dishes, from a woodsy version with wild mushrooms, capers, and orange juice, to a more ethereal presentation with saffron and rice. Another historic footnote: The Spanish Socialist Workers' Party (PSOE) was founded here in 1879.

Calle Tetuán, 12. ✆ **91-531-00-81.** www.casalabra.es. Main dishes 12€–19€. Taberna service daily 9:30am–3:30pm and 5:30–11pm; restaurant service daily 1:15–3:30pm and 8:15–10pm. Metro: Vodafone Sol.

La Huevería del Ganso ★★ SPANISH   The game at this tongue-in-cheek taberna right outside Plaza Santa Ana is duck-duck-goose—or maybe goose-goose-duck. As the name suggests, great big goose eggs figure prominently in the kitchen's reinterpretation of the classics of Spanish bar food. Goose or duck takes the place of the more traditional pork in most cases, and super chef Dani García was even amused enough to give the Jimenez Herrara brothers a couple of tapas recipes for their launch in July 2013. The flavors and textures remain remarkably similar—goose "ham" is a lot like pig ham. This being a Spanish kitchen, some ham from Iberian pigs does creep onto the menu. Goose egg *estrellitas* (broken fried egg, usually oozing over fried potatoes), for example, are served over crisp-fried potato straws with thin slices of air-dried Iberian ham. When the geese stop laying in the heat of summer, the kitchen substitutes duck eggs.

Calle Echegaray, 26. No phone. Main dishes 3.50€–12€. Daily 1pm–midnight. Metro: Antón Martín.

4

MADRID | Where to Eat

tapas bars AROUND PLAZA SANTA ANA

Most tapas restaurants outside Spain encourage customers to settle in at a table and order lots and lots of small plates of food. But tapas are ideally eaten standing at a bar and should be a movable feast: Enjoy the specialty of the house, and then move on to the next stop. Plaza Santa Ana has one of the best concentrations of tapas bars. They begin serving food between noon and 2pm and remain open until the last customer staggers out in the early morning. Peak hours for tapas are usually 6 to 9pm, and a place that was empty at 5pm will have people drinking in the street by 7pm. We find tapas-hopping ideal for eating an early dinner. It's also a great way to try food you're not sure you'll like (like callos, or tripe), or specialties that are too expensive for a full meal. Many tapas bars don't take credit cards, even if their attached restaurants do. Cash keeps the pace moving. You should do the same.

Las Bravas ★ Fried potatoes smothered in a spicy red paprika-based sauce are a staple in bars all over Spain. This one claims to have invented the dish—known as patatas bravas—and even has a patent on the sauce. At Las Bravas, you can also get a pig's ear, fried baby squid, chicken wings, and even a whole 6-inch tortilla española smothered in it. We always grab a ledge on the mirror-covered wall so we can keep track of how much sauce we've dripped on ourselves.

Calle Espoz y Mina, 13. ℭ **91-521-35-07.** Tapas 4€–9€. Noon–1am. Cash only. Metro: Sevilla.

Méson Cinco Jotas ★ "Cinco Jotas" (or "5J") refers to the highest possible score in a ham grading system employed in Jabugo in Andalucía. The 5J ham sells at a premium, but once you've tasted it, it's as hard go back to generic jamón serrano as to switch from single-malt Scotch to cheap beer. Try it here, where the 5J tapa consists of three paper-thin squares of ham to wrap around five conical crackers. If you like the gamy taste more than the gummy texture, order the caña de lomo 5J tapa for a larger helping of sausage made from the same grade of ham.

Plaza Santa Ana, 1. ℭ **91-522-63-64.** www. mesoncincojotas.com. Tapas 4€–18€. Noon–1am. Metro: Antón Martín.

La Venencia ★ If you're among the fortunate, you'll score standing room at the bar or one of the seats on the elevated platform in the back. If so, you're in for

Lateral ★ TAPAS The fifth of a small local group of tapas restaurants, this 2008 branch of Lateral is perfectly situated in Plaza Santa Ana to offer a sleek, cocktail bar look for diners making the rounds of the square. The menu consists of all the greatest hits of Spanish tapas along with innovations like melted brie with air-dried ham, vegetable tempura with a yogurt dipping sauce, and a ham-encased roll of salmon, cheese, and caramelized apple served on toast. It's just inventive enough to encourage you to drink gin and tonic or a cosmo instead of beer and wine.

Plaza Santa Ana, 12. ℭ **91-420-15-82.** www.lateral.com. Plates 3.50€–8€. Sun–Wed noon–midnight; Thurs–Sat noon–2am. Metro: Vodafone Sol or Antón Martín.

La Mallorquina ★ PASTRY This pastry shop at the edge of Puerta del Sol has been a classic hangout for the *merienda* (coffee break) since it opened its doors in 1894. If you can pull yourself away from the downstairs display cases, you'll find a about as Andalucían a drinking experience as you can find in Madrid. La Venencia serves fino, oloroso, and amontillado sherries straight from the cask—or famous marques from the bottle. (Cask sherry is common in Andalucía, but rare in Madrid.) Drinking is primary here, and eating secondary. We like to nibble some pickled sardines or roasted peppers while savoring the taste of Spain's most famous wines.

Calle Echegaray, 7. ✆ **91-429-62-61.** Tapas 3€–5€. Noon–midnight. Cash only. Metro: Sevilla.

Cervecería La Fábrica ★

On a Sunday afternoon, it seems like everybody here is tossing back draft beer and munching on *montaditos* (tasty bites mounted on a diagonal slice of baguette). The variety is jaw dropping, especially if you like fish. Most flavor for the euro are the smoked tuna and the combination of blue cheese with salt-packed anchovies.

Calle Jesus, 2. ✆ **91-369-30-67.** Montaditos 2€–3€. Daily 1:30pm–1am. Metro: Antón Martín.

La Trucha ★

The quintessential fish tapas of Madrid, however, belong to La Trucha, located slightly off the northeast corner of Plaza Santa Ana. If you want to try the house specialty of a slice of smoked trout on toast, order a single slice, but most people order a whole plate of smoked trout toasts. To save a few euros, try the salad of mixed smoked fish. All that smoke and salt will make you thirsty, but draft beers are some of the cheapest in the neighborhood.

Calle Manuel Fernández y González, 3. ✆ **91-429-58-33.** Tapas 2€–14€. Daily noon–1am. Metro: Antón Martín.

La Casa del Abuelo ★

Grandpa really gets around, as "Grandpa's House" is found in three separate locations, all within sight of each other. The main bar is on Calle Victoria, and keeps the longest hours. The others open to accommodate overflow. Choose the original to savor the patina of age—it opened in 1906 and has been serving shrimp specialties ever since. It is good that they accept credit cards, because the bill mounts quickly. We like our gambas plainly grilled (*gambas a la plancha*) or grilled with garlic (*gambas al ajillo*), but many customers prefer the smaller plates of breaded shrimp deep-fried in olive oil. The house wine is a steal.

Calle Victoria, 12. ✆ **91-521-23-19.** Also Calle Nunez de Arce, 5; Calle Goya, 57. www.lacasadelabuelo.es. Daily 1:30pm–1am. Metro: Sevilla.

little tearoom upstairs where you can order sandwiches, pastries, or ice-cream concoctions. A window seat gives you a great view of the hubbub in Puerta del Sol.

Puerta del Sol, 8. ✆ **91-521-12-01.** Sandwiches 3€–7.50€; pastries 2€–4€. Tearoom 9am–9pm. Metro: Vodafone Sol.

Taberna Alhambra ★ TAPAS   Andalucía gave Spain bullfighting and sherry, and it also gave Madrid a certain style of tavern, of which Alhambra is a prime example. Founded in 1929, it has retained all the color of a Granada barroom down to the extravagant scenes on the tiled walls designed by Alfonso Romero, who also created the tiles for Las Ventas bullring. Dishes are largely charcuterie—sausages, air-dried hams or beef, smoked and dried tuna. Most come in a choice of tapas, *raciones* (meal-size plates), or *media raciones* (half-size). We don't know the secret, but Taberna Alhambra makes the tastiest meatballs (albóndigas) in Madrid.

Calle Victoria, 9. ✆ **91-521-07-08.** www.tabernaalhambra.es. Plates 2€–11€. Daily noon–1am. Cash only. Metro: Sevilla.

Plaza Mayor & La Latina

MODERATE

Restaurante Botín ★ SPANISH   Ernest Hemingway really did eat at Botín, and he certainly set a scene here at the end of "The Sun Also Rises." The establishment has been trading on that publicity ever since, along with the determination by the Guinness Book of World Records that it is the world's oldest restaurant still in business (since 1725). It's a charming tourist trap with good-tasting but expensive food. As you enter, peek into the kitchen to see rack after rack of suckling pigs ready to go into the wood-fired oven. If your party is large enough to order a whole pig, it is brought to the table with great ceremony and then—bam!—smashed on top to break up all the parts. The daily menu gets you garlic soup as a starter, a serving of roast suckling pig, a drink, and ice cream. But you can enjoy the authentic 18th-century atmosphere of this restaurant in the street beneath Plaza Mayor and eat just as well on roast chicken for about a third the price. Roast milk-fed lamb is another house specialty, but most diners go for the pork.

Calle de Cuchilleros, 17. ℰ **91-366-42-17.** www.botin.es. Reservations recommended. Main courses 15€–32€; fixed-price menu 42€. Daily 1–4pm and 8pm–midnight. Metro: Ópera or Vodafone Sol.

Casa Lucio ★ CASTILIAN   Lucio Blázquez started working here at age 12 and eventually came to own the place. Now a venerable figure in the Madrid restaurant trade, he has maintained Casa Lucio as the model ancient Madrileño dining room. His meat-heavy menu has barely changed over the years, from the churrasco of grilled veal to the capon roasted until the meat falls off the bone. The bar has a classic Spanish look, with hams hanging from rough-hewn beams. Lucio's chief nod to more modern sensibilities is the "panache" of fresh vegetables cooked al dente. The big plate includes Swiss chard, broccoli, green beans, carrots (and just because it is Spain) lots and lots of artichoke hearts. Oldtimers take care of the annoying crunch by asking to have their panache further sautéed with olive oil and garlic.

Cava Baja, 35. ℰ **91-365-32-52.** www.casalucio.es. Reservations required. Main courses 16€–28€. Sun–Fri 1–4pm; daily 9–11:30pm. Closed Aug. Metro: La Latina.

Julián de Tolosa ★★ BASQUE   Maybe the most elegant restaurant along Cava Baja, this superb Basque asador has become a Madrid fixture over the last quarter century. Pretty much everything you'll order here will arrive with grill marks on it, so the house keeps the menu rather simple. Meat eaters can order a sirloin steak or a thick chop, fish eaters get a choice of hake or monkfish. There are two principal side dishes: grilled piquillo peppers, which taste both smoky and sweet, and fat stalks of Lodosa asparagus from the upper reaches of the Río Ebro. The ambiance is more fine steakhouse than tavern, with large plate glass windows making the street level dining room a showcase. Many diners prefer the lower dining room with its exposed brick walls and the radiant heat of the wood grill. The wine list here is spectacularly good, not just on the expected Riojas but also on the wines of Navarre.

Calle Cava Baja, 18. ℰ **91-365-82-10.** http://juliandetolosa.com. Main dishes 22€–30€. Daily 1:30–4pm; Mon–Sat 9pm–midnight. Metro: La Latina.

INEXPENSIVE

Alquezar ★★ MOROCCAN   If you thought you knew couscous because you've made it from a box of dried semolina, you need to eat at this modest restaurant with soccer matches on the TV to see what the dish is really like. Try to visit this friendly, family run restaurant on the weekend when the mother of the clan hand-rolls her own couscous and simmers delicious chicken or lamb tagines to accompany it. During the rest of the week, you'll have to settle for beef or chicken kebab plates accompanied by a pilaf of rice studded with vegetables, raisins, and almonds. By your second visit, the proprietors might hug you like family.

Calle Lavapiés, 53. (C) **91-527-72-61.** Meals 9€–12€. Daily 1:30–6pm and 8pm–midnight. Cash only. Metro: Lavapiés.

Cervecería Plaza Mayor ★ TAPAS   Because this spot is basically a beer hall with food rather than a restaurant with drinks, it's always been our first choice for enjoying the atmosphere of Plaza Mayor without having to break the bank. The tapas and *raciones* are utterly traditional, and equally dependable. A few slices of fried chorizo, a slice of tortilla española, maybe a plate of diced potatoes fried with garlic. All you need to make it a meal is a beer. FYI, the draft beer is about half the cost of the bottled suds here, and if you're really frugal, you'll eat inside standing up at the bar to avoid the surcharge for table service and the additional surcharge for table service on the plaza.

Plaza Mayor, 2. (C) **91-365-06-46.** Plates 4€–12€. Daily 7am–1am. Cash only. Metro: Ópera or Vodafone Sol.

Taberna Almendro 13 ★★ ANDALUCIAN   A Hollywood set designer couldn't imagine a more "typical" Spanish bar, from the dark wood and florid 19th-century tiles down to the barrel of manzanilla that you can order for a pittance per glass. In fact, when you enter, it will take a while for your eyes to adjust to the reduced illumination. The perfect complement to that mild sherry is an inexpensive plate of sheep's milk cheese with *membrillo* (quince paste). For a meal, it's hard to beat the ratatouille with fried egg. For authenticity's sake, do your eating and drinking while standing.

Calle Almendro, 13. (C) **91-365-42-52.** Main dishes 4€–11€. Daily 1:30–4:30pm and 8pm–1am. Cash only. Metro: La Latina.

Taberna Txakoli ★ TAPAS   Not to be confused with the upscale suburban Basque restaurant Txacoli, this tapas bar with two rooms down the street from each other has a winning formula of inexpensive but excellent Basque wine served with inexpensive but delicious Basque tapas. The most popular plates are brochettes of either squid, cod, or beef sirloin tips, while the most expensive is the "Bomba"—a heap of mashed potatoes studded with meat and swimming in mushroom gravy. You'll have to muscle your way to the bar to order, then back through the crowd to a place where you can eat standing up.

Calle Cava Baja, 26; Calle Cava Baja, 42. (C) **91-366-48-77.** Tapas 2€–8€. Daily 1:30–4pm and 8pm–2am. Cash only. Metro: La Latina.

Ópera & Palacio Real
MODERATE

Asador Real ★★ BASQUE   This classic Basque grill house is easy to find: Just look for the golden arches. The same building on Plaza Isabel II houses a McDonald's at street level. Asador Real is downstairs and its entry faces Calle Escalinata. Given the proximity to the Teatro Real, the emphasis on substantial cuts of meat, and the formality of the restaurant, Asador Real has surprisingly reasonable prices. If you're so inclined, you can watch the grill masters prepare your food. The best deal is on a quarter lamb or pig, which serves two generously.

Plaza Isabel II, 1. ℂ **91-547-11-11.** www.asadorreal.com. Main dishes 14€–24€. Daily 1:30pm–midnight. Metro: Ópera.

La Bola Taberna ★ CASTILIAN   This is possibly the most Madrileño restaurant in the whole city and it is one of the last that makes an old-fashioned *cocido* of long-boiled mixed cuts of meat and sausages. The stew is usually served in three stages—as meat, as vegetables, and as broth. The big pots of *cocido* simmer away over charcoal and entire families come on Sunday afternoon to make a ceremony of the heavy stew. It's unlikely that the menu has changed since La Bola opened in 1870, although (to the dismay of purists) the cooks no longer emphasize organ meats or some of the more gelatinous cuts in the *cocido*.

Calle Bola, 5. ℂ **91-547-69-30.** www.labola.es. Main dishes 12€–26€. Reservations recommended on weekends. Daily 1–4pm; Mon–Sat 8:30–11pm. Cash only. Metro: Ópera.

Café de Oriente ★ SPANISH   We've always thought of the outdoor cafe tables at Oriente as Madrid's seats of power. They overlook the Palacio Real and the Plaza de Oriente sculpture garden, and there's a courtly decorum to both the menu and the service. You will certainly not gain weight eating the dainty sandwiches such as the house special of lettuce, tomato, pickled pepper, mayo, ham, cheese, and asparagus. But that means you won't be too full to enjoy a pavlova with freshly whipped cream and fruit or a fancy ice cream dish. A meal is hardly the point here. You sit down at Café de Oriente so you can feel like (and are treated like) you own the world. We're less fond of the indoor dining room where the food is French and the prices are extravagant, even for traditional fare.

Plaza de Oriente, 2. ℂ **91-541-39-74.** http://cafedeoriente.es. Cafe plates 6€–18€. Cafe daily 10am–1am. Metro: Ópera.

Casa Marta ★★ SPANISH   If you're the sort of traveler who always looks for the "home cooking" sign when you're on the road, then Casa Marta is your kind of place. Although the menu is longer than it would be in most Madrid households, the plain and simple recipes are the sort that home cooks have made since the place was founded in the 1920s as Casa Eladio. We've always held that you can judge a casual restaurant by its croquetas, and these are excellent: Lots of flaky tuna, a slight crunch of onion, and a béchamel that's thick enough to hold its shape and thin enough to explode in your mouth. Other classic, homey plates include calf's liver smothered in onions, stewed chicken thighs, and roasted green peppers stuffed with ground meat and onion.

Calle Santa Clara, 10. ℂ **91-548-28-25.** www.restaurantecasamarta.com. Main courses 8€–14€. Tues–Sun 1:30–4pm; Tues–Sat 9pm–midnight. Metro: Ópera.

Restaurante Sandó by Arzak Instruction ★★★ SPANISH   One Spanish gastronome hit the nail on the head when he called Sandó the ready-to-wear version of famed chef Juan Mari Arzak's high cuisine couture in San Sebastián. Of course, the off-the-rack version won't have the hand-stitching or the luxuriant fabric of the runway piece, but it has the style and panache. The dishes at Sandó, which opened in summer 2013, represent some of the classics that Juan Mari and daughter Elena have created in their "laboratory" at Arzak, then served frequently enough to work out all the kinks. In classic Arzak style, they marry two seemingly incompatible flavors with great success, like white anchovies and sweet strawberries. One thing is for sure: You can eat a

FOR dipping

At some point, all of Madrid comes into **Chocolatería San Ginés** for a cup of the almost fudgy hot chocolate and the fried dough sticks known as churros. When the music stops in the wee hours of the morning, disco queens from Joy Eslava next door pop in for a cup, and later on, before they head to the office, bankers in three-piece suits order breakfast. There's sugar spilled everywhere on the tables, yet the marble counters are an impeccable tableau of cups lined up with the handles all facing at the same angle and a tiny spoon on each saucer. Dipping the sugar-dusted churros into the hot chocolate is de rigueur, and, yes, it's OK to have the snack in the afternoon. Pasadizo San Ginés, 5. ℰ **91-365-65-46.** Daily 9am–6am. Cash only. Metro: Vodafone Sol or Ópera.

tasting menu here for about a quarter the price of Arzak, and it will still include inventive plates like foie gras ravioli with melon and a spinach vinaigrette, or roasted monkfish and chorizo with a vegetable sauce sweetened with honey. If you consider yourself a foodie (or even if you don't), Sandó is a treat you should not miss. "Arzak Instruction" (the Arzak family company) also runs the bar here at the fabulously renovated Hotel Santo Domingo. For an amazing bargain, try a lunch of two inventive tapas plates and a beer for as little as 10€.

In Hotel Santo Domingo, Calle Isabel la Católica, 2–4. ℰ **91-547-99-11.** Main dishes 18€–26€. Restaurant Tues–Sun 1–4pm; Tues–Thurs 8–11pm; Fri–Sat 8pm–midnight. Bar Mon–Thurs 10:30am–11pm; Fri–Sat 10:30am–midnight. Closed 3 weeks in Aug. Metro: Santo Domingo.

Taberna del Alabardero ★★ SPANISH   This handsome restaurant and tapas bar named for the royal guards known as "Beefeaters" opened in 1974 in a historic tavern where nobles and literati rubbed shoulders before the Civil War. There are several small and rather formal dining rooms, including one in the cellars often used for private parties. The dining room menu represents a fairly light approach to contemporary Spanish cooking with dishes like bream roasted in a salt crust and served with a sauce of fresh tomatoes and basil, or oxtail stewed with honey and cinnamon. It's a terrific place to have a civilized Spanish meal. In the bar, on the other hand, you'll probably have to stand and might have to shout to carry on a conversation, but the food is even lighter (chilled almond soup with prawns and grapes, "meat" balls of fish and shellfish, brochettes of pork with mushrooms and pineapple). The sherry collection behind the bar is terrific.

Calle Felipe V, 6. ℰ **91-547-25-77.** www.grupolezama.es. Reservations required for restaurant. Bar tapas 3€–12€. Restaurant main courses 17€–25€; tasting menu 46€. Daily 1–4pm and 9pm–midnight. Metro: Ópera.

Gran Vía, Chueca & Malasaña
MODERATE
Restaurante Casa Salvador ★ SPANISH/ANDALUCÍAN   Too bad Hemingway didn't live long enough to eat at Casa Salvador. The place is an instant immersion in Andalucian décor and the cult of the bullfight. The owner is, you might say, an aficionado of the *corrida* and has photos of bulls, bullfighters, and bullfights all over the place. The food, however, is as simple and unaffected as the atmosphere is

overwhelming. House specialties include a delicious soupy casserole of white beans and ham. If the bull photos don't bother you, opt for a grilled veal chop or a gristly but flavorful sirloin steak.

Calle Barbieri, 12. ☏ **91-521-45-24.** Reservations recommended. Main courses 10€–28€. Mon–Sat 1:30–4pm and 9–11:30pm. Closed 2 weeks July–Aug. Metro: Chueca.

INEXPENSIVE

Antigua Casa Ángel Sierra ★ TAPAS   Nowhere in Chueca is the transformation of the neighborhood more obvious than at the working-man's bar that one of the bartenders once assured us was "the most ancient, the most beautiful." When the tavern opened in 1917 as an outlet for a vermouth maker south of the city, laborers from the gritty neighborhood would bring in their own bottles to be filled from the barrels. Nowadays it's a much more primped crowd in tight jeans and jaunty earrings who stop off for a few excellent tapas, the retro kick of a glass of Spanish vermouth (very much an acquired taste), and a chance to admire the elaborate Andalucían tiles and the cellar full of vermouth barrels. The house vermouth is potent and rough but it goes well with smoked anchovies, chunks of tuna with onions and capers in vinaigrette, or a plate of sardines in olive oil.

Calle Gravina, 11. ☏ **91-531-01-26.** Tapas 2€–5€. Daily noon–2am. Cash only. Metro: Chueca.

Babel Restaurante B&B ★ SPANISH/AMERICAN   The American grill restaurant is a concept the Spanish have always admired. Fortunately, when they imitate it, they can't help but make the place far more Spanish than they realize. Some of Babel's burgers, for example, come with caramelized onions, slices of foie gras, or a fried egg. The pizzas include a New Yorker, which for some inexplicable reason has dill pickles and mesclun salad mix on top. It all sounds a little funny until you taste the dishes and realize that they are very pleasing to the Spanish palate. One of the menu standards is the Argentine parrillada de carne, which is a non-stop parade of meat and sausage cooked over charcoal on metal skewers and brought to the table until you cry "uncle." We're more fond of the intentionally Spanish dishes, like a grilled piece of hake served with clams and a parsley green sauce. The prices are very low for such quality and pleasant service.

Calle de la Libertad, 23. ☏ **91-521-61-37.** www.bb-restaurante.com. Main dishes 8€–14€, weekday lunch menu 15€. Tues–Sun 1–4pm; Tues–Sat 8–11pm. Metro: Chueca.

Bazaar Restaurant ★ SPANISH   This restaurant shocked the neighborhood by getting locals to break with tradition and line up at 8pm for dinner—truly early-bird hours for Madrileños. The dishes are eclectic, light, and most are under 10€, making Bazaar a perfect spot for impecunious young folks out on a date or for traveling families with kids. The broad menu includes a lot of kid-friendly plates like spaghetti with cheese sauce, chicken couscous, or mushroom croquetas The salads are huge, while the dishes with meat and fish tend to be small. We figure three plates serve two people well. Service is super-fast and so is the kitchen, so don't plan to linger. On a good night, Bazaar will serve four seatings at a single table.

Calle Libertad, 21. ☏ **91-523-39-05.** www.restaurantbazaar.com. Main dishes 7€–13€. Daily 1:15–4pm and 8:30–11:45pm. Metro: Chueca.

Bocaito ★ SPANISH   This bar-restaurante has one of the stranger physical layouts we've ever encountered. There are two entries, each into a barroom serviced by the same bartenders who stand in the middle surrounded by bar stools. This made sense in the days when it was a boon to have a smoking and non-smoking bar, but now both sides fill up equally. The menu is cheaper if you stand at the bar or even if you score one of the barroom seats. But it costs little more to dine sitting down inside one of the three dining rooms, including the new "garden" room that's filled with blue and white Andalucían tiles. The food is traditional working class bar-restaurante fare—a quarter roasted chicken with fried potatoes, pork sweetbreads with green beans, or a grilled pork chop with vegetable of the day—but it's done very well and priced fairly. The tapas plates include the usual Andalucían specialties (chicken livers, sardines, anchovies in vinegar) as well as small sandwiches on buns—called "bocaitos."

Calle Libertad, 4–6. ☎ **91-532-12-19.** www.bocaito.com. Main dishes 8€–11€. Mon–Fri 1–4:30pm; Mon–Sat 8:30pm–midnight. Metro: Chueca.

Nebraska ★ SPANISH The Gran Vía flagship of this small chain of "American" restaurants looks like a cafeteria with its clusters of booths and Formica-topped tables. One of the first Madrid restaurants to copy the "American" look and menu, specializing in hamburgers and ice cream sundaes, it is one of the last of the early adopters still standing. The menu emphasizes breakfast egg dishes at all hours, grilled cheese sandwiches, hot dogs baked into a bun ("pigs in a blanket"), and "platos combinados," which are inexpensive combo plates with meat (pork steak, chicken breast, beef steak tips), starch (fried potatoes or red rice), and the vegetable of the day (best overlooked). The food is freshly and quickly prepared—and they still serve those great ice cream sundaes. It's a sensible compromise when your kids want Mickey D's and you want something Spanish with a cold beer.

Gran Vía, 55. ☎ **91-547-16-35.** www.gruponebraska.com. Main dishes 4€–13€. Daily 8am–1am. Metro: Gran Vía or Santo Domingo.

Salamanca
EXPENSIVE

Alkalde ★★ BASQUE If you dine on the sidewalk terrace at this tony end of Calle Jorge Juan, you'd never suspect that the main dining rooms downstairs have stone walls and the dark, homey feel of a Basque tavern. This family-run establishment opened nearly a half century ago to bring Basque cuisine to their homesick countrymen. Over time, the cooking has become ever more modern and sophisticated without deviating from the tried and true formula of buying the best available products and being careful not to mess them up. There are some Basque classics that need no updating, including the *sopa de txanguerro* (a spider crab soup), *bacalao a pil pil* (cod in an emulsification of olive oil and dish juice), and turbot in garlic sauce.

Calle Jorge Juan, 10. ☎ **91-576-33-59.** www.alkalderestaurante.com. Reservations required. Main courses 17€–40€; menu del dia 52€. Daily 1:30–11pm. Metro: Retiro or Serrano.

dASSA bASSA ★★ SPANISH Anyone who has caught chef Darío Barrio on television knows that he's a flamboyant ham. Fortunately, he cooks with as much panache as he emotes for daytime TV. This is a man who likes food, and likes to have fun with it. The entrance to his restaurant is on a small street (a little hard to find) off Puerta de Alcalá, and the restaurant itself is below grade in a room of whitewashed brick with twinkly LED lights leading the way down the stairs. It's meant to be a bit disorienting—as if you've been spirited away to a dyslexic speakeasy where the staff is determined to feed you dishes you've never tried before. The simple market-based menu features five starters, four meats, and four fish dishes, but what Barrio does with the market provender is complex. He loves to plop salmon eggs or flying fish roe on fish dishes to literally make them pop when you take a bite. Trout eggs even find their way into his watermelon gazpacho with scallops. Crepes filled with oxtail stewed in red wine and chocolate are a menu perennial. To enjoy the theater for a relative pittance, opt for the three-course "executive" menu of starter, main dish, pastry of the day, and a glass of wine for only 25€.

Calle Villalar, 7. ✆ **91-576-73-97.** www.dassabassa.com. Reservations required. Fixed-price menus 25€–80€. Tues–Sat 1:30–4pm and 9–11:30pm. Closed Aug 1–21. Metro: Retiro.

La Paloma ★ BASQUE/FRENCH Chef Segundo Alonso hails from that part of Basque territory where they consider San Sebastián on the Spanish side and Biarritz on the French to be part of the same country. It's certainly part of the same cuisine, and Alonso serves the powerful rustic food of the mountainous countryside, like a tartare of red deer or beef sirloin with a mustard sauce. Perhaps the most celebrated dish is foie-gras-stuffed pigeon roasted in a bed of salt. But when the weather calls for it, Alonso can go light as air with an exquisite cold lobster salad with a coriander vinaigrette or poached eggs on puff pastry with smoked salmon. Most dishes are available as full and half portions, which can be good for the diet as well as the wallet.

Calle Jorge Juan, 39. ✆ **91-576-86-92.** www.lapalomarestaurante.es. Reservations recommended. Main courses 20€–45€. Mon–Sat 1:30–4pm; Tues–Sat 8pm–11:45. Closed Aug. Metro: Velázquez or Vergara.

MODERATE

La Colonial de Goya ★ SPANISH It's nice to find a casual and comparatively inexpensive place to eat lunch (or dinner, for that matter) in Salamanca, and Colonial de Goya hits the mark. The closer you stick to Spanish classics, though, the better. Chicken brochettes with sweet and sour sauce, for example, are not half as tasty as the spiced lamb brochettes, which consist of lamb brisket pounded thin and rolled in North African spices. Sea bream with tangerine sauce and sautéed artichokes is a thoroughly successful "light" dish. Even traditionally weighty dishes like foie gras get a little lighter touch. Here it's served as a terrine with peach jam.

Calle Jorge Juan, 34. ✆ **91-575-63-06.** www.lacolonialdegoya.com. Main dishes 11€–14€. Mon–Sat 1–4pm and 8pm–midnight. Metro: Velázquez.

Iroco ★★ SPANISH It's hard to tell which is leafier—the dining room walls covered with botanical prints or the back garden terrace where tables sit among potted trees and shrubs. Either is a good place to enjoy contemporary Spanish cooking that sometimes borrows ingredients from around the globe. The delicious plate of paella-style rice with cilantro and crisply fried squid is stained black with *huitalacoche* (corn smut) to make a lighter and more original version of a Catalan *arròs negre,* or black rice. One of the most succulent treatments of kid you'll find anywhere is Iroco's slow-roasted, boneless kid glazed with honey and served with a turnip purée. Service in the garden carries a 10 percent surcharge.

Calle Velázquez, 18. ✆ **91-431-73-81.** www.restauranteiroco.es. Reservations required. Main courses 15€–25€. Daily 1:30–4pm and 8:30pm–midnight. Metro: Goya.

Cervecería José Luís ★★ SPANISH This is the original in the group of José Luís restaurants, and it has had a shoeshine man in attendance since it opened in 1957. The founder believed that a gentleman should always have clean and shiny shoes, so they can stand at the bar near the door to get their brogues polished. The adjacent dining room has a genial elegance, but many patrons favor the bar side where you can perch on a stool and have a complete meal of soup, salad, fish, and dessert. The cervecería also has a great selection of *pinchos,* including a signature egg and shrimp salad on a small roll.

Calle Serrano, 89. ℂ **91-563-09-58.** www.joseluis.es. Main dishes 13€–22€; tapas 3€–5€. Bar daily 9am–1am. Dining room daily noon–4pm and 8pm–midnight. Metro: Gregorio Marañón.

La Terraza ★★ SPANISH   One of Spain's most celebrated chefs, Pedro Larumbe is credited with pioneering a modern, ingredient-driven take on traditional Spanish cooking. His elegant flagship restaurant, Pedro Larumbe, sits on the top floor of the ABC shopping center in Salamanca. La Terraza shares that floor, but it's only open from spring to fall (and closed on the rare rainy day) because all the tables are on a rooftop terrace looking down on Paseo de la Castellana. The skyline views are amazing—and so is the food. The lunch menu feature light and breezy fare, such as a club sandwich, a chicken breast with lemon and baked potato, or a salad of white asparagus. As the day begins to cool, Larumbe serves a set menu of starter, two mid-sized plates, dessert, bread, water, and coffee. Expect imaginative dishes like duck ravioli with cassis-soaked pears.

Paseo Castellana, 34, 4th floor. ℂ **91-575-11-11.** Lunch dishes 8€–18€; dinner menu 37€. Tues–Sat 1:30–4pm and 8pm–midnight.

Viavélez ★★★ SPANISH   Asturian Paco Ron walked away from a Michelin star in the little fishing village of Viavélez to make his assault on the big city in 2008. This restaurant, named for the town he left behind, may not have attracted the French starmakers, but it has certainly drawn Madrid gourmets who have always been partial to the cold-water fish cuisine of the country's northern Atlantic coast. Ron wisely splits the establishment between a casual taberna and a more formal restaurant. The tavern has a short menu of "canapes" (tapas, really) like bonito tuna with sweet red pepper, and some simple dishes like steamed mussels, steamed cockles, and pieces of fried cod. The restaurant dishes have a bit more finesse and include treats like squid meatballs, grilled hake with al dente green beans and tomato salad, and, for dessert, a dark chocolate cake with dried tart cherries.

Avenida General Perón, 10. ℂ **91-579-95-39.** www.restauranteviavelez.com. Reservations required. Main courses 18€–27€. Tues–Sun 2–4pm; Tues–Sat 9pm–midnight. Closed 3 weeks in Aug. Metro: Santiago Bernabeu.

INEXPENSIVE

Harina ★ BAKERY CAFE   The watchword here is "healthy." Most dishes are based on the excellent artisanal breads—some not-too-cheesy pizzas, for example, and several kinds of tostas, like goat cheese with tomato jam. We love the "anticrisis" menu, which provides six different choices of inexpensive complete meals. The location near the Puerta de Alcalá gate to Parque del Retiro makes Harina a good spot for lunch before or after a park visit. The cakes are better and richer than most in Madrid. There's a bright and cheerful dining room inside the bakery, and a few dozen sidewalk tables where the waiters are a bit overworked.

Plaza de la Independencia, 10. ℂ **91-522-87-85.** www.harinamadrid.com. Main dishes 7€–14€. Mon–Sat 11am–9pm; Sun 11am–4pm. Metro: Retiro.

EXPLORING MADRID

Madrid may be a sprawling city, but it seems to have grown organically. Exploring is easy if you think of the neighborhoods as clusters. Plan your day and then take public transit to a central spot and hoof it from there. An excellent and inexpensive Metro system makes it easy.

One of the oldest clusters radiates from Puerta del Sol and its principal Metro stop, known as **Vodafone Sol** through at least June 2016. (The financially strapped city government began selling naming rights to public services in mid-2013.) This area includes **Puerta del Sol** itself and the immediate uphill neighborhood known as **Barrio de las Letras** for its association with the writers of Spain's Golden Age. Here you'll find many of Madrid's historic theaters and some of its greatest tapas bars.

Plaza Mayor is one of the city's main gathering spots and the streets behind it flow downhill into the neighborhood known as **La Latina,** as its Metro stop is called. This is another excellent district for tapas bars and nightlife, but is also the site of some of Madrid's oldest structures. The **Museo de Origines** marks the spot where Madrid's patron saint, San Isidro Labrador, and his wife lived in the early 12th century. The city's famous flea market, **El Rastro,** takes over many of the streets on Sunday.

A few blocks away, several attractions cluster around the **Palacio Real.** In addition to the palace, they include royal gardens, the **Teatro Real** (Opera) itself, and the **Convento de las Descalzas Reales,** the beautiful convent founded by the sister of a Spanish king. The main Metro stops are **Ópera** and **Santo Domingo.** Nearby but north of the major boulevard **Gran Vía** are the neighborhoods of **Chueca and Malasaña.** Trendy shops, recently renovated museums, and vibrant gay nightlife signal that the neighborhoods' gentrification is well underway. The useful Metro stops here are **Gran Vía, Chueca, Tribunal,** and **Noviciado.**

The **Paseo del Prado** between the **Atocha** and **Banco de España** Metro stops is the mother lode for art lovers with no less than the **Museo del Prado,** the **Museo Thyssen-Bornemisza,** the **Real Jardines Botánicos,** and the **CaixaForum** a few blocks from each other. Practically just around the corner on the Carlos V traffic circle ("glorieta" in Spanish) stands the **Museo Nacional Centro de Arte Reina Sofía.** The most useful Metro stops here are Atocha, Banco de España, and Colón.

The largely 20th-century neighborhood of **Salamanca** is much larger and the distances between attractions are greater. Fortunately, good Metro service makes visiting most attractions an easy proposition. This area includes the **Parque del Retiro,** the **Museo Sorolla,** and the **Museo Lázaro Galdiano.** The most useful Metro stops include **Retiro, Serrano, Velázquez,** and **Núñez de Balboa.**

MADRID'S TOP SIGHTS

ICONIC SIGHTS

Museo del Prado ★★★ (p. 86)
Museo Reina Sofía ★★★ (p. 88)
Museo Thyssen-Bornemisza ★★★ (p. 89)
Palacio Real ★★★ (p. 98)
Parque del Retiro ★★ (p. 104)
Plaza Mayor ★★★ (p. 95)
Plaza Santa Ana ★★ (p. 92)
Puerta del Sol ★★ (p. 92)

MUSEUMS & ART CENTERS

CaixaForum ★ (p. 83)
Casa de Lope de Vega ★ (p. 91)
Fundación Juan March ★ (p. 102)
Matadero Madrid ★ (p. 95)
Museo Arqueológico ★★ (p. 86)
Museo de América ★★ (p. 105)
Museo de Arte Publico ★ (p. 102)
Museo de Historia de Madrid ★ (p. 101)

Museo de los Orígines ★ (p. 95)
Museo del Romanticismo ★ (p. 101)
Museo del Traje ★ (p. 105)
Museo Lázaro Galdiano ★★ (p. 103)
Museo Naval ★ (p. 89)
Museo Sorolla ★★ (p. 103)
Real Academia de Bellas
Artes ★★ (p. 91)

ARCHITECTURAL MASTERWORKS
Basilica de San Francisco
el Grande ★ (p. 94)
Casa de la Villa ★ (p. 94)
Catedral de la Almudena ★ (p. 96)
CentroCentro ★★ (p. 83)
Circulo de Bellas Artes ★ (p. 99)
Monasterio de las Descalzas
Reales ★★ (p. 97)
Palacio Real de El Pardo ★ (p. 105)
Panteón de Goya ★★ (p. 104)
Plaza de Toros de
Las Ventas ★ (p. 106)

OTHER ATTRACTIONS
Carrusel Serrano Madrid ★ (p. 102)
Casa de Campo ★ (p. 104)
Casa Patas ★★ (p. 91)
Hammam al Andalus (p. 94)
Mercado de la Paz ★★ (p. 102)
Mercado de San Miguel ★★ (p. 95)
Monasterio de la
Encarnación ★ (p. 97)
Parque de Atracciones ★ (p. 107)
Plaza Dos de Mayo ★ (p. 101)
El Rastro ★ (p. 96)
Real Fábrica de Tapices ★ (p. 90)
Real Jardín Botánico ★ (p. 90)
Teatro Caser Calderón (p. 93)
Teatro de la Zarzuela (p. 93)
Teatro Español (p. 93)
Teatro Monumental (p. 93)
Teatro Nuevo Apolo (p. 93)
Teatro Real ★★ (p. 99)
Teleférico de Madrid ★ (p. 107)
Zoo Aquarium de Madrid ★ (p. 107)

Arts District & Paseos

CaixaForum ★ MUSEUM It took 5 years to transform the 1901 Mediodia electrical power plant across the Paseo del Prado from the Real Jardín Botánico into a dynamo for contemporary art. Pritzer Prize winners Jacques Herzog and Pierre de Meuron managed to multiply the floor space by five-fold while creating a brick structure that seems to levitate (it's actually cantilevered) above its plaza. It's such a curious building that you might not immediately notice the 24-meter-high (79-ft.) Jardin Vertical—a wall covered with 250 species of plants that flourish without soil. The interior of the building is equally amazing. The floors are hung on the spine of a winding white central staircase that widens as it rises (a trick achieved with rubber molds). Although La Caixa has permanent collections, it is known for its constantly changing exhibitions of contemporary art. Usually three major exhibitions are on display at any given time. Some of the strongest shows are large format photography, often featuring leading Spanish photographers such as José Manuel Ballester. Many exhibitions are accompanied by lectures, concerts, panel discussions, or other public events.

Paseo del Prado, 36. ℂ **91-330-73-00.** http://obrasocial.lacaixa.es. Building admission free; exhibition halls 4€, free for visitors under 16. Daily 10am–8pm. Metro: Atocha. Bus: 10, 14, 27, 34, 37, or 45.

CentroCentro ★★ MUSEUM A truly palatial Baroque Revival building that once housed the central post office and the city's telecommunications agency, the Palacio de Cibeles became Madrid's City Hall in 2007. Even the city councilors didn't need something quite this huge, so much of the building was recently converted to a series of galleries, a concert hall, and other public spaces called CentroCentro. A reading area has daily papers and free PCs with Internet access. You'll also find lockers, coat check, public rest rooms, an excellent store selling Madrid-oriented books and gifts, and a tourist information area. If you're hungry, there's a cafeteria for a quick bite

Madrid Attractions

CaixaForum Madrid **39**
Campo del Moro **3**
Carrusel Serrano
  Madrid **23**
Casa de Campo **2**
Casa de la Villa **12**
Casa Museo
  Lope de Vega **34**
Casa Patas **19**
Catedral de Santa María la
  Real de la Almudena **5**
CentroCentro,
  Palacio de Cibeles **26**
Círculo de Bellas Artes **28**
El Rastro **15**
Ermita de San Antonio
  de Florida **2**
Fundación Juan March **24**

Hammam Al Ándalus Madrid **16**	Museo del Traje **1**	National Archaeological Museum of Spain **22**	Real Academia de Bellas Artes de San Fernando **29**
Matadero Madrid **41**	Museo de los Orígenes **14**	Palacio Real **4**	Real Fábrica de Tapices **42**
Mercado de la Paz **24**	Museo Lázaro Galdiano **21**	Parque de Atracciones Pta. Principal **2**	Real Jardín Botánico **38**
Mercado de San Miguel **11**	Museo Nacional Centro de Arte Reina Sofía **40**	Parque del Retiro **37**	Real Monasterio de la Encarnación **6**
Monasterio de las Descalzas Reales **8**	Museo Naval **27**	Plaza de Toros Monumental de Las Ventas **25**	San Francisco el Grande Basílica **13**
Museo de Arte Público **21**	Museo Sorolla **21**	Plaza Dos de Mayo **20**	Teatro Caser Calderón **17**
Museo de Historia de Madrid **20**	Museo Thyssen-Bornemisza **31**	Plaza Mayor **10**	Teatro Español **32**
Museo Nacional del Prado **36**	Museum of the Americas **1**	Plaza Puerta del Sol **9**	Teatro Monumental **35**
National Museum of Romanticismo **20**		Plaza Santa Ana **33**	Teatro Nuevo Apolo **18**
			Teatro Real **7**

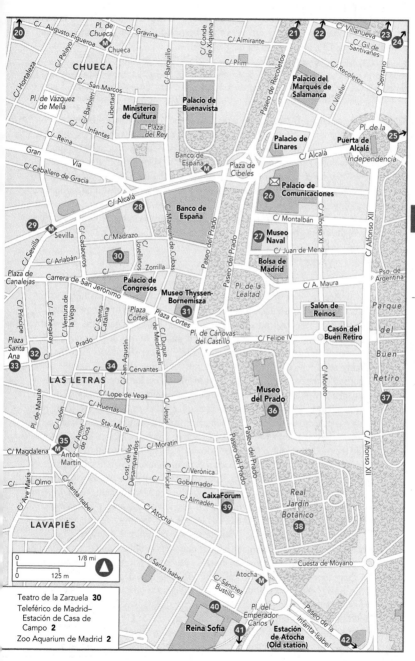

Teatro de la Zarzuela **30**
Teleférico de Madrid–
Estación de Casa de
Campo **2**
Zoo Aquarium de Madrid **2**

and **Restaurante Palacio de Cibeles** (p. 68), run by Toledo master chef Adolfo Muñoz, for a more leisurely meal. The Mirador Madrid is perhaps the grandest delight of the whole complex. An elevator whisks you to the seventh floor where you can walk around on the open-air balcony for one of the best bird's-eye views of the city, and especially of the Cibeles fountain on the plaza below.

Plaza de Cibeles, 1. *©* **91-480-00-08.** http://centrocentro.org. Building admission free; admission charged to some exhibitions. Mirador de Madrid 2€, 0.50€ under 12. (Purchase at entry level.) Building Tues–Sun 8am–8pm; Mirador de Madrid Tues–Sun 10am–1pm and 4:30–7:30pm, weather permitting. Metro: Banco de España. Bus: 1, 2, 5, 9, 10, 15, 20, 27, 34, 45, 51, 52, 53, 74, 146, or 150.

Museo Arqueológico Nacional ★★ MUSEUM   Set to re-open in early 2014, Spain's principal archaeological museum spent more than 5 years redesigning its 140-year-old palace and its exhibits. Unlike some parts of the world, Spain recognized the value of its buried culture early on and managed to keep most of the treasures in the country. They range from wonderful Celto-Iberian statues like La Dama de Elche and La Dama de Baeza to a wealth of Roman sculpture. The Moorish collections are also outstanding. Possibly the most surprising finds are the Visigothic crowns and other royal jewels. To build suspense, the museum has been keeping the new exhibition halls under tight wraps. But given the treasures in the museum vaults, the exhibitions will be world-class.

Calle Serrano, 13. *©* **91-577-79-12.** http://man.mcu.es. Admission and hours to be determined. Metro: Serrano or Colón. Bus: 1, 9, 19, 51, or 74.

Museo del Prado ★★★ MUSEUM   There was a very quiet revolution at the Prado in 2013, when the museum rehung the galleries of paintings by **Diego Velázquez** (1599–1660), making his psychological masterpiece, "Las Meninas," the sun at the center of its artistic solar system. They placed it among his royal portraits directly opposite the entry door of Sala 12 on the second level of the Villanueva building. You have probably seen reproductions of this portrait of Felipe IV's royal family (with shadowy portrait of the painter himself) a thousand times, but the sheer scope and power of the actual canvas will bowl you over. The focus of the painting is on the young infanta Margarita (daughter of Felipe IV) and her diminutive ladies in waiting, including one of the many royal dwarves whom Velázquez never tired of painting. "Las Meninas" is easily the most popular painting in the Prado. (Before you leave the Prado, stop by the bookstore in the modern addition by Rafael Moneo to pick up a postcard of "Las Meninas." When you visit Barcelona, you'll want a copy to compare to Picasso's homage in the Museu Picasso.) If you want to see "Las Meninas" without someone standing in front of you, be among the first to enter in the morning—a Madrid Card, Paseo del Arte pass, or printout of an online ticket purchase lets you to skip the line.

Even before the rearrangement, there was a logic to gravitating first to Velázquez. Felipe VI ordered the creation of the Prado in 1819 to consolidate the royal art collections (hence all those portraits of Spanish kings and their families), and to prove to the rest of Europe that Spanish art was the equal of any other nation. He was right, and while the Prado has some priceless works by Fra Angelico, Titian, Rembrandt, and Hieronymus Bosch, the Spaniards dominate the collection and we can't think of a better place to see their work. No matter what else interests you, we suggest focusing first on Velázquez and then turning your attention to Francisco de Goya.

From 1623 until his death in 1660, Velázquez was court painter to Felipe IV, a king only a few years his junior. He painted the king as a vacuous-looking young man, as a thoughtful king in middle age, and as an aging ruler weary from grief and depression— a remarkable psychological progression that the painter witnessed firsthand, and

ARE passes A GOOD DEAL?

Don't jump at either of the Madrid discount cards before you have an idea of what you want to see. The offers all sound good on the surface, but you may not reap significant savings.

The most clear-cut is the **Tarjeta Paseo del Arte** (25€), which will save you 25 percent off the admission prices for the Museo Nacional del Prado, Museo Nacional Centro de Arte Reina Sofia, and the Museo Thyssen-Bornemisza and enable you to skip the lines. You can purchase it at any of the museums. The card is good for a year, but allows just one entry to each museum and is not worth it if you are not going to visit all three.

The big three are among the 50 or so museums and monuments included on the **Madrid Card** (www.madridcard.com; 42€ for 24 hr., 51€ for 48 hr., 61€ for 72 hr., 70€ for 120 hr.). Using the Madrid Card will also let you bypass the ticket lines, which is a good thing since you might need to hustle to make the pass worthwhile. Several of the attractions listed, by the way, are always free and the restaurant and shop savings are not very significant. But the card does allow you to take the Discover Madrid tour offered by the tourist office (see above) for free and includes free admissions to Bernabéu stadium and the Plaza de Toros de las Ventas. You'll also get small discounts for the flamenco shows (p. 110) at Cardamomo and Corral de la Morería and on your purchases at El Corte Inglés (p. 109) department store.

By the way, you can also skip the lines at the Prado, Reina Sofía, and Thyssen-Bornemisza by buying your tickets in advance online. When making your decision about the discount passes, also keep in mind that Madrid has a number of free museums and some of the major ones have generous free hours, but are more crowded during that time. If you are on a tight budget, it could be worth your while to work those free admission hours into your touring plans.

perhaps shared. His early works, hung in **Sala 9A,** show great technique but little reflection. The more palpably human portraits by Francisco de Zurbarán hung in the same room may lack the brush strokes, but carry far more emotion. But Velázquez gets better as the gallery numbers rise. His religious paintings in **Sala 14** derive amazing intensity from the geometric rigor of their compositions. The dead body on the cross in "Cristo Crucificado," nailed up with four rather than three nails, as 17th scholarship suggested, has ceased to be either man or god—he has been transfigured into the devotional icon of Spanish Catholicism.

Most paintings by Velázquez were never seen by anyone but the royal family until they were deposited in the Prado, but **Francisco de Goya** (1746–1828) did get to study them when he began working for the crown in the late 1770s. For the rest of his life, he cited Velázquez as one of his most important influences. Goya's mature work, especially after Carlos IV made him court painter in 1799, shows an understanding of character on a par with Velázquez. "The Family of Carlos IV" in **Sala 32,** painted around 1800, shows a burly king uncomfortable in his finery who would rather hunt than rule. In 1808, Carlos abdicated when the going got tough, and his foolish son invited Napoleon in to tidy up Spain.

Goya's cheerful side is on full display in his paintings of countryside idylls that he made as cartoons for tapestries to cover the walls of the royal palace at El Pardo. It was his first royal commission and he did his level best to be cheerful and witty. Head to **Salas 90-94** to experience this youthful joy.

On the darker side, Goya captured the horrors of the French occupation in "Dos de Mayo," which shows the popular uprising in Puerta del Sol on May 2, 1808, and "El Tres de Mayo," which depicts the executions of the Spanish partisans by firing squad on Principe Pío hill the following day. These late paintings that made his modern reputation are found in **Salas 64-65** on the ground level. The somber "Dark Paintings" that he made on the walls of his house in the years after 1819 in fits of depression and madness fill adjacent **Salas 66-67.** These nightmarish images, such as "Saturn Devouring One of His Sons" and the heart-breaking "Half Drowned Dog," did not reach the Prado until late in the 19th century, where they became inspirations for German Expressionism and for Surrealism.

Goya wasn't the first Spaniard with a fantastical imagination. At the opposite end of the Villanueva building from the Dark Paintings are a number of Gothic and Romanesque rooms radiating from the central rotunda. Be sure to visit **Sala 51C** and wait for your eyes to adjust to the dim illumination. The room re-creates a chapel from the 1125 A.D. Iglesia de la Vera Cruz Maderuelo outside Segovia. Animals high on the wall include the artist's conception of a bear and an elephant—a beast he had heard described but had clearly never seen. The creatures are so abstract they could have been painted by Joan Miró.

In 2014, the Prado will have a blockbuster exhibition featuring the works of **El Greco** (ca. 1541–1614) in honor of the 400th anniversary of the painter's death. The Prado exhibition is coordinated with another at Museo de Santa Cruz in Toledo (p. 122), which actually owns the more extensive collection of El Greco's works. Prado curators of the 19th century considered Crete-born Doménikos Theotokópoulos a foreign painter, so the museum did not actively collect his work until the 20th century.

Paseo del Prado. © **91-330-28-00.** www.museoprado.es. Admission 14€ adults, 7€ seniors, free for students and children 17 and under, free for all visitors Mon–Sat 6–8pm, Sun 5–8pm. Mon–Sat 10am–8pm; Sun 10am–7pm. Closed Jan 1, Good Friday, May 1, and Dec 25. Metro: Atocha. Bus: 9, 10, 14, 19, 27, 34, 37, or 45.

Museo Nacional Centro de Arte Reina Sofía ★★★ MUSEUM

It's about a 3-block walk—and a much larger aesthetic leap—from the Prado to the Reina Sofia, which holds Spain's most significant collection of 20th- and 21st-century works. In fact, that collection has swelled so extensively in recent years that it now uses the two 19th-century exhibition palaces in the Parque del Retiro (p. 104) as spaces for temporary shows (often installation art) that require large physical spaces. The main museum consists of the neoclassical 18th-century former General Hospital designed by Francisco Sabatini, and the post-modern non-rectilinear addition by Jean Nouvel that opened in 2002.

Every few years the Reina Sofía curators rethink how to present the permanent collection. It is hung in rough chronological order but with various "movements" grouped by room. The movements and their accompanying wall texts change, even when the art remains the same. For the time being, two floors of the Sabatini building contain "permanent" chronological exhibits: "The Irruption of the 20th Century: Utopias and Conflicts (1900–1945)" fills Level 2 ("Guernica" is in Gallery 206); and "Is the War Over? Art in a Divided World (1945–1968)" occupies Level 4. The missing chronological gap is found on Level 1 of the Nouvel building, where "From Revolt to Postmodernity (1962–1982)" covers art as it lost its boundaries with pop culture, and includes a lot of work by American pop artists, just as the 1945-1968 galleries have several Abstract Expressionist works, also by Americans.

Current pedagogy declares that in modern art, context is everything because the horrors of the 20th century invalidated old Platonic concepts of art as a reflection of eternal beauty. Abstractions aside, that means that paintings by Picasso, Juan Gris, Joan Miró, and Dalí are surrounded by photographs, posters, advertising art, and short films that provide context for the world in which the art was created. This approach is particularly effective in the galleries that deal with art related to the Spanish Civil War, including "Guernica." Picasso's response to the unprovoked bombing of a small Basque village remains one of the most powerful antiwar statements ever made.

This courtyard of the Sabatini building is open during warm weather for light sculpture and light snacks. (Contrary to expectation, the coffee cart, which also sells wine and beer, is not a performance installation.) Note that admission to blockbuster temporary exhibitions, like the Salvador Dalí retrospective of 2013, is usually through the Sabatini entrance. Those interested only in the permanent collection enter through the courtyard of the Nouvel building. Pay attention to signage or you could wait an hour or more in the wrong line. Having a Paseo del Arte pass, Madrid Card, or advance online purchase provides priority admission.

Sabatini entrance: Calle Santa Isabel, 52. Nouvel entrance: Ronda de Atocha, s/n. ✆ **91-774-10-00.** www.museoreinasofia.es. Admission 8€ adults; 4€ seniors, students, and visitors 17 and under; 4€ for temporary exhibitions only; free for all Apr–Sept Mon and Wed–Sat 7pm–closing and Sun 3pm–closing. Apr–Sept Wed–Mon 11am–9pm; Oct–Mar Wed–Mon 10am–6pm. Metro: Atocha. Bus: 6, 10, 14, 19, 26, 27, 32, 34, 36, or 37.

Museo Naval ★ MUSEUM We're rarely fans of military museums but this institutional gem, on the ground level of Spanish Navy headquarters, is worth making an exception. The museum covers the greatest hits of Spanish naval preeminence, including the discovery and exploration of the Americas, the exploitation of the Pacific trade routes, the Spanish Armada, and the feared Spanish galleons of the 17th and 18th centuries. A scale model of Columbus's flagship, the *Santa Maria,* shows what a fat little tub it was. By contrast, the large cutaway models of a circa-1700 galleon bristling with cannons can be seen as the birth of the modern battleship. The detailed coverage of the Battle of Trafalgar could make you forget that the Spanish lost. We marvel over Juan de la Cosa's handwritten map of 1500, said to be the oldest map of Europe that shows the Americas—including such inhabitants as men with faces in their stomachs. Only 300 visitors at a time are allowed inside; on weekends arrive early to avoid a wait. Security is tight here. You will need to show your passport and allow your bags to be x-rayed.

Paseo del Prado 5. ✆ **91-523-87-89.** www.armada.mde.es/museonaval. Free admission. Tues–Sun 10am–2pm. Metro: Banco de España. Bus: 6, 10, 14, 19, 26, 27, 32, 34, 36, or 37.

Museo Thyssen-Bornemisza ★★★ MUSEUM In a city where the Prado and the Reina Sofía are your neighbors, the Thyssen-Bornemisza has to try a little harder than it might elsewhere. The museum has made summer even better for art lovers, keeping its temporary exhibitions open until 10pm Tuesday through Saturday and until 9pm Sunday and Monday from mid-June through mid-September. (The permanent collection closes 2 hr. earlier.) During the same months, the open-air Terrasse bar-restaurant remains open until 2am so you can discuss the art over drinks. That's a good thing, because this museum, dominated by the tastes of two strong personalities, can prompt plenty of conversation.

The original collection was compiled by the Baron Thyssen-Bornemisza. Covering European art from the 13th through 20th centuries, it was one of the world's great private art collections, which he sold to Spain at a bargain in 1993. Before he sold it, though, he gave some major pieces to his Spanish wife, Carmen, who continued collecting until she donated her collection in 2004. Altogether, their collections represent the best art money could buy in the mid–20th century. That means that the Dutch Masters were pretty well picked over but a lot of Impressionist art was on the market. The breadth of the collections is astounding, and so is their weight. We advise focusing on the strengths—the Baron amassed great works of Italian and German Gothic art and 20th-century German Expressionism. The Baroness also bought some outstanding German Expressionist works, some beautiful Impressionist paintings, and showed a real affinity for the Spanish Moderns (Picasso, Dalí, and Miró) as well as Abstract Expressionist works by Americans. The museum has also begun to mount blockbuster shows that require borrowing from other collections. These temporary exhibitions have a separate ticket.

Palacio de Villahermosa, Paseo del Prado 8. ✆ **90-276-05-11.** www.museothyssen.org. Admission 9€ adults, 6€ students and seniors, free for children 11 and under; permanent collection free to all Mon noon–4pm. Mon noon–4pm; Tues–Sun 10am–7pm. Metro: Banco de España. Bus: 1, 2, 5, 9, 10, 14, 15, 20, 27, 34, 45, 51, 52, 53, 74, 146, or 150.

Real Fábrica de Tapices ★ FACTORY TOUR Visiting this working tapestry factory is like opening a time capsule. In a fit of royal rivalry, it was founded by Felipe V in 1721 to give Spain its own version of the Gobelins Manufactory in Paris. Almost 3 centuries later, you will still find skilled artisans making rugs and wall tapestries at the original hand looms. Watching their fast-moving fingers will give you a new appreciation for this time-honored craft. Francisco de Goya seemed to have his hand in all things artistic in the mid–18th century and even designed cartoons for tapestries that still grace the walls of the Palacio Real (p. 98) and the Palacio de El Pardo (p. 105). When you've finished observing the workers, you can view some of his original cartoons as well as tapestries from the 18th through 20th centuries. You'll find the factory on the far side of the Atocha train station from the Prado.

Calle Fuenterrabia, 2. ✆ **91-434-05-50.** www.realfabricadetapices.com. Admission 4€ adults; 3€ children. Guided tours Mon–Fri 10am–2pm. Closed Aug. Metro: Menéndez Pelayo. Bus: 10, 14, 26, 32, 37, 102, or C.

Real Jardín Botánico ★ GARDEN The Age of Enlightenment lives on in these formal gardens next to the Museo del Prado and at the southwest corner of the Parque del Retiro. Carlos III, the so-called mayor-king, had Juan de Villanueva (architect of the Prado and the Paseos) design the gardens as a collection of temperate zone plants from around the world. The king himself opened the gardens in 1781. Today the meticulously maintained gardens contain more than 104 species of trees and 3,000 types of plants. Also on the premises are an exhibition hall and a library specializing in botany. There is a lot to see, but you can select among nine self-guided tours to focus your interests.

Plaza de Murillo, 2. ✆ **91-420-30-17.** www.rjb.csic.es. Admission 3€ adults, 1.50€ students, free for seniors and children 9 and younger. May–Aug daily 10am–9pm; Mar and Oct daily 10am–7pm; Apr and Sept daily 10am–8pm; Nov–Feb daily 10am–6pm. Closed Dec 25 and Jan 1. Metro: Atocha. Bus: 10, 14, 19, 26, 27, 32, 34, 37, 45, 57, 146, or 150.

Puerta del Sol & Barrio de las Letras

Puerta del Sol is the hub of old Madrid and the principal crossroads of the city's transport systems. It is also the square where Madrileños have always flocked when trouble was afoot—from the uprising against Napoleon in 1808 to the economic protests of

May 2011—and when there was a party to be had (the May feria or Halloween, for example). The square was originally the eastern gate of the medieval city. Just uphill on the south side are the old streets of the Barrio de las Letras, or "neighborhood of letters," which the city defines as bounded by Calles Atocha and Cruz, the Paseo del Prado, and Carrera de San Jerónimo. Those narrow streets and shady alleys, now paved instead of cobbled, are the same 16th- and 17th-century paths walked by poet and playwright Tirso de Molina (1579–1648), by Miguel de Cervantes (1547–1616), and by the grandest rascal of them all, Félix Lope de Vega y Carpio (1562–1635). Now as then, the neighborhood is home to many of Madrid's finest theaters and numerous bars. Cervantes' home was razed long ago, although he does have a street named for him where the Cervantes Institute has mounted a plaque showing where he lived and died. This neighborhood is served mainly by the Metro stops of **Vodafone Sol, Sevilla,** and **Antón Martín.**

Casa de Lope de Vega ★ HISTORIC HOME

Félix Lope de Vega may have been a more complex and fascinating character than any that he invented in his plays. He purchased this house in 1610 when he was already an established playwright and lived here—close to the theaters of his day—for the last 25 years of his life. Just as in the theater, suspend your disbelief and you may be able to get a sense of the daily life of the author, husband, father, and notorious womanizer who also became a priest at age 50. The three-story house was badly damaged in the Civil War and may not have been restored to full historic accuracy, but it has been furnished to reflect the inventory of contents in Lope de Vega's will. It's a good chance to see how a well-off figure lived in Habsburg Madrid. Based on his own writings, he was particularly fond of his little walled garden with a covered well. To us, the most telling details are the low, Moroccan-style furnishings in the women's gathering room and by the window in his bedroom that overlooks his in-house chapel. All tours are guided and you are supposed to book in advance, although we've walked in off the street during slow seasons. For a tour in English, book at least 2 days ahead.

Calle Cervantes, 11. 🕐 **91-429-92-16.** www.madrid.org. Free admission. Tues–Sun 10am–3pm. Metro: Antón Martín. Bus: 6, 9, 10, 14, 26, 27, 32, 34, 37, 45, or 57.

Casa Patas ★★ SHOW

To see authentic flamenco in the company of enthusiasts, head to this Andalucían-style club co-founded by members of the jazz-flamenco band, Pata Negra. You might catch a newly discovered singer-guitarist duo or see members of the Amaya, Montoya, or Habichuela royal families of flamenco. Either way, the performance will be top rate. The bar starts filling up with *flamencos,* as those who live the life of the music are called, about an hour before the nominal start time for a performance. Unshaven men sporting long black ponytails and dressed all in black nurse glasses of sherry amid chic Madrileños in designer jeans tossing back Scotch on the rocks. Show times vary, usually occurring at 10:30pm Monday to Thursday, with shows at 9pm and midnight on Friday and Saturday, and more frequent shows during Madrid's major fiesta month of May. Tapas—priced at 4€ to 18€—are available at the bar, and you're welcome to come in for a drink and a tapa anytime after 8pm.

Calle Cañizares, 10. 🕐 **91-369-04-96.** www.casapatas.com. Mon–Sat 8pm–2:30am. Cover 19€–40€. Metro: Tirso de Molina or Antón Martín. Bus: 6 or 26.

Museo de la Real Academia de Bellas Artes de San Fernando ★★

MUSEUM   The smaller scale and more intimate galleries of the Royal Academy Museum are a nice change of pace in a city with three really big art museums. Founded in 1752 to aid in the education of students at the academy of fine arts, the museum has amassed a fine collection of paintings and sculptures from the Renaissance period to the present. Spanish artists, naturally, are the best represented, but in some cases you can compare their work to that of their Italian and Flemish contemporaries. So good, in fact, is the collection that some pieces have been transferred to the Prado. The Forrest Gump–like Goya became director of the museum in 1795 and the collection features 13 of his paintings, including an equestrian portrait of Fernando VII and an absorbing scene of the Spanish Inquisition. Most revealing are the two self-portraits, one painted when he was not quite 40 and another painted in 1815, several years before he succumbed to the madness that drove his "Dark Paintings." The museum also preserves Goya's paint-covered final palette. But it doesn't ignore other Spanish masters, and you will find works by Zurburán, El Greco, Juan Gris, and Picasso, as well as a striking collection of drawings from the 16th through 20th centuries. The collections of 19th- and 20th-century art on the second and third levels (sometimes closed due to staff shortages) include more modern temporary exhibitions, including occasional striking photography shows.

Calle Alcalá, 13. © **91-524-08-64.** www.realacademiabellasartessanfernando.com/en. Admission 5€ adults, 2.50€ students, free for children 17 and under; free for all visitors Wed. Tues–Sat 9am–3pm. Metro: Vodafone Sol or Sevilla. Bus: 3, 5, 15, 20, 51, 52, 53, or 150.

Plaza Santa Ana ★★ SQUARE   Sooner or later you'll have a drink or two on Plaza Santa Ana and probably wonder what took you so long to discover the place. The neighborhood has been Madrid's theater district since the Corral des Comedias de Principe, one of Spain's first theaters, began packing in the crowds in 1583. The open-air theaters of that era were famous for producing the plays of Lope de Vega (who lived nearby) and other satirists. When the Teatro Español (see below) was erected here in the mid–19th century, it made Plaza Santa Ana as hip then as it is now. Since the square was firmly established as an entertainment district, dozens of bars and cafes popped up. They (or their successors) are still there and still constitute one of the city's most varied and most civilized tapa scenes.

Metro: Antón Martín.

Puerta del Sol ★★ SQUARE   Some visitors liken Puerta del Sol to New York's Times Square, but we think that's a canard because Puerta del Sol is smaller and friendlier. Alas, the signature neon sign of Puerta del Sol (a colorful rendition of the Tío Pepe sherry bottle) was removed when the old Hotel Paris was sold to developers who are replacing the hotel that Hemingway loved with an Apple Store. Moreover, in July 2013, the Metro stop here became officially known as "Vodafone Sol," after the mobile phone service provider. That prompted one clerk at the Madrid Tourist Information office to comment that, "Yes, soon we will all have to walk around with 'Sony' stamped on our foreheads." Ah, the fallout of the economic crisis. Fortunately, amid all those bankruptcies and loan defaults, Madrid was able to complete its overhaul of the square to make it a central hub for Metro lines and for commuter rail. Auto traffic was further curtailed, the central pedestrian plaza was greatly enlarged, and a new Louvre-like glass entrance was created for the steps down to the trains. The beloved statue of a bear and a madroña tree (pictured on the city's coat of arms) was moved out to the middle of the plaza. Embedded in the pavement in front of the old Casa de Correos building is the **Zero Kilometer marker** from which all distances in Spain are calculated. The clock on the former post office displays Spain's official time. When it strikes midnight on New Year's Eve, Spanish revelers in the square eat a dozen grapes—one for each chime.

ALL THE neighborhood's A STAGE

The earliest record of a theater in Madrid is the Corral de Príncipe, an open-air venue that began offering performances in 1583. More than 400 years later, the same Plaza Santa Ana neighborhood remains the hub of theatrical activity in the city. No less than five historic theaters are either on the plaza or in the vicinity. Performances are in Spanish, of course, but you'll find broad comedy and musical theater in its various forms (opera, zarzuela, American-style musicals) really don't depend on a perfect grasp of the language.

Teatro Caser Calderón This is the largest theater in Madrid, with a seating capacity of 2,000. In the past this venue included everything from dramatic theater to flamenco, but in recent years it has taken a more serious turn by presenting mostly opera.

Calle Atocha, 18. © **90-200-66-17.** www.teatrocalderon.es. Tickets 5€–50€. Metro: Tirso de Molina or Vodafone Sol. Bus: 6, 9, 10, 14, 26, 27, 32, 34, 37, 45, or 57.

Teatro Español This exquisite 19th-century theater continues to anchor the east side of Plaza Santa Ana and presents performances of dance, orchestral and chamber music, and live theater. Medallions on the facade depict the pantheon of Spanish playwrights, from Calderón de la Barca (1600–81) on the right to Federico García Lorca (1898–1936), appropriately enough on the far left.

Calle Príncipe, 25. © **91-360-14-84.** www.teatroespanol.es. Most tickets 15€–30€. Metro: Antón Martín or Tirso de Molina. Bus: 6, 26, 32, 57, 65, 15,150, 3, 5, 9, 20, 51, 52, or 53.

Teatro de la Zarzuela If you're curious about Spain's equivalent of Broadway musicals, this theater is the principal venue for the art form known as *zarzuela*. It mixes sketch theater, opera, popular song, and spoken narrative—all in Spanish, of course. This theater of potent nostalgia also produces ballet and an occasional opera. Most Wed performances are half price.

Calle Jovellanos, 4. © **91-524-54-00.** http://teatrodelazarzuela.mcu.es. 5€–50€, up to 336€ for boxes. Metro: Banco de España, Sevilla. Bus: 5, 9, 10, 14, 15, 20, 27, 34, 37, 45, 51, 53, or 150.

Teatro Monumental Now that the city's most prestigious symphonic orchestra, Orquestra Sinfónica de Madrid, has moved to the Teatro Real (p. 99), this acoustically splendid theater has become home of the Orquesta Sinfónica de Radio Televisión Española, or Spanish Radio and Television Symphonic Orchestra. The RTVE Symphony plays a series of concerts from September through June, and it's worth the price of admission just to see the theater, which was built in 1923 as a lavish movie house.

Calle Atocha, 65. © **91-429-81-19.** www.rtve.es/orquesta-coro. Tickets 11€–20€. Metro: Antón Martín. Bus: 6, 26, 32, or 57.

Teatro Nuevo Apolo Nuevo Apolo is the permanent home of the renowned Antología de la Zarzuela company. It is on the restored site of the old Teatro Apolo, where these musical variety shows have been performed since the 1930s.

Plaza de Tirso de Molina. 1. © **91-369-06-37.** www.teatronuevoapolo.com. Tickets 15€–60€. Metro: Tirso de Molina. Bus: 6, 26, 32, 57, or 65.

Plaza Mayor & La Latina

Madrid was born in La Latina. The neighborhood's boundaries conform largely to the walled medina of the 10th-century citadel village known as al-Majrit, or "place of water" in Arabic. When Alfonso VI of Castilla y León conquered the citadel in 1085,

GET SOAKED (that's a good thing)

Many North Africans have settled in La Latina and the adjacent neighborhood of Lavapiés in the last few decades, so it was really only a matter of time before a traditional Arabic bath, a hammam, opened in the neighborhood. **Hammam al Andalus** is modeled on the baths of Moorish Andalucía, and shares the traditional design of arched brick and tile chambers with grillwork windows to let in light. Alternating hot and cold rooms, a warm room where attendants scrub you with soap, a super-hot steam room, and the option of a massage with aromatic oils round out the sensual experience.

Calle Atocha, 14. *©* **90-233-33-34.** http://hammamalandalus.com. Rates vary with services 30€–73€. Daily 10am–noon, 2–4pm, 6–8pm and 10pm–midnight. Metro: Tirso de Molina or Vodafone Sol. Bus: 3, 17, 18, 23, 31, or 35.

he turned the mosque into a church (predecessor of the Almudena cathedral; see p. 96) and left the walls in place. Four centuries would pass before they were fully torn down to let the village grow, and the neighborhood left in the place of the old medina retained its medieval Moorish street pattern. Even today, this original Madrid neighborhood is defined by narrow 10th-century streets punctuated almost randomly by little plazas. The Plaza Mayor was originally the market square on the outskirts, but since the 17th century it has been Madrid's town square. In many ways, it functions as a broad gate from Puerta del Sol into La Latina.

Basilica de San Francisco el Grande ★ CHURCH This immense house of worship was completed in 1760 on the site of a Franciscan convent that, tradition has it, was founded by St. Francis of Assisi himself in 1217. The basilica served as Madrid's leading church until 1993, when Catedral de la Almudena (p. 96) was finished after more than a century of construction. The basilica boasts several architectural superlatives (largest cupola in Spain, for example), and it has some wonderful art, including the recently restored ceiling murals of Mary Queen of Heaven.

Plaza de San Francisco, s/n. *©* **91-365-38-00.** Tourism visits Tues–Sat 11am–1pm and 4–6:30pm. 3€ adults; 2€ students. Metro: La Latina. Bus: 3, 60, or 148.

Casa de la Villa ★ HISTORIC SITE Remnants of some Madrid's oldest buildings sit on the tiny Plaza de la Villa. The plaza on Calle Mayor midway between Plaza Mayor and Plaza del Oriente has been the site of city government since medieval times, and the Casa de la Villa, the old town hall, is located here. The original medieval structure was rebuilt in Renaissance style in 1645, and further modified when Spanish baroque became all the rage. Subsequent modifications, including a stained glass roof over the courtyard, continued to gild the lily. A free tour in both Spanish and English, offered at 5pm on Mondays by the Madrid Tourism Board, includes the grand staircase and some municipal treasures, such as the silver monstrance (receptacle for the Host) traditionally carried in the Corpus Christi procession. The highlight is Goya's painting, "La Alegoria de Madrid," which personifies the city as a woman standing next to the municipal coat of arms. The tiny plaza is also crowded with two other notable buildings, the Mudéjar-style, 15th-century Casa Lujones and the Casa Cisneros, constructed for the nephew of the powerful cardinal and statesman in the 16th century.

Plaza de la Villa, 4–5. *©* **91-588-10-00.** www.esmadrid.com. Mon 5pm. Free admission. Metro: Ópera. Bus: 3 or N16.

Matadero Madrid ★ MULTI-USE VENUE   Talk about edgy—this city-run contemporary arts center is located in a former slaughterhouse. It functions as a combination think tank and incubator for the arts and has a number of different spaces where artists can unleash their creativity through interactive exhibits, theater, performance art, and exhibitions of large-scale visual art. Overall, the space is so large that it can accommodate just about any artistic idea, no matter how avant-garde, and half the fun of visiting is that you don't really know quite what to expect. The Cineteca is devoted exclusively to non-fiction film and video. Free guided tours of the facility in Spanish or English are available by advance reservation.

Plaza de Legazpi, 8. ✆ **91-517-73-09.** http://mataderomadrid.org. Free admission. Tues–Fri 4–10pm; Sat–Sun 11am–10pm. Metro: Legazpi. Bus: 6, 8, 18, 19, 45, 78, or 148.

Mercado de San Miguel ★★ MARKET   Just outside the walls of Plaza Mayor, the long-dormant Beaux Arts food market has been updated for 21st-century shoppers, with more than three dozen vendors sheltered under the gigantic wood-and-iron roof. The Mercado originally opened in 1916, when it was meant to evoke Les Halles in Paris. Servants and homemakers of the time flocked here to stock their larders. Today the vendors sell everything from fresh pastas and homemade pastries to cooking utensils and even fresh fish. Consider the place a stopover for an inexpensive lunch, as it offers a cafe, a beer tavern where tapas are sold, and a pastry shop selling freshly baked apple strudel, among other goodies. At night Madrileños show up here for beer, tapas, wine, and even champagne and oysters.

Plaza de San Miguel. ✆ **91-542-49-39.** www.mercadodesanmiguel.es. Sun–Wed 10am–midnight; Thurs–Sat 10am–2am. Metro: Ópera, Vodafone Sol, or Tirso de Molina. Bus: 3 or 148.

Museo de los Orígines ★ MUSEUM   Renamed from the Museo de San Isidro in 2013, this museum nonetheless occupies a late medieval palace on the site where San Isidro Labrador and his wife, Santa Maria de la Cabeza, were said to have lived in the 12th century. The humble farmer was elevated to the patron saint of Madrid (which celebrates him with a festival in May) and of agriculture. Legend says their son fell into their well and was miraculously rescued by their prayers—the first public evidence of their holiness. The well remains as one of the museum's chief exhibits. Isidro and Maria's remains are buried nearby in Basilica de San Isidro (Calle Toledo, 37). This municipal museum also deals with the secular prehistory and history of Madrid from the arrival of the first humans who hunted along the Río Manzanares some 300,000 years ago through Madrid's apotheosis as Spain's capital. Signage is in Spanish, but the museum makes very good use of portrait reproductions to literally put a face to many of the city's most important movers and shakers. Historic photographs capture the quick growth of the city in the 19th century.

Plaza de San Andrés, 2. ✆ **91-366-74-15.** www.munimadrid.es/museosanisidro. Free admission. Sept–July Tues–Sun 9:30am–8pm; Aug Tues–Fri 9:30am–1:30pm. Metro: La Latina. Bus: 3, 17, 18, 23, 35, 60, 65, or 148.

Plaza Mayor ★★★ SQUARE   When the sun shines beneficently down, you'd think Plaza Mayor had been custom-built for outdoor dining and arcade souvenir shopping. But the site was originally a food market just outside the city walls, and the current square was constructed in 1619 as the mass gathering spot for the city. People came to Plaza Mayor to see bullfights, attend political rallies, celebrate royal weddings, shop for bread and meat, watch hangings, and witness the torture-induced confessions of victims of the Spanish Inquisition. With apartments on the square, the royal family had ringside seats. Little remains of that original square, as the buildings surrounding it burned in 1631, 1672, and again in 1790. The plaza was fully enclosed in 1854, creating the great arches that now serve as its gates. Madrileños come to the plaza for the Sunday morning coin and stamp market and for the annual Christmas market. The plaza's acoustics are excellent, and musicians often perform in the center near the equestrian statue of Felipe III. The zodiac murals decorating the Casa de Panadería (originally home to the all-powerful Bakers' Guild) on the north side look appropriately ancient, but they date only from 1992. The most dramatic of the gates is the Arco de Cuchilleros (Arch of the Knife-Sharpeners), on the southwest corner, which leads to the street of the same name. Beneath Plaza Mayor are the "cave" restaurants that have lured tourists since the days when Washington Irving commented on the spectacle of roast piglet feasts accompanied by copious flagons of wine. Perhaps the best known of these ancient purveyors of food and drink is **Restaurante Botín** (p. 74), celebrated by Ernest Hemingway and certified by the "Guinness Book of World Records" as the world's oldest restaurant.

Metro: Vodafone Sol, Ópera, or Tirso de Molina. Bus: 3, 17, 18, 23, 31, or 35.

El Rastro ★ MARKET   Foremost among Madrid's street markets, El Rastro (translated as either "flea market" or "thieves' market") occupies a roughly triangular district of streets and plazas a few minutes' walk south of Plaza Mayor. Its center is Plaza Cascorro and Ribera de Curtidores. The market comes alive every Sunday morning and will delight anyone attracted to a mishmash of fascinating junk interspersed with antiques, bric-a-brac, paintings, and cheap scarves from India. Real bargains can still be had, but you'll need to use your haggling skills. Don't expect to find a piece that would light up the eyes of appraisers on TV antiques shows, but you could find something that you want to buy and someone else wants to sell. We often find good buys on flamenco CDs, for example. Take care with your belongings. Pickpockets do work the crowds here.

Plaza Cascorro and Ribera de Curtidores. www.elrastro.org. Sun 7am–2:30pm. Metro: La Latina. Bus: 3 or 17.

Ópera & Palacio Real

As you approach the regal quarter of Madrid, the dark and narrow streets of the old city open into sun-splashed plazas. Comparisons to the Paris Opera and the palace of Versailles are inevitable: Everything you see was built under Bourbon kings with French taste. From the Metro stop at Ópera, stairs will deliver you to Plaza Isabel II on the back of Teatro Real. The broad expanse between theater and palace is Plaza de Oriente, constructed in the first half of the 19th century and peopled with statues of Spanish kings and queens. If Plaza Mayor is where people sit at cafes in their shirtsleeves to catch some rays, Plaza de Oriente is where they sit at fancier cafe tables in smart suits to be seen and admired. Main Metro stops are Ópera and Santo Domingo.

Catedral de la Almudena ★ CHURCH   Wars, rebellions, political chaos, and a sheer lack of cash delayed the completion of Madrid's cathedral for 110 years after ground was broken in 1883. In keeping with Spanish tradition, it was built on the site of Madrid's chief mosque under Moorish rule. It was named for the Virgen de la Almudena, whose icon was found on the site when Alfonso VI re-conquered the city under the sign of the cross in 1085. The cathedral was originally designed as a neo-Gothic building but when architect Fernando Chueca took over the construction, he altered the plans to make it neoclassical—a better fit with the adjacent Palacio Real. Spanish television had a field day with the colorful "pop art" stained-glass windows

WATCH OUT FOR wednesdays

Unless you are a European citizen, you're probably wondering why we are telling you that the **Monasterio de Las Descalzas Reales, Real Monasterio de La Encarnación,** and **Palacio Real** are free on Wednesdays for citizens of European Union countries. But free admission swells visitation on those days and can create a real logjam, especially at the two monasteries, both of which keep short hours and limit entry to a few people at a time. Plan accordingly. If you're thinking of doing day trips, note that the same deal applies at the royal palaces at El Pardo (p. 105), and El Escorial (p. 111).

and multicolored ceiling during the wedding of Prince Felipe to newscaster Doña Letizia in May 2004.

Calle Bailén 10. © **91-542-22-00.** www.catedraldelaalmudena.es. Suggested donation 1€. Summer daily 10am–1pm and 6–8pm; off season daily 9am–9pm. Metro: Ópera. Bus: 3, 6, 17, 18, 23, 26, 31, 32, 35, 50, 51, 60, 65, or M-1.

Monasterio de las Descalzas Reales ★★ MUSEUM In the 16th century, the daughters of nobility had two choices: to be married off to forge alliances among powerful men or to opt for a life behind the walls of a convent. Many of the wealthiest chose this convent, founded by the powerful and charismatic sister of Felipe II, Juana de Austria. As the widow of the Prince of Portugal, she took over a palace of the royal treasurer in 1557 to establish this Franciscan convent as her own retreat from the world. Each of the noblewomen who took the veil brought a dowry as a bride of Christ, and their treasures still fill the convent. Ironically, by the mid–20th century, all the nuns came from poor families and were literally starving to death in midst of a priceless art collection that they were forbidden to sell. The state intervened, and Rome granted special dispensation to open the convent as a museum, allowing the public to see the riches. The large hall of the nuns' former dormitory, for example, is hung with 20 tapestries woven in Brussels from cartoons by Rubens. (Take a moment to notice the floor tiles that delineate each nun's tiny sleeping area.) This is still a working convent, home to about 20 nuns. You can easily imagine them gliding silently along the upper cloister, praying at the tiny chapels, and shivering against the chill of the tile floors and stone walls after the visitors are gone. Guided tours are solely in Spanish, but one glimpse of the massive staircase, with its magnificent murals of saints, angels, and Spanish rulers, immediately explains the conjunction of art, royalty, and faith that defines Spanish history. The guided tour takes at least 1 hour—more if you have to wait for enough people to assemble before the guide will start. Tours are limited to 20 visitors at a time.

Plaza de las Descalzas Reales s/n. © **91-454-88-00.** www.patrimonionacional.es. Admission 7€ adults; 4€ children 5–16 and seniors 65 and older; free for children 4 and under. Tues–Sat 10am–2pm and 4–6:30pm; Sun 10am–3pm. Closed Jan 1, Jan 6, Holy Week, May 1, May 15, Sept 9, Nov 9, Dec 21, and Dec 24–25. Metro: Ópera. Bus: 3, 25, 39, or 148. From Plaza del Callao, off Gran Vía, walk down Postigo de San Martín to Plaza de las Descalzas Reales; the convent is on the left.

Real Monasterio de la Encarnación ★ CONVENT If you have visited the Descalzas, you might find its sister institution something of letdown. An Augustinian convent, founded in 1611 by Marguerite of Austria, wife of Felipe III, its main attraction is the harmonious design by royal architect Ventura Rodriguez, who rebuilt it after

4

MADRID | Exploring Ópera & Palacio Real

a fire in 1767. But between the privacy needs of the cloistered nuns and the painfully slow restoration that has been going on for decades, you see little but religious paintings on the 1-hour guided tour in Spanish. The highlight is the reliquary room, packed floor to ceiling with purported True Cross splinters, personal objects of saints, and innumerable chalices and monstrances. Perhaps the most intriguing relic is a vial of the blood of Saint Pantaleon. According to legend, it liquefies on July 26 each year, the eve of his feast day. If it does not, guides glumly warn, disaster is in the offing.

Plaza de la Encarnación, 1. ℰ **91-547-05-10.** www.patrimonionacional.es. Admission 7€ adults; 4€ children 5–16 and seniors 65 and older; free for children 4 and under. Tues–Sat 10am–2pm and 4–6:30pm; Sun 10am–3pm. Closed Jan 1, Jan 6, Holy Week, May 1, May 15, Sept 9, Nov 9, Dec 21, and Dec 24–25. Metro: Ópera. Bus: 3, 25, 39, or 148.

Palacio Real ★★★ PALACE Those Bourbons certainly knew how to build a palace! When the old royal palace—which was a dank, dark, and rather plain alcázar captured from the Moors in 1086—burned down in 1734, Felipe V ordered a new palace designed to rival the one his French cousins inhabited at Versailles. Having wrested the throne from the Habsburg line in the War of Spanish Succession, it was important for this first king of the Bourbon line to eclipse the previous royal dynasty. He was literally minting money with the gold and silver flowing from the New World colonies, so price was no object and the finished product is one of the grandest, most heavily decorated palaces in Europe. Construction began in 1738, and Felipe's younger son, Carlos III, finally moved into the 2,000-plus-room complex in 1764. Most rooms are reserved for state business, but a significant portion of the palace is open for tours. Although it remains the official residence of the royal family, no monarch has lived here 1931 when Alfonso XIII and his wife, Victoria Eugénie, fled Spain.

Unless you are a VIP, you'll enter on the south side of the palace complex. When you walk into the blinding sunlight of the Plaza de la Armería, everyone else in your line will make a mad dash for the palace. Ignore them and cross the plaza to start at the Armory. You can truly take the measure of the Spanish nobility since the plate and chain armor were individually tailored. Felipe I, the Austrian who married Juana la Loca (daughter of Fernando and Isabel) in 1496, was a medium-slender man nearly 6 feet tall—a giant in his day. Many other royals were almost a foot shorter; generally speaking, the shorter the noble, the larger his metal codpiece by way of compensation.

Once you enter the palace, you're not allowed to backtrack on the rigidly delineated tour. Move quickly through the first few ceremonial rooms until you enter the Throne Room (or Hall of Ambassadors), which marks the start of the Carlos III era. Tiepolo takes political flattery to new heights in the vault fresco, "The Apotheosis of the Spanish Monarchy." It's easy to be overwhelmed by the next sequence of rooms, where the décor morphs from baroque into rococo, but you also get a sense how the royals lived amid such splendor. You see the drawing room where Carlos III usually had lunch, the over-the-top Gasparini Room where he dressed, and the bedroom where he died. The Yellow Room, which had been Carlos III's study, is rich with avian and floral tapestries woven at the Real Fabrica de Tapices (p. 90). Finally, you'll reach the grand dining hall, which was first used by Alfonso XII in November 1879 to celebrate his marriage.

Some of the smaller, more intimate rooms on the tour are not always open, but they show Alfonso XIII as a more domestic king, screening movies with the family on Sunday afternoons. What remains of royal silver and china is also on display (Napoleon's brother Joseph Bonaparte sold the best pieces to finance French military adventures).

Unless you have a lot of time, skip the Farmacia Real's numbing collection of apothecary jars in favor of a walk in the the **Jardines de Sabatini** ★. Construction of the gardens began in the 1930s on the site of the former royal stables. The formal gardens, dotted with statues of Spanish kings, were opened to the public by King Juan Carlos I in 1978, just a couple of years after he assumed the throne.

Note that the changing-of-the-guard ceremony at noon on the first Wednesday of the month is free to the public.

Plaza de Oriente, Calle de Bailén, 2. ⓒ **91-454-88-00.** www.patrimonionacional.es. Admission 10€ adults, 5€ students and children 16 and under, free to all last 2 hr. of each day. Oct–Mar daily 10am–6pm; Apr–Sept daily 10am–8pm. Metro: Ópera. Bus: 3, 25, 39, or 148.

Teatro Real ★★ THEATER   One of the world's finest acoustic settings for opera, the up-to-date technical side of this theater is as impressive as its 19th-century over-the-top ornamentation. Elaborate stage designs and special effects are possible thanks to state-of-the-art equipment. Today the building is the home of the Compañía del Teatro Real, which specializes in opera, as well as the Orquestra Sinfónica de Madrid, which plays classical concerts and accompanies opera and ballet. On November 19, 1850, under the reign of Queen Isabel II, the Royal Opera House opened its doors with Donizetti's "La Favorita." The best way to appreciate the grand space is to attend a performance, of course, but three different tours are also available. The general tour (limit of 25) shows you the lobby, the Café de Palacio, the formal rooms, the Ballroom restaurant, and the main auditorium (with a peek at the royal box). The "artistic" tour (limit of 15) is a behind-the-curtain look at dressing rooms, rehearsal rooms, the choir, the orchestra pit, and costume workshops. The guide customizes this tour based on the shows being performed at the time. The technical tour (limit of 12), new in 2013, is for equipment geeks who love ropes and pulleys, wire cables, bars and hooks, and all the other machinery that makes stage magic.

Plaza Isabel II, s/n. ⓒ **91-516-06-60.** www.teatro-real.es. Performance tickets 8€–294€. General tour 8€ adults, 6€ for visitors under 26 or over 65; tours daily 10:30am–1pm on the half-hour. Artistic tour 12€ adults, 10€ for visitors under 26 or over 65; tours daily 9:30am and 9:45am. Technical tour 16€ adults, 14€ for visitors under 26 or over 65; tours daily 9:30am. Metro: Ópera. Bus: 3, 25, 39, or 148.

Gran Vía, Chueca & Malasaña

The slashing diagonal of Gran Vía was built to be Madrid's "modern" street. Alfonso XIII himself ceremonially inaugurated the demolition work in 1910 with the announced intention of creating a boulevard to rival any in Paris. (Economic collapse in 1929 scaled back the plans.) But Gran Vía was Madrid's first street built for motorcars, and through the first two-thirds of the 20th century, banks, movie theaters, and upscale businesses lined its broad expanse between the Cibeles fountain and Plaza de España. The street began a long, slow slide in the 1970s and has never quite recaptured its erstwhile glamour, although the opening of some good hotels in recent years has been a step in the right direction. At the same time, the two neighborhoods immediately to its north, Chueca and Malasaña, are much further along on their revitalization and have become destinations for shopping, dining, and nightlife.

Circulo de Bellas Artes de Madrid ★ ARCHITECTURE   This cultural center from the age of "tertulias" (formal discussion groups that resembled book clubs in suits) has forged bravely into the digital age with conferences on media arts to augment a terrific program of repertory film showings and exhibits of contemporary photography and graphic arts. The center also maintains a vigorous publishing program of

art ON THE WALLS

In the early 20th century, shopkeepers began the marvelous practice of covering their establishments with beautiful tiled scenes to advertise their products and services. Three great examples still bring life to their surrounding streets.

Farmacia Juanse (Calle San Andres, 5) sits on the corner of Calle San Vicente Ferrer, which gave the ceramic artists plenty of surface to cover with lively scenes of men, women, and children partaking of Juanse's own formulations to cure everything from toothaches to rheumatism. The Malasaña drugstore focuses on more modern medicine, but who would change such a colorful exterior?

Not to be outdone, the proprietors of the **Huevería,** or egg shop, around the corner in Malasaña (Calle San Vicente Ferrer, 32) embellished their establishment with images of sprightly hens. The spot is now a restaurant and tapas bar—and a felicitous spot to enjoy a slice of tortilla española.

Farther afield in La Latina, **La Pelquería Vallejo** (Calle Santa Isabel, 22) was founded in 1908 and, a few years later, added its tiled facade of men and boys being attended to by barbers. Tile signs announce that the services also include hair cuts for women as well as electric and facial massages. The advertising must have worked, as the barbershop is still open and still owned by the same family.

Keep your eye out for colorful tile ornamentation on buildings throughout Madrid. You'll find a number that have been enhanced by the work of Segovia-based master ceramist Daniel Zuloaga, whose family museum is in Segovia (p. 137). For his contribution to advertising art, he created the sign and the beautiful tile clock on the facade of the building that held the printing press of the ABC newspaper. It's now the **ABC Serrano** shopping center (Calle Serrano, 61). But Zuloaga was more artist than ad man. Look for his floral designs and classical motifs on the **Palacio de Cristal** (p. 104) and the **Palacio de Velázquez** (p. 104) in the Parque del Retiro.

You'll find two other wonderful buildings as you tapas hop around Plaza Santa Ana. The restaurant and flamenco tablao **Villa Rosa** (Plaza de Santa Ana, 15; p. 110) is encrusted with tiled scenes of landmark Spanish buildings and monuments, including Madrid's Cibeles fountain and Granada's La Alhambra. Similar scenes are depicted on **Bar Viva Madrid** (Calle Manuel Fernández y González, 7), though the artists found room to work in reminders that passersby could stop in for "Cervezas, Refrescos Y Cafe." You should do the same, if only to see the original tin counter, dark woodwork, and Andalucían-style patterned tiles of the interior.

monographs and proceedings from its conferences on the state of art and culture. But for all its forward-looking programming, much of the appeal of the Circulo de Bellas Artes de Madrid is the building, which was constructed in 1920. The interior architecture shows all the foment and contradiction of that age, with a grand marble staircase and classical statuary, the great domed rotunda of the Salon de Baile, and plentiful bas-relief decoration where classical motifs blend into Art Deco style. The cafe windows open directly onto Gran Vía at the most elegant street corner in the city: where the wedgelike Metropolis building across the street points the way to the Cibeles fountain. It's the only cafe we know where you pay an entry fee. For even better views, the rooftop terrace is open when weather permits. (That's an additional entry fee.)

Calle Alcalá, 42. ☎ **91-360-54-00.** www.circulobellasartes.com. General admission to building and cafeteria 1€; admission to cafeteria and roof terrace 3€; admission to cafe and exhibitions 3€; combined admission to everything 4€. Cafeteria daily 9am–1am; exhibition halls Mon–Sun 11am–2pm, Mon–Sat 5–9pm. Metro: Banco de España. Bus: 1, 2, 3, 5, 9, 46, 51, 52, 53, 74, 146, 150, or 202.

Museo de Historia de Madrid ★ MUSEUM

This museum recreates the Madrid of days gone by without waxing nostalgic about it. It was partially closed for several years as restoration work was carried out on the marvelous Baroque building. At the same time, curators took the opportunity to digitize the entire collection. Then, when it fully reopened in 2013, they brought back some of our favorite old-fashioned exhibits. There really is no substitute for the topographic scale model of the city that was meticulously assembled in 1830. It remains better than any paper or digital map in its overview of the streets of the historic center. You can go up on a balcony above the model for an aerial view. Get your bearings by locating the Palacio Real, Plaza Mayor, and Puerta del Sol, and you're good to go. Exhibitions trace the evolution of Madrid since it was first selected as the national capital in 1561, drawing on a collection of more than 60,000 artifacts. It is instructive to see paintings of Plaza Mayor through the ages, for example. The stage set of the plaza barely changes—its inhabitants are simply wearing different costumes.

Calle Fuencarral, 78. ☎ **91-701-18-63.** www.madrid.es. Free admission. Sept–June Tues–Sun 9:30am–8pm; July–Aug Tues–Fri 9:30am–2pm, Sat–Sun 9:30am–8pm. Metro: Bilbao or Tribunal. Bus: 3, 21, 40, 147, or 149.

Museo del Romanticismo ★ MUSEUM

We love it when a "renovation" of a museum takes a fresh look at the collection. This institution set in the 1776 palace of the Marquis and Marchionessa of Matallana used to be the Museo Romántico, established by the great dandy and founder of the Royal Tourism Commission, the Marquis de Vega-Inclán. In truth, he needed a place to park his immense collection of "typical" folk art, porcelain representations of Spanish "types," and visual art from the early 19th century, much of it by the prolific Anonimo. A wonderful if odd mish-mash of objects, the museum had hardly changed in three-quarters of a century when it closed in 2001. When it reopened under the current name in 2009, curators had exorcised the Marquis' ghost. They now use the palace and its collections to give visitors a peek at the upper middle class lifestyle during the reign of Isabel II (1830–68). Spanish Isabelline has a lot in common with British Victorian, despite the very different personalities of the monarchs, but this collection is hardly humdrum because it has the advantage of the Marquis's keen eye for quality.

Calle San Mateo, 13. ☎ **91-448-10-45.** http://museoromantico.mcu.es. Admission 3€. May–Oct Tues–Sat 9:30am–8:30pm, Sun 10am–3pm; Nov–Apr Tues–Sat 9:30am–6:30pm, Sun 10am–3pm. Metro: Tribunal or Alonso Martínez. Bus: 3, 37, 40, or 149.

Plaza Dos de Mayo ★ SQUARE

Rebellion echoes through the ages here. The arch in this Malasaña park marks the spot of the Monteleón artillery barracks. When the people of Madrid rose up against Napoleon's troops on May 2, 1808, Spanish troops were ordered to remain confined to barracks. The artillery under command of Luis Daoiz de Torres and Pedro Velarde y Santillán defied the crown and joined the popular uprising. In return, the French reduced the Monteleón barracks to rubble, killed most of the Spanish soldiers, and made martyrs of the leaders. The square also has marble statues honoring captains Daoíz and Velarde. At the end of the Franco era, this park in a largely bohemian neighborhood became a flash point for rebellion against Spanish authoritarianism. In a May 2, 1976, uprising of sorts, a couple undressed on top of the statues to the delight of a crowd—an event often cited as the beginning of the "movida Madrileña." Those heady days are gone; today the plaza is skateboard turf by day, and a center of cafe life at night.

Metro: Bilbao or Tribunal.

Salamanca

After walking in the narrow streets of Madrid's old city, Salamanca is a welcome change of pace. The Marquis de Salamanca, a legendary financier and bon vivant, began constructing this quarter in the 1870s and, by the time it was completed around 1920, Salamanca was Madrid's premier address. The neighborhood of broad, tree-lined streets laid out in an orderly grid is lined with elegant buildings, many girded with wrought-iron balconies. Situated east of Paseo de Castellana and north of Parque del Retiro, Salamanca was the first barrio to feature such modern conveniences as electric lights, elevators, and central heating. Today it's a lot like contemporary Spanish fashion: a lively mix of classic formality and radical modernism. The large grid of Salamanca is dotted with Metro stations, but the most useful for sightseeing and shopping are Retiro, Serrano, Velázquez, Rubén Dario, and Núñez de Balboa.

Carrusel Serrano Madrid ★ CAROUSEL Also known as "Carrusel de Belle Epoque" for its late-19th-century styling, this vintage merry-go-round operates on a plaza in front of Salamanca's branch of El Corte Inglés department store. Definitely a step up from the conventional street attraction, it has horses with real horsehair tails and such exotic animals as a camel and a tiger. It also features a wonderfully whimsical flying pig and an elephant carriage.

Calle Serrano, 47 (corner of Calle Marques de Villamagna). No phone. 1.90€ per ride. Mon–Fri 11am–2pm and 5–9pm; Sat–Sun 11am–10pm.

Fundación Juan March ★ ARTS CENTER This family-run foundation dedicated to the sciences and humanities has a number of free programs. Most notable is its music series, and while the schedule could change, concerts are generally held on Wednesday and Friday evenings at 7:30pm and at noon on Saturday. It is also worth checking the web site for upcoming art exhibitions from the foundation's collection. If you're confident in your Spanish, look also for panel discussions, poetry readings, and lectures.

Calle Castelló, 77. ℰ **91-435-42-40.** www.march.es. Metro: Núñez de Balboa. Bus: 1, 9, 19, 29, 51, or 74.

Mercado de la Paz ★★ MARKET It is no surprise that of Madrid's traditional food markets, Salamanca's is the most beautiful and carries some of the most expensive luxury items. No other market can match it for the presentation of just-misted fresh fish and shellfish, perfect vegetable specimens, carefully aged meats, perfectly ripe fruit, decadent pastries, and dozens of different varieties of olives. If you consider yourself a foodie, come here to see the provender that the top restaurants use and to buy saffron in bulk to take home.

Calle Ayala, 28; Calle Claudio Coello, 48. ℰ **91-435-07-43.** www.mercadodelapaz.com. Mon–Fri 9am–8:30pm; Sat 9am–2:30pm. Metro: Velázquez.

Museo de Arte Publico ★ MUSEUM This open-air museum of public sculpture brings whimsy and delight to what would otherwise be a rather bleak set of steps between Calle Serrano and the busy Paseo de Castellana. The works represent two generations of the Spanish avant-garde (a dangerous thing to be in the Franco years) including Joan Miró and the so-called Generation of 1950, a defiant group of artists who picked up the mantle of abstraction. Our favorite is the waterfall/fountain of alternating wave forms (it's called *Barandillas en "S"*) created in 1972 by Eusebio Sempere. You can't miss it—the rushing water makes you think that Madrid has suddenly sprung a leak.

Paseo de la Castellana, 41 (beneath Calle Juan Bravo overpass at Calle Eduardo Dato). © **91-467-50-62.** www.munimadrid.es/museoairelibre. Free admission. Open 24 hr. Metro: Serrano.

Museo Lázaro Galdiano ★★ MUSEUM   This highly personalized collection of often extraordinary art ultimately forms a sketch of its collector: José Lázaro Galdiano (1862–1947), a financier, intellectual, collector, and editor. The collections he amassed in a long and fruitful career fill the beautiful Palacio Parque Florido, named in honor of his wife Paula Florido. The museum preserves the mural decorations and room layout of the main floor, but during recent renovations the upstairs rooms were modified to better display and preserve the collections. (Each room has a photo showing how the room was decorated and used in Lázaro's day.) As an art aficionado and editor of the journal "Goya," Lazaro held two tenets dear: Painting was the most important of the arts, and every country had a national painting style. He championed—and collected, when he could—the works of Spanish masters, including El Greco, Velázquez, Zurbarán, Ribera, Murillo, and Valdés-Leal. He also collected sculpture and decorative arts that he felt spoke to the Spanish spirit, notably ceramics, silverware, and crystal. But he held special affection for Goya, and managed to acquire an important canvas from the witches' sabbath series Goya painted in 1798 for the Duchess of Osuna. Lazáro did not stop at the Pyrenees, though. He managed to buy several important Dutch and Flemish paintings, including a uncharacteristically meditative image of John the Baptist in the desert painted by Hieronymous Bosch. Several English portrait and landscape paintings by Reynolds, Gainsborough, and Constable were his indulgence of his wife's taste. The museum continues on the upper floors with individual cases of swords and daggers, royal seals, Limoges crystal, Byzantine jewelry, and even some medieval armor. It is too much to take in at a single visit, but fear not: In 2013 the museum put high-resolution images of 109 paintings on the Google Art Project, so you can visit anytime you have Internet access.

Calle de Serrano, 122. © **91-561-60-84.** www.flg.es. Admission 6€ adults, 3€ students and seniors, free for children 12 and under; free for all Mon and Wed–Sat 3:30–4:30pm, Sun 2–3pm. Mon and Wed–Sat 10am–4:30pm; Sun 10am–3pm. Metro: Rubén Darío. Bus: 9, 12, 16, 19, 27, 45, or 51.

Museo Sorolla ★★ MUSEUM   Now offering art workshops for aspiring adult painters, this enchanting house and studio was built between 1910 and 1911 by Joachín Sorolla (1863–1923). The museum is technically on the wrong side of Paseo de la Castellana to be in Salamanca, but the haute bourgeois sensibility is a perfect fit. The house offers a charming window into the comfortable world of the successful painter, who seemed to have mastered the ability to balance his work and domestic life. The home includes three studios with access to the beautiful Andalucían-style garden, as well as large living and dining areas on the main floor, maintained as the family used them. There are also four bedrooms on the second floor, now used as galleries. It's easy to imagine the artist at work at one of the unfinished paintings on the easels in the studio and the galleries display a good range of his work from portraits and folkloric paintings to the seascapes at which the Valencian-born artist excelled. But perhaps most telling is the angelic mural of his wife, Clotilde García del Costillo, and children on the dining room ceiling. It was Clotilde who decided to turn the property into a museum as a memorial to her husband. Most visitors fantasize about moving right in.

General Martínez Campos 37. ⓒ **91-310-15-84.** http://museosorolla.mcu.es. Admission 3€ adults, 1.50€ students, free for children 17 and under; free for all Sat 2–8pm and all day Sun. Tues–Sat 9:30am–8pm; Sun 10am–3pm. Metro: Iglesia, Gregorio Marañón, or Rubén Darío. Bus: 5, 7, 14, 16, 27, 40, 45, 61, 147, or 150.

Parque del Retiro ★★ PARK To meet Madrileños at their most relaxed, plan to spend a Sunday among the families enjoying Parque del Retiro. Originally a royal playground for the Spanish monarchs and their guests, the park covers 140 hectares (346 acres), but most of the main attractions are located adjacent to the central pathway, best accessed by the gate at the Puerta de Alcalá traffic circle. The park is big enough to be a playground for much of Madrid—whether they want to rent rowboats on the small lake where Felipe IV used to stage mock naval battles, watch puppet shows, practice tai chi, play cards or chess, have their fortunes told, or just lounge on the grass. Even winter chills don't discourage Madrileños with their kids and their dogs. Now, visitors can also view contemporary art. The Reina Sofia museum mounts large-scale exhibitions in the two grand buildings constructed for the 1887 Philippines Exposition. The **Palacio de Cristal** is literally a glass palace, while the **Palacio de Velázquez** is as opaque as the Cristal is transparent. It was constructed of brick and marble with florid tilework in the Mudéjar Revival style. From May through September, there are free concerts in the park on Saturday and Sunday evenings; look for the program posted at the major entrances.

Free admission. Summer daily 7am–midnight; winter daily 7am–10pm. Palacio de Cristal and Palacio de Velázquez Apr–Sept daily 11am–9pm; Oct–Mar daily 10am–6pm. Metro: Retiro.

Outlying Attractions

Casa de Campo ★ PARK Children love the zoo and the Parque de Atracciones (see "Madrid for Families," p. 106), both in this park formed from former royal hunting grounds south of the Palacio Real across the Río Manzanares. You can see the gate through which the kings rode out of the palace grounds, either on horseback or in carriages, on their way to the tree-lined park. The lake inside Casa de Campo is usually filled with rowers, and you'll find a snack bar here for drinks and light refreshments by the water. A playground by day, the park gets rather dangerous at night.

Daily 8am–9pm. Metro: Lago or Batán.

Ermita de San Antonio de la Florida–Panteón de Goya ★★ CHURCH Goya's tomb reposes in this little hermitage on the banks of the Río Manzanares north of the Palacio Real. The church also contains one of the painter's masterpieces: an elaborately beautiful fresco depicting the miracles of St. Anthony on the dome and cupola. Perhaps because he had to paint on scaffolding, the paintings are sometimes called Goya's Sistine Chapel. He worked in the labor-intensive fresco technique of applying fresh plaster to the surface, incising his design based on a "cartoon" drawing, and then applying pigment with a sponge instead of a brush. Many early viewers were shocked that Goya used his inordinate skill to include image of prostitutes, beggars, and hardworking common folk. But the patron, Carlos IV, approved and the work has certainly stood the test of time. The tomb and frescoes are on the right as you enter. Magnifying mirrors on the floor help you see the ceiling without straining your neck.

Glorieta de San Antonio de la Florida, 5. ⓒ **91-542-07-22.** www.munimadrid.es/ermita. Free admission. Tues–Sun 9:30am–8pm. Metro: Príncipe Pío. Bus: 76, 46, or 41.

Museo de América ★★ MUSEUM   Five hundred years later, it is hard to imagine the shock waves that spread through Europe when Christopher Columbus stumbled on a "new" and previously unimagined world. This earnest museum, in an old Spanish colonial-style church, draws on its significant holdings of objects from scientific research trips and archeological digs to present a picture of the European interaction with the Americas. Exhibits recreate a "cabinet of curiosities" similar to the one prized by Carlos III back when the sun never set on Spain's empire, and it's easy to imagine how exciting it would have been to see a beautiful Mayan stone carving or golden funerary figure from Colombia for the first time. But the museum does an admirable job of using its holdings to try to understand and record the rich cultures that would never be the same after contact with Europeans. It also deals with the exploration of the new world (the progression of knowledge as captured on maps is fascinating) and the life of Spanish colonists in the new world.

Avenida de los Reyes Católicos, 6. ✆ **91-549-26-41.** http://museodeamerica.mcu.es. Admission 3€ adults, 1.50€ seniors and students, free for children 17 and under; free for all Sun. May–Oct Tues–Sat 9:30am–8:30pm, Sun 10am–3pm; Nov–Apr Tues–Sat 9:30am–6:30pm, Sun 10am–3pm. Metro: Moncloa. Bus: 1, 2, 16, 44, 46, 61, 82, 113, 132, or 133.

Museo del Traje ★ MUSEUM   Don't talk to a Spaniard about French or Italian fashion—Spain's been making stylish clothes since the cave dwellers at Altamira introduced the drop-shoulder fur. Shoes don't get quite the attention they could, given Spanish footwear innovation, but this museum does trace the evolution of Spanish dress from the 1800s forward. Spain's modern fashion designers are, in many ways, the culmination of that arc. Look especially for the work of the visionary designer Balenciaga (1895–1972), whose influence is still felt today. While many of the textiles are fragile and must be displayed in low light, the collection also includes jewelry and other accessories.

Avenida Jean de Herrera, 2. ✆ **91-550-47-00.** http://museodeltraje.mcu.es. Admission 3€ adults, free for children 17 and under; free for all Sat 2:30–7pm and all day Sun. Tues–Sat 9:30am–7pm; Sun 10am–3pm. Metro: Moncola. Bus: 46, 82, 83, 132, or 133.

Palacio Real de El Pardo ★ PALACE   One of the less imposing of the royal palaces, El Pardo is worth a visit just to see some of the early Goya tapestries, the other decorative arts, and the gardens. Built in the 16th century as a hunting lodge and backup fortress where Carlos V could feel safe from his many enemies, the palace sits only 10km (6¼ miles) from the Palacio Real in central Madrid. It was an easy morning's ride on horseback, now a quick trip on the bus. Yet El Pardo remains surprisingly bucolic, thanks to the royal protection of the surrounding forests. When the palace burned in the 18th century, Carlos III had it rebuilt by Francisco Sabatini and decorated with full Enlightenment grace. A young Francisco de Goya was chosen to paint the cartoons for a number of rather sweet tapestries showing country idylls. (The paintings themselves are in the Museo del Prado.) The tapestries were woven at the Real Fábrica de Tapices (p. 90) and in many cases cover the walls like wallpaper. Alas, Carlos V was not the only one who considered El Pardo a safe haven. Francisco Franco made it his home after the Civil War and many Spaniards still find the association with the dictator to be offputting. Others shrug and enjoy the grounds—and the rotisserie restaurants on the nearby roads.

Calle Manuel Alonso, s/n. ✆ **91-376-15-00.** www.patrimonionacional.es. 9€ adults; 4€ seniors and students; free for children 5 and under. Apr–Sept daily 10am–8pm; Oct–Mar Tues–Sun 10am–6pm. Bus: 601 from Moncloa station.

Plaza de Toros Monumental de Las Ventas ★ BULLRING   This grand Mudéjar-style bullring of red brick, tile, and ornate ironwork is not the largest in the world (that's in Mexico), but it is arguably the most important. It opened in 1931 and seats 24,000 people. The best bullfighters face the best bulls here—and the fans who pack the stands are among the sport's most passionate and knowledgeable.

Although many Spaniards, including the queen, dislike (or simply have no interest) in the sport, the *corrida* remains an essential element of Spanish history and identity. If you would like to try to gain an understanding of the spectacle, it's worth visiting this storied site. Audio guide tours begin at the ceremonial Grand Portal. After a match, matadors who have earned the highest honors are carried through the portal by jubilant fans and assume a kind of stardom that can only be compared to rock stars. The tour also includes the stands, the ring itself, and the patio where matadors pause with their admirers before entering the chapel to pray before they enter the ring.

Calle Alcalá, 237. ℂ **91-356-22-00.** www.las-ventas.com. July–Aug daily 10am–7pm; Sept–June daily 10am–6pm. Mar–Oct tours close 4 hr. before corrida. 10€ adults, 7€ children under 12. Tickets for Sun matches go on sale Fri; box office hours 10am–2pm and 4–7pm, expect to pay 7€–36€ for reasonable seats. Metro: Ventas.

Madrid for Families

Parque del Retiro (p. 104) is the classic family weekend outing, with rowboats to glide over a small lake, puppet shows, street musicians, pony rides, and lots of green grass for simply running around. The wide, paved paths are also one of the few good places in the city for a family bike ride. You can rent bikes at nearby **Rent and Roll** (Calle Salustiano Olozaga, 14; www.rentandroll.es; ℂ **91-576-35-24;** from 5€; Metro: Retiro). While you're in the park, you can also pause to see the temporary art exhibitions organized by the Museo Nacional Centro de Arte Reina Sofia in the park's beautiful 19th-century exhibition halls, the glass house of the **Palacio de Cristal** (p. 104) and the neo-Mudéjar **Palacio de Velázquez** (p. 104). Admission is free, so it won't hurt to spend a few minutes.

In fact, you can use the free admission hours at some of Madrid's best museums to work short visits into your day without breaking the bank or taxing your children's attention spans. At the **Museo del Prado** (p. 86), for example, admission is always free for children and free for all from 6-8pm Mon-Sat and 5-8pm on Sundays. You might want to take your young kids to see the "cartoons" (full-sized colored drawings) that Francisco de Goya created for tapestries. Many of them feature children and animals in bucolic settings. Teenagers, on the other hand, are usually engrossed by Pablo Picasso's "Guernica" in the **Museo Nacional Centro de Arte Reina Sofia** (p. 88), which is also always free for children and (from spring through early fall) free for all from 7pm until closing during the week, 3pm until closing on Sundays. Your children might also enjoy seeing the grand neoclassical fountains of Cibeles and Neptuno as you stroll along the Paseo del Prado. For a bird's eye view of Cibeles, take them up to the observatory at **CentroCentro** (p. 83) for grand rooftop views. If your children accompany you on a shopping trip to Salamanca, let them run around and touch the artwork (one of the few places where it is allowed) in the outdoor **Museo de Arte Publico** (p. 102). From there, it's just a short walk to the **Carrusel Serrano Madrid** for a ride on the classic merry-go-round.

Madrid's other celebrated gathering place, **Plaza Mayor** (p. 95), is also a fine spot for families. Kids will find plenty of entertainment watching artists at work under the arcade, street musicians, and "living statues" posing for change. Since the plaza is enclosed on all sides, you might be able to keep an eye on your children—and the passing scene—from a cafe table.

In addition, there are several notable attractions specifically geared to families that work well as a cluster.

Parque de Atracciones ★ AMUSEMENT PARK This amusement park opened in 1969 with about 30 rides for youngsters, older children, and adults. It has continued to remodel and add new attractions to keep up with the times. You'll find mini-fire engines for tykes, graceful "flying chairs," water rides, the "cave of tarantulas," and a twisting roller coaster called "Abismo" that climbs to 200m (656 ft.) and reaches a maximum speed of 105kmph (65 mph). For riders who can keep their eyes open, the city skyline views are amazing.

Casa de Campo. ✆ **90-234-50-01.** www.parquedeatracciones.es. Admission 30€ adults, 23€ children, 16€ seniors; significant discounts available for online advance ticket purchase. July–Aug daily noon–midnight, variable days and hours the rest of the year. Metro: Linea 10. Bus: 33 or 65.

Teleférico de Madrid ★ CABLE CAR A fun way to reach the Parque de Atracciones (see above), the Teleférico is also an attraction in its own right. It was built in 1969 to connect the fairgrounds of the Casa de Campo (p. 104) with the eastern edge of Parque del Oeste, not far from the Palacio Real. The Disneyland-style cable cars take passengers on an 11-minute ride high above the city with views of parks, buildings, the Río Manzanares, and the Palacio Real. Passengers jump in as the cars slow down and children under 14 must ride with an adult. Weather junkies will be interested to know that the cable cars operate in rain and snow.

Paseo del Pintor Rosales. ✆ **91-541-74-50.** www.teleferico.com. Fare 4€ one-way, 5.75€ round-trip, free for children under 3. June–Aug daily noon–11pm; variable days and hours the rest of the year.

Zoo Aquarium de Madrid ★ ZOO When this zoo opened in 1972, it was in the forefront of thinking about how to best let animals and people interact, with animals in simulated natural habitats separated from humans by pits or moats. We like to think that this respectful approach has been a factor in the success of the zoo's breeding programs, which include the first panda born by artificial insemination outside China and the third rhino born by artificial insemination in the world. In all, the zoo is home to about 6,000 animals from 500 different species. Lovers of marine mammals will not be disappointed, as the zoo also has a tropical marine aquarium and a dolphin aquarium.

Casa de Campo. ✆ **90-234-50-14.** www.zoomadrid.com. Admission 23€ adults and children 8 and over, 19€ seniors and children 3–7; significant discounts for online advance ticket purchase. Summer Thurs–Sat 10:30am–midnight, Sun–Wed 10:30am–8:30pm, variable hours and days rest of year. Metro: Linea 10 or Linea 5. Bus: 33.

Organized Tours

The Plaza Mayor tourist information center (Plaza Mayor, 27; www.esmadrid.com/officialguidedtours; ✆ **90-222-14-24;** Metro: Vodafone Sol or Ópera) is practically one-stop shopping for guided tours in several languages, including English. **Walking tours** (5.90€) in English primarily focus on Madrid's history, but new options include historic taverns and a ghost tour. A **bicycle tour** (6.90€, without bike rental) covers that same historical ground at a quicker pace. **Rollerblade tours** (6.90€, without skate rental) follow the banks of the Río Manzanares, for example, or explore historic gardens. Tours operate all year, but sizes are limited, so book ahead. Note that rollerblade tours and more specialized bicycle and walking tours are not usually offered in English. Dust off your high school Spanish and you'll expand your choices.

4

MADRID | Organized Tours

Many travelers opt for the double-decker **Madrid City Tour** (p. 50) as a convenient, hop-on, hop-off mode of transportation to major tourist attractions. You might also simply ride the two routes and take advantage of the recorded commentary. Special versions for children are a particularly nice touch.

More traditional motorcoach tours offered by **Trapsatur** (Calle San Bernardo, 7; www.trapsatur.com; ℰ **91-541-63-21;** Metro: Santo Domingo) depart from their headquarters at Plaza de Santo Domingo. A 2½-hour sightseeing tour is 23€ adults, 18€ seniors, and 11€ children. If you prefer to see the city's buildings and fountains illuminated at night, a panoramic night tour is 19€ adults, 15€ seniors, and 11€ children. Other options allow you to add on tours of the Palacio Real, Bernabéu football stadium, or Las Ventas, the city's Mudéjar-style bullring to the general city tour. Trapsatur also offers an array of tours to surrounding areas, such as a full-day tour of Toledo (63€ adults, 48€ seniors, 38€ children) or a seasonal full-day tour to Ávila and Segovia (70€ adults, 53€ seniors, 36€ children).

SHOPPING IN MADRID

There are surprising discoveries to be made throughout Madrid, which is why you should keep your schedule flexible enough that you can stop in the store that catches your eye as you make your way from one attraction to the next. That said, two neighborhoods stand out for their shopping opportunities.

Salamanca (p. 102) is the more chic, with the tasteful boutiques of Spain's top designers as well as international luxury brands that you will find in similar districts around the world. If you want to keep it local, check out the beautiful tasseled bags, wallets, jackets, and other goods at **Loewe** (Calle Serrano, 26; ℰ **91-577-60-56;** and Calle Serrano, 47; www.loewe.com; ℰ **91-200-44-99;** Metro: Serrano) or handle a truly well-made shoe at custom-maker **Gaytan** (Calle Jorge Juan, 15; ℰ **91-435-28-24;** Metro: Serrano or Velázquez). Not surprisingly, Madrid's nicest shopping mall **ABC Serrano** (Calle Serrano, 61; www.abcserrano.com; ℰ **91-577-50-31;** Metro: Serrano) is also in the neighborhood. Even if the goods are too dear for your wallet, you might pick up a few style tips to employ elsewhere. Wherever you shop, keep in mind one of our favorite Spanish words: "rebajas." Translated loosely as "reductions," it signals that a sale is in progress. (Citywide sales generally take place Jan–Feb and July–Aug.)

Shoppers with more limited means will have more luck—and more fun—in the recently trendy neighborhood of **Chueca** (p. 99). It's worth exploring side streets for shops of up-and-coming designers looking for a lower rent. But the main drag of Calle Augusto Figueroa is shoe central, since a number of top-end Spanish shoe manufacturers, including **Barrats** (Calle Augusto Figueroa, 20; ℰ **91-531-65-37;** Metro: Chueca) have outlets here. We have found discounts of 30–60 percent.

Also in the neighborhood, is the outlet store of **Salvador Bachiller** (Calle Gravina, 11; www.salvadorbachiller.com; ℰ **91-523-30-37;** Metro: Chueca) a great source for luggage, purses, travel accessories, and other small leather goods. You can get great buys here (especially on brightly colored merchandise), but watch for flaws, such as broken zippers.

If your style runs more to T-shirts, a number of fashion designers and other Madrid notables have designed shirts that celebrate their city. Look for them at the Plaza Mayor tourist information center (see "Organized Tours," above). For souvenirs, the store at **CentroCentro** (p. 83) may the best general gift shop in the city. It stocks a good range of Spanish cookbooks in English, jewelry by local designers, and all kinds of clever household goods and novelty items. Our favorite? Mini wind-up toreadors and bulls.

In Puerta del Sol, the city's main branch of **El Corte Inglés** (Calle Preciados, 3; ✆ **91-379-80-00;** Metro: Vodafone Sol) department store is another good bet for one-stop souvenir shopping. It carries some fairly predictable merchandise such as embroidered shawls, damascene jewelry, and mass-produced pottery. It's best to think more broadly. Flamenco CDs (for some of the top artists, see p. 35) or specialty food items like saffron (expensive) and smoked paprika (cheap, but packed in charming tins) are easy to pack and make novel gifts. In addition, the city's venerable perfumería Alvarez Gómez closed its retail shop in 2013, but many of the products are available at El Corte Inglés, including a lovely line of soaps scented with Mediterranean flowers and concentrated bath gel that is great for travel.

For more choices, follow some of the streets that radiate out from Puerta del Sol. On Calle Preciados, for example, you'll find an outlet of **Zara** (Calle Preciados, 18; www.zara.com; ✆ **91-521-09-58;** Metro: Vodafone Sol or Callao), the clothing manufacturer that has gained a huge following for its on-trend yet affordable styles. For more timeless fashion, walk uphill to **Capas Seseña** (Calle Cruz, 23; www.sesena.com; ✆ **91-531-68-40;** Metro: Vodafone Sol), which has been making beautiful capes since 1901. If they suit your style, they are worth the investment.

But there are other, less costly, icons of Spanish style, including the constructed Basque cap, Spain's answer to the French beret. **La Favorita** (Plaza Mayor, 25; www.lafavoritacb.com; ✆ **91-366-58-77;** Metro: Vodafone Sol or Ópera) has a range of colors and styles for men and women. And right off Plaza Mayor, you can shop for hand-sewn espadrilles at local favorite **Casa Hernanz** (Calle Toledo, 18; ✆ **91-366-54-50;** Metro: La Latina). Bring a color swatch if you want to match a particular outfit.

Before you leave Plaza Mayor, stop at **El Arco de los Cuchilleros Artesania de Hoy** (Plaza Mayor, 9; ✆ **91-365-26-80;** Metro: Vodafone Sol or Ópera), which is devoted to contemporary craft items from throughout Spain. If you have a particular interest in Spain's great ceramics traditions, do not miss **Antigua Casa Talavera** (Calle Isabel La Catolica, 2; ✆ **91-547-34-17;** Metro: Santo Domingo), where the beautiful tile facade of the building is only a prelude to the artful ceramics inside. Spanish artisans also excel at guitar-making. The best of the best is **Guitarras Ramirez** (Calle de la Paz, 8; www.guitarrasramirez.com; ✆ **91-531-42-29;** Metro: Sevilla), which was founded in the 1880s and has created instruments for everyone from Andrés Segovia to Eric Clapton. Other good options include **Conde Hermanos** (Calle Arrieta, 4; www.condehermanos.com; ✆ **91-429-93-33;** Metro: Ópera), makers of classical and flamenco guitars, and **El Flamenco Vive** (Calle Conde de Lemos, 7; www.elflamencovive.com; ✆ **91-547-39-17;** Metro: Ópera), the city's tiny but indispensable flamenco hub, with guitars, sheet music, CDs, and more.

Be sure to set aside some of Sunday morning for Madrid's famed flea market **El Rastro** (p. 96). We once saw Madrileñas stocking up on armloads of fake pashminas here and you might find other fun fashion pieces among the mix of bric-a-brac. Enjoy the scene, but keep a close eye on your belongings, as pickpockets like to work the crowd. If you are a serious antiques collector, it's better to return to the neighborhood on a weekday and check out the shops gathered in **Mercado Galerias Piquer** (Calle Ribera de Curtidores, 29; no phone; Metro: Puerto de Toledo).

Madrid's most beautiful food market is **Mercado de la Paz** (p. 102) in Salamanca, where you can peruse the fresh goods and shop for packaged items to take home. On the other hand, Madrid's best market for the beautiful people is **Mercado de San Miguel** (p. 95). This long-shuttered fresh food market has assumed a new identity as a lifestyle emporia with all sorts of specialty food items to eat on premises or take away.

In 2013, **Real Madrid**, surpassed Great Britain's Manchester United to become the most valuable soccer team in the world. According to "Forbes," Madrid's beloved team is worth $3.3 billion. You can add a bit to the coffers by picking up some of the team's training jerseys and shorts, scarves, socks or hoodies. For the truly obsessed, there are also blankets, sheets, mugs, coasters, electric toothbrushes, and rubber duckies. We joke, but a piece of the colorful merchandise will make a good conversation starter when you get home. Official stores include Tienda Carmen (Calle Carmen, 19; ✆ **91-521-79-50;** Metro: Vodafone Sol or Callao), Tienda Goya (Calle Goya, 77; ✆ **91-435-79-04;** Metro: Goya) and Tienda Gran Vía (Gran Vía, 31; ✆ **91-755-45-38;** Metro: Callao or Gran Vía). Check the web site at www.realmadridshop.com.

ENTERTAINMENT & NIGHTLIFE

If you are only going to hit the town for 1 night, you should see a flamenco show. Madrid is at the forefront of the flamenco revival and much of the credit goes to **Casa Patas** (p. 91), which presents established artists and rising stars. But we also have great respect for some of the showier and more touristic offerings, which help introduce people to the art form. Good choices include **Cardamomo** (Calle Echegaray, 15; www.cardamomo.es; ✆ **91-369-07-57;** 39€; Metro: Vodafone Sol) which often features well-known performers and **Corral de la Morería** (Calle Morería, 17; www.corraldelamoreria.com; ✆ **91-365-84-46;** 39€; Metro: Ópera) which is located near the Palacio Real and has championed flamenco since 1956. Prices above are for the show and one drink. Dinner is available, but you are better off eating elsewhere. For a more casual performance, try **Villa Rosa** (Plaza Santa Ana, 15; www.villa-rosa.es; ✆ **91-521-36-89;** 15€; Metro: Antón Martín), which occupies an historic tiled building on Plaza Santa Ana.

If you prefer cool jazz to hot flamenco, check out **Cafe Central** (Plaza del Angel, 10; www.cafecentralmadrid.com; ✆ **91-369-41-43;** Metro: Antón Martín), which has been presenting touring musicians since the early 1980s. The Malasaña mega-club **Clamores** (Calle Alburquerque, 14; www.clamores.es; ✆ **91-445-7-38;** Metro: Bilbao) often programs live jazz in the early evening, before it turns into a late-night disco. In nearby Chueca, Madrid's premier gay bar **Black & White** (Calle Libertad, 34; www.discoblack-white.net; ✆ **91-531-11-41;** Metro: Chueca) features a basement disco and a street-level bar with drag shows, male strip tease, and other entertainment. For a more centrally located dance club, **Disco-Teatro Joy Eslava** (Arenal 11; www.joy-eslava.com; ✆ **91-366-37-33;** Metro: Vodafone Sol or Ópera) occupies a 19th-century theater near Puerta del Sol. For a late-night chocolate and churros hangover cure, Joy Eslava is conveniently located near **Chocolatería San Gines** (p. 77).

For classical music lovers, **Teatro Real** (p. 99) is known for the fine acoustics that enhance its offerings of opera and classical music. Madrid's largest concentration of theaters is in the vicinity of Plaza Santa Ana (see sidebar on p. 93). For classical music concerts, check **Teatro Monumental** or **Teatro Español,** which schedules dance, orchestral, and chamber music concerts as well as live theater. Both the **Teatro Nuevo Apolo** and the **Teatro de la Zarzuela** specialize in zarzuela, the Spanish form of musical entertainment that mixes opera, popular song, and spoken narrative. Performances are in Spanish, of course, but they are so expressive that the language barrier is not necessarily an impediment to enjoying the action.

SAVE ON THAT seat

Sometimes it pays to wait until the last minute. **Taquilla Ultimo Minuto** (www. taquillaultimominuto.com) offers up to 60 percent discounts on selected theater performances and other entertainment. You check the offerings on the web site and make a purchase with a credit card. Then you use that same credit card to collect your tickets at any Caja Madrid ATM. Present those tickets at your selected venue up to 1 hour before the show.

One of our favorite ways to improve our language skills is to watch American films dubbed into Spanish. **Cine Ideal** (Doctor Cortezo, 6; www.yelmocines.es; $\mathcal{C}$ **90-222-09-22;** Metro: Tirso de Molina) screens current films, including 3D, in their original language, with Spanish subtitles when appropriate.

DAY TRIPS FROM MADRID

The two destinations below offer a real switch of attitude and ambiance from central Madrid. Each is key to the Spanish psyche, but they could not be more different. The monastery palace at San Lorenzo de El Escorial, a gigantic mass of heavily decorated stone, might be the weightiest attraction in the country. It is also the embodiment of the religious fervor that seized and motivated some of the Spanish monarchs. Alcalá de Henares, by contrast, is a pleasantly dusty, flat little town on the plains east of the city where some of the greatest minds of Spanish culture studied and taught.

San Lorenzo de El Escorial ★★

Set in the Guadarrama mountains about 51km (31 miles) northwest of Madrid, El Escorial can be surprisingly cooler than the city. After Toledo, a visit to its austere royal palace and monastery is the second most popular day trip from Madrid. The pleasant weather has also made the town a favorite summer getaway for Madrileños. But if you don't own a breezy summer home here, plan to spend a half day at the royal site.

ESSENTIALS

GETTING THERE   More than two dozen **cercanías** (commuter trains) depart daily from Madrid's Atocha, Nuevos Ministerios, Chamartín, and Recoletos railway stations. During the summer another dozen trains are added. For schedules and information, call $\mathcal{C}$ **90-232-03-20,** or visit www.renfe.es. A one-way fare costs 4.50€, round trip is 6.60€. Trip time is a little more than 1 hour. The railway station is about a mile outside town along Carretera Estación. The Herranz bus company meets all arriving trains to shuttle passengers to and from Plaza Virgen de Gracia, about a block east of the monastery's entrance.

Empresa Herranz (Calle del Rey, 27, in El Escorial; $\mathcal{C}$ **91-890-19-15**), runs some 50 **buses** per day back and forth between Madrid's Moncloa station and El Escorial. On Sunday, service is curtailed to 10 buses. Trip time is an hour, and the one-way fare is 6€.

If you're driving, follow the N-VI highway (marked on some maps as A-6) from the northwest perimeter of Madrid toward Lugo, A Coruña, and San Lorenzo de El Escorial. After about a half-hour, fork left onto the C-505 heading toward San Lorenzo de El Escorial. Driving time from Madrid is about an hour.

The **tourist information office** (Calle Grimaldi, 4; www.sanlorenzoturismo.org; ✆ **91-890-53-13**) is open Tuesday to Saturday 10am to 2pm and 3 to 6pm, and Sunday 10am to 2pm.

EXPLORING SAN LORENZO DE EL ESCORIAL

Real Monasterio de San Lorenzo de El Escorial ★★★ HISTORIC SITE

Felipe II ordered the construction of this granite and slate behemoth in 1563, 2 years after he moved his capital to Madrid. This monument to the Habsburg line was completed in only 21 years. After the death of the original architect, Juan Bautista de Toledo, the structure was completed by Juan de Herrera, often considered the greatest architect of Renaissance Spain. It is an important landmark of Spanish Renaissance style, but the complex does have a rather institutional look, and due to its sheer size can seem intimidating. The buildings, which include a basilica, a monastery, the royal palace, and a library are arranged in a quadrangle. You might want to consider the optional guided tour to get an overview and then explore on your own and admire the impressive royal art collection. Felipe II was a particular fan of Titian and the artist's "Last Supper" is one of the highlights. Spain, however, is well-represented with El Greco's "Martyrdom of St. Maurice" and Velázquez's "La Tunica de José."

Guides will almost certainly linger in the basilica, which has 43 ornate altars beneath a dome that emulates St. Peter's in Rome. Habsburg and Bourbon monarchs, including Carlos V, the father of Felipe II, lie at rest in royal vaults beneath the basilica. Much of the mural work in the complex is quite impressive—from the frescoes of Habsburg battle victories in the royal palace to the incredible vaulted ceiling in the library painted with allegorical scenes depicting the Liberal Arts and the Sciences. In the midst of this splendor, the monarch's private quarters are very modest, but a window does provide a view of the main altar of the basilica.

Calle Juan de Borbón, s/n. ✆ **91-890-59-03.** http://patrimonionacional.es. Admission 10€ adults, 5€ students and children; audio guide 4€; guided tour additional 7€. Apr–Sept Tues–Sun 10am–6pm; Oct–Mar Tues–Sun 10am–5pm.

Alcalá de Henares ★★

The buildings are old and the population is young—as befits the city where the Spanish Renaissance was born when the university was founded here by Cardinal Francisco Jiménez de Cisneros in 1499. While the Inquisition was closing minds, Alcalá was opening them. The progenitor of the modern Spanish language, Miguel de Cervantes, was also born here in 1547. Although the Cervantes family left Alcalá when Miguel was a boy, the central square of the old town is called Plaza de Cervantes and boasts a heroic bronze of the author. The original university moved to Madrid in the 1800s, and the town went into decline. It has established a new identity with residential study programs for several American universities. Great commuter rail connections have nearly turned the college town into a suburb, earning the nickname "the bedroom of Madrid."

ESSENTIALS

GETTING THERE   **Trains** travel from Madrid's Chamartín station to Alcalá de Henares four times per day. A one-way fare costs 3€ to 10€, depending on the train. Trip time is 21-45 minutes. The train station (www.renfe.es; ✆ **90-232-03-20**) in Alcalá is at Paseo Estación.

Buses from Madrid depart from Avenida de América 18 (Metro: América) every 15 minutes. A one-way fare is 5€. Bus service is provided by Continental, and the Alcalá bus station is on Avenida Guadalajara, 36 (✆ **90-242-22-42**), 2 blocks past Calle Libreros.

Alcalá lies adjacent to the main national highway (N-II), connecting Madrid with eastern Spain. As you leave central Madrid, follow signs for Barajas Airport and Barcelona.

VISITOR INFORMATION The **tourist information office,** Callejón de Santa María, 1 (www.turismoalcala.com; ✆ **91-889-26-94**) is open daily 10am to 2pm and 4 to 6:30pm (until 7:30pm July–Sept). It is closed on Monday in July and August.

EXPLORING ALCALÁ DE HENARES

You can easily explore Alcalá in a day, walking everywhere. From February to August, keep an eye out for about 100 pairs of storks that nest on the rooftops and in the bell towers.

Capilla de San Ildefonso ★ CHURCH   Next door to the Colegio (see below) is the Capilla de San Ildefonso, the 15th-century chapel of the old university with an artesanado (artisan's) ceiling and intricately stuccoed walls. It houses the Italian marble tomb of Cardinal Cisneros, the founder of the original university.

Plaza San Diego, s/n. ✆ **91-885-41-85.** Admission included in tour of Colegio Mayor de San Ildefonso. Mon–Fri 11am–1pm and 5–7pm; Sat–Sun 11am–2pm and 5–7:30pm.

Colegio Mayor de San Ildefonso ★★ HISTORIC SITE   Adjacent to Plaza de Cervantes (the main square) is the Colegio Mayor de San Ildefonso, where Lope de Vega and other famous Spaniards studied. You can see some of their names engraved on plaques in the examination room. The old university's Plateresque **facade** dates from 1543. From here, walk across the Patio of Saint Thomas (from 1662) and the Patio of the Philosophers to reach the Patio of the Three Languages (from 1557), where Greek, Latin, and Hebrew were once taught. The **Paraninfo** (great hall or old examination room) has a Mudéjar carved-panel ceiling and is now used for special events. The Paraninfo is entered through the restaurant Hostería del Estudiante.

Plaza San Diego. ✆ **91-885-41-85.** www.uah.es. Guided tour 4.50€; audio guides 3€. Tours in Spanish or English Tues–Sat noon, 1pm, 5pm, 6pm, and 7pm; Sun noon and 1pm.

Museo Arqueológico Regional ★★ MUSEUM   Clear signage and vivid exhibits make this one of the most rewarding archaeological museums in the country. Its coverage includes natural history as well as human occupation. While storks seem to be the most common form of wildlife these days, the beasts were considerably more ferocious some 780,000 years ago, judging by the bones of saber-toothed tigers, urwolves and rhinoceros on display. Don't miss the wonderful murals recovered from Alcalá's Roman era when it was known as Complutum, founded 1 B.C.

Plaza Bernardas, s/n. ✆ **91-879-66-66.** www.madrid.org. Free admission. Tues–Sat 11am–7pm; Sun 11am–3pm.

Museo Casa Natal de Cervantes ★ MUSEUM   Miguel de Cervantes, the creator of "Don Quixote," was born in Alcalá in 1547 and the city remains proud of its association with Spain's literary giant. In the 1940s, research by a Cervantes biographer suggested that this country estate may have been his birthplace and the city moved quickly to reconstruct the building and establish it as a museum. The handsome brick and stone dwelling has a small courtyard and well. Cervantes' father was a barber-surgeon and the interior of tile floors, white walls, and carved wooden doors conjures the lifestyle of a comfortable family of the time. Displays of Cervantes' manuscripts help to cement the connection to the author. If you are inspired to read Cervantes' picaresque tale, copies are available in the gift shop.

Calle Mayor, 48. ✆ **91-889-96-54.** www.museo-casa-natal-cervantes.org. Free admission. Tues–Sun 10am–6pm.

SIDE TRIPS
FROM MADRID

M adrid is surrounded by legendary cities whose names echo
down the ages in story and song. These were the frontier
fortresses in the prolonged battle between the cross and
the crescent for the body and soul of Iberia. As you approach these
central Spanish cities, imagine that you are leading an invading
army. After a long march across a flat plain with no place to hide,
you finally reach the outskirts of Toledo, Cuenca, Segovia, Ávila, or
Zamora. (Unfortified Salamanca is another story.) You crane your
neck to look up at the walled fortress city high on the hill. Its defenders have been watching your approach for days, and their swords
are ready. . . . It is the tale of central Spain written over and over—
only the names of the invaders and defenders changed.

5

Whoever seized the plains of La Mancha or the hilltop cities always
acted audaciously. Roman engineers channeled water from distant mountains to make Segovia bloom. Centuries later, a string of rulers named
Alfonso and Sancho and Fernando plotted power in the name of a Christian
god and fortified every high spot, giving the region its enduring name,
Castilla, or land of castles. They carried the battle of the Reconquista from
castle to castle across the searing center of the Iberian peninsula, mustering
the military might, religious fervor, and brilliant scholarship that made
them the most powerful rulers in this corner of Europe—and ultimately
kings of Spain.

This chapter includes La Mancha's Toledo, with its medieval streets, El
Greco masterpieces, and lingering Moorish influences; Segovia, with its
clifftop fairytale castle and iconic Roman aqueduct; Ávila, with its mystical
religious sites and the dizzying ramparts of its ancient walls; and the bluff-
top city of Cuenca, where abstract modern and contemporary art is as big
a draw as the casas colgadas, or "hanging houses" cantilevered off the side
of the city nearly 200 feet above a river gorge. It also ventures farther into
the heart of Castilla y León to the learned city of Salamanca, where thousands of non-Spaniards flock to learn the language, and Zamora, the Río
Duero borderland city where Romanesque churches thrust up their crosses
like pikes against southern invaders.

The construction of the medium-distance high-speed rail lines has made
travel to these cities from Madrid both easy and inexpensive. While the rail
links make day trips possible, these cities merit more than a quick "hello-
goodbye." Plan to spend at least 1 night to experience their magic in the
evening and in the early morning.

TOLEDO ★★★

If you can make only one excursion, go to Toledo, where even its medieval Arab, Jewish, and Christian elements have not entirely eclipsed the Roman and Visigothic eras. The hilltop Old City is a UNESCO Heritage site and surprisingly little of its appearance has changed since El Greco painted his adopted home in the 16th century. Even then it was ancient.

The close medieval streets were deliberately constructed to be barely wide enough for a man and his donkey to pass, but they are strikingly practical—offering cool, welcome shade in the summer and a shield from winter winds. Wrapped on three sides by a bend in the Tagus River, Toledo overlooks the arid plains of La Mancha from a high bluff. This outcrop provided a natural fortress in the center of the Iberian Peninsula. The Romans made it the capital of central Iberia, and the Visigoths made it the capital of their kingdom. For roughly a century, it was the capital of a regional Muslim kingdom before it was reconquered by Alfonso VI in 1085. The Castilian kings ultimately made Toledo the capital of Spain. Even after the court moved to Madrid in 1561, Toledo remained the national religious center as the seat of the primate of Spain. As the governing city of so many cultures, it retains more layers of history than almost anywhere else in Spain.

Although most of Toledo's medieval defensive walls have been taken down, the city still has the feel of a hilltop fortress. So approach it in that manner, beginning your visit with a circumnavigation of the roads that once lay just inside the walls, eerily marked by the preserved ceremonial gates, notably the Arabic archway of **Puerta del Sol** on the north side. To better understand how defenders could watch potential enemies as they approached, spend some time surveying the surrounding plain from **Mirador Barrio Nuevo** across the street from the **Museo Sefardí** (see below). Once you begin spiraling into the city interior, two key squares are the centers of life in Toledo. You'll find Toledo children playing street soccer or learning to ride bicycles (as well as travelers visiting the tourist office) at the **Plaza del Ayuntamiento,** southwest of the **cathedral. Plaza de Zocodover,** northeast of the cathedral, is filled with outdoor cafes popular both with visitors and, at night, with young Toledanos. Both squares serve as reference points, as they represent transitions between neighborhoods within the city. Plaza de Zocodover is also the central point where local buses stop in the old city.

Essentials

GETTING THERE   High-speed RENFE Avant **trains** run frequently every day. Those departing Madrid's Atocha railway station for Toledo run daily from 6:50am to 9:50pm; those leaving Toledo for Madrid run daily from 6:50am to 9:30pm. Travel time is approximately 35 minutes. The fare one-way is 12.50€. For train information in Madrid, visit www.renfe.com or call ✆ **90-232-03-20.** To reach the old city from Toledo's bus station, take bus 5 to the Plaza de Zocodover (1.40€); a taxi from the station is about 8€.

From Madrid, it's also feasible to take the **bus** instead of the train. The main service is provided by **Alsa** (www.alsa.es; ✆ **90-242-22-42**). Buses depart daily, from Madrid's Estación de Plaza Elíptica, Avenida Vía Lusitana, between 6:30am and 11pm at 15- to 30-minute intervals. Travel time is 50 minutes to 1¼ hours, and a one-way transit costs 5.65€ and can be purchased only at the station. Once you reach Toledo, you'll be deposited at the Estación de Autobuses, which lies beside the river, about 1.2km (¾ mile) from the historic center. Although many visitors opt to walk, be ready to climb a hill. Buses 5 and 6 run from the station uphill to Plaza de Zocodover, charging 1.40€ for the brief ride. Pay the driver directly. By **car,** exit Madrid via Cibeles (Paseo del Prado) and take the N-401 south.

VISITOR INFORMATION   The **tourist information office,** Plaza del Consistorio, 1 (www.toledo-turismo.com; ✆ **92-525-40-30**), is open daily 10am to 6pm.

Where to Stay

Parador de Toledo ★★★   This parador occupies a handsome stone building with tile roof from the 14th century, but travelers choose it less for its historic ambience and more for its stupendous view. The property sits on a hilly ridge about 4km (2½ miles) from the city center—the perfect vantage point to take in Toledo in all its architectural glory, whether you are sunning by the outdoor pool or enjoying the city lights at night while eating dinner on the patio. The restaurant serves all the standards of Castilla-La Mancha, including partridge, roast lamb, honey ice cream, and *mazapán*. Guestrooms depart from the usual parador approach of antique reproduction furnishings for clean-lined modern pieces that don't detract from the city or countryside views. The only disadvantage of this location across the Río Tajo is that you will probably want to take taxi rides back and forth to the city center.

Cerro del Emperador. ✆ **92-522-18-50.** www.parador.es. 76 units. 120€–180€ double; 190€–232€ suite. Free parking. **Amenities:** Restaurant; bar; outdoor pool; room service; free Wi-Fi.

Hostal del Cardenal ★★   You will be immediately charmed when you make your way through an entrance in the thick city walls and find yourself in the tranquil Andalucian-style garden of this former summer home of a very lucky archbishop. The hotel is near the Bisagra Gate on the northern end of the city, roughly 15 minutes on foot from the cathedral. Truthfully, it's a bit difficult to find, but worth the effort for its effortless combination of history and elegance. You will probably find yourself spending a lot of time in the garden or the traditionally furnished sitting areas. The standard double rooms, while bright and cheerful, are somewhat small.

Paseo de Recaredo, 24. ✆ **92-522-49-00.** www.elhostaldelcardenal.com. 27 units. 70€–120€ double; 130€–300€ suite. Free street parking about 10-min. walk away. Bus: 5 or 6 from rail station. **Amenities:** Restaurant; bar; free Wi-Fi.

Hotel Santa Isabel ★★   There's an old European tradition that travelers may spend the night unmolested within the shadow of the church. While this delightful B&B inn is not quite as cheap as the cathedral doorway, it's not far from the church and a whole lot more comfortable. It occupies a medieval building across from the Convent of Santa Isabel and near the cathedral. Some guestrooms, in fact, have cathedral views, while the rooftop terrace (reached by a spiral staircase) has panoramic city views. The building became a lodging in 1990 and careful restoration retained the ancient facade while creating a more fresh and airy modern interior. Guest rooms are small but well furnished and maintained. Room 215, with a glassed-in balcony, is perhaps the nicest.

Calle Santa Isabel, 24. ✆ **92-525-31-20.** www.hotelsantaisabel.net. 42 units. 40€–98€ double. Underground parking 10€. Bus: 5 or 6. **Amenities:** Free Wi-Fi.

Hotel Pintor El Greco ★★★   One of the city's most romantic lodgings, this hotel is built around the core of a classic 17th-century Toledo house (and former bakery) constructed of brick and stucco both inside and out. Carved wooden furniture upholstered in patterned woven fabrics, wrought-iron banisters and light fixtures, and

Toledo

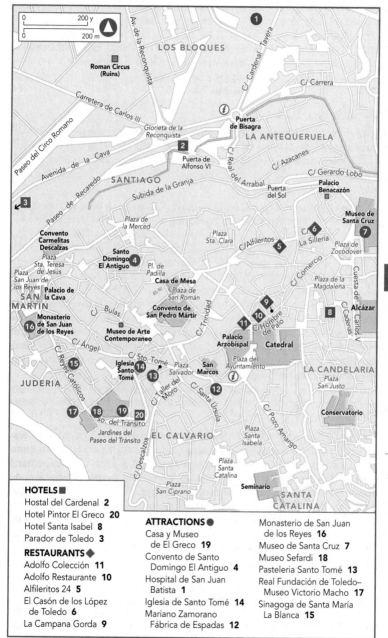

0 ——— 200 y
0 ——— 200 m

LOS BLOQUES

Av. de la Reconquista

1

C/ Cardenal Tavera

C/ Carrera

Roman Circus
(Ruins)

Carretera de Carlos III

Glorieta de la
Reconquista

2 Puerta
de Bisagra

(i)

LA ANTEQUERUELA

Paseo del Circo Romano

Avenida de la Cava

Puerta de
Alfonso VI

C/ Azacanes

C/ Real del Arrabal

Puerta
del Sol

C/ Gerardo Lobo

Palacio
Benacazón

SANTIAGO

Subida de la Granja

Paseo de Recaredo

3

Plaza de
la Merced

Museo de
Santa Cruz

7

Convento
Carmelitas
Descalzas

Plaza
Sta. Teresa
de Jesús

Santo
Domingo
El Antiguo **4**

Pl. de
Padilla

Plaza
Sta. Clara

C/ Alfileritos

5

La Sillería

6

Plaza de
Zocódover

Plaza
San Juan de
los Reyes

Palacio de
la Cava

**SAN
MARTÍN**

C/ Bulas

Casa de Mesa

Plaza de
San Román

Convento de
San Pedro Mártir

Plaza de la
Magdalena

C/ Comercio

8

Alcázar

Cuesta de Carlos V

C/ Cadenas

16 Monasterio
de San Juan
de los Reyes

C/ Ángel

Museo de Arte
Contemporaneo

C/ Trinidad

9
10
11 Palacio
Arzobispal

C/ Hombre
de Palo

Catedral

15

C/ Reyes Católicos

Iglesia
Santo
Tomé **14**
13

C/ Sto. Tomé

Plaza
Salvador

San
Marcos

Plaza del
Ayuntamiento

(i)

LA CANDELARIA

Plaza
San Justo

JUDERÍA

17
18
19
20

C/ Taller del
Moro

C/ Santa Úrsula

12

Po. del Tránsito

Jardines del
Paseo del Tránsito

EL CALVARIO

C/ Descalzos

Plaza
Santa
Isabela

Plaza
Santa
Catalina

Conservatorio

Plaza
Pozo Amargo

Plaza
San Ciprano

Seminario

**SANTA
CATALINA**

HOTELS ■
Hostal del Cardenal **2**
Hotel Pintor El Greco **20**
Hotel Santa Isabel **8**
Parador de Toledo **3**

RESTAURANTS ◆
Adolfo Colección **11**
Adolfo Restaurante **10**
Alfileritos 24 **5**
El Casón de los López
de Toledo **6**
La Campana Gorda **9**

ATTRACTIONS ●
Casa y Museo
de El Greco **19**
Convento de Santo
Domingo El Antiguo **4**
Hospital de San Juan
Batista **1**
Iglesia de Santo Tomé **14**
Mariano Zamorano
Fábrica de Espadas **12**

Monasterio de San Juan
de los Reyes **16**
Museo de Santa Cruz **7**
Museo Sefardi **18**
Pasteleria Santo Tomé **13**
Real Fundación de Toledo–
Museo Victorio Macho **17**
Sinagoga de Santa María
La Blanca **15**

sunny colors sponged on stucco walls conjure up fine living in old Toledo. The new addition, which doubled the size, is as ultra-modern as the original is traditional, with contemporary dark wood and leather furniture, bright splashes of saturated color in pillows and wall decor, white marble floors, and flat-screen TVs. Ironically, many guests prefer the older section for its historical ambiance. The location on the west side of town in the old Jewish Quarter near the Sinagoga del Tránsito and the Convento de San Juan de los Reyes is quiet, but it's only a short walk to the cathedral.

Calle Alamillos del Tránsito, 13. ℭ **92-528-51-91.** www.hotel-pintorelgreco.com. 60 units. 60€–185€ double. Parking 14€. Bus: 2. **Amenities:** Free Wi-Fi.

Where to Eat

Toledo's cuisine relies heavily on mushrooms foraged from the river gorges, artichokes raised in the dry fields below the city, and wild game. The striking signature dish *perdiz a la Toledana* (partridge cooked with herbs, olive oil, and white wine) is widely imitated all over Spain. The local olive oil is also highly prized, and you may find some dishes dressed with nothing else.

Adolfo Restaurante ★★ LA MANCHAN   Sometimes it takes just one chef to turn around a city's dining habits. In Toledo, that would be Adolfo Muñoz, the charismatic and talented champion of modernized La Manchan cooking. This flagship of his restaurant group, located in a late medieval structure near the cathedral, offers what might be considered the greatest hits of Toledan cuisine: the dishes served all over Spain but always attributed to Toledo. Game is first and foremost, of course, with a glorious version of *perdiz a la Toledana,* the classic pickled partridge slow-cooked in olive oil. Muñoz serves it with a puddle of reduced cooking juices and a circle of intensely red rice and herbs. Part of what makes Toledan cuisine distinctive is the use of fruit, both fresh and dried, in many savory dishes. It's part of the Moorish heritage of the city and Muñoz nods to it by accompanying roast suckling pig with a side of sliced green apples quickly sautéed in pork fat. He also sometimes serves the rack of venison with a sauté of onions, carrots, and dried fruits.

Calle Hombre de Palo, 7. ℭ **92-522-73-21.** www.adolforestaurante.com. Reservations recommended. Main courses 27€–45€; tasting menu 90€–110€. Daily 1–4pm; Mon–Sat 8pm–midnight. Bus: 5 or 6.

Adolfo Colleción ★ LA MANCHAN   You don't need to pay haute prices to enjoy star chef Adolfo Muñoz's creative cooking (and some fabulous wines from central Spain) if you head to his bargain-priced wine bar and shop across from the cathedral. It serves light meals in a hip, casual setting with seating for just 16 people. Game figures prominently, with such treats as rolled, stuffed venison with herbs. It's also a good place to try the typical Toledano dish, *carcamusas,* which is a stewed meat casserole, in this case pork, tomatoes, and green peas, served with fried potatoes. The *menu del día* (two courses and dessert, but no wine) is always a bargain. More than 300 wines are available, many by the glass.

Calle Nuncio Viejo, 1. ℭ **92-522-42-44.** www.grupoadolfo.com. Most main dishes under 10€. Daily 11am–11:30pm. Bus: 5 or 6.

Alfileritos 24 Taberna Restaurante ★★ SPANISH   Old Toledo and new Spain come together in this establishment that even has separate rooms for its split personality. It's in a medieval building on a very narrow street almost in the geographic center of Toledo. The tavern side, one of the favorite watering holes for Toledo professionals, can get a bit rowdy on weekends, but it offers one of the best cheap breakfasts in the mornings and a *menu del día* (two courses, dessert, and choice of drink) for a song (10.50€). Starters could include a salad of tuna and white asparagus or mixed cheeses and dried fruits with a honey vinaigrette. For a main course, choose the deer tacos with mushroom salsa. Prices go up and table settings get more elegant on the restaurant side, where you might find a grilled fish with green pepper sauce or rounds of venison filet mignon with quince and Parmagiano cheese on the 18.50€ menu. All dishes can also be ordered a la carte.

Calle Alfileritos, 24. ℰ **92-523-96-25.** www.alfileritos24.com. Main dishes 7€–18€. Daily 9am–4pm and 8pm–midnight.

Casón de los López ★★ LA MANCHAN This restaurant is something of a campy museum piece, right down to the antique furnishings (most of which are for sale), the splashing fountain, and the caged songbirds. But the flair is mostly reserved for the décor. The kitchen serves traditional La Manchan dishes and is particularly adept at farmed and wild game. Game dishes best suited to non-Spanish tastes (in other words, not too gamy) are casseroles such as wild hare with mushrooms, partridge in red-wine sauce, or squab with vegetables. For a more elegant treatment, try the duck confit with apple purée and a tart sherry vinegar sauce.

Calle Sillería, 3. ℰ **90-219-83-44.** www.restaurante-toledo.es. Reservations required. Main courses 18€–26€; tasting menu 42€–72€. Daily 1:30–4pm; Mon–Sat 8:30–11:30pm. Bus: 2.

Cervecería Restaurante La Campana Gorda ★ LA MANCHAN Join Toledo shopkeepers having lunch on such traditional specialties as pickled partridge and vegetables in this dining room near the cathedral. The beer hall in the front room has a long, curving marble bar that is quite beautiful. It serves tapas and raciónes such as plates of anchovies in vinegar, wild mushrooms sautéed in butter, or paper-thin slices of air-dried venison. As a general rule, skip the fried food and concentrate on dishes that are either steamed or roasted.

Calle Hombre de Palo, 13. ℰ **92-521-01-46.** Restaurant main dishes 12€–20€, beer hall tapas and raciónes 6€–19€. Daily noon–4pm and 8–11pm. Bus: 2.

Exploring Toledo

Catedral de Toledo ★★★ CATHEDRAL Filled with treasures of religious art and freighted with history as the first cathedral to reclaim central Spain for Christianity, this cathedral remains the ecclesiastical seat of the Roman Catholic Church in Spain, long after the political capital moved to Madrid. Set at the center of the hilltop old city, this structure is one of just three High Gothic cathedrals in Spain and is considered by some critics as the finest example. Construction began in 1226 and was more or less finished in 1463. Keeping with Spanish tradition, the cathedral was built on the site of Toledo's chief mosque, which was in turn built on the foundations of a Visigothic cathedral. The Gothic bones are sometimes hard to see for all the ornate Baroque decoration. Oddly enough, you can't enter from any of the logical doorways that open onto broad plazas. The main entrance is off Calle Hombre del Palo (look for the clock tower), and ensures that you pass through the well-stocked cathedral store.

From an art historical point of view, the church is rather like a great old-fashioned antique store stuffed with treasures, each remarkable by itself but only tangentially related to its neighbor. So rather than looking for a harmonious assemblage, concentrate on specific beautiful pieces. The heavily gilded main altar, for example, shows the influence that Moorish damascene decoration would ultimately exert on over-the-top Spanish Baroque. The backs of the lower tier of the seats in the choir, carved by

Rodrigo Alemán in 1495, depict the conquest of Granada just a few years earlier. His extraordinary carving of the seat arms in images of knights deep in prayer or thought (some of them hooded like Death himself) may be the most moving statues in a cathedral filled with statuary. VIP tombs—kings Alfonso VII, Sancho II, and Sancho III, as well as Cardinal Mendoza; among others—fill the outer walls.

Fans of Baroque carving are especially enamored of the *transparente*—a wall of marble and alabaster sculpture long overlooked because the cathedral was so poorly lit. The sculptor who created it, Narciso Tomé, cut a hole in the ceiling so a shaft of light would illuminate the translucent stonework. The window has been restored, throwing highlights on a group of angels, a "Last Supper" rendered in alabaster, and a Virgin ascending into heaven. The side chapels contain some of the cathedral's greatest artistic treasures in rooms small enough to get close to the work and study it.

For an extra fee, you can visit the cathedral museums. The Sacristy contains the modest-sized El Greco portraits of each of the 12 apostles, as well as his 1577–79 masterwork, "El Espolio" ("The Disrobing of Christ"). The Treasure Room, as the name suggests, is crammed with precious metals and jewels. The main attraction here is the 500-pound gilded monstrance paraded through the streets on the Feast of Corpus Christi. Note that after years of tourists disobeying the "no flash" rule, the cathedral now bans all photography, filming, and use of cell phones.

Calle Cardenal Cisneros, 1. ℂ **92-522-22-41.** www.catedralprimada.es. Free admission to cathedral; admission to Sacristy and Treasure Room 11€. Mon–Sat 10am–6pm; Sun 2–6pm. Special hours during feast days. Bus: 2.

Hospital de San Juan Bautista ★ ART MUSEUM Cardinal Juan Pardo de Tavera, the 16th-century Toledo archbishop who was a close confident of Emperor Carlos V, was not one to hide his light beneath a bushel. He had this elegant Renaissance palace with beautiful arcaded twin courtyards built in far more grandiose a style than necessary to serve as a hospital for the indigent—but maybe just grandiose enough to serve as a pantheon recalling the greatness of its patron. The building represents the finest mature work of local architect Alonso de Covarrubias, who also designed the Hospital de Santa Cruz, now the Museo de Santa Cruz (below). Cardinal Tavera's mausoleum, designed by Alonso Berruguete, is within the adjacent church, but the hospital now houses the striking Fundación Medinaceli collections of Spanish paintings from the 15th through 18th centuries. Among them are five works by El Greco, including a portrait of Tavera and versions of "The Holy Family" and "The Baptism of Christ." The building itself is clearly visible in an unfinished state in El Greco's "View and Plan of Toledo" in the Museo del Greco (see below). A portrait of Carlos V by Titian dominates the banquet hall.

Calle Cardenal Tavera, 2. ℂ **92-522-04-51.** www.fundacionmedinaceli.org. Admission 4.50€. Mon–Sat 10am–1:30pm and 3–6:30pm; Sun 10am–2:30pm. Closed Dec 25 and Jan 1. Bus: 2.

Iglesia de Santo Tomé ★ CHURCH This modest little 14th-century chapel, situated on a narrow street in the old Jewish Quarter, holds two treasures: a de Graaf pipe organ that makes it a choice venue for organ concerts and El Greco's masterpiece **"The Burial of the Count of Orgaz"** ★★★, created in 1586. The painting is no longer displayed inside the church; it is mounted in a separate entranceway to accommodate both visitors to the painting and the congregants who use the church for worship. Bus groups often descend on the El Greco painting en masse. To avoid big crowds, go when the chapel first opens.

Plaza del Conde, 4. ℂ **92-525-60-98.** www.santotome.org. Admission 2.30€. Daily 10am–6:45pm (closes at 5:45pm in winter). Closed Dec 25 and Jan 1. Bus: 2.

Mariano Zamoraño Fábrica de Espadas y Armas Blancas ★ SHOP Medieval Toledo craftsmen rediscovered the ancient techniques for making weapons of hardened steel, making a sword of "Toledo steel" the gold standard for a crusading knight going to do battle in the Holy Land. The ubiquitous modern souvenir swords are a waste of money, but connoisseurs of fine blades can still find a handful of swordmakers practicing the venerable profession. Mariano Zamorano's family started making swords in Toledo in the late 19th century, and he continues hammering and honing fine steel just a few blocks from the cathedral. Visit the workshop in the winter and you can see the artisans heating steel bars red-hot on a bed of charcoal, then stretching and shaping the steel into the final blades. During the rest of the year, the swordmakers attend to less heat-intensive tasks, such as creating foils and tangs, sharpening blades, or painstakingly polishing the high-nickel steel into a mirror finish. (Unlike souvenir swords, Zamaraño's blades are not plated with chrome.) The shop produces everything from fencing rapiers to sabers and cutlasses to ceremonial presentation swords. They also make some kitchen cutlery. Every authentic piece bears the stylized MZ mark.

Calle Ciudad, 19. ✆ **92-522-26-34.** www.marianozamorano.com. Mon–Sat 10am–2pm and 4–6pm.

Monasterio de San Juan de los Reyes ★★ MONASTERY There are no El Grecos in this early Renaissance monastery, but the cloisters work their own kind of magic. Fernando and Isabel had the convent built to mark their 1476 victory over the Portuguese and originally intended to be buried here—until the symbolic importance of being buried in Granada trumped that plan. It is the epitome of a Franciscan retreat—the cloister's junglelike central garden is filled with birdsong, and the high-vaulted Renaissance arches flood the arcades with reflected light. The convent was not finished until 1504, when it was dedicated to St. John the Evangelist and turned over to the Franciscans. Heavily damaged during Napoleon's invasion, it stood vacant until the late 19th century, when restoration began. In 1954, the state returned the property to the Franciscans and it has been a working friary every since. Located at the western edge of the old city, midway between the San Martín bridge and the Cambrón gate, it's worth seeking out for the serenity of the courtyard and for the exquisitely graceful stone carvings on the columns of the lower cloister.

Calle Reyes Católicos, 17. ✆ **92-522-38-02.** www.sanjuandelosreyes.org. Admission 2.30€ adults; 1.80€ seniors; free for children 4 and under. Daily 10am–6:30pm (closes 5:30pm in winter). Bus: 2.

Museo Convento de Santo Domingo el Antiguo ★★ CHURCH This monastery church is not the grandest religious site in town, nor does it have the most famed art works. But it does have the distinction of having lured El Greco to Toledo in 1577 with a commission for nine paintings. The rest, as they say, is history. Be sure to see El Greco's "Assumption" over the altar. It's one of the works that made observers sit up and take notice of his talent. The painter and the city proved a good match and he spent the rest of his life in Toledo, marrying and raising a family. He is buried in the crypt beneath the church. Take the museum tour and you will be able to gaze through the ultimately unsatisfying peephole in the floor at what is purported to be the underground tomb. The museum also contains many other works of art, including some interesting carved wooden statues and painted retablos, but El Greco is the main reason to visit.

Plaza Santo Domingo El Antiguo, s/n. ✆ **92-522-29-30.** Museum admission 4€. Mon–Sat 11am–1:30pm; daily 4–7pm.

Museo del Ejército ★★ MUSEUM   As you might imagine for a city that has changed hands many times over the centuries, the Alcázar, or main fortress of Toledo, was rebuilt constantly over the centuries every time the city fell. The fortress last endured battle in the early months of the Spanish Civil War, when a 70-day siege and bombardment nearly destroyed it. It took more than 70 years of engineering and archaeology to completely reconstruct the historic building and add a modern extension. Given the building's symbolism during the Civil War, it also took some deft political maneuvering to open the Alcázar as Spain's military museum, the **Museo del Ejército.** The modern portion is devoted to changing exhibits, while the old walls contain some striking collections of Spanish military history, including what is claimed to be the personal sword of El Cid. The Spanish armor collection is second only to that at the armory in Madrid's **Palacio Real** (p. 98), and there are some real curiosities, including objects carried by conquistadors Francisco Pizarro and Hernán Cortés, a piece of the cross that Columbus took ashore to claim the New World in the name of Spain, and a tent that sheltered Carlos V in his Tunisian campaign against the Ottoman Empire. Perhaps most stirring, though, are the exhibits on the Siege of the Alcázar, which was ended when Francisco Franco arrived from Morocco with his Army of Africa. It ensured Franco's ascendancy among the Nationalist generals.

Cuesta de Carlos V, 2, near the Plaza de Zocodover. ℭ **92-523-88-00.** www.ejercity.mde.es. Admission 5€ adults; 2.50€ seniors and students; free for children 18 and under. Thurs–Tues 11am–5pm. Closed Jan 1 and 6; May 1, 9, 24, and 25; and Dec 31. Bus: 2.

Museo del Greco ★ ART MUSEUM   With Spain's art world celebrating 2014 as the fourth centenary of El Greco's death, this fine little museum adjacent to the old synagogue is finally coming into its own. It opened in 2011 as a remake of the shabby (and frankly inauthentic) "El Greco House." It contains a series of period gardens, Mudéjar-style cave rooms, and a number of the painter's later works. While the main exhibitions in 2014 are taking place at the **Museo del Prado** in Madrid (p. 86) and the Museo de Santa Cruz (below), attendance is expected to soar at the Museo del Greco. The museum claims to be the only one in Spain devoted exclusively to El Greco and does an admirable job of tracing the artist's impact on his adopted city—and vice versa. Among the most notable pieces in the collection are a set of portraits of the apostles, the retablo of San Bernardino, and one version of the celebrated "View and Plan of Toledo." But the museum has wisely collected work by other Mannerist and Baroque painters that serve to place El Greco in a broader artistic and historic context.

Paseo del Tránsito, s/n. ℭ **92-522-36-65.** http://museodelgreco.mcu.es. Admission 3€ adults; 1.50€ students; free for seniors and children 17 and under; free for all Sun and Sat after 4pm. Apr–Sept Tues–Sat 9:30am–8:30pm, Sun 10am–3pm; Oct–Mar Tues–Sat 9:30am–6:30pm, Sun 10am–3pm.

Museo de Santa Cruz ★★★ ART MUSEUM   If you want to get close to masterpieces by El Greco, make this museum your first stop. The museum has been the repository for dozens, perhaps hundreds, of 16th- and 17th-century paintings that once decorated Toledo churches and convents. About a dozen of them are by El Greco, and the greatest of the lot is "La Asunción de la Virgen" ("Assumption of the Virgin"), painted 1607–13. If you stand about 18 inches from this late masterpiece, you can see how the paint flows like tiny rivers. You don't have to be religious—or even an art fan—to appreciate the electric excitement in this progenitor of "action painting."

TOLEDO AS el greco SAW IT

While wandering through the heart of Toledo is a delight, it's almost as memorable to view Toledo from afar. In many respects, it still looks as it did when El Greco painted it. For the best perspective, you will need a car. Take the **Carretera de Circunvalación,** the road that runs 3km (1¾ miles) on the far bank of the Tagus. This road makes a circular loop of the river from the Alcántara to the San Martín Bridge. Clinging to the hillsides are farmsteads (cigarrales) with rustic dwellings and extensive olive groves. The cigarrales of the Imperial City were immortalized by Tirso de Molina, the 17th-century dramatist, in his trilogy **"Los Cigarrales de Toledo."**

This massive former hospital, an early architectural design by Alonso de Covarrubias, features elaborate carved and painted coffered ceilings—some in the Mudéjar style influenced by Muslim decorative arts, some in a pure Renaissance fashion. It was commissioned by Cardinal Mendoza, whom some historians credit as the mastermind behind the political machinations of Fernando and Isabel. The museum is divided into three sections, with the ground level devoted to archaeological fragments from Roman, Visigoth, and Muslim periods in Toledo. Another portion of the museum is devoted to examples of popular culture and traditional local crafts, including ceramics, glass, and jewelry. The Carranza collection of ceramics of the Iberian peninsula is a thorough but not overwhelming survey of colorful Spanish and Portuguese tile work from the reconquest of Valencia in 1238 through the 19th century.

The fine art galleries—which include the El Greco works—are the principal reason for visiting. Recent additions to the collection include works by Toldeo-born avant garde sculptor Alberto Sanchez (1895-1962).

Calle Miguel de Cervantes, 3. © **92-522-10-36.** www.toledo-turismo.com/es/santa-cruz_70. Free admission. Mon–Sat 10am–6:30pm; Sun 10am–2pm. Bus: 5 or 6. Pass beneath the granite archway on the eastern edge of Plaza de Zocodover and walk about 1 block.

Museo Sefardí (Sephardic Museum) ★★★ MUSEUM/SYNAGOGUE It only took 500 years after the expulsion of the Jews from Spain for this museum to open, in an attempt to explain Judaism and Jewish history to a city where the Jewish population was essential to the functioning of the court and the country for centuries. Since 1992, it has blossomed into one of the most visited spots in Toledo. The most important section is the **Sinagoga del Tránsito,** built in 1355 by Samuel Leví with a special dispensation from Pedro I. Leví had significant influence with the king, having served Pedro as royal treasurer, among other roles. It was the only Toledo synagogue untouched in the 1391 attacks on the city's Jewish ghetto. The building was Christianized after 1492, so only some of the scrollwork on the walls is original. Restorations in 1910 and again in 1992 filled in most of the blanks in the original scripts, which include psalms inscribed along the tops of the walls and a poetic description of the Temple on the east wall. Museum display cases chronicle the Jewish communities on the Iberian peninsula from the Roman era to 1492. One gallery deals with slow changes in 19th-century Spanish law, from the 1802 edict that allowed Jewish religious observances to the 1869 formal retraction of Fernando and Isabel's expulsion order. A new quarterly lecture series discusses the contributions of minority groups often overlooked in traditional historic accounts. The museum fits nicely with the Museo del Greco next door and San Juan de los Reyes across the street to make a full morning.

Calle Samuel Leví, s/n. ☏ **92-522-36-65.** http://museosefardi.mcu.es. Admission 3€ adults; 1.50€ students; free for seniors and children 17 and under; free for all Sun and daily after 2pm. Tues–Sat 9:30am–8:30pm (closes 6:30pm in winter); Sun 10am–3pm. Closed Jan 1, May 1, June 7, Dec 24–25, and Dec 31. Bus: 2.

Museo Victorio Macho ★ ART MUSEUM   One of Spain's finest modern sculptors, Macho fled the country at the outbreak of the Civil War and made his name in Latin America. When the Franco regime began courting expatriate artists, he moved back to Toledo in 1953 to build a home and studio on a dramatic rock outcrop over the Tagus River, just 150 meters from the Sinagoga del Tránsito. Following his death in 1966, the beautiful site was donated to the city as a museum. Displays include several of Macho's smaller bronzes, some bronze reliefs, and many, many drawings and sketches. The city often uses the site for small art conferences. Visit for the serene gardens and fabulous view of the river below the city walls.

Plaza Victorio Macho, 2. ☏ **92-528-42-25.** Admission 3€. Mon–Sat 10am–7pm; Sun 10am–3pm. Bus: 2.

Santo Tomé Obrador de Mazapán ★ SHOP   The nuns of Toledo began making the sugar and ground-almond confection known elsewhere as marzipan (but called *mazapán* here) in the early 13th century to preserve eggs as emergency rations. The tradition still flourishes, but the nuns face stiff competition from small commercial operations. Some of the best *mazapán* pastries in the city come from this company, founded in 1856. Its principal shop remains in the original location near the Santo Tomé church. Unlike the convents, which sell their pastries in prepackaged boxes, Santo Tomé allows you to assemble your own assortment from the display cases—or just buy one piece for a quick shot of sugar (1.50€–5€). The Plaza de Zocodover location is known for extravagant mazapán sculptures in the main display window.

Calle Santo Tomé, 3; ☏ **92-522-37-63.** Plaza de Zocodover, 7. ☏ **92-522-11-68.** www.mazapan.com.

Sinagoga de Santa María la Blanca ★ SYNAGOGUE   This small synagogue is believed to be the oldest European synagogue still standing. It was built in 1203 in the elegant Almohad style with horseshoe arches and intricately carved moldings. Fortunately, when it was converted to a Christian church, five naves and much of the elaborate decoration were preserved. The decorative style modestly echoes La Mezquita in Córdoba, the grandest of the Iberian mosques. The Roman Catholic Church maintains the building as an ecumenical museum. The structure is very minimal, with little decoration. Visitors are split on whether it seems barren or more spiritual than the later, far more elaborate Sinagoga del Tránsito a few blocks away.

Calle Reyes Católicos, 4. ☏ **92-522-72-57.** Admission 2.30€. Daily 10am–6:45pm (closes 5:45pm in winter). Bus: 2 or 12.

CUENCA ★★★

Poised between earth and sky, this small mountaintop city is as improbable as it is beguiling. Moorish soldiers constructed it in 714 on a high limestone spur with a 15-story drop down gorges of the Júcar and Huécar rivers, which converge here. They assumed that their fortification could command every strategic pass between the mountains and the plains of La Mancha. They were right—until Alfonso VIII of Castilla came marching up the hill in 1177. Only a crumbling wall and the Arco de Bezudo

Cuenca

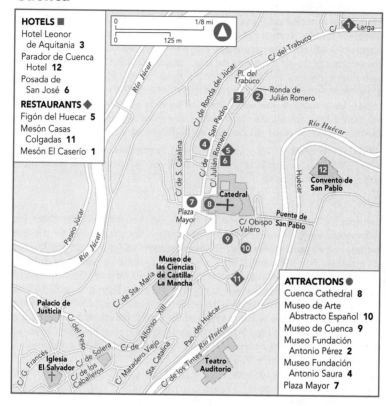

HOTELS ■
Hotel Leonor
   de Aquitania **3**
Parador de Cuenca
   Hotel **12**
Posada de
   San José **6**

RESTAURANTS ◆
Figón del Huecar **5**
Mesón Casas
   Colgadas **11**
Mesón El Caserío **1**

0 _____ 1/8 mi
0 _____ 125 m

C/ Larga
C/ del Trabuco
Pl. del Trabuco
Ronda de Julián Romero
Río Huécar
C/ de Ronda del Júcar
C/ de San Pedro
C/ de S. Catalina
C/ de Julián Romero
Río Júcar
Huécar
12 Convento de San Pablo
Catedral
Paseo Júcar
8
Plaza Mayor
Puente de San Pablo
C/ Obispo Valero
Museo de las Ciencias de Castilla-La Mancha
C/ de Sta. María
Palacio de Justicia
C/ del Peso
C/ G. Francés
Iglesia El Salvador
C/ de Solera
C/ de los Caballeros
C/ de Alfonso XIII
C/ Matadero Viejo
Sta. Catalina
Pso. del Huécar
Río Huécar
C/ de los Tintes
Teatro Auditorio

ATTRACTIONS ●
Cuenca Cathedral **8**
Museo de Arte
   Abstracto Español **10**
Museo de Cuenca **9**
Museo Fundación
   Antonio Pérez **2**
Museo Fundación
   Antonio Saura **4**
Plaza Mayor **7**

remain from the Muslim fortress, but the Christian conquerors shoe-horned wonderful Gothic and Renaissance palaces into the medieval street plan. Under Christian rule, Cuenca filled with convents and monasteries. It has always been a place where passion and contemplation walk hand in hand, where the life of the mind meets the unlikely realities of geography.

Although the city hemorrhaged population during and after the Spanish Civil War, it never lost its dramatic appearance as a hilltop fantasy of angular vertical buildings built right to the edges of the gorges. (It is known for its dramatic *casas colgadas,* or "hanging houses," that are cantilevered over the gorges.) The Spanish abstract artists of El Grupo Paso (formed in 1957) discovered Cuenca's abstract jumble of angles and peculiar tricks of light and many relocated here for at least part of the year. Like their art, Cuenca is a city that is more about gesture than image, vector than target, and about finding a place where creativity can take root. The legacy of the art scene has meant more art museums per capita than any other place in central Spain. Simultaneously romantic and artistic, Cuenca became a favorite getaway for middle-class Madrileños even before high-speed rail cut the travel time to under an hour.

Essentials

GETTING THERE   Ten high-speed RENFE AVE and ALVIA trains leave Madrid's Atocha railway station daily and arrive about 50 minutes later at Estación AVE Fernando Zóbel in the modern part of town at Cerro de La Estrella. The fare one-way begins at 29.40€. For train information, visit www.renfe.com or call ✆ **90-232-03-20.** The local bus to the old town from the train station costs 1.20€. There are also about eight intercity **buses** from Madrid every day. Buses arrive at Calle Fermín Caballero 20 (www.avanzabus.com for information and schedules; ✆ **96-922-70-87** or 96-922-11-84). A one-way fare costs 12€ to 15€. Cuenca is the junction for several highways and about a dozen lesser roads that connect it to towns within its region. From Madrid, take the N-III to Tarancón, and then take the N-400, which leads directly into Cuenca.

VISITOR INFORMATION   The city **tourist information office,** Calle Alfonso VIII, 2 (http://turismo.cuenca.es; ✆ **96-924-10-51**), is open daily 9am to 8pm. Its city map is a must for exploring.

Where to Stay

Leonor de Aquitania ★   If you are an early riser, you might want to request one of the rooms with a view of the Huécar River gorge so that you can open the windows and take in the magnificent sunrise. This hotel occupies an 18th-century building that sits high enough on a hillside to offer views of both the old town and the jaw-dropping gorge. If you want to take it all in, splurge on the *Hebrea Hermosa* (Beautiful Jewish Maiden) suite with a private terrace. In any case, the rooms feature handsome red tile floors that are cool underfoot, pale walls, traditional wooden furnishings, and colorful fabrics. They are similar in size to those at the nearby Posada de San José—large enough, but not exactly roomy. While you almost expect a prayer book next to the bed at the Posada, at the Leonor each room is equipped with a copy of "Don Quixote" (in Spanish, of course) on the bedside table.

Calle San Pedro, 60. ✆ **96-923-10-00.** www.hotelleonordeaquitania.com. 49 units. 103€–120€ double; 178€–199€ suite. Weekend lodging/dining specials available. Free parking. **Amenities:** Restaurant; bar; babysitting; room service; free Wi-Fi.

Parador de Cuenca ★★   It's hard to imagine a hotel with a more dramatic location than the Parador de Cuenca. It sits on a high rocky outcrop sandwiched between the deep gorge of the Huécar River and sheer, rocky cliffs. Yet this lodging in a 14th-century convent has an air of permanence and is the best choice in town if you seek quiet luxury. You can even get a sense of monastic life in the church and cloister and relax in the cafe in a former chapel. The mid-size rooms feature traditional dark wood furniture and some have views of the *casas colgadas,* right across the gorge in Cuenca's old town. The parador and the old town are connected by a pedestrian bridge over the gorge, making the parador convenient for sightseeing, despite its remove from town. But if you are bothered by open heights, this might not be the best lodging choice.

Subida a San Pablo, s/n. ✆ **96-923-23-20.** www.parador.es. 63 units. 155€–194€ double; 310€–336€ suite. Parking 18€. **Amenities:** Restaurant; bar; exercise room; outdoor pool; room service; sauna; outdoor tennis court; free Wi-Fi.

Posada de San José ★★★   Antonio and Jennifer Cortinas have run this lodging in an 18th-century building since 1983 and we like the fact that they have not succumbed to the common practice of decorating the public areas in modern style. Quite the contrary—the public areas of this former boys choir school maintain a rich, ecclesiastical air, with religious frescoes on the walls and statues of saints standing in corners. The rooms are all different shapes and sizes but feature simple, plain wooden furnishings against white walls and paintings by local artists. It's impossible to imagine them any other way. If you're willing to forgo a private bathroom, you can get a double room very inexpensively, and if you're traveling with kids, a couple of these rooms that share one bath may be a good budget option. If you prefer a private bathroom, try to get one of the rooms overlooking the Huécar gorge. They have great views and enjoy cool night breezes. Should you feel the need for a large unit with separate sitting room, TV, and coffee bar, ask for Room 12 or Room 33 (which also has an outdoor terrace). They are among the most expensive but can accommodate an extra bed.

Calle Julián Romero, 4. ℰ **96-921-13-00.** www.posadasanjose.com. 22 units (18 with private bath). 40€–50€ double without bathroom, 78€–157€ double with bathroom. Bus: 1 or 2. **Amenities:** Restaurant; bar. No Wi-Fi.

Where to Eat

The cuisine of Cuenca reflects its position at the border between the mountains to the east and the plains of La Mancha to the west. Wild game and foraged mushrooms figure prominently, and virtually every eatery offers two Cuenca specialties: *morteruelo* (a pâté of rabbit, partridge, ham, pork liver, pine nuts, clove, and caraway), and *ajoarriero* (a creamy pâté of potato, flaked codfish, oil, and garlic). Both are usually spread on bread or toast as a starter and one serving makes a fine appetizer for two people. Since this is sheep country, lamb appears on most menus. If you're adventurous, try the *zarajos,* or grilled lamb intestines, sometimes translated on the English menu as "lamb tripe." Chewy and richly flavored, they're usually served coiled like a ball of yarn around a grapevine shoot.

Figón del Huécar ★★ CASTILIAN Fans of José Luis Perales must get a big kick out of dining in his former home. But even if you are not familiar with the singer-songwriter and composer, you will enjoy your meal in this venerable home where the décor is as smooth as his voice and as elegant as his guitar. For summer dining, try for a table on the outdoor terrace. Inside, the most sought-after tables are those with views of the Huécar gorge, but we also enjoy dining in the book-lined library. While the kitchen pays homage to tradition (*morteruelo, ajoarriero,* salad with pickled partridge—all available as starters), it brings modern creativity to Cuencan cuisine, with dishes like a creamed squash soup with a hint of cheese and parsley-infused oil, or grilled veal sirloin with a Manchego cheese sauce. The restaurant also offers a very reasonable three-course *menu del día.* The wine bar is a good spot to taste the well-made reds now being produced in the D.O. Cuenca region. Take a hint from the staff, who all wear dark suits and ties, and dress for dinner.

Calle Julián Romero, 6. ℰ **96-920-00-62.** www.figondelhuecar.com. Reservations recommended. Main courses 19€–25€; menu del día 26€. Tues–Sat 12:30–4pm and 7–11pm. Bus: 1 or 2.

Mesón Casas Colgadas ★★ CASTILIAN Practically next door to the abstract art museum, this longtime Cuenca favorite produces elegant renditions of classic Castilian dishes and serves them in a dining room in one of the last surviving medieval "hanging houses." This is a place to linger over both the food and the views of the river gorge and the surrounding hills. Most travelers end up opting for the grand classics of the Castilian table: roast suckling pig or roasted suckling lamb. This isn't pig country, but there is a lot to be said for the lamb. Cuenca is surrounded by herds of sheep, and the extraordinarily tender lamb tastes of the wild rosemary that the ewes browse on the hillsides. Cuenca is so high and dry that blisteringly hot days can turn into very chilly nights. If so, try the robust lamb stew. If you're on a budget, you can enjoy a drink and the view in the street-level tavern.

Calle Canónigos, s/n. ℭ **96-922-35-09.** www.mesoncasascolgadas.com. Reservations recommended. Main courses 17€–25€; fixed-price menus 27€–38€; tasting menu 40€. Wed–Mon 1–4pm; Wed–Sun 9–11pm. Bus: 1 or 2.

Mesón El Caserío ★★★ CASTILIAN   As your nose will tell you as you walk up the hill, this casual restaurant just outside the old Moorish gate specializes in wood-grilled meat and vegetables. You can sit indoors at the bar or in the dining room, but you might be alone, as almost everyone gravitates to the casual tables outside. If you have to wait for a table, get a drink at the bar and carry it across the street to the scenic overlook to enjoy great views of the city. None of the savory, smoky meat will put much of a dent in your budget. Beef sirloin steak or a plate of four lamb chops is about as expensive as it gets (under 17€), and big plates of grilled asparagus that have been drizzled in olive oil are less than half that. *Zarajos* are a popular bar snack here, usually heavily dosed with black pepper and accompanied by a glass of cold beer.

Calle Larga, 25. ℭ **96-923-00-21.** Wed–Mon noon–4:30pm and 8:30pm–2am. Main courses 7€–17€. Bus: 1 or 2.

Posada de San José ★★ CASTILIAN   There's a strong local flavor to the menu at this inn dining room, and many diners start with a small plate of *zarajos* or share a bowl of *morteruelo*. If you've grown tired of organ meats and wild game, order the pork tenderloin braised with apples in cider. The most desirable tables are outside on the terrace surrounded by rose bushes and an olive tree. But the view of the Huécar gorge is just as impressive from the windows of the semi-formal dining room. Like the rest of the property (see above), the restaurant strikes a fine balance between simple, heavy, monastic furniture and outstanding abstract graphic art by contemporary Spanish masters. The restaurant is open to the general public, not just guests of the inn, and tables fill far in advance on the weekends, so reserve early.

Calle Julián Romero, 4. ℭ **96-921-13-00.** www.posadasanjose.com. Reservations required. Tues–Sun 7:30–10:30pm. Main courses 12€–17€. Bus: 1 or 2.

Exploring Cuenca

The new city that puddles at the base of Cuenca is of limited interest, except for its bus and train stations. Plan to spend your entire time in the old town, a vertical fantasy where medieval foundations have accreted Gothic, Romanesque, and Renaissance upper stories. The sharp angles and exposure to the high-altitude sun give the physical city the look of a cubist puzzle. In fact, spending time in Cuenca feels very much like inhabiting an abstract modern painting. The streets (often cobbled, and always lined with grooves for the rainfall runoff) are narrow and steep, and even athletic visitors may find themselves flagging as they hike around. Persist and pace yourself; Cuenca is worth the effort.

Plaza Mayor ★★ LANDMARK   This square is the social center of the old city. It is flanked by the *Ayuntamiento* (City Hall) on one side and the cathedral on the other. Only local traffic is permitted in the plaza during most of the day, making it safer for walking around. Cafes spill out into the plaza at mealtimes. **Calle Alfonso VIII** heads downhill from the plaza. Painters and photographers love the faded pastel colors of the houses, many of which have medieval crests above their ancient doors. Be sure to walk (or take the bus for 0.20€) to the top of the hill by the **Arco de Bezudo** for almost unbelievably long vistas. Different but just as dramatic views can be found at the **Mirador de San Miguel,** northwest of Plaza Mayor. It overlooks the Júcar gorge and its green hillsides. Deep gorges give Cuenca an unreal quality, and eight old bridges span two rivers at the bottom to connect the medieval city with the booming new town. Assuming that you're not prone to vertigo, take the leap of faith into thin air and walk across the **Puente de San Pablo ★,** a footbridge between the old city and the parador that crosses a 60m (197-ft.) drop. It gives a great perspective on the *casas colgadas* ★, which are illuminated at night. In the summer, the intense heat of the day suddenly dissipates at night and the streets of Cuenca become so cool that you may want a jacket or sweater. At dusk and dawn, thousands of swallows swoop and dart in the high air of the gorges.

Catedral de Cuenca ★★ CATHEDRAL   As soon as Alfonso VIII conquered Cuenca, he commissioned this Anglo-Norman cathedral to please his homesick wife, Eleanor Plantagenet (daughter of England's Henry II and Eleanor of Aquitaine). The masons he brought from Normandy constructed it in the same style as the cathedral at Chartres, which was built at precisely the same time. Major renovations during the Renaissance have obscured the original mystical purity of form, and reconstruction after a partial collapse in the 20th century has required further alterations. But the original soaring alabaster columns are still standing, and there's not another Gothic church like it in Spain. Artistic highlights include the neoclassical altar by Ventura Rodriguez (architect of the Prado), stunning Flemish tapestries, a Gothic statue of Virgen del Sagrario that dates from around the cathedral's founding, and a number of powerful religious paintings (including a pair of El Grecos). Many of the stained-glass windows, which date from the 1990s, were designed by Cuenca's resident abstract artists. The multilingual audio guide provides a blow-by-blow account of 37 paintings and sculptures; fortunately, it has a fast-forward button so you can move on to the next point of interest.

Plaza Mayor de Pío XII. ℰ **96-922-46-26.** Free admission during Mass; other times 2.80€ adults, 2€ students and seniors. Paid admission includes audio guide and admission to museum. July–Sept Mon–Fri 10am–2pm and 4–7pm, Sat 10am–7pm, Sun 10am–6:30pm; Oct–Apr daily 10:30am–2pm and 4–7pm; May–June Mon–Sat 10:30am–2pm and 4–7pm, Sun 10:30am–2pm and 5–6:30pm. Bus: 1 or 2.

Fundación Antonio Pérez ★★ ART MUSEUM   Spanish-born Antonio Pérez (b. 1934) has divided much of his life between Cuenca and Paris, but, fortunately, chose Cuenca as the site of his foundation. He is usually described as a collector, editor, and artist, and we also suspect that he has a profound sense of humor. His own art works fall into the category of found art and often employ common objects to make funny and surprising commentary. For example, he titled three bells without their clappers "Castrati." Large, airy galleries carved out of a former convent of the Barefoot Carmelites display Peréz's work as well as highlights of his collection of Spanish artists (many of whom are also featured in the Saura foundation and the abstract art museum, both below) and international artists including Andy Warhol. Not surprisingly, Pérez is a big fan of pop art. Two even more extensive collections—one of found objects, the other of graphic art—belong to the Fundación Antonio Pérez but are displayed in a Renaissance palace in the town of San Clemente, 109km (68 miles) south of Cuenca. Objects from each sometimes show up in Cuenca in temporary exhibitions.

Ronda de Julian Romero, 20. ℰ **96-923-06-19.** www.dipucuenca.es/fap/fundacion.asp. Free admission. Wed–Mon 11am–2pm and 5–9pm (winter closes 8pm). Bus: 1 or 2.

Fundación Antonio Saura ★★ ART MUSEUM   Of all the artists inspired by the improbable beauty of Cuenca, Antonio Saura (1930–98) had the most personal connection to the city. He had tuberculosis as a teenager and began coming to Cuenca for his health at age 18. He became fascinated by the view from his sickbed window and it became seminal in his artistic vocabulary. This foundation was established 10 years after the death of this master Abstract Expressionist painter. It displays his own work as well as that of his contemporaries, including other members of El Grupo Paso, which Saura helped found. In a late interview, Saura noted that all his life, without realizing it, he had been painting "the hypnotic mask between the rocks—the blackberry eyes. The curve of the mountain looks like the mound where the head of Goya's dog emerges."

Plaza de San Nicolas, 4. ✆ **96-923-60-54.** www.fundacionantoniosaura.es. Free admission. Summer Mon and Wed–Sat 11am–2pm and 4–8pm, Sun 11am–2pm; winter daily 11am–2pm and 4–7pm. Bus: 1 or 2.

Museo de Arte Abstracto Español ★★★ ART MUSEUM   You are in for a double treat here. Cuenca's first contemporary art museum, opened in 1966, occupies the largest of the casas colgadas and offers a first-hand look inside one of these late Gothic engineering marvels. As if that weren't enough, it also has a vivacious collection of mid-20th-century Spanish abstract art. It's hard to know where to look first—at the details of the building, out the windows to the stomach-lurching gorge, or at the aggressive art on the walls. Studying the art that Cuenca has embraced does, in fact, demonstrate how to look beyond the picturesque to the play of angle and color. Although the museum's art represents an era of pure abstraction, it also echoes the city. Dense, knotlike black snarls on the canvases of Antonio Saura, for example, could be maps of the city's tangled alleyways. The segmented color blocks of José Guerrero resemble the painted walls of the old houses. The thrusting gestures of Fernando Zóbel (founder of the museum) mimic the verticality of the Cuenca streets. The works span a broad period in the output of the artists; while Saura's late work was purely abstract, he went through a much earlier semi-representational surrealist phase represented by a grotesque portrait of Brigitte Bardot that makes the French actress look like an escapee from Picasso's "Guernica."

Calle los Canónigos, s/n. ✆ **96-921-29-83.** www.march.es. Admission 3€ adults; 1.50€ students and seniors. Tues–Sat 11am–2pm; Sun 11am–2:30pm; Tues–Fri 4–6pm; Sat 4–8pm. Bus: 1 or 2.

Museo de Cuenca ★ MUSEUM   A stark contrast to all the contemporary art museums in the city, this regional history museum takes a broad view, harking back to the Neolithic period with Celtic idols excavated from burials in the region. Most exhibit rooms are below street level and they feel like a cave of many chambers. The Cuenca area was an important mining district for lead and silver, and Iron Age exhibits show a number of Carthaginian, Greek, and Phoenician artifacts that found their way to Cuenca through a vigorous trade with the Mediterranean coast. The Romans made peace with the local leaders because the mines were so important to the empire, ushering in a long period of Roman life under Ibero-Celt leadership. Ceramics in the North African style help detail the period of Moorish dominance. Rooms devoted to the medieval period and the 14th through 16th centuries show how Cuenca emerged as a major wine and wool center.

Calle Obispo Valero, 12. ✆ **96-921-30-69.** 1.20€ adults, 0.60€ students, free Sat–Sun. Jun 15–Sept 15 Tues–Sat 10am–2pm and 5–7pm, Sun 11am–2pm; rest of year opens afternoons at 4pm.

SEGOVIA ★★★

Poor Segovia! Because the city's Roman aqueduct appears on every checklist of Spanish monuments, the city often suffers from drive-by tourism. It's easy to park near the aqueduct, take a picture, maybe stop for lunch, and then move on. But Segovia is more than just a pretty face. Outside the perimeter of its old walls lie important religious communities and a mystical shrine of the Knights Templar. In the city proper, Segovia displays a monumental drama from the arches of its Roman aqueduct on one end to the fantasy castle of its Alcázar on the other. The city is built on a large rocky outcrop, resulting in narrow, winding streets that have to be covered on foot to visit the Romanesque churches, early Renaissance palaces, and medieval Judería. This ancient city is located at the heart of the castle-rich part of Castilla. Isabel herself was proclaimed queen of Castilla here in 1474.

Essentials

GETTING THERE   Seventeen **trains** leave Madrid every day. Five take over 2 hours to reach Segovia, but the high-speed trains arrive in 26-29 minutes. The five slow commuter trains leave from Chamartín station; a one-way fare is 7.50€. The high-speed trains leave from Atocha station and cost 12.50€ (for the AVANT) to 24.10€ (for the AVE or the ALVIA). The traditional rail station at Segovia is on Paseo Obispo Quesada s/n (www.renfe.com; ✆ **90-232-03-20**). It's a 20-minute walk southeast of the town center but you can take bus no. 3 (1€), departing every quarter-hour for the Plaza Mayor. The high-speed train arrives at Segovia-Guiomar, 4km (2½ miles) from downtown but served every 15 minutes by bus no. 11 (1€) to the aqueduct.

   Buses arrive and depart from **Estacionamiento Municipal de Autobuses,** Paseo de Ezequiel González 10 (✆ **92-142-77-06**), near the corner of Avenida Fernández Ladreda and the steeply sloping Paseo Conde de Sepúlveda. It's about a 7-minute walk to the aqueduct. There are 20 to 35 buses a day to and from Madrid (which depart from Paseo de la Florida, 11; Metro: Norte), and about four a day traveling between Ávila and Segovia. One-way tickets from Madrid cost 8€.

   If you're driving, take the N-VI (on some maps it's known as the A-6), in the direction of A Coruña, northwest from Madrid, toward León and Lugo. At the junction with Rte. 110 (signposted SEGOVIA), turn northeast (AP-61 or N-603).

VISITOR INFORMATION   The **Visitor Reception Center,** Plaza del Azoguejo, 1 (www.segoviaturismo.es; ✆ **92-146-67-20**), is open daily 10am to 8pm and offers a free city map and sightseeing advice. It's a good place to start if you arrive at the Roman aqueduct. Follow calle Juan Bravo toward Plaza Mayor where you'll find the **Tourist Information of Castilla y León,** Plaza Mayor, 10 (www.turismocastillayleon.com; ✆ **92-146-03-34**), which is open daily from 9am to 3pm and from 5 to 7pm. This regional office's city map is easier to use. If you're going to visit Ávila, ask for that city's map as well.

Where to Stay

Hostería Ayala Berganza ★★★   Whether you select a room in the 15th-century former noble home or in the modern addition, you will find a feeling of ease and retreat from the modern city. This lodging does lie outside Segovia's ramparts, but it is within easy walking distance to the aqueduct and the center of town. Décor varies from room to room, but all share the same approach of incorporating lovely fabrics and nice details, such as mini-canopies on the beds or handsome carved headboards. For a romantic stay, book the suite that occupies the building's tower and has its own balcony.

Calle Carretas, 5. ✆ **92-146-04-48.** www.hosteriaayalaberganza.com. 17 units. 65€–175€ double; 165€–255€ suite. Parking 10€. **Amenities:** Restaurant; bar; free Wi-Fi.

Hostería Natura ★★   The owners of this 17th-century palace, just steps from Plaza Mayor, kept the historic exterior intact but took colorful, creative liberties with the interior. The cheerful stylishness almost makes you forget that there's no elevator. Bargain priced rooms 101, 102, and 112 are unusually large quarters furnished with two twin beds, but their airshaft windows don't open. Romantic room 103 has a high, carved-wood four-poster bed, a little private balcony, and walls sponged a deep red. Equally romantic room 114 has a salmon-tinged canopy on the wrought-iron four-poster bed. Room 111 can easily sleep up to five, making it a good bet for families. Parents get a private bath and bedroom suite with a queen-size bed and a balcony overlooking the park next door. It's connected to a narrow interior room with three twin beds lined up along the wall and a separate bath for the kids.

Calle Colón, 5 and 7. ✆ **92-146-67-10.** www.naturadesegovia.com. 17 units. 40€–90€ double; family room 90€–105€. No parking. **Amenities:** Free Wi-Fi.

Hotel Sercotel Infanta Isabel ★   If you like being in the thick of things, this hotel is a good option. It sits on Plaza Mayor right across from the cathedral and some rooms have balconies overlooking the square. The Infanta Isabel (1851–1931), the great-great aunt of King Juan Carlos, used to make a stopover here as she traveled to the summer palace in La Granja. She would probably still recognize the grand staircase of the otherwise updated property and would probably appreciate the combination of luxurious traditional style and modern amenities. Six triple rooms are good for families.

Plaza Mayor. ✆ **92-146-13-00.** http://hotelinfantaisabel.com. 39 units. 55€–135€ double; 92€–177€ triple; 157€–209€ suite. Parking 15€. **Amenities:** Restaurant; bar; babysitting; room service; free Wi-Fi.

Hotel Palacio San Facundo ★★★   This hotel in a 16th-century former noble palace exudes character. Sensitive renovations have maintained its Renaissance-era grace while creating 33 unique rooms that surround the central courtyard. They all have tub showers, glass-slab sinks on stained-wood bases, and flat-screen TVs. Headboards run either to wrought iron or padded dark brown leather, with soft leather trim on the decorative pillows. On the second floor, both 202 and 204 have small balconies with a view of the plaza out front. Many third-floor rooms have even more character, with exposed pine beams on the slanting ceilings and skylights with remote-controlled shades. One especially popular room is 306, with a large bed and decor in deep aubergine tones. Sizes vary a bit, of course. Whatever room you choose, you will want to spend time in the glassed-over central courtyard with soaring columns and lots of comfortable seating.

Plaza San Facundo, 4. ✆ **92-146-30-61.** www.hotelpalaciosanfacundo.com. 33 units. 100€–120€ double; 200€–250€ jr. suite. Parking 15€. **Amenities:** Bar; room service; free Wi-Fi.

Where to Eat

Segovia is justifiably proud—some would say even possessive—of what it considers the city's great contribution to Spanish cuisine: roast suckling pig. There's even a special certification for the dish, *Marca de Garantía "Cochinillo de Segovia,"* indicating that the restaurant only uses milk-fed local pigs less than 21 days old that have

Segovia

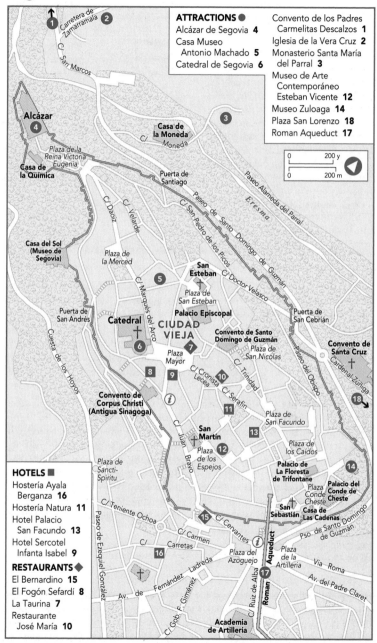

ATTRACTIONS ●
Alcázar de Segovia **4**
Casa Museo
 Antonio Machado **5**
Catedral de Segovia **6**

Convento de los Padres
 Carmelitas Descalzos **1**
Iglesia de la Vera Cruz **2**
Monasterio Santa María
 del Parral **3**
Museo de Arte
 Contemporáneo
 Esteban Vicente **12**
Museo Zuloaga **14**
Plaza San Lorenzo **18**
Roman Aqueduct **17**

0   200 y
0   200 m

Carretera de
Zamarramala

1   **2**

C/ San Marcos

Alcázar
4

Plaza de la
Reina Victoria
Eugenia
Casa de
la Química

Casa de
la Moneda
C/ Moneda

3

Puerta de
Santiago

Paseo Alameda del Parral

Eresma

C/ Daoiz

C/ Velarde

Paseo de Santo Domingo de Guzmán

C/ San Pedro de los Picos

Casa del Sol
(Museo de
Segovia)

Plaza de
la Merced

San
Esteban

C/ Doctor Velasco

5

Plaza de
San Esteban

C/ Marqués del Arco

Palacio Episcopal

Puerta de
San Andrés

Catedral

CIUDAD
VIEJA

6

7

Plaza
Mayor

Convento de Santo
Domingo de Guzmán

Plaza de
San Nicolás

Puerta de
San Cebrián

Convento de
Santa Cruz

Paseo del Obispo

Cardenal Zúñiga

Cuesta de los Hoyos

8

9

C/ Cronista
Lecea

10

C/ Serafín

C/ Trinidad

Convento de
Corpus Christi
(Antigua Sinagoga)

i

11

Plaza de
San Facundo

13

San
Martín

C/ Juan Bravo

12

Plaza
de los
Espejos

Plaza de
los Caídos

Palacio de
La Floresta
de Trifontane

14

Palacio del
Conde de
Cheste

Plaza de
Sancti-
Spíritu

Plaza
Conde
Cheste

San
Sebastián

Casa de
Las Cadenas

Paseo de Ezequiel González

C/ Teniente Ochoa

C/ Carmen

15

C/ Cervantes

i

Pso. de Santo Domingo
de Guzmán

C/

Carretas

16

Plaza del
Azoguejo

17

Plaza
de la
Artillería

Vía Roma

Av. del Padre Claret

C/ Fernández Ladreda

C/ Gob. F. Giménez

Av. de

C/ Ruiz de Alba

Aqueduct

Roman

Academia
de Artillería

HOTELS ■
Hostería Ayala
 Berganza **16**
Hostería Natura **11**
Hotel Palacio
 San Facundo **13**
Hotel Sercotel
 Infanta Isabel **9**
RESTAURANTS ◆
El Bernardino **15**
El Fogón Sefardí **8**
La Taurina **7**
Restaurante
 José María **10**

5

SIDE TRIPS FROM MADRID | Segovia

bargains ON SEGOVIAN ROAST SPECIALTIES

Most restaurants offer roast suckling pig as a huge plate with a lot of accompaniments and roast baby lamb only as a dish for two. But two of our favorite casual dining spots serve these Segovian specialties as *raciones*—entrée size plates with no side dishes. We like **Restaurante la Churrería de San Lorenzo ★** because it's in an atmospheric neighborhood outside the old city. Named for its ancient, almost crumbling church, San Lorenzo is about a 10-minute walk from the aqueduct, and La Churrería is the most popular family restaurant on the plaza. The bar looks as if it was built for a tavern scene in "Man of La Mancha."

Plaza San Lorenzo. ℭ **92-143-79-84.** Roast piglet or lamb 20€. Open daily 8am–4pm and 8pm–midnight.

La Taurina ★, located right on Plaza Mayor, organizes each course of the meal as a stage in a bullfight—no great surprise considering the bullfight-themed tiles on the wall and the profusion of matador memorabilia. Unadorned plates of suckling pig or baby lamb are what most people order, though the full menu that adds some sides, bread, dessert, and wine is only 3€ more. On a nice night, sit outside and enjoy a view of the cathedral with your meal.

Plaza Mayor, 8. ℭ **92-146-09-02.** Roast piglet or lamb 18€–20€. Daily noon–5pm and 8pm–midnight.

been processed and cooked in accordance with a strict set of standards. Restaurants without a special oven will fry the piglet, a dish known as *cochifrito*. As if that were not enough, Segovia is also known for its local lamb, usually offered as *chuletóns de cordero,* or lamb chops, sometimes as *chuletillas de lechal,* or chops from milk-fed lambs. Two common starters on Segovia menus are *sopa castellana*—a soup usually made with a chicken broth base to which chopped ham, bread, sweet paprika, and eggs are added—and *judiones de La Granja,* a dish of white broad beans, chorizo sausage, fresh ham, and onion.

El Bernardino ★ CASTILIAN   Just inside the walls of the old city from the aqueduct, this traditional *asador* (meat roaster) has been keeping the faith with the Segovian roasting tradition since it opened in 1939. As you look around the dining room (or around at other tables on the terrace), you'll see large wooden platters with roast piglets splayed out on top. You'll also notice that the other diners are having a festive time, scraping off big servings of super-tender pork. The restaurant gives the same wood-fired oven treatment to *cordero lechal* (milk-fed baby lamb), lamb quarters from yearlings, and whole chickens. The rest of the menu is almost a catalog of Castilian mountain food, from the chicken-garlic soup to the "floron" (a kind of Segovian cake) served on a puddle of vanilla cream.

Calle Cervantes, 2. ℭ **92-146-24-77.** www.elbernardino.com. Reservations recommended. Main courses 12€–18€. Daily 1–4pm and 8–11pm.

La Fogón Sefardí Restaurante ★★ SPANISH/MIDDLE EASTERN   The most formal of the dining options at the Casa Mudéjar hotel, "the Sephardic cook" takes the unusual step of incorporating a lot of traditional Spanish Jewish dishes into the otherwise Castilian menu. So while one table might be feasting on the ubiquitous suckling pig, the next will be enjoying a sort of strudel of layers of eggplant with curried lamb and tiny baby vegetables. The kitchen also makes some rather modern dishes, including salmon tacos with a basil-cream sauce. Dessert is the classic: *ponche* *segoviano*. It's a cake drenched in syrup with the layers separated by a golden custard. The entire dessert is then encased in marzipan.

Hotel Casa Mudéjar, Calle Judería Vieja, 17. ② **92-146-62-50.** www.lacasamudejar.com. Main courses 7€–19€; menu del día 23€. Daily 1:30–4:30pm and 8:30–11:30pm.

José María Restaurante ★★★ CASTILIAN   Ask any Segoviano where his or her family goes for *cochinillo* and you'll get a big smile and a rambling reverie about the crackling skin and succulent meat served at this culinary landmark. Simply put, in pig-roasting circles, chef-proprietor José María Ruiz is the man. As a result, you'll pay a little more for the privilege of eating in the formal white-tablecloth interior dining room, but if you're going to "pig out," it might as well be on the best. Ruiz also excels at roast suckling lamb *(cordero lechal asado)*. To the (mock) horror of Spanish dining purists used to overcooked green beans and canned artichokes and white asparagus, he also invents entire dishes to highlight seasonal vegetables.

Calle Cronista Lecea, 11. ② **92-146-11-11.** www.rtejosemaria.com. Reservations recommended. Main courses 14€–35€. Daily 1–4pm and 7–11pm.

Exploring Segovia

Segovia is shaped like a wedge of cake plopped on its side. The aqueduct is at the point, while the Alcázar stands atop the thick end above all the frosting. The cathedral and Plaza Mayor are in the middle. You'll find the best shopping in the old city between the Roman aqueduct, the cathedral, and the Alcázar. For local ceramics and souvenirs, cruise **Calle de Juan Bravo, Calle Daoiz,** and **Calle Marqués del Arco.** Thursday is market day on Plaza Mayor.

Alcázar de Segovia ★★ CASTLE   Check out the Alcázar first from below, at the junction of the Clamores and Eresma rivers. It is an impressive, noble vision. It's also terribly misleading. There is a good reason why this fortress looks like a late-19th-century romantic ideal of a medieval castle. Most of it burned in 1862 and it was rebuilt to emulate the storybook castles of 16th-century northern Europe rather than the messy fortress-castle of Spain's warrior monarchs of the 1300s. The reconstruction was carried out during shaky political times to burnish the otherwise tarnished image of the monarchy. In effect, it is a museum of the nobler side of the reconquista.

As you enter (from the city side), the first thing you'll spy are suits of German plate armor for knights and two of their steeds. Spanish monarchs have cultivated this chivalrous image ever since the Habsburgs came to the throne in the 1500s. The castle was a favorite residence of Castilian monarchs throughout the medieval period, and the sumptuous decoration of tapestries, tiles, and Mudéjar woodwork conjures "days of old when knights were bold."

Isabel took refuge in the original fortress in 1474 when word came that her brother Enrique IV had died. A mural in the Galley Chamber tells the rest of that story: Having mustered the support of the royal army, she marched out of the Alcázar to Segovia's Plaza Mayor to be proclaimed queen of Castilla. She also first met Fernando II of Aragón here, but wisely held onto her rights when they married.

The most dramatic room of the castle is the Hall of Monarchs, with its ceiling-level frieze in a style usually reserved for the depictions of saints. Each king or queen in the Castilian line from Pelayo (Pelagius in Latin) of Asturias, credited with starting the reconquista in the 720s, to Juana la Loca, Isabel's mad daughter, is shown seated on a golden Gothic throne. This incredible piece of art and history was commissioned by Juana's grandson, Felipe II, to cement his lineage's claim to the Spanish crown. Felipe married his fourth wife, Anne of Austria, here.

Walk the battlements of this once-impregnable castle, from which its occupants hurled boiling oil onto the enemy below. Ascend the hazardous stairs of the tower, originally built by Isabel's father as a prison, for a panoramic view of Segovia.

Plaza de la Reina Victoria Eugenia. ⓒ **92-146-07-59.** www.alcazardesegovia.com. Admission 4.50€ adults; 3€ children 6–16; free for children 5 and under. Apr–Sept daily 10am–7pm; Oct Sun–Thurs 10am–6pm, Fri–Sat 10am–7pm; Nov–Mar daily 10am–6pm. Bus: 3. Take Calle Vallejo, Calle de Velarde, Calle de Daoiz, or Paseo de Ronda.

Cabildo Catedral de Segovia ★ CATHEDRAL Segovia's original Gothic cathedral was destroyed in 1520 during the short-lived uprising of the Castilian cities against the Habsburg kings. When the smoke cleared and the lords of Segovia were crushed, Carlos V ordered it rebuilt in the same style, making it Spain's last Gothic cathedral. Just to be on the safe side, he also moved it to Plaza Mayor from its old spot next to the Alcázar. Construction began in 1525, and it was finally consecrated in 1768. Even on the brightest days, the interior is gloomy, but it is worth visiting to see the swirling, gold-encrusted altar created by José de Churriguera for the Santisimo Sacramento chapel circa 1700, as well as the stained-glass windows, elaborately carved choir stalls, and 16th- and 17th-century paintings. The **cloisters ★** date from the original cathedral.

Plaza Catedral, Marqués del Arco, s/n. ⓒ **92-146-22-05.** www.obispadodesegovia.es. Admission to cathedral, cloisters, museum, and chapel room 3€ adults; free for children 13 and under; free admission to cathedral Sun 9am–1:15pm. Daily 9:30am–6:30pm (closes 5:30 in winter).

Casa-Museo Antonio Machado ★ MUSEUM The great Spanish poet lived in this boardinghouse from 1919 to 1932, when he taught French in Segovia. The modest structure is more a remembrance—almost a shrine—than a true museum. Documents, drawings, and other mementos try to conjure the poet, but they aren't half as evocative as the little courtyard overgrown with flowering cacti and hollyhocks gone to seed where a canary sings as he flits from perch to perch in his cage.

Calle Desamparados, 5. ⓒ **92-146-03-77.** Admission 1.50€; free Wed. Guided tours Wed–Sun 11am, noon, 1pm, 4:30pm, 5:30pm, and 6:30pm. Closed Mon–Tues.

Convento de los Padres Carmelitas Descalzos ★ MONASTERY The 16th-century mystic and theologian San Juan de la Cruz founded and personally helped build this monastery in 1586. Upon his death in 1591, his body was returned here for burial, where it still rests in the left side chapel of the convent's church. Saint John of the Cross was the confessor of Santa Teresa of Ávila and one of the most significant theologians of the Counter-Reformation. His teachings found new audiences among Roman Catholics in the late 20th century, and clergy in Segovia speak of him as if he was merely away for the weekend. His central axiom was that a person must empty his or her soul of "self" in order to be filled with God—a mystical tenet akin to Zen Buddhism. The monastery's Casa de Espiritualidad (House of Spirituality) offers an extensive program of themed retreats (conducted only in Spanish), for men, women, and couples. It is also possible to simply visit the church and San Juan's grave.

Paseo de Segundo Rincón, 2. ⓒ **92-143-19-61.** www.ocdcastilla.org. Admission by donation. Church daily 10am–1:30pm; Tues–Sun 4–8pm.

Iglesia de la Vera Cruz ★ CHURCH Built in the 12th century by the Knights Templar, this is the most fascinating Romanesque church in Segovia. Essentially a shrine rather than a parish church, it still resonates with the rough faith of the warrior monks who founded it. The 12-sided shape (copied from Jerusalem's Church of the Holy Sepulchre), the style of the niches, and the fragmentary wall murals all had special significance in the mystic beliefs of the crusader order that built the church to house a piece of the True Cross. Consecrated in 1246 (1208 on the Gregorian calendar), the church's very existence illustrates the strong bond between military and religious life in Segovia. The site was abandoned when the Knights Templar were disbanded by Pope Clement V in the early 14th century, but the structure has been partially restored under the care of the Knights of Malta.

Carretera de Zamarramala. © **92-143-14-75.** Admission 2€. Tues–Sun 10:30am–1:30pm and 3:30–7pm (closes 6pm in winter). Closed Nov.

Monasterio Santa María del Parral ★ MONASTERY

The restored "Monastery of the Grape" was established for the Jerónimos by Enrique IV, king of Castilla (1425–74) and half brother to Isabel I. The monastery lies across the Eresma River about a half-mile north of the city and it's worth visiting for the exquisite carvings and paintings in the church, which is a medley of Gothic, Renaissance, and Plateresque styles. The facade was never completed, and the monastery itself was abandoned when religious orders were suppressed in 1835. Today, it's been restored and has been returned to the Jerónimos, Hieronymite priests and brothers. This cloistered order, which emulates the hermit St. Jerome in its rejection of most physical comforts, welcomes men on retreats for up to a week of prayer and reflection while they work to help restore and maintain the property. Write for details. A large facility with extensive gardens, the monastery once housed dozens of monks but only a handful remain. Inside, a robed novitiate will show you the order's treasures, including a polychrome altarpiece and the alabaster tombs of the Marquis of Villena and his wife—all the work of Juan Rodríguez, also known to art history as Juan de Segovia.

Calle del Marqués de Villena (across the Eresma River). © **92-143-12-98.** Free admission. Mon–Sat 10am–12:30pm; Sun 10–11:30am; daily 4–6:30pm. Take Ronda de Santa Lucía, cross the Eresma River, and head down Calle del Marqués de Villena.

Museo de Arte Contemporáneo Esteban Vicente ★ ART MUSEUM

The economic crisis has hit this small museum harder than most, resulting in hours being truncated on short notice and long gaps between exhibitions. Call ahead to make sure it is open, but it is definitely worth a visit. Spanish-born Estéban Vicente (1903–2001) found his artistic niche as a member of the pioneering New York School of Abstract Expressionist artists, but chose to donate a significant body of work to his home country. The collection includes oil paintings, collages, a tapestry, and a number of small sculptures. To house and display the collection, the mid-15th-century palace of Enrique IV of Castilla y Leon (Isabel I's older half-brother) was converted to a white-walled, unadorned, contemporary gallery space. Fortunately, the architects preserved the intricately carved wooden ceiling of the former chapel, now the auditorium. Although Vicente died in New York, his ashes, along with those of his wife, are in a quiet garden, open to museum visitors. The museum tries to further the spirit of artistic inquiry that characterized the first generation of Abstract Expressionism through temporary exhibitions which often focus on video.

Plazuela de las Bellas Artes. © **92-146-20-10.** www.museoestebanvicente.es. Admission 3€ adults, 1.50€ seniors and students, free for children 11 and under; free for all Thurs. Tues–Fri 11am–2pm; Tues–Wed 4–7pm; Thurs–Fri 4–8pm; Sat–Sun 11am–8pm.

Museo Zuloaga ★★ ART MUSEUM

This fascinating little museum occupies the medieval Iglesia San Juan de los Caballeros, where ceramic artist Daniel Zuloaga based his family pottery studio starting in 1908. The firm made many of the scenic tiles that decorate the building facades all over Spain, and museum exhibits elucidate the entire artistic process, with an emphasis on the Zuloaga family's masterful painting. Other exhibits highlight the history of the church. Although the church is largely 14th century, parts of it date from the A.D. 6th century, making it one of the oldest Christian sites in this part of Spain.

Plaza de Colmenares. ℂ **92-146-33-48.** Admission 1.20€ adults, free for seniors and students; free to all Sat–Sun. July–Sept daily 10am–2pm and Tues–Sat 5–8pm; Oct–June daily 10am–2pm and Tues–Sat 4–7pm.

Roman Aqueduct (Acueducto Romano) ★★★ ARCHITECTURE   Roughly 2,100 years ago, Roman engineers constructed this architectural marvel—a 15km (9⅓-mile) conduit to bring water from the Guadarrama mountains to Segovia. The graceful feat of engineering remains as impressive as it was in the age of the Caesars. While much of the original aqueduct was a ground-level canal, the concluding segments arch high over the city and then continue underground all the way to the Alcázar. The entire structure was built of granite blocks without mortar. Following restorations in the 15th and 16th centuries, it continued to supply the city's water into the late 19th century. The highest of the 166 arches is 28m (92 ft.), and seems even higher when you stand under it and look up. Follow the aqueduct uphill and you'll find pleasant residential neighborhoods where the city's feral cats scamper along the much shorter arches. Perhaps the most striking vantage for photographing the aqueduct is from the overlook just off Plaza Avendaño, which places you above the arches. The neighborhood surrounding this half-hidden mirador is the erstwhile noble quarter where wealthy clergy and nobles built many elegant in-town Renaissance palaces.

Plaza del Azoguejo.

ÁVILA ★★

A UNESCO World Heritage site, the ancient city of Ávila draws pilgrims for its physical wonders—most notably the well-preserved 11th-century walls and battlements—and for its spiritual history. It was the home base of dynamic mystic reformer Santa Teresa, co-founder (with San Juan de la Cruz; see p. 136) of the *Carmelitas Descalzos* (Barefoot Carmelites). She was born here in 1515, entered the Carmelites at 19, and began her reform of the order at age 45. Both a prolific writer and a brilliant organizer, Santa Teresa became the practical and political mover of the Spanish Counter-Reformation, while her compatriot San Juan de la Cruz tended to the inner spiritual life of the reform movement. Several sites associated with Santa Teresa remain in Avila, and the pious visit them as a pilgrimage. If you are coming to Ávila to see the walls, make it a daytrip. If you want to delve into the religious history, plan on staying the night.

Essentials

GETTING THERE   More than two dozen **trains** leave daily from Madrid for Ávila, about a 1½- to 2-hour trip each way. Trains depart from Madrid's Chamartín station. Tickets cost from about 9€ to 12€. The Ávila station is at Avenida José Antonio (www.renfe.com; ℂ **90-232-03-20**), 1.6km (1 mile) east of the old city. You'll find taxis lined up in front of Ávila's railway station and at the more central Plaza Santa Teresa. For taxi information, call ℂ **92-035-35-45.**

Buses leave Madrid daily from Estación Sur de Autobuses at Calle Méndez Álvaro. In Ávila, the bus terminal (www.avanzabus.com; ℂ **90-202-00-52**) is at the corner of avenidas Madrid and Portugal, northeast of the center of town. A one-way ticket from Madrid costs 11€.

5 SIDE TRIPS FROM MADRID | Ávila

Ávila

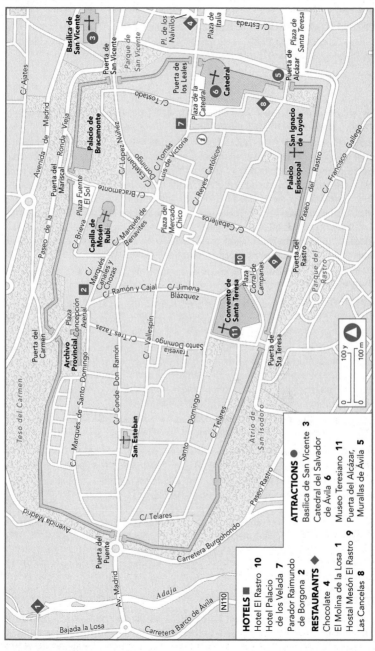

HOTELS ■
Hotel El Rastro **10**
Hotel Palacio
de los Velada **7**
Parador Raimundo
de Borgona **2**

RESTAURANTS ◆
Chocolate **4**
El Molina de la Losa **1**
Hostal Mesón El Rastro **9**
Las Cancelas **8**

ATTRACTIONS ●
Basílica de San Vicente **3**
Catedral del Salvador
de Ávila **6**
Museo Teresiano **11**
Puerta del Alcázar,
Murallas de Ávila **5**

To drive here, exit Madrid at its northwest perimeter and head northwest on Highway N-VI (A-6) toward A Coruña, eventually forking southwest to Ávila. Driving time is around 1¼ hours.

VISITOR INFORMATION   The **tourist information office,** Av. Madrid 39 (www.avila-turismo.com; ℂ **92-022-59-69**), is open daily 9am to 2pm and 5 to 8pm. July to September it's open Monday to Thursday 9am to 8pm, and Friday and Saturday 9am to 9pm.

Where to Stay

Ávila attracts many religious pilgrims, but the hotels are few. Book ahead, especially for July and August, when Spaniards make their pilgrimages and the searing heat means you will certainly want air-conditioning.

Hotel El Rastro ★   The folks who run this hotel seem to have all the lodging (and most of the dining) bases covered in and near Ávila. The hotel is a charming but modern adaptation of an old building that's part of the city walls. Exposed walls of brick and stone and floors covered in large tiles in the public areas create an air of antiquity. Bedrooms, however, have been modernized with plastered walls, wooden floors, and small tiled bathrooms with porcelain fixtures. If the hotel is full, the nearby Mesón del Rastro (below) has another 10 very modest rooms over the restaurant. And if *that* isn't adequate, they'll offer you a house in the countryside. Personally, we'd stick with the hotel for price, comfort, and convenience.

Calle Cepedes, s/n. ℂ **92-021-12-18.** www.elrastroavila.com. 19 units. 47€–65€ double. Free parking. **Amenities:** Restaurant; bar; free Wi-Fi.

Hotel Palacio de Los Velada ★★★   With a tiled floor and graceful arched colonnades, the central courtyard of this hotel is one of the most lovely in the city. The 16th-century noble palace turned hotel is located near the cathedral and makes an ideal base for exploring the city. Everything is so close that you can easily return to enjoy one of the comfortable sofas in the courtyard whenever you feel like taking a break. The guest rooms circle the courtyard and mix comfort with a sense of formality that suits the setting. Many rooms feature unique architectural details such as slanting wooden ceilings or big windows framed by stone arches.

Plaza de la Catedral, 10. ℂ **92-025-51-00.** www.veladahoteles.com. 145 units. 80€–140€ double. Parking 17€. **Amenities:** Restaurant; bar; room service; free Wi-Fi.

Parador Raimundo de Borgoña ★★   Located just inside the city walls 2 blocks northwest of Plaza de la Victoria, this hotel can be hard to find. But once you are settled, it makes a good base for exploring the city. Like most properties in rambling historic buildings it features wonderful public spaces, including a lovely central courtyard and a formal garden with some archaeological remnants. Some of the nicest rooms look out on the garden. They all have traditional furnishings that can sometimes seem more dated than evocative of a historic past. Although limited, the free outdoor parking is a plus.

Marqués de Camales de Chozas, 2. ℂ **92-021-13-40.** www.parador.es. 61 units. 133€–252€ double; 300€–324€ suite. Garage 15€; free outside parking. **Amenities:** Restaurant; bar; room service; free Wi-Fi.

Where to Eat

Ávila is famous throughout Spain for the quality of its veal ribeye steaks, known as *chuletón de Ávila.* The cuisine here is otherwise rather typical Castilian—red meat, dark sauces, wild game, and the potent red wines of the region. Rarely do you need a reservation for dinner—except on Friday and Saturday nights and midday Sunday.

Chocolate ★★ CASTILIAN   You don't need to spend a lot to enjoy a splendid *chuletón de Ávila* at this stylish bar-restaurant with foodie aspirations. The steak (about a half-kilo, or 1 lb.) literally hangs over the edge of the plate and comes with roasted red peppers and oven-fried potatoes. Located in a quiet plaza outside the walls, Chocolate seems to have taken its decor from a candy box: dark brown walls, brown banquettes, chocolate brown napkins on the red plastic tables, and Philippe Starck red acrylic chairs. (There are even red "crystal" plastic chandeliers.) Chocolate's other house specialty is a massive hamburger.

Plaza de Nalvillos, 1. ℭ **92-021-16-79.** Main courses 9€–15€. Daily 11am–4pm and 8:30–11:30pm. Cash only.

Las Cancelas ★★ CASTILIAN   The best part of this venerable lodging is the terrific, if slightly expensive restaurant that occupies its central courtyard. The heavy wooden tables are set casually with paper covers for the midday meal, but the restaurant turns romantic at night when candles flicker on linen table settings on the patio surrounded by stone columns. Specialties of the house all issue from the wood-fired oven, and include the crusty loaves of hearth breads as well as leg or shoulder of lamb, the inescapable roast suckling pig, or the classic veal chops of Ávila *(chuletón de Ávila)*. It's a popular spot with well-heeled locals, and you'll find the wines of the nearby Castilian countryside to be very good.

Hotel Las Cancelas, Calle Cruz Viejo, 6. ℭ **92-021-22-49.** www.lascancelas.com. Main courses 14€–24€. Daily 1:30–4pm and 8:30–11pm.

Mesón del Rastro ★ CASTILIAN   The inn run by the Hotel El Rastro crew (see above) is a more rustic affair than the hotel, and it's very popular with tourists from other parts of Spain who know good if greasy roast meats when they encounter them. The suckling pig almost goes without mentioning, but the real focus here is on many different roasted preparations of lamb, veal roasts, and—one dish done on top of the stove—pan-fried sweetbreads.

Plaza del Rastro 1. ℭ **92-021-12-18.** www.elrastroavila.com. Main courses 9€–24€; fixed-price menu 26€. Daily 1–4pm and 9–11pm.

El Molino de la Losa ★★ CASTILIAN   Outside the walls and across the river, this 15th-century mill converted to a restaurant has a large dining room that retains its rustic origins—a wooden ceiling, wrought iron chandeliers—as well as a smaller, modern dining room with a nice view of the Río Adaja and its old bridge. While the kitchen does its part to keep up the image of Ávila as carnivore heaven (oven-roasted lamb, baby pig, veal, and duck), the chefs also clearly love vegetables and present them with care and panache. The selection of grilled seasonal vegetables is an excellent option for vegetarians, although at some times of year, it might be an entire plate of different mushrooms!

Bajada de la Losa, 12. ℭ **92-021-11-01.** www.elmolinodelalosa.com. Main courses 13€–32€. Tues–Sun 1:30–4pm and 9–11pm.

Exploring Ávila

A Cubist jumble of Gothic convents and palaces slumping down the top of a hill and entirely surrounded by imposing, castellated stone walls, Ávila is the perfect stage set of a Castilian city. It seems a unified whole, making a stronger impression than its individual parts. No visitor can—or should—miss the Murallas, or walls. After that, let your heart and your devotion dictate which of the holy spots to visit.

Basílica de San Vicente ★★★ CHURCH   One of Spain's greatest Romanesque churches, this faded sandstone basilica with a huge nave and trio of apses stands outside the medieval ramparts—a defiant Christian structure intended to claim this high ground in the name of the cross. Its fiercely moralistic carvings, especially on the cornice of the southern portal, play out the eternal struggle between good and evil. The **western portal ★★**, dating from the 13th century, has exquisite Romanesque carvings. Inside is the tomb of San Vincente, martyred on this site in the 4th century. The tomb's medieval carvings, which depict his torture and subsequent martyrdom, are fascinating, if somewhat disturbing and terribly revealing of medieval Spanish institutional anti-Semitism. The story casts "a rich Jew" as the villain, and hastens to note that he was saved by repenting, converting to Christianity, and building this church.

Plaza de San Vicente. ℂ **92-025-52-30.** Admission 1.60€. Daily 10am–1:30pm and 4–6:30pm.

Carmelitas Descalzas de San José (Barefoot Carmelites of St. Joseph) ★ CONVENT   Also known as the Convento de las Madres (Convent of the Mothers), this is the first convent founded by Santa Teresa in 1562 when she began her reform of the Carmelite order. There are two churches: a primitive one, where the first Carmelite nuns took the habit; and one built by Francisco de Mora, architect for Felipe III, after the saint's death. The convent's peculiar little museum, consisting of several rooms behind plate glass, holds personal artifacts of Santa Teresa, including her collarbone and the saddle on which she rode around Spain founding convents. One room re-creates her original cell at the convent, including the window seat where she sat to write and a narrow bed with a log pillow. In the tiny convent church, you might hear the disembodied voices of the cloistered nuns as they sing their prayers.

Calle de las Madres, 4. ℂ **92-022-21-27.** www.sanjosedeavila.es. Admission to museum 1.50€. Apr–Oct daily 10am–1:30pm and 4–7pm; Nov–Mar daily 10am–1:30pm and 3–6pm. From Plaza de Santa Teresa and its nearby Church of San Pedro, follow Calle del Duque de Alba for about 2 blocks.

Catedral del Salvador ★★ CATHEDRAL   Built into the old ramparts of Ávila, this cold, austere cathedral and fortress (begun in 1099 under Alfonso VI) bridges the gap between the Romanesque and the Gothic and, as such, enjoys a certain distinction in Spanish architecture. One local writer compared it to a granite mountain. So heavy is the fortified church that a veritable forest of columns in the local mottled red and white stone supports it from within, obscuring many sight lines. Nine hundred years of entombments have filled every nook and cranny of the voluminous cathedral. Dutch artist Cornelius designed the seats of the choir stalls in the Renaissance style. Behind the main chapel is Vasco de Zarza's masterpiece: the beautifully sculpted tomb of Bishop Alonso de Madrigal—nicknamed "El Tostado" ("the toasted one") for his dark complexion. A prominent theologian of his day, he was the powerful bishop of Ávila from 1449 to 1455. A side altar, naturally enough, honors local celebrity Santa Teresa. Be sure to stop in the Capilla del Cardenal to marvel at the polychrome wooden statues of saints created by anonymous artists in the 12th and 13th centuries.

Plaza de la Catedral. ℂ **92-021-16-41.** Admission 4€ adults, free for children 9 and under. Apr–Oct Mon–Fri 10am–6pm, Sat 10am–7pm, Sun noon–5pm; Nov–Mar Mon–Fri 10am–5pm, Sat 10am–6pm, Sun noon–5pm.

Murallas de Ávila (Walls of Ávila) ★★★ ARCHITECTURE   Ávila's defensive walls are among the best preserved in Europe. They were begun in 1190 on orders of Alfonso VI as part of the reconquest of Spain. Since the builders used the foundations of an earlier Roman fortification, they were able to complete the brown-granite construction in 1199, although embellishments continued into the 14th century. Averaging 10m (33 ft.) in height, the walls have 88 semicircular towers and more than 2,300 battlements. Of the nine gateways, the two most famous are the San Vicente and the Alcázar, both on the eastern side. In many respects, the walls are best viewed from the west. You can hire a taxi to drive alongside the walls' entire length of 2km (1¼ miles). Better yet, you can walk the ramparts, looking eye to eye with storks nesting on rooftops and chimneys. Be aware that there are many rough stone steps and some tricky footing, and despite railings, some fully exposed heights. The views are unsurpassed, and it's easy to imagine the frustration of invading armies thwarted by the soaring fortifications.

Carnicerías, Alcázar, or Ronda Vieja gates. ✆ **92-025-50-88.** http://muralladeavila.com. Admission 5€ adults; 3.50€ seniors and students. Daily 10am–8pm (closes 6pm in winter).

Museo Teresiano ★★ MUSEUM   Located below the Convento de Santa Teresa, which was built on the site of her childhood home, this scholarly museum preserves the garden where Teresa recalled her childhood joy at playing with her siblings. Among some of the museum's more striking artifacts are painted portraits of Teresa by artists who were her contemporaries, as well as letters between Santa Teresa (strong and forceful penmanship!) and San Juan de la Cruz (a more meticulous but rather florid hand). The museum does a good job of placing Teresa in the context of 16th-century Roman Catholicism, and then tracing the influence of her thought down to the present day.

Calle La Dama, s/n. ✆ **92-021-10-30** or 92-022-07-08. Admission 2€. Museum Nov–Mar daily 10am–1:30pm and 3:30–5:30pm; Apr–Oct closed Mon.

SALAMANCA ★★★

When the sun is low in the sky, the sandstone cathedrals, convents, and university buildings of Salamanca take on a luminous golden glow. The soft stone lends itself to carving, and virtually every civic structure in the city has been gloriously embellished with flora and fauna, dreams and nightmares, or fables to instruct the illiterate. Only the remnants of a Roman wall suggest historic fortifications—as a university city since 1218, Salamanca has tended to fortify itself with wit and arm itself with wisdom. Instead of archers' battlements or rusted cannons, look for the good-luck frog on the university portal, narrative reliefs of Bible stories on the churches, and sudden surprises of angels or gargoyles overhead.

The University of Salamanca attracts scholars and students from all over the world—including a large contingent of Americans in summer—and their inquiring minds also go out to play, ensuring a full complement of inexpensive diversions and a lively nightlife. Although greater Salamanca's population exceeds 180,000, the compact old city retains a charming provincial aura. Most attractions are within walking distance of Plaza Mayor, so the best way to explore Salamanca is on foot.

GETTING THERE   Seven **trains** travel directly from Madrid's North station to Salamanca daily (trip time: 2¾ hr.), arriving northeast of the town center on Plaza de la Estación de Ferrocarril (www.renfe.com; ✆ **90-232-03-20**). The fare is 23€. More frequent are the rail connections between Salamanca and the cities of Ávila, Ciudad Rodrigo, and Valladolid (around six trains each per day). There is also frequent daily **bus** service from Madrid (trip time: 2½–3 hr.). The fare is 16€ to 23€. Salamanca's bus terminal is at Av. Filiberto Villalobos, 71 (✆ **92-322-60-79**), northwest of the town center. If you're driving from Madrid, take the N-VI northwest, forking off to Salamanca on the N-501.

The **Oficina Municipal de Turismo de Salamanca,** Plaza Mayor, 32 (www.salamanca.es; ☎ **92-327-83-42**), is open July to mid-September Monday to Friday 9am to 2pm and 4:30 to 8pm, Saturday 10am to 8pm, Sunday 10am to 2pm; mid-September to June Monday to Friday 9am to 2pm and 4 to 6:30pm, Saturday 10am to 6:30pm, Sunday 10am to 2pm. The regional **Oficina de Información Turistica de Castilla y León,** Rúa Mayor at Casa de las Conchas (www. turismocastillayleon; ☎ **92-336-85-71**), is open mid–September to June daily 9am to 2pm and 5 to 8pm; July to mid-September Sunday to Thursday 9am to 8pm, Friday and Saturday 9am to 7pm.

Where to Stay

To take full advantage of Salamanca, you'll want to stay within the old city to avoid a long walk from a hotel on the outskirts. Besides the usual ultra-high seasons of Christmas and Easter, Salamanca hotels also command a premium from late September through October during a succession of festivals and annual conferences.

Abba Fonseca Hotel ★★   Adjoining a classic 17th-century university college, this efficiently modern hotel hides inside a massive golden sandstone facade that makes it look as if it had been part of the university campus for generations. The immediate neighborhood consists of graduate colleges, making on-street parking easy, and the grad-school and scholarly conference clientele guarantee a truly usable desk, plenty of outlets to plug in your gear, and internet that actually lives up to its high-speed billing. The beds are some of the best we've encountered in Spain, and the hotel is only a short walk to the cathedrals, yet sufficiently removed from the main student areas that it's extremely quiet at night.

Plaza San Blas, 2. ☎ **92-301-10-10.** www.abbahotels.com. 86 units. 65€–140€ double; 120€–215€ suite. **Amenities:** Restaurant; bar; babysitting; fitness center; sauna; room service; free Wi-Fi.

Apartahotel Toboso ★   Bargain-hunters and families rejoice at finding this apartment hotel in the heart of the city near the Plaza Mayor. The furnishings are clean and modern, but hardly stylish. The space, however, is hard to beat. In addition to 23 double rooms, the Toboso has seven apartments—four with two bedrooms that sleep three, and three with three bedrooms that can sleep up to five. The apartments also have kitchens with full-sized stoves and refrigerators and a washing machine to get caught up on your travel laundry. The bathrooms are shiny and new, if a little gaudy with all that red marble. There are two possible drawbacks. Some rooms are over a cabaret/music bar—ask for digs overlooking the quiet interior courtyard instead. Secondly, there is no air conditioning. The thick stone walls keep it fairly cool even in the summer, but it's not for travelers who can't sleep in a room that isn't chilly.

Calle Clavel, 7. ☎ **92-327-14-62.** www.hoteltoboso.com. 30 units. 40€ double; 70€ 2-bedroom suite, 100€ 3-bedroom suite. **Amenities:** Bar-cafeteria; free Wi-Fi.

Microtel Placentinos ★★   Aptly named—with just nine rooms it really is a micro-hotel—Placentinos is a marvel of design and interior decorating. There are three single rooms and six doubles in this tiny 16th-century building amid the looming blocks of the old university. Most rooms have at least one wall of exposed stone. Open the shutters on the windows and you may be shocked to discover that those sandstone walls are almost a foot deep. Comfortable but contemporary furniture may strike a muted palette, but the simple rooms are anything but spartan. Bathrooms in the doubles

Salamanca

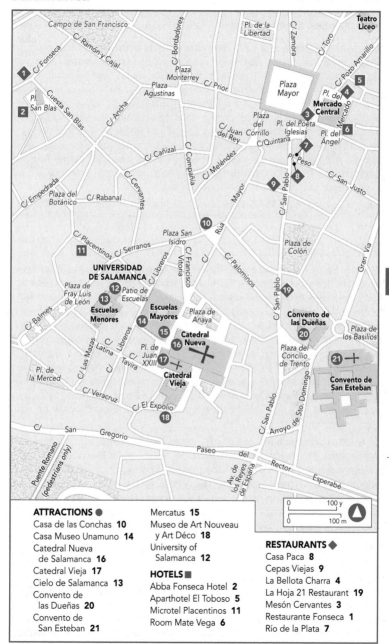

Campo de San Francisco
C/ Fonseca
C/ Ramón y Cajal
C/ Bordadores
Pl. de la Libertad
C/ Zamora
Teatro Liceo
C/ Toro
1
Pl. San Blas
Cuesta San Blas
2
Plaza Monterrey
C/ Prior
Plaza Agustinas
Plaza Mayor
Pl. del
4
C/ Pozo Amarillo
5
Mercado
Mercado Central
C/ Ancha
Plaza del Corrillo
Pl. del Poeta Iglesias
3
Pl. del Ángel
6
C/ Juan del Rey
C/ Quintana
Pl. Peso
7
C/ Cañizal
Compañía
C/ Meléndez
8
C/ San Justo
C/ Empedrada
Plaza del Botánico
C/ Rabanal
C/ Cervantes
Mayor
C/ San Pablo
9
10
Rúa
Plaza de Colón
C/ Placentinos
C/ Serranos
Plaza San Isidro
C/ Francisco Vitoria
C/ Palominos
C/ San Pablo
Gran Vía
11
C/ Libreros
UNIVERSIDAD DE SALAMANCA
Plaza de Fray Luis de León
12 Patio de Escuelas
13
Escuelas Menores
Escuelas Mayores
Plaza de Anaya
19
Convento de las Dueñas
Plaza de los Basilios
C/ Balmes
14
15
Catedral Nueva
C/ Las Mazas
C/ Latina
C/ Libreros
16
Pl. de Juan XXIII
17
Catedral Vieja
Plaza del Concilio de Trento
20
21
Convento de San Esteban
Pl. de la Merced
C/ Veracruz
C/ El Expolio
18
Arroyo de Sto. Domingo
C/ San Pablo
C/ San Gregorio
Puente Romano (pedestrians only)
Paseo del Rector
Av. de los Reyes de España
Esperabé

0   100 y
0   100 m

5

SIDE TRIPS FROM MADRID | Salamanca

have whirlpool tubs and some even have a sauna shower. The location is spectacular—steps from the cathedrals.

Calle Placentinos, 9. (C) **92-328-15-31.** www.microtelplacentinos.com. 57€–100€ single; 73€–122€ double. **Amenities:** Guest Jacuzzi on terrace; cable high-speed Internet.

Room Mate Vega ★★ All the boutique hotels in the Room Mate group are design-centric, and this one picks up the city's muted sand tones, contrasting them with graphic bed covers and gigantic color art photos in the rooms. Vega is located near the city's fresh food market and about a 90-second walk from Plaza Mayor, making the location extremely convenient for sightseeing. The building is a quirky one, so rooms are all a little different in size and configuration. Most are doubles with two full beds, sometimes pushed together to look like a king. If you opt for an executive room, you get more room to spread out, sometimes with a reading nook, other times with a small balcony. All rooms share the rooftop terrace. There are some tiny singles here, but single travelers should inquire if Room 003 on the ground level is available, as it has a tiled terrace almost as big as the rest of the room.

Plaza del Mercado, 16. (C) **92-327-22-50.** www.room-matehotels.com. 38 units. 36€–90€ single; 50€–113€ double; 70€–133€ executive. **Amenities:** Bar; room service; free Wi-Fi; free business center.

Where to Eat

Although Salamancan cuisine is similar to Segovia and Ávila, the university city does have a few distinctive specialties: the thinly sliced dry mountain ham from Guijuelo; a spicy, crumbly sausage called *farinato* that is more bread crumbs than meat; and a pastry stuffed with cheese, sausage, and ham, called *hornazo*. Students traditionally feasted on these meat pies during Easter week to celebrate the return of prostitutes to the city after Lent, but the dish is now available year-round and is no longer consumed only by young men with raging hormones. Tourist restaurants along **Rúa Mayor** offer acceptable if uninspired meals at slightly inflated prices, and the restaurants lining **Plaza Mayor** attract tourists and locals alike. To join Salamantinos in a more tranquil setting, walk up to **Paseo Carmelitas** between calle La Fuente and Puerta de Zamora. The leafy green park that lines the street is full of terraces that are popular for afternoon drinks and snacks.

La Bellota Charra ★★ CASTILIAN About as casual and local as restaurants get in Salamanca, this dining room that specializes in sausages is located next door to a sausage maker and across the street from the city fresh market. It's very basic—pale wooden tables and chairs, a tile floor, fluorescent lights—but the food is good and it's inexpensive. In addition to various sausage plates, you can order a whole meal of meat pâtés and vegetable terrines for a relative song. Beer is always a good choice, but the restaurant stocks some excellent and inexpensive red wines from the nearby Arribes del Duero region, which recently received D.O. (Denominación de Origen) status. Like wines all up and down the river, they are made primarily from the Tempranillo grape.

Plaza del Mercado, 8–10. (C) **92-321-96-57.** Plates 7€–11€. Daily 1:30–4pm and 8–11:30pm.

Casa Paca ★★ CASTILIAN The classic choice among Salamantino restaurants, Casa Paca has been serving its meat-heavy menu since 1928. Ancient dishes like *alubias* (white beans stewed with pig's tails and ears) and *cocido* (a meat stew of all the trimmings from several kinds of animals) are on the menu, but diners making a night of it tend to ask for meats *a la brasa volcánica,* or cooked on the wood-fired grill. Favorites include suckling pig, thick beef steaks, and racks of baby goat chops. The

chilling ON PLAZA MAYOR

On hot summer nights, you'll find as many people eating ice cream as dining on Plaza Mayor. If you want a cone, join the line outside **Café Novelty** (Plaza Mayor, 2; ✆ **92-321-49-56;** daily 8am–midnight). During colder months, an arty crowd convenes in the Art Nouveau interior, and you might want to go in, just to have a look. Local specialty cold drinks can be just as refreshing, and we like the plaza tables of **Cafetería Las Torres** (Plaza Mayor, 26; ✆ **92-321-44-70;** daily 8am–midnight) for sipping *leche helada* (a smooth concoction with hints of vanilla, cinnamon, and citrus rimmed with whipped cream) or *blanco y negro* (vanilla ice cream melting in a double shot of espresso).

---

atmospheric dining room with alternating wood-paneled and ancient stone walls is a real throwback to old Castilla. Honestly, we find it all a little overwhelming and usually opt to eat and drink on the bar side, where some of the most generous tapas in central Spain are provided "free" with drinks. (Beer and wine go up to 3.50€–5€ at meal times.) There's an array of tapas displayed—slices of tortilla española, farinato sausage with scrambled eggs, pig's ears in tomato sauce *(orillas)*, pastry squares filled with goat cheese and quince jam, small casseroles of meatballs, cod-stuffed red peppers, potato salad. You only have to ask (or point) when you order your drink.

Plaza del Peso, 10. ✆ **92-321-89-93.** www.casapaca.com. Main courses 12€–27€. Daily 2–4:30pm and 9–11:30pm. Bar daily 11am–midnight.

Cepas Viejas ★ CONTEMPORARY SPANISH   Originally a design-centric wine bar with a good and somewhat innovative tapas menu (sliced pickled octopus, small fried sausages, breast of dove, or tuna topped with roasted red pepper), Cepas Viejas has expanded its interior dining room to offer a chef-driven creative cuisine built around oven-roasted meats and fish. The restaurant's motto translates as "when the barrel is empty, the heart has no joy." Not surprisingly, it boasts one of the most extensive wine lists in the city.

Calle Felipe Espino, 6. ✆ **92-326-23-36.** Tapas 2€–3€, main courses 14€–22€. Daily 1–4pm and 8:30pm–midnight.

La Hoja 21 ★★ CONTEMPORARY SPANISH   One of the things we love about the menu at La Hoja 21 is the chef's penchant for cooking with fresh vegetables. Maybe that's because the establishment is just steps from the city's farmer's market. The tasting menu changes only in the seasonal ingredients, but almost always features mushroom risotto with fresh veggies, and braised cheeks of the local heritage beef called Morucha. You can also expect crab crepes and little pasta purses filled with cheese, shrimp, and minced vegetables. One of the regional specialties here is roasted leg of mutton with potato cakes. The most popular dessert is an international classic: the fallen chocolate cake.

Calle San Pablo, 21. ✆ **92-326-40-28.** www.lahoja21.com. Reservations recommended. Main courses 14€–20€; tasting menu 33€. Tues–Sun 2–4:30pm; Tues–Sat 9–11:30pm.

Méson Cervantes ★ CASTILIAN   Combination plates are the mainstay of dining on Plaza Mayor, and this venerable restaurant offers some of the best prices as well as some of the best food. For about 10€, you can get a small steak with two fried eggs and fried potatoes while lamb chops with lettuce, tomato, and fries might set you back

5

SIDE TRIPS FROM MADRID

Salamanca

147

a few euros more. It's one of the few spots serving generous vegetarian plates—our favorite includes white asparagus, green beans, peas, lettuce, tomato, marinated artichokes, and steamed squash. The darkly atmospheric upstairs bar (the restaurant has no plaza-level dining room) is jammed at midday with locals drinking beer and eating such plates as rice-filled blood sausage with red peppers or scrambled eggs and farinato drizzled with honey.

Plaza Mayor, 15. © **92-321-72-13.** www.mesoncervantes.com. Combination plates 10€–17€; main dishes 15€–21€. Daily 10am–midnight or later.

Restaurante Fonseca ★★★ SPANISH Every major college town has a restaurant where faculty and staff take guests for inexpensive meals in a fancy setting. In Salamanca, it's this beauty in the formal 16th-century courtyard of the Colegio Arzobispo. The tables are set in pristine white linens and you'll be dining with dons and university administrators. The *menu del día* is clearly subsidized, offering a choice of two first plates (typically a salad or a rice dish) and two second plates (sole or chicken, for example), along with wine, bread, and a pastry.

Plaza Fonseca, 4. © **92-326-02-70.** Main dishes 10€–24€; *menu del día* 11€–13€. Daily 1:30–4pm and 9–11:30pm.

Río de la Plata ★ CASTILIAN Rafael and Josefa Andrés Lorenzo opened this basement restaurant in 1958, naming it in honor of Josefa's native Argentina. Over the years, it became a favorite hangout for the bullfight crowd and those ubiquitous Americans, Ernest Hemingway and Orson Welles. Still serving the same homemade Castilian fare generations later, it remains a popular dining room for a certain arty university crowd as well as curious tourists. Josefa's daughter Paulina oversees the kitchen these days, offering homey dishes like a simple garlic soup, grilled sausages, or local trout with ham. If you hanker for Castilian dishes not available at most restaurants, consider the brains fried in batter or stewed kid with almonds.

Plaza del Peso, 1. © **92-321-90-05.** Reservations recommended. Main courses 10€–27€; *menu del día* 24€. Tues–Sun 1:30–3:30pm and 9pm–12:30am. Closed 2 weeks in July.

Exploring Salamanca

You probably won't want to visit Salamanca in August, when the scorching midday makes even the lizards dash across the plazas in search of a sliver of shade. But at any other time, this is a stroller's city where new delights catch the eye at every turn. The **Plaza Mayor ★★★** is the heart of the community and in true academic fashion, it embodies the conflicting spirits of Spanish intellect. José Benito Churriguera's design of the square is rational, cool, and neoclassical—but the decoration is utterly Baroque. Salamantinos gather here at all hours of the day and night to connect with each other, to talk, and (most of all) to eat and drink. On a hot day, the drink of choice is *leche helada*—vanilla-and-almond ice milk. When the sun sets and the stone plaza begins to cool, cafe tables spill out from beneath the arcades and "tunas" (student singers in old-fashioned academic cloaks) wander from table to table singing for tips.

About a quarter of the old city is devoted to buildings of the University of Salamanca, which reached its apex of influence in the 15th and 16th centuries but remains one of Spain's most prestigious centers of scholarship. Courtyards around university buildings are generally open to the public, and the **Patio de Escuelas Menores** is a popular gathering point for tour groups as well as Salamantinos. Standing proudly in the center is a statue of 16th-century poet and scholar **Fray Luis de León,** the city's poster boy for intellectual freedom and defiance of tyranny. Imprisoned for 4 years by the Inquisition for translating the Biblical "Song of Solomon" into Castilian, the scholar began his first lecture after returning to the classroom, *"Decíamos ayer . . . ,"* or "as we were saying yesterday. . . ."

Casa de las Conchas (House of Shells) ★ ARCHITECTURE It's hard to miss this restored 1483 house on the street between the University and Plaza Mayor because the facade consists of 400 simulated scallop shells, the symbol of Santiago (St. James), the patron saint of the Reconquista. It was created by a medical professor at the university as a tribute to the pilgrimage city of Santiago de Compostela in Galicia. You can visit the courtyard daily, but only in the evening on Sundays. The region of Castilla y León maintains a tourist office here (see above).

Calle de la Compañía, 2. ℂ **92-326-93-17.** Free admission. Courtyard Mon–Fri 9am–9pm; Sat 9am–2pm; Sat–Sun 5–8pm. Bus: 1.

Casa-Museo Unamuno ★★ HISTORIC HOME The financial crisis has severely limited hours at this delightful little house museum, but make a point of visiting nonetheless if you want to understand the intellectual, humanistic side of the city. Poet, philosopher, and novelist Miguel de Unamuno lived in this 18th-century home during his first term as university rector. A man of principle, he had to leave the country when dictator Primo de Rivera came to power and demanded that he censor his scholarship. When de Rivera fell, he returned exultant, but the euphoria was short-lived. Never have we seen a home where the life of the mind was so manifest, from his library of world masterpieces in many languages to his own photographs showing him with the top intelligentsia of his era. Unamuno was the symbol of a humanistic era of lofty values and high ideals crushed in Spain's descent into chaos. Indeed, he died of an apparent broken heart shortly after the Civil War began. Unamuno loved his adopted city deeply, once writing in a poem, "I keep your very soul in my heart. And you, my golden Salamanca, will keep my memory when I die." And so it has.

Calle de Libreros, 25. ℂ **92-329-44-00.** Admission 4€ adults; 2€ students. Tues and Thurs 10am–noon. Bus: 1.

Catedral Nueva (New Cathedral) ★★ CATHEDRAL Salamantinos started constructing their "new" cathedral in 1513 in an old-fashioned style that made it "the last gasp of Gothic style," as architectural historians put it. Located in the south end of the old town, about 5 blocks south of Plaza Mayor at the edge of Plaza de Anaya, it is the largest and highest building in the city. The soaring spaces inside welcome pious contemplation. All three Churriguera brothers (see box above) served as supervising architects of the late stages of the cathedral's long construction (it wasn't consecrated until 1733), so many of the surface details and twisted-rope columns are truly Churrigueresque. One bas-relief column, for example, resembles a cluster of palm trees. The tradition of inspired stone carving continues. When the lower portion of the Puerta Ramos on the west side was rebuilt in 1992, the stonemason and restorers decided to update the carvings with the image of an astronaut floating in space. a monkey eating an ice cream cone, and a stork carrying a branch in its beak. (Panhandlers hanging out near the entrance will point them out for a tip.)

Plaza Juan XXIII. ℂ **92-321-74-76.** www.catedralsalamanca.org. Free admission. Apr–Sept daily 9am–8pm; Oct and Mar daily 9am–1pm and 4–6pm; Nov–Feb Sun 9am–1pm. Bus: 1.

Catedral Vieja (Old Cathedral) ★★★ CATHEDRAL Functioning more as a museum than a house of worship, the old cathedral is a squat Romanesque structure begun in 1140, and its sight lines to the altar are obscured by the sheer bulk of its

A twisted FAMILY

Spanish Baroque architecture takes the impulse for distortion to an extreme. The Churriguera family carved out a name for themselves with a family style that owes a great deal to the forms assumed by twisted rope. **José Benito Churriguera** (1665–1725) and his brothers **Joaquin** (1674–1724) and **Alberto** (1676–1750) were stone sculptors who became architects. Their work in Salamanca, especially with altarpieces and the stucco work on building facades, spawned many imitators in Spain as well as in Mexico—hence the term, Churrigueresque.

interior supports. Nonetheless, it retains some powerful religious art, most notably the mid-15th-century altarpiece of 53 compartmentalized scenes painted by Nicholas of Florence to delineate the life of Christ and scenes of the Virgin Mary. It is not uncommon to see pilgrims entranced by the masterpiece, spending hours on their knees in prayer in the medieval gloom as they contemplate each scene. After viewing the church, stroll through the enclosed cloisters with their Gothic tombs of long-forgotten bishops. Two chapels are of particular note: the Capilla de San Martín with frescoes painted in 1242, and the Capilla de Santa Catalina, replete with gargoyles.

Plaza Juan XXIII. (✆ **92-321-74-76.** www.catedralsalamanca.org. Admission 4.75€. Apr–Sept daily 10am–7:30pm; Oct–Mar daily 10am–12:30pm and 4–5:30pm. Bus: 1.

Cielo de Salamanca ★★ MUSEUM Sometimes the best attempts at understanding the universe turn out to be bad science but deserve to survive because they are simply beautiful. This fresco of the night sky painted by Francisco Gallego in 1474 is just such an example. It covers part of the ceiling of the old university library and is located just off the plaza that separates the university's graduate school from its undergraduate campus. Working without the benefit of the explorations by Copernicus and Galileo, the artist attempted to merge myth, science, and religion by enjambing astrology and night-sky astronomy. You'll have to wait a few minutes after entering for your eyes to adjust to the low light, but the vision is the very definition of magic.

Patio de Escuelas Menores, s/n. No phone. Free admission. Tues–Sat 10am–2pm and 4–8pm; Sun 10am–2pm.

Convento de las Dueñas ★★★ CONVENT Unlike the brothers, the Dominican nuns are cloistered, but the cloister and intensely fragrant rose garden of their convent are open to visitors. Originally a noble palace, it was donated to the order in 1419 and has been subsequently altered and enlarged. The 16th-century cloister designed by Rodrigo Gil de Hontañón is a hidden treasure. The capitals on the arcade pillars represent some of the most inspired stone carving in the entire city, and any fan of gargoyles or modern graphic novels should make the effort to see them. They're a sample book of contorted human bodies, angels, griffons, devils, flying goat heads, winged horses, and other fantastic creatures. The carvings are so vivid that it's hard to believe the poor nuns can sleep at night.

Plaza del Concilio de Trento, s/n. (✆ **92-321-54-42.** Admission 1.50€. Mon–Sat 10:30am–12:45pm; Mon–Fri 4:30–6:45pm. Bus: 1.

Convento de San Estéban ★ MONASTERY Religious belief and humanist philosophy converge at this historically significant monastery. Dominicans from this monastery accompanied Columbus on his voyages. Not only did they proselytize to the

5

SIDE TRIPS FROM MADRID | Salamanca

SIDE TRIPS FROM MADRID

150

natives of the New World, they argued that indigenous people around the world had souls and human rights. While the dignity of all persons seems common sense in the 21st century, it was a radical concept in the 16th, and the Dominicans of Salamanca suffered for it. Nonetheless, they persevered and continue to agitate for social and economic justice, finally convincing the pope to declare indigenous people as human beings. Their convent is a pleasure to tour, highlighted by the elaborate gilded José Benito Churriguera altar in the church and the stunning Baroque choir with an illustrated hymnal big enough that all 118 monks could read the music from their seats.

Plaza del Concilio de Trento, s/n. ⓒ **92-321-50-00.** http://sanesteban.dominicos.es. 3€ adults; 2€ seniors and students. Daily 10am–2pm and 4–7pm. Bus: 1.

Mercatus ★ STORE The official university store has the usual branded merchandise, but it also sells some terrific souvenirs and/or gifts that won't embarrass you once you get home. If you became enamored of the student singing groups, or "tunas," one night on Plaza Mayor, you can purchase CDs here. Silk scarves that reproduce the Cielo de Salamanca in all its mysterious beauty are worth a splurge, but you can also purchase T-shirts, tote bags, puzzles, and drink coasters emblazoned with the same image. Or go tacky and buy your budding scholar a bright stuffed frog, the good-luck talisman of Salamanca students.

Cardenal Plá y Deniel, s/n. ⓒ **92-329-46-92.** http://mercatus.usal.es. Mon–Sat 10am–7pm; Sun 10am–2pm.

Museo de Art Nouveau-Art Déco ★ MUSEUM Masterful Art Nouveau glass by Émile Gallé and René Lalique are the artistic highlights, but the 1,500-plus piece collection of the Manuel Ramos Andrade Foundation also embraces jewelry, paintings, furniture, and marble and bronze figurines. All the works date from the late 1880s through the 1930s, and while some are mainstream Art Nouveau or Art Deco, others are Spanish outliers of the two styles. Many visitors are surprised to also find a collection of more than 400 porcelain dolls. Manuel Ramos Andrade was a major doll collector and the pieces represent the top European manufacturers. Since the onset of the financial crisis, the museum has supplemented its income by sponsoring numerous fashion shows and photo shoots.

Calle El Expolio, 14. ⓒ **92-312-14-25.** www.museocasalis.org. Admission 4€ adults; 2€ students; free for children 13 and under. Apr to mid-Oct Tues–Fri 11am–2pm and 5–9pm, Sat–Sun 11am–9pm; mid-Oct to Mar Tues–Fri 11am–2pm and 4–7pm, Sat–Sun 11am–8pm. Bus: 1.

Museo de Salamanca ★ MUSEUM Only steps from the grandly carved main entrance of the University, this attractive little museum is packed with religious art confiscated from convents and monasteries in the mid–19th century. Most of the churches from which the 15th- to 17th-century carvings and paintings were taken no longer exist, and in a few cases, the art is exhibited with the altar or niche from its original church. The contrast between rude architecture and polished artistry is striking—a reminder that for rural people, the church was often the most beautiful thing in their lives. One highlight is a golden Churrigueresque altarpiece crafted between 1697 and 1704. In addition to the permanent collections, the museum has begun a very active program of thematic exhibitions combining pieces from its collection with works borrowed from other municipal and regional museums around the region of Castilla y León.

Patio de las Escuelas, 2. ⓒ **92-321-22-35.** www.museoscastillayleon.jcyl.es/museodesalamanca. Admission 1.20€ adults, free for seniors and children; free to all Sat–Sun. Oct–June Tues–Sun 10am–2pm, Tues–Sat 4–7pm; July–Sept Tues–Sun 10am–2pm, Tues–Sat 5–8pm.

Universidad de Salamanca ★ HISTORIC SITE Established in 1213 and granted its full charter in 1254, Salamanca was organized on the model of the University of Bologna—that is, it gave precedence to humanistic scholarship over the study of theology favored by the University of Paris. Its intellectual heyday was in the 15th and 16th centuries, but it remains a major force in Spanish intellectual life and the most popular place in the country for foreigners to study the Spanish language. The original college, the Escuelas Mayores, boasts one of the **best carved portals** ★★★ in a city of pretty impressive doorways. The entryway was carved in 1534 at the height of Salamanca's finest stone carving. This "doorway to heaven" was intended to emulate the goldsmith's art. The main medallion in the first register depicts the Catholic monarchs Isabel and Fernando. Crowds gather to scrutinize the fine details, but they are not looking for the Catholic monarchs. They are looking for the carved frog perched on a human skull on the right hand side of the door. Legend holds that students who can spot it will do well on their exams. Although Salamanca is not known for its business school, Salamantino entrepreneurs have capitalized on the legend by making the *rana* (frog) a whimsical if unofficial symbol of Salamanca. Every imaginable trinket can be purchased emblazoned with its likeness.

Given such a great entrance, it's a little disappointing that the only tour inside the university is restricted to a self-guided walk around the Renaissance arcades of the Escuelas Mayores, the original college of the university. Let your nose lead the way. The chapel has the lingering odor of sanctity (actually, frankincense), while the wonderful old library on the upper level smells of paper and old leather, even through the closed glass doors. You can also visit the lecture hall of Fray Luis de León, fitted with crude wooden benches. The university is 2 blocks from the cathedral in the south end of the old town.

Patio de las Escuelas, 1. ℂ **92-329-44-00.** www.usal.es. Admission 4€. Mon–Sat 9:30am–1pm; Sun 9am–1pm; Mon–Fri 4–7pm; Sat 4–6:30pm. Enter from Patio de las Escuelas, a widening of Calle de Libreros. Bus: 1.

ZAMORA ★

If you've ever doubted the profound effect of the Reconquista on the Spanish landscape and psyche, come to Zamora and see the Christians still standing sentinel on the Peñas de Santa Marta ridgeline above the Duero River. Twenty-four spires of Romanesque churches line up along the ridge, turning their crosses against the long-vanished Moorish soldiers on the south side of the river. When León finally captured the city from the Moors in the 11th century, the king repopulated the area with settlers from Burgundy, planted vineyards all along the river, and began building churches.

As a border land, Zamora reclaimed the soil of Spain with the cross and the vine as well as the sword. Until the recent installation of high-speed rail, few North Americans beyond architecture buffs ever visited Zamora. Although it does have some modern hotels and terrific restaurants, the city seems little changed since its years of dusty decline in the 17th century, when the majority of its populace emigrated to South America, establishing several Zamoras across that continent. Scholars sometimes refer to Zamora as an open-air museum of Romanesque architecture, and the old churches—most of them well-preserved and still functioning as neighborhood parishes—are powerfully moving. The processions, or *pasos,* during Holy Week (the week before Easter) are some of the largest and most spectacular in Spain. Reserve far ahead if you're planning to visit during this period.

Zamora

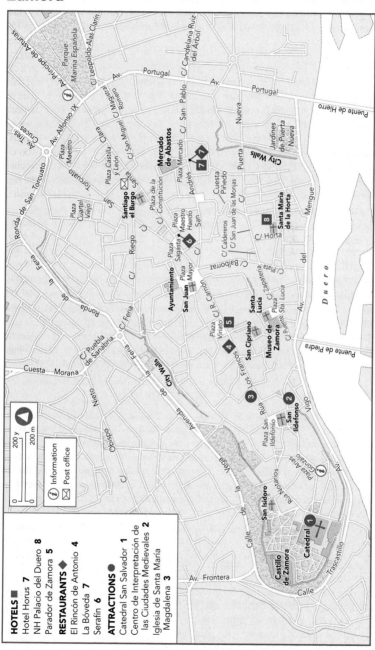

HOTELS ■
Hotel Horus **7**
NH Palacio del Duero **8**
Parador de Zamora **5**

RESTAURANTS ◆
El Rincón de Antonio **4**
La Bóveda **7**
Serafín **6**

ATTRACTIONS ●
Catedral San Salvador **1**
Centro de Interpretación de
las Ciudades Medievales **2**
Iglesia de Santa Maria
Magdalena **3**

0   200 y
0   200 m

ⓘ Information
☒ Post office

It is surprising that Zamora's monuments have survived so many centuries, as the city was also the scene of fierce battles in the 15th-century war between Isabel I and Juana la Beltraneja, Isabel's illegitimate half-niece—a struggle whose memory is preserved in the old Spanish proverb *No se ganó Zamora en una hora,* or "Zamora wasn't won in an hour."

Essentials

GETTING THERE   There are three high-speed **trains** to and from Madrid every day. They take just under 2 hours and cost 25€ to 31€. The railway station is at Calle Alfonso Peña (www.renfe.com; ☏ **90-232-03-20**), about a 15-minute walk from the edge of the old town. Ten to twenty-three **bus** connections a day from Salamanca are very convenient. The express takes 50 minutes (6.30€) while the regular bus (5.25€) takes 1 hour. The town's bus station lies a few paces from the railway station, at Calle Alfonso Peña, 3 (☏ **98-052-12-81**). Call ☏ **90-202-00-52** for bus schedules and price information. If you're driving from Madrid, take the A-6 superhighway northwest toward Valladolid, cutting west on the N-VI and west again at the turnoff onto 122.

VISITOR INFORMATION   The **Oficina Municipal de Turismo,** Plaza de Arias Gonzalo, 6 (www.zamora.es/lang; ☏ **98-053-36-94**), is open daily 10am to 2pm and 4 to 7pm.

Where to Stay

Hotel Horus ★   Set in the former Banco de España building from the 19th century, this handsome hotel was transformed into a rich merchant's mansion in the early 20th century and later served as a newspaper headquarters. Just before the financial crisis struck, it was converted into a boutique hotel that retains the Art Nouveau decoration of the original building but upgrades the interiors in a minimalist modern style. Even the smallest rooms are spacious and airy, and the largest rooms are huge. Just a 2-minute walk from the Plaza Mayor, the location is ideal for seeing Zamora's sights.

Plaza del Mercado, 20. ☏ **98-050-82-82.** www.hotelhorus.com. 45 rooms. 58€–86€ double; 85€–101€ jr. suite. **Amenities:** Bar; restaurant; room service; spa; free Wi-Fi.

NH Palacio del Duero ★★   Barely outside the old city walls of Zamora, the NH Colección hotel (the group's top grade) occupies the 14th- to 15th-century convent of San Juan de Jerusalem as well as the 16th-century Comendadores convent and part of a 20th-century winery. All those properties have been nicely integrated, but the path to some rooms seems a bit like a maze. The rooms themselves are spacious, modern, and serene, and some have private terraces while others open onto a hidden courtyard where some guests like to sunbathe. Given the number of churches in Zamora, it's no surprise that the hotel stands next to the 12th-century Santa Marta de la Horta.

Plaza de la Horta, 1. ☏ **98-050-82-62.** www.nh-hotels.com. 49 units. Doubles 54€–85€. **Amenities:** Bar; restaurant; free Wi-Fi.

Parador de Zamora ★   Medieval armor, heavy tapestries, hanging lanterns, and reproduction antique furniture give this parador a *gravitas* that other lodgings in Zamora lack. Built in the mid–15th century on the site of an earlier Roman fortress, the building features a beautiful staircase and a dignified wood and stone interior courtyard with a well in the center. The two levels of guest rooms are arrayed around the central patio and most have big windows with heavy wooden shutters. The décor mixes richly colored fabrics with dark wood furnishings for a modern interpretation of traditional style. The location is within convenient walking distance of attractions and restaurants.

Plaza de Viriato, 5. ✆ **98-051-44-97.** www.parador.es. 52 units. 110€–155€ double, 230€ superior double. **Amenities:** Restaurant; bar; outdoor pool; room service; free Wi-Fi.

Where to Eat

Zamora sits on the north bank of the Río Duero just downstream from the wine districts of Rueda and Toro (and just upstream from Portugal's port vineyards). To the north, the landscape rises rapidly into mountain woodlands that supply the foraged mushrooms and wild trout often found on Zamoran menus. Historically, the city was an important stop on the Roman "silver road" to Galicia, and the Galician penchant for octopus continues even in this dusty Castilian city.

La Bóveda ★★ CONTEMPORARY SPANISH Located in the old Banco d'España vault at the Hotel Horus, La Bóveda (which translates as The Vault) is a treasure. The chef adapts a number of classic Spanish dishes from different regions— *bacalao al pil-pil* with piquillo peppers from Basque country, for example, or suckling pig with crispy skin from Castilla—and gives them a modern twist. The wine list features the splendid reds from nearby Toro. Although it's perhaps the dressiest restaurant in Zamora, La Bóveda offers exceptional value for the price.

Plaza del Mercado, 20. ✆ **98-050-82-82.** www.hotelhorus.com. Reservations recommended. Main dishes 12€–22€. Daily 1:30pm–3pm; Mon–Sat 9pm–midnight.

El Rincón de Antonio ★★ CASTILIAN The chef at this atmospheric restaurant proves the adage that everything old is new again. He has resurrected some of the classic dishes of this corner of Castilla y León—like garbanzo beans in a garlicky sauce with local boletus (porcini or cep mushrooms) or candied artichokes with ham and a mushroom purée. Other Castilian classics like veal tongue and leg of lamb are also featured prominently. Although the menu can be parsed a la carte, almost everyone who dines in the bustling, close-quartered dining rooms, or the greenhouselike extension, orders one of the tasting menus. There is a vegetarian option as well as five- and six-course menus with meat and fish. The tapas tasting menu of four small plates, wine, dessert, and coffee is one of the best light meals in town—available only in the bar.

Rúa de los Francos, 6. ✆ **98-053-53-70.** www.elrincondeantonio.com. Reservations recommended. Main dishes 14€–28€; fixed-price menus 32€–60€; tapas tasting menu 11€. Daily noon–4pm; Mon–Sat 8pm–midnight.

Serafín ★★ SPANISH Zamora is famous for its rice dish, *arroz al la zamoraña,* and the kitchen at Serafín makes the best version in town. Staff sometimes have trouble explaining the dish to non-Spanish speakers, so you should know that in addition to the minced bits of pig's trotters and pig's ears that characterize the dish, it is redolent with sweet paprika and a combination of sautéed onion and cubed turnip. The restaurant is an unusual hybrid—combining a skillful execution of the roast meat dishes of Castilla y León (accompanied by hearty reds from D.O. Toro) and simple presentations of superb fish and shellfish from the Cantabrian coast on the Bay of Biscay. (With the fish, you drink Rueda whites, from about 40 miles east.) Local fish include trout from the mountains north of Zamora, frog legs (an amphibian, but treated as fish on the menu), and sweet river crab.

Plaza Maestro Haedo, 10. ✆ **98-053-14-22.** www.restauranteserafin.com. Main courses 12€–20€; fixed-price menu 17€ and 24€. Fri–Wed 1–4:30pm and 8:30pm–midnight.

Exploring Zamora

Zamora's Romanesque churches are a delight to explore, but you'll have to check the doors for the hours of Masses to get inside most of them. They may be priceless monuments that are 700-800 years old, but they are still active parish churches. A handful open for prayers in the mornings at 10am, close before lunch, and open again in the early evening before dinner, 5–8pm. It's also a treat to explore the city walls. The **Portillo de la Traición** (Treason Gate) on the northwest corner of the city commemorates the duplicitous assassination of Castilian king Sancho II in 1072 when he and El Cid were laying siege to the city in a battle over succession to the crown of León. The upshot of Sancho's death was that his brother Alfonso united the crowns of Castilla and León.

Catedral San Salvador ★★ CATHEDRAL   With its ribbed blue-and-white Byzantine-style dome, there's no mistaking Zamora's cathedral. Built swiftly between 1151 and 1174 (although the transept wasn't finished until 1192), it has a stylistic unity that is unusual in Spain, where cathedrals were generally completed over centuries rather than decades. Set on the high point of Zamora's ridge, the cathedral looks as much like a fortress as a church when viewed from the riverbanks below. Yet it opens into the city with a harmonious plaza that gives viewers the distance to appreciate its full grandeur. Some Gothic towers have been added to the Romanesque temple, of course, and the interior decorations stretch out across the centuries. The choir stalls, carved 1512–16 by Juan de Bruselas, are especially notable for their lively scenes of country life in addition to the usual images of saints and famous figures from antiquity. The cathedral's museum is located inside the cloister, and it contains the city's greatest artistic treasure, the so-called "Black Tapestries" woven in Flanders in the 15th century. They illustrate scenes from the Trojan War as well as Hannibal's campaign in Italy. They are called "black" because several show people about to be decapitated.

Plaza de la Catedral. ✆ **98-053-06-44.** http://catedraldezamora.wordpress.com. Admission 4€ adults, 2€ seniors and students, 1€ photo permit (no flash). Cathedral admission free during Mass. Mar–Sept daily 10am–2pm and 5–8pm; Oct–Feb daily 10am–2pm and 4:30–6:30pm.

Centro de Interpretación de las Ciudades Medievales ★ MUSEUM   Since so much of Zamora remains medieval, it was a logical spot to open this center for the study of medieval cities. The cutting-edge facility built into the exterior of a city wall as it descends toward the river has a series of galleries that explore the historical, social, and cultural side of medieval life in central Spain with dioramas, scale models, and multi-lingual panels. You'll make your way down to the lowest level of the museum, which is known as the Zen overlook, or "Mirador Zen." It overlooks the Rio Duero from a softly lit room filled with faint music.

Cuesta del Pizarro, s/n. ✆ **98-053-62-40.** Free admission. Daily noon–2pm and 5–8pm.

Iglesia de Santa María-Magdalena ★ CHURCH   One of the most beautiful of the many Romanesque churches in Zamora, the Magdalena was begun in 1157 for the Order of San Juan and completed early in the 13th century. The form is a simple parish church of its era—a single narrow rectangular nave with a semicircular apse. What sets this church apart (beyond the extensive restoration carried out in the late 20th c.) are the remarkable stone carvings. The capitals of the four pairs of columns supporting the main door are embellished with dragons that have both human and animal heads. The exquisite carvings continue inside the church, with laughing heads on the moldings over the arches. Two tabernacles are embedded in carved stone, and there is a magnificent tomb of a now-anonymous woman watched over by a pair of carved angels.

Rua de los Francos, s/n. No phone. Free admission. Daily 10am–1pm and 5–8pm.

BARCELONA

The Catalan language has a verb that must have been invented for Barcelona. "Badar" translates (more or less) as to walk around with your mouth wide open in astonishment. You'll be doing a lot of that in Barcelona. The city's artists have always had a fantastical vision—from the gargoyles along the roofline of the cathedral, to Antoni Gaudí's armored warrior chimneys on La Pedrera, to the surreal amoeboid sculptures of Joan Miró. (They're on a roof, too.)

Barcelona really is an original, with its own unique history, language, gastronomy, and overall sense of style. When Madrid was still a dusty fortress village on the Río Manzanares, Barcelona was already a force to be reckoned with on the Mediterranean. It has been at the intersection of cultures—Iberian, Roman, Visigothic, Moorish, French, and Aragonese— for 2,000 years. Today it is the capital of the autonomous region of Catalunya, forever chafing to leave the federal fold of Spain but enjoying near-country status within the European Union.

Having won back its identity from Spain, Barcelona is profoundly Catalan, yet generous about conducting business and pleasure alike in Catalan and Castilian—as well as in English. Whatever tongue its visitors speak, Barcelona knows how to impress. Whether you are floating above the city on a cable car, rambling the medieval streets of the Barri Gòtic, devouring peel-and-eat shrimp at a beachside cafe, or sipping fresh strawberry-melon juice at La Boqueria, just remember to keep your eyes wide open.

You never know what will amaze you next.

ESSENTIALS

Arriving

BY PLANE   Barcelona's international airport (BCN) is **El Prat,** located in El Prat de Llobregat (www.aena.es; ✆ **90-240-47-04**), 12km (7½ miles) southwest of the city center. It has two currently operating passenger terminals connected by shuttle buses. The newer, flashier terminal is T1, which opened in 2009, and serves the majority of international carriers, including Air Canada, Air Europa, Air France, Alitalia, American Airlines, British Air, Delta Airlines, El Al, Emirates, Iberia, KLM, Lufthansa, Qatar, Scandinavian Airlines, Swiss International, TAP Portugal, Turkish Airlines, United Airlines, and low-cost carrier Vueling. Most other international carriers—most notably discount airlines Ryanair and easyJet—operate from T2 (formerly terminals A, B, and C).

Most U.S. travelers to Barcelona fly to Madrid and change planes there, although there are seasonal direct flights to Barcelona on American Airlines from New York and on Delta Airlines from New York and Atlanta. Less expensive routes are sometimes available on Lufthansa, British Air, and Air France with changes elsewhere in Europe. Bargain hunters willing to do the research and put up with some inconvenience can often find the cheapest overall airfare by flying to Ireland or the United Kingdom and taking easyJet, Ryanair, or Vueling from there to Barcelona. **Iberia** (www.iberia.com; ✆ **800/772-4642**) offers many daily shuttle flights between Barcelona and Madrid—every half hour at weekday peak hours. Generally cheaper than Iberia, **Air Europa** (www.air-europa.com; ✆ **90-240-15-01**) also runs shuttles between Madrid and Barcelona.

A train runs between the airport and Barcelona's Estació Central de Barcelona-Sants every 15 to 30 minutes daily from 5:40am (the first airport departure) to 11:10pm (from Sants) or 11:40pm (the last city departure). The 20-minute trip costs 3.80€. If your hotel is near Plaça de Espanya or Plaça de Catalunya, it might be worth the slight extra expense to take an **Aerobús** (www.aerobusbcn.com; ✆ **93-415-60-20**). It runs daily every 5 minutes between 6:10am and 1am from the airport, and until 12:30am from the Plaça de Catalunya. The fare is 5.90€ single trip, 10€ round-trip. A taxi from the airport into central Barcelona costs about 30€.

BY TRAIN   Barcelona has two major railway stations. Most national and international trains arrive at **Estació Central de Barcelona-Sants,** Plaça de Països Catalanes (Metro: Sants-Estació), including the high-speed AVE trains from Madrid and the high-speed Trenhotel from Paris. Some slower trains from northern Spain and just over the French border arrive at **Estació de França,** Avenida Marqués de L'Argentera (Metro: Barceloneta, L3). For general RENFE (Spanish Railways) information, log on to www.renfe.com or call ✆ **90-232-03-20.** It's best to purchase tickets, especially on high-speed trains, in advance. There are two train options between Barcelona and Madrid—"express trains" that take 8½ to 9½ hr. and cost 41€–45€ and the high-speed AVE trains that take 2¾ to 3¼ hr. and cost 128€–180€.

BY BUS   Bus travel to Barcelona is possible, but it's pretty slow and less comfortable than the train. Barcelona's Estació del Nord, Carrer d'Alí Bei, 80 (Metro: Arc de Triomf) serves **Alsa** (www.alsa.es; ✆ **90-242-22-42**) buses to and from southern France and Italy. Alsa also operates 27 buses per day to and from Madrid (trip time: 7½– 8½ hr.). A one-way ticket from Madrid costs 33€ to 40€.

Linebús (www.linebus.com; ✆ **90-233-55-33**) offers six trips a week to and from Paris. **Eurolines Viagens,** Carrer Viriato (www.eurolines.es; ✆ **93-490-40-00**), operates seven buses a week to and from Frankfurt and another five per week to and from Marseille.

BY CAR   From **France** (the usual European road approach to Barcelona), the major access route is at the eastern end of the **Pyrenees.** You have a choice of the express highway (E-15) or the more scenic coastal road. If you take the coastal road in July and August, you will often encounter bumper-to-bumper traffic. You can also approach Barcelona via **Toulouse.** Cross the border into Spain at **Puigcerdà** (where there are frontier stations), near the Principality of Andorra. From there, take the N-152 to Barcelona.

From **Madrid,** take the N-2 to Zaragoza, and then the A-2 to El Vendrell, followed by the A-7 freeway to Barcelona. From the **Costa Blanca** or **Costa del Sol,** follow the E-15 north from Valencia along the eastern Mediterranean coast.

BY FERRY   **Trasmediterránea,** Muelle de Sant Bertran s/n (www.trasmediterranea. es; ✆ **90-245-46-45**), operates daily trips to and from the Balearic Islands of Mallorca (trip time: 8 hr.) and Menorca (8 hr.). In summer, it's important to have a reservation as far in advance as possible.

Visitor Information

Barcelona has two types of tourist offices. The Catalunya regional office deals with Spain in general and Catalunya in particular, with basic information about Barcelona. It has two locations at the airport, **El Prat** (Terminal 1: ✆ **93-478-47-04;** Terminal 2: ✆ **93-478-05-65**), both in the Arrivals hall after you pass Customs. Hours are daily 8:30am to 10pm. These offices are co-managed with **Turisme de Barcelona** (see below). There is another large office in the center of Barcelona at the **Palau de Robert,** Passeig de Gràcia, 107 (www.gencat.net; ✆ **93-238-80-91**), where there are often exhibitions. It's open Monday to Saturday 10am to 8pm, Sunday and holidays 10am to 2:30pm.

The **Oficina de Informació de Turisme de Barcelona,** Plaça de Catalunya 17-S (www.barcelonaturisme.com; ✆ **93-285-38-34**), deals exclusively with the city of Barcelona. The main office is located underground on the southeast corner of the plaza. In addition to getting detailed information about the city, you can purchase the **Barcelona Card** (p. 199) here. Sharing the same space is the **FC Barcelona** shop that sells tickets to the matches along with all the souvenirs imaginable, and the information desk for the **Ruta de Modernisme** (p. 199). The office is open daily 9am to 9pm, although the Modernisme desk is open 10am to 6pm.

City Layout

Barcelona is a port city surrounded by two small mountains (**Montjuïc** on the southwest, **Tibidabo** on the north) that form a natural bowl around the port. Although the city sprawls on its east side, the main sections of interest to most travelers are the **waterfront,** the **Ciutat Vell** (old city), **L'Eixample** and **Gràcia** (the 19th-c. extensions inland from the old city), and **Montjuïc.**

The central artery of the Ciutat Vell is **Les Rambles,** a broad avenue with a pedestrian center strip. It begins at the waterfront at Plaça Portal de la Pau, with its 50m-high (174-ft.) monument to Columbus, and stretches north to Plaça de Catalunya, changing names several times along the way. Along this wide promenade you'll find bookshops and newsstands, stalls selling birds and flowers, and benches or cafe tables where you can sit and watch the passing parade. West of Les Rambles is **El Raval,** a sector of the old city that has been spruced up in recent years and is developing an interesting restaurant and bar scene. Just off Les Rambles to the east is **Plaça Reial,** the most harmoniously proportioned square in Barcelona. The neighborhood immediately east of Les Rambles is the **Barri Gòtic** (or Gothic Quarter), and east of the **Barri Gòtic** are the neighborhoods of **El Born** (where the waterfront transitions into the medieval city) and **La Ribera.**

Plaça de Catalunya is intersected by **Gran Via Corts Catalanes,** which is the approximate divider between the old and new cities. The plaza is a major intersection for bus and Metro routes and is ringed with hotels and restaurants. North of Gran Via, the streets of L'Eixample assume an orderly grid. **Passeig de Gràcia** is the most elegant of the north-south boulevards. The exception to the grid is the grand slash across "new" Barcelona, the **Avinguda Diagonal,** which separates the grid of L'Eixample from the grid of Gràcia.

FINDING AN ADDRESS/MAPS Finding a Barcelona address can be difficult. The city abounds with long boulevards and a complicated maze of narrow, twisting streets. Knowing the street number, if there is one, is essential. The designation s/n *(sin número)* means that the building has no number. It's crucial to learn the cross street if you're seeking a specific address. The rule about street numbers is that there is no rule. Most streets are numbered with odd numbers on one side, even numbers on the other.

But because each building counts as a single number and some buildings are much wider than others, consecutive numbers (like 41 and 42, for example) may be a block or more apart.

Arm yourself with a good map before setting out. The free maps given out at the tourist office will do, but they often leave off the names of many of the small streets. The Barcelona Streetwise map from **Falk** is good as well as durable. It is available at most newsstands and kiosks. However, finding your way with a massive folding map is usually impractical and, frankly, makes you more vulnerable to pickpockets. **Google Maps** (http://maps.google.com) are very detailed for Barcelona and largely accurate. If your phone or tablet has local cellular service, you can use them while walking around. Otherwise, download an app that allows you to save the maps for offline reference.

The Neighborhoods in Brief

LES RAMBLES & EL RAVAL

Les Rambles, as famous a promenade as Madrid's Paseo del Prado, was originally the drainage canal that ran down the western edge of the city walls erected by Jaume I in the 13th century. Now it's a broad avenue with a large pedestrian strip down the middle. Street entertainers, flower vendors, news dealers, cafe patrons, and strollers flow along the length of Les Rambles. It is a little like a Fellini movie at times, its 1.5km (1-mile) length between the waterfront and Plaça de Catalunya simultaneously embracing sophistication and a kind of crude vitality.

In the 15th century, convents and monasteries were built on the southwest side of Les Rambles. The last of them was razed in the 19th century, but the succession of names along the promenade—Rambla de Santa Mònica, Rambla dels Caputxins, Rambla de Sant Josep, Rambla dels Estudis, and Rambla de Canaletes—recalls the religious orders. When they left, the brothels moved in, and **El Raval,** west of Les Rambles, became Barcelona's red light district. Nonetheless, a few important landmarks of Modernisme were constructed in Raval and by the late 20th century, the city spruced up the quarter. Today it is a resurgent neighborhood where the university campus and contemporary arts scene on the north end encourage both inexpensive restaurants and interesting design shops. The newly developed Rambla del Raval provides a charming neighborhood park complete with Fernando Botero's giant bronze cat, "El Gato del Raval," and a loud flock of wild monk parrots that nest in the trees.

BARRI GÒTIC

East of Les Rambles is Barcelona's main medieval quarter, the **Barri Gòtic.** King Jaume I fortified it with an encircling wall in the 13th century, of which little remains. Built atop the old Roman city of Barcino, it is a tangle of narrow, cobbled streets that radiate from and connect to slightly larger plazas around the cathedral and a series of other Gothic churches. Buried deep within the Barri Gòtic are the remnants of the **Call,** the medieval Jewish neighborhood. The Barri Gòtic is perhaps the most atmospheric sector of Barcelona, where thoroughly modern shops stand cheek by jowl with museums and historic churches.

LA RIBERA & EL BORN

La Ribera—literally, the shore—was constructed in medieval times in the area east of the city walls where the sea encroached. Part of it was destroyed to build a fortress, now the Parc de la Ciutadella. **El Born** was the name given to the streets west of the fortress that formed the transition between La Ribera and Port Vell. The entire area consists of small, ancient streets, with the straight north-south **Via Laietana** forming its western boundary, and the equally straight **Passeig de Sant Joan** and **Parc de la Ciutadella** forming the eastern boundary. Somewhat more open than the cramped quarters of the Barri Gòtic, this is the area where the **Museu Picasso** stands.

L'EIXAMPLE & GRÀCIA

North of Plaça de Catalunya and Gran Via de les Corts Catalanes, **L'Eixample** is the elegant planned "expansion" that unfolded in the late 19th and early 20th centuries. Catalan Modernisme, a colloquial and localized version of Art Nouveau architecture, reached its apex here. Famous landmark buildings include Antoni Gaudí's **Basilica de la Sagrada Familia** and **Casa Milà,** nicknamed La Pedrera (the stone quarry). The main north-south axis is **Passeig de Gràcia.** At its northern end, it is transected by the broad swath of **Avinguda Diagonal.** North of the Diagonal is the working class neighborhood of **Gràcia,** which consists of several formerly rural villages annexed by Barcelona over the years.

LA BARCELONETA & THE WATERFRONT

Back when Barcelona was a sailor's town, the waterfront was colorful but a little iffy after dark. The 1992 Olympics changed all that, bringing a complete redevelopment of the Port Vell—now basically a yacht harbor—and installing **L'Aquarium Barcelona** and the massive **Maremagnum** shopping center on a newly created island, the Moll d'Espanya. Another moll, or quay, was transformed into the **Moll de la Fusta,** one of the most popular walking and cycling paths in the city. At the east end of Moll de la Fusta, **Passeig de Joan de Borbó** goes down to the tip of **La Barceloneta.** Once the neighborhood of Barcelona fishermen, Barceloneta has become one of the hippest bohemian addresses in the city and is noted for its seafood restaurants and sandy beaches. Follow the beaches east to **Port Olimpic,** developed for the boating events of the 1992 Olympics.

MONTJUÏC

In some ways disconnected from the rest of the city, **Montjuïc** is a small mountain that doesn't seem so small when you're walking up it in the summer heat. It begins at **Plaça d'Espanya,** a traffic rotary where the city's new convention center is located, and goes up past fountains to the old Palacio Nacional, now the stunning **Museu Nacional d'Art de Catalunya.** The mountain was used for the 1929 Barcelona International Exposition, which created the roadways, many of the gardens, and the **Poble Espanyol** area of "typical" architecture from around Spain. Many of the events of the 1992 Olympics were also held here, leaving behind a stadium and a state-of-the-art swimming facility. It is also the home of the **Fundació Joan Miró.**

GETTING AROUND

On Foot

You can walk most places in Barcelona's old city, or through the main districts of interest in L'Eixample. But it's a good idea to use public transport to a starting point and then set off on foot to explore.

By Public Transit

Barcelona's public transit system includes extensive and interlinked networks of buses, subway trains, trams, and "rodalies" (local commuter rail). For a full overview, check the website of **Transports Metropolitans de Barcelona** (www.tmb.cat). This site, available in Catalan, Spanish, and English, has a very useful tool that recommends ways to get from one place to another using any combination of public transit and walking. Individual tickets on subway and buses within the central city cost 2€.

By Subway

Barcelona's Metro system consists of six main lines; it crisscrosses the city more frequently and with greater efficiency than the bus network. Service operates Sunday to Thursday from 5am to midnight, and Friday and Saturday from 5am to 2am. Each

Metro station entrance is marked with a red diamond. The major station for all subway lines is **Plaça de Catalunya.**

By Bus

About 190 bus lines traverse the city and, not surprisingly, you don't want to ride them at rush hour. Most buses operate daily from 5:30am to 10pm; some night buses go along the principal arteries from 11pm to 4am. You can buy your ticket when boarding. Red buses cut through the city center during the day, and yellow ones operate at night.

By Barcelona Bus Turistic

The most established of the sightseeing buses, the double-decker **Barcelona Bus Turistic** makes a circuit on three routes that can deliver you to almost every major tourist attraction in the city. The bus includes running commentary (through headsets) in 10 languages, and a choice of outdoor seating with great views and indoor seating with heat or air conditioning. It also claims free Wi-Fi on board, but it never worked on any buses where we tried it. The circuits on the red route (old city, Montjuic, and the waterfront) and the blue route (L'Eixample and Gràcia) each take about 2 hours. The green route, which shuttles along the neighborhoods and beaches east of Port Olimpic, takes 40 minutes. You can get on and off all day, but be forewarned that you can wait as much as a half-hour to get onto a crowded bus during high season. It's useful if you don't want to use regular public transportation, but it's quite a bit less efficient. One day on the bus, however, will get you a booklet of discounts good on many attractions including La Pedrera and La Sagrada Familia. The cost is 26€ for 1 day, 34€ for 2 days (15€ and 19€ for ages 4–12).

By Taxi

Each yellow-and-black taxi bears the letters SP *(Servicio Público)* on its front and rear. A lit green light on the roof and a LIBRE sign in the window indicate the taxi is free to pick up passengers. Make sure that the meter is at zero when you enter. The basic rate begins at 2€. Each additional kilometer costs 1€. Supplements might apply—1€ for a large suitcase placed in the trunk, for instance. Rides to the airport carry a supplement of 3.10€. For a taxi, contact **Ràdio Taxi** (www.radiotaxi033.com; ✆ **93-303-30-33**).

By Funicular & Rail Links

It takes some planning to visit the mountains of Tibidabo or Montjuïc. To visit Tibidabo by public transport, you'll have to take the **Funicular de Tibidabo.** The fare is 7.10€, or 4.10€ if you're also purchasing admission to the Tibidabo amusement park. The funicular operates every 15 to 20 minutes. From mid-April to September service is daily 10am to 8pm. In the off season it usually operates only Saturday and Sunday 10am to 6pm. To get to the funicular, take Metro Line 7 to Avinguda Tibidabo. Exit onto Plaça Kennedy and take either the 1901 tram called **Tramvía Blau** (Blue Street-car) or **Bus 196** to the funicular. The bus is the usual 2€ fare. Tickets on the **Tramvia Blau** are 4.70€.

Getting to Montjuic by funicular is a simple ride from the Paral.lel Metro station and is considered part of the Metro network, although you need to change and use a new 2€ ticket. Once you're on the mountain, you can ride a cable car to the castle on top. Tickets on **Telefèric de Montjuïc** are 7.30€ one-way, 10€ round-trip (5.50€ or 7.40€ for ages 4–12).

By Car

Driving and trying to park in congested Barcelona is not worth the hassle. Use public transportation and save car rentals for excursions and moving on. Avis and Hertz have offices at the airport and downtown. **Avis,** Carrer Corçega 293–295 (www.avis.es; 𝄃 **90-211-02-75**), is open Monday to Friday 8am to 9pm, Saturday 8am to 8pm, and Sunday 8am to 1pm. **Hertz,** Carrer de Viriat, 45 (www.hertz.es; 𝄃 **93-419-61-56**), is located adjacent to the Estació Barcelona-Sants rail station and keeps the same hours. It is usually cheaper and easier to arrange your car rental before leaving home. Given the consolidation in the rental car industry, prices vary little among companies, so stick with whichever one dovetails with your frequent-flyer program.

[FastFACTS] BARCELONA

Banks & ATMs You can usually find a bank—or at least an ATM—wherever crowds gather in Barcelona, especially in shopping districts and around major Metro stations. Most permit cash withdrawals via MC or V, and many are linked into international networks that will let you access your home bank account. Most offer a choice of language, almost always including English. The most prominent banks with large ATM networks in Barcelona are **La Caixa** and **Banco Santander.** Major overseas banks with a presence include **Deutsche Bank** and **Citibank.** Note that most Spanish ATMs only accept 4-digit PINs, so if you have a longer PIN, change it at least a week

before departure. Many banks now have "dynamic currency conversion," which means the bank will offer to charge your withdrawal in dollars rather than euros. The exchange rate is even worse than the one your bank at home will give you, so always answer "NO" and ask to be charged in euros. With the proliferation of ATM networks, cash exchanges are uncommon and should be avoided as they usually offer poor exchange rates and/or high service charges.

Business Hours Opening hours are in flux in Barcelona. The lunch break is vanishing faster here than in the rest of Spain, but expect small shops and some old-fashioned places

to open at 10a.m, close 2–5pm for lunch, and open again 5–8:30pm. Other businesses stay open through the midday.

Consulates National embassies are all located in Madrid, but some consular offices are found in Barcelona. The **U.S. Consulate,** Carrer Reina Elisenda, 23 (𝄃 **93-280-22-27;** train: Reina Elisenda), is open Monday to Friday 9am to 1pm. The **Canadian Consulate,** Plaça de Catalunya, 9 (𝄃 **93-412-72-36;** Metro: Plaça de Catalunya), is open Monday to Friday 9am to 12:30pm. The **U.K. Consulate,** Avinguda Diagonal, 477 (𝄃 **93-366-62-00;** Metro: Hospital Clínic), is open Monday to Friday 8:30am to 1:30pm. **Australia** and **New Zealand** have only honorary consuls in Barcelona.

Doctors & Dentists

Barcelona has many hospitals and clinics, including **Clínic Barcelona** (www.hospitalclinic.org; ✆ **93-227-54-00**) and **Hospital de la Santa Creu i Sant Pau,** at the intersection of Carrer Cartagena and Carrer Sant Antoni María Claret (✆ **93-291-90-00;** Metro: Hospital de Sant Pau). For dental needs, contact **Clínica Dental Barcelona,** Passeig de Gràcia, 97 (✆ **93-487-83-29;** Metro: Diagonal), open daily 9am to midnight.

Emergencies

Call ✆ **112** for general emergencies. To report a fire, call ✆ **080;** to call an ambulance, ✆ **061;** to call the police, ✆ **088.**

Internet Access

Most lodgings offer free Wi-Fi access, at least in public areas, if you have your own laptop, tablet, phone, or other device. Typically, bandwidth on free hotel Wi-Fi is good enough to surf the web, use email, look up maps, and sometimes even make VOIP phone calls. It is not adequate for streaming video or music. Some hotels give away basic Wi-Fi but charge for faster access. Somewhat slower free Wi-Fi access is usually available in cafes and some stores. The city government also provides free Wi-Fi at 109 hotspots in L'Eixample and 61 spots in the old city. You will have to sign up for a free account to use it, however, and it is limited

by intention to minimal service to "respect the marketplace." Buses and some Metro lines also have free Wi-Fi. If you are planning to use a phone or tablet, download the GOWEX Free Wifi app for iOs from the Apple Store or for Android from the Google Play Store. With the proliferation of free hotspots, Internet cafes are vanishing—usually they are coupled with long-distance phone services in immigrant neighborhoods. Expect to pay 2€ to 4€ per hour.

Language

Catalunya has two official languages: Catalan and Castilian Spanish. Catalan (Catalá in its own language) takes precedence for signage, television and radio, and most publications. As a romance language, it resembles both Spanish and French. Indeed, most Spanish speakers read Catalan with little difficulty and the languages can sound very much alike. Note, for example, that a Catalan word ending in an accented vowel is pronounced as if there were a nasal "n" at the end. English is widely spoken in the tourism sector, although you might be better off resorting to your high school or college Spanish once you step away from the bright lights. Many Barcelona websites offer pages in English.

Mail & Postage

The main post office is at Plaça d'Antoni López (www.correos.es; ✆ **93-486-80-50;** Metro: Jaume I). It's open Monday to Friday 8:30am to 9:30pm and

Saturday 8:30am to 2pm for sending letters and telegrams. Sending a postcard or letter to the U.S. starts at 0.90€. To calculate the price, visit http://correos.es. You can also buy stamps at any place that sells tobacco.

Newspapers & Magazines

The Paris-based "International New York Times" (formerly the "International Herald Tribune") is sold at most newsstands in the tourist districts, as are "USA Today" and European editions of "Time" and "Newsweek." British papers abound on the same newsstands. Barcelona's own leading daily newspapers, which often list cultural events, are "El Periódico" and "La Vanguardia."

Pharmacies

Farmacia Montserrat, Les Rambles, 118 (✆ **93-302-43-45;** Metro: Liceu), is the most centrally located. It's open daily 9am to 8pm. Pharmacies take turns staying open late at night. Those that aren't open post the names and addresses of pharmacies in the area that are.

Safety

Barcelona is a big city with a lot of slightly disoriented tourists paying scant attention to their belongings. Pickpockets and purse-snatchers treat the unwary like the weak antelopes straggling at the back of the herd. Don't be one of them. Be careful with cameras, purses, and wallets wherever there are crowds, especially on Les Rambles.

WHERE TO STAY

Hotels in Barcelona are among the most expensive in Spain but that doesn't mean you can't find good values. Many visitors gravitate to hotels on or near **Les Rambles** for convenience in getting around, but somewhat better bargains can be found in **El Raval** as well as in the **Barri Gòtic.** Although not quite as convenient to public transit, lodgings in **La Ribera** and **El Born** tend to offer the best combination of price and value. Hotels along the **Waterfront** tend to be new and flashy, and priced accordingly. **L'Eixample** hotels, while typically more expensive than in the old city, are also usually more spacious.

Les Rambles & El Raval

The Ciutat Vella (Old City) forms the monumental center of Barcelona, taking in Les Rambles, Plaça de Sant Jaume, Vía Laietana, Passeig Nacional, and Passeig de Colom. It contains some of the city's best hotel bargains. Most of the glamorous, and more expensive, hotels are here.

EXPENSIVE

Casa Camper ★   The Camper shoe company took its offbeat shoe design aesthetic and used it to convert a 19th-century Raval tenement building near the contemporary art museum into a designer hotel. Rooms have a breezy and playful décor, and each one features a rope hammock as well as a bed. They're designed to appeal to well-heeled hipsters—just spare enough to be modern, not so empty as to look barren and each is a mini-suite, with separate sleeping and sitting areas. There's also one real suite on each floor where the living and sleeping areas are linked through a pocket sliding door. Should you feel overwhelmed by the city, you can catch a nap in a hammock on the roof terrace. The lobby has a buffet of snacks available around the clock.

Carrer Elisabets, 11. ☎ **93-342-62-80.** www.casacamper.com. 25 units. 194€–282€ double; 236€–330€ suite. Metro: Plaça de Catalunya. **Amenities:** Bar; babysitting; bikes; restaurant; room service; free Wi-Fi.

H1898 ★   Superb soundproofing makes the elegant rooms on this, the loudest stretch of Les Rambles, surprisingly quiet. As for décor, the owners re-created the opulence of imperial Spain but with 21st-century conveniences, and named the hotel for the year that Spain lost the Philippines in the Spanish-American War. (The building once served as the headquarters of the Philippines Tobacco Company.) The broad rooftop terrace even features a full lap pool. Rooms are graded in five levels, but even the lowliest is sumptuous and comfortable. Upgrade only if you need a lot of extra space.

Les Rambles, 109 (entrance on Pintor Fortuny). ☎ **93-552-95-52.** www.hotel1898.com. 169 units. 195€–435€ double; suites from 485€. Free parking. Metro: Plaça de Catalunya. **Amenities:** Restaurant; bar; concierge; exercise room; 2 heated pools (1 indoor); spa; free Wi-Fi.

Hotel Bagues ★★★   There are more expensive and even fancier hotels in Barcelona, but we think this is the best choice in the old city for a romantic getaway. Why? The answer is in both its looks and its high level of hospitality. The staff provides friendly and helpful service without putting on airs. And the hotel's Modernista design is a holdover from the building's heyday as a jewelry store; the modern comforts don't detract one iota from the stunning visuals of the original designs. The walls and wardrobes in the rooms, for example, are enhanced with gold leaf accents and panels of Madagascar ebony. The hotel even has a Masriera Museum, showcasing the jewelry of

Abba Rambla Hotel **13**
Actahotels Antibes **40**
Avenida Palace **2**
Axel **37**
Banys Orientals **28**
Barcelona Hotel
  Colonial **26**
Casa Camper **8**
Casa Fuster **33**
Chic & Basic Born **30**
Citadines
  Aparthotel **9**
Ciutat Barcelona
  Hotel **29**
Duquesa de Cardona
  Hotel **25**
Europark Hotel **39**
Eurostars Ramblas
  Boqueria **12**
H1898 **10**
HC Ramblas **5**
Hesperia Ramblas **14**
Hostal Girona **31**
Hotel Adagio **17**
Hotel Arts **22**

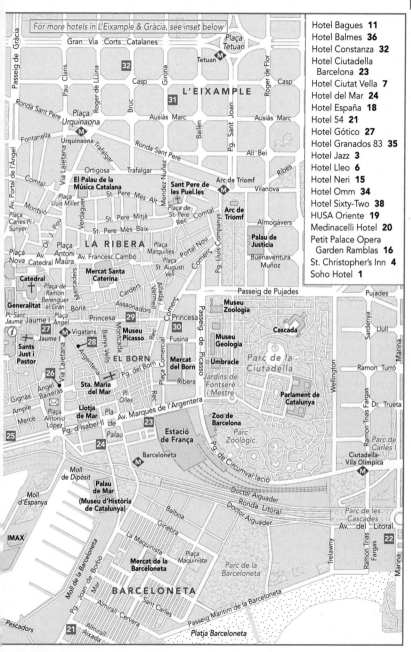

For more hotels in L'Eixample & Gràcia, see inset below

Hotel Bagues **11**
Hotel Balmes **36**
Hotel Constanza **32**
Hotel Ciutadella
  Barcelona **23**
Hotel Ciutat Vella **7**
Hotel del Mar **24**
Hotel España **18**
Hotel 54 **21**
Hotel Gótico **27**
Hotel Granados 83 **35**
Hotel Jazz **3**
Hotel Lleo **6**
Hotel Neri **15**
Hotel Omm **34**
Hotel Sixty-Two **38**
HUSA Oriente **19**
Medinacelli Hotel **20**
Petit Palace Opera
  Garden Ramblas **16**
St. Christopher's Inn **4**
Soho Hotel **1**

the Art Nouveau master. By the way, the bulk of the rooms are called "standard," but in this case, they are larger than most hotel suites.

Les Rambles, 105. ℂ **93-343-50-00.** www.derbyhotels.com. 31 units. 175€–280€ double; suites from 310€. Metro: Plaça de Catalunya. **Amenities:** Bar; restaurant; room service; business center; outdoor swimming pool; solarium; spa; gym; limousine service; free Wi-Fi. Dogs allowed on request.

MODERATE

Abba Rambla Hotel ★   Built in 2005, this sleekly modern and friendly hotel was a pioneer of fine lodging in El Raval, an area once known for super-budget pensions. It fronts on the park of La Rambla del Raval, an up-and-coming cafe district. Rooms are compact but extremely well-designed with adequate space and contemporary bathrooms, most with tub-showers. Set just far enough off Les Rambles to avoid the crowds, it's still convenient to walk to the contemporary art museum as well as most attractions in the Barri Gòtic.

Carrer La Rambla del Raval, 4C. ℂ **93-505-54-00.** www.abbahotels.com. 49 units. 110€–140€ double. Parking 22€. Metro: Liceu. **Amenities:** Bar; cafeteria; business center; solarium; free Wi-Fi.

Citadines Aparthotel ★★   At the upper end of Les Rambles near the Plaça de Catalunya, these self-sufficient apartments, constructed in 1994, were renovated floor to ceiling and completely refurnished in late 2013. With gray wood floors, muted earth tone bedspreads and draperies, dark wood furniture, large showers in the bathrooms, and a fully equipped if compact kitchen, even the smallest of these units is twice the size of most Barcelona hotel rooms. Having the kitchen makes it easy (and cheaper) to prepare breakfast and gives you a wonderful excuse to shop at La Boqueria. Just steps from the Plaça del Pi in the Barri Gòtic, the location is prime. Much bigger than it looks from the street, the aparthotel has two buildings that share a gym and coin-op laundry. There's no minimum stay, but prices per night decline with longer bookings.

Les Rambles, 122. ℂ **93-270-11-11.** www.citadines.com. 131 units. 100€–245€ studio apt, 200€–490€ 1-bedroom apt. Metro: Plaça de Catalunya. **Amenities:** Gym; free Wi-Fi and high-speed cable Internet.

Eurostars Ramblas Boqueria ★   If the bright colors of the décor in this new hotel remind you of a summertime fruit salad, you're thinking like the designer. Since it's right next to La Boqueria, the hotel employs a color palette of Mediterranean fruits and vegetables and even has a lobby mural depicting broccoli and carrots. That's Barcelona whimsy for you. The building is a 19th-century palace that's been transformed into a compact hotel of 30 rooms of very modest dimensions and minimalist décor. The location is great, and the new construction is as close to soundproof as it can be. All rooms either overlook Les Rambles or La Boqueria and all have pocket balconies or terraces.

Les Rambles, 91–93. ℂ **93-343-54-61.** www.eurostarshotels.com. 30 units. 70€–200€ double. Metro: Liceu. **Amenities:** Bar-cafeteria; fitness room; free Wi-Fi.

HC Ramblas ★★   Of all the HC hotels in Barcelona, we think this one offers the best value for the price. It is a large business hotel right off Plaça de Catalunya, so rooms are furnished in quiet, modern style without the pops of color featured at design hotels. But the beds are comfortable, the desks are functional, and there's plenty of room to place your luggage. Moreover, the staff is efficient and polite. The building is vaguely Modernista, dating from the early 20th century, but those design features do not carry through inside. Nonetheless, location and price make it a good alternative, and because it is large, rooms are almost always available.

Carrer Pelai, 28. ℂ **93-316-84-00.** www.hoteles-catalonia.com. 221 units. 120€–260€ double. Metro: Plaça de Catalunya. **Amenities:** Restaurant; bar; business center; concierge; exercise room; pool; free Wi-Fi. Pets allowed on request.

Hesperia Ramblas ★   This very modern hotel is, in some respects, the antithesis of its surroundings. Tucked onto a corner in El Raval, it stands out for its pale gray concrete mass amid the older stone buildings. Inside, the furnishings evoke the showroom of Design Within Reach—lots of molded plastic furniture and contemporary design lighting fixtures. The rooms, though, are soothing oases of gray and white—unless you select a Pink Room, designed for female executives. In its own way, it embodies the Barcelona love affair with Scandinavian post-modernism.

Carrer Hospital, 26. ℂ **93-151-61-00.** www.hesperia-ramblas.com. 70 units. 100€–170€ double. Metro: Liceu. **Amenities:** Business center; free Wi-Fi.

Hotel España ★   Erected as a rooming house in 1859, this handsome structure just steps from Les Rambles was transformed into a Modernista hotel in 1903 by Lluís Domènech i Montaner. Guests get a discount on the guided architectural tour (see "Exploring," below). The hotel was completely renovated in 2010 to restore its Modernista flair while also installing contemporary technology and plumbing. The styling is serene and simple, with dark wood tones and taupes that coordinate nicely with the Modernista design. The smallest rooms are a little tight (roughly 12×12 ft.), but most are larger.

Carrer Sant Pau, 9–11. ℂ **93-550-00-00.** www.hotelespanya.com. 82 units. 103€–238€ double. Metro: Liceu. **Amenities:** Bar; restaurant; business area; terrace; swimming pool; free Wi-Fi.

Hotel Jazz ★   A member of the same group as the H1898 (see above), the Jazz aims for a more modern comfort without the trappings of empire. Located off Plaça de Catalunya near the contemporary art museum and the downtown campus of the University of Barcelona, the Jazz is true to its name, evoking the Rat Pack era (for some reason, a Spanish fascination) without exactly replicating it. Indeed, the new renditions of retro design are timeless. This is an unusually family-friendly design hotel, even providing complimentary cradles for infants. In an odd nod to an old-fashioned amenity from the Fifties, the rooms offer piped-in music—a feature that can be easily turned off.

Carrer Pelai, 3. ℂ **93-532-96-96.** www.hoteljazz.com. 108 rooms. 150€–200€ double. Parking 30€. Metro: Plaça de Catalunya. **Amenities:** Bar-cafe; business center; outdoor pool; rooftop terrace; room service; free Wi-Fi.

INEXPENSIVE

Hotel Ciutat Vella ★★   The red-white-and-black color scheme gives this smart little boutique hotel a lot of visual pop, which is only fitting for a new hostelry around the corner from the contemporary art museum. Rooms have an uncluttered but functional design that has the color and ease of use of a good web page. The clientele tends to skew young, but that could be because the art school and university are also nearby. It might be the brightest and airiest lodging in El Raval, and the low-season prices make it one of the best bargains.

Carrer Tallers, 66. ℂ **93-481-37-99.** www.hotelciutatvella.com. 40 units. 70[e]–140€ double. Metro: Plaça de Catalunya or Universitat. **Amenities:** Free lobby snacks and drinks available 24 hr.; rooftop terrace with Jacuzzi and solarium; free Wi-Fi.

Hotel Lleó ★   Surrounded by a bevy of designer boutique hotels where all the furnishings are dark wood, all the floors are Pergo, and all the soft goods are shades of brown and taupe, the Lleó is a Spanish throwback of blond wood furniture, tan walls, and hardwood floors. It's like finding a caramel in a box of chocolates—different but just as good in its own way. Maybe better in this case, since the hotel lacks a star in the official ratings (no restaurant) and is thus cheaper. Rooms are adequately sized with decent desks to go with comfortable beds and small but well-designed bathrooms.

Low-season prices are a steal, and in summer, the rooftop terrace and pool are a welcome surprise in this price range.

Carrer Pelai, 22 y 24. ✆ **93-318-12-12.** www.hotel-lleo.com. 92 rooms. 75€–145€ double. **Amenities:** Rooftop terrace and pool; business center; Jacuzzi; billiards room; Wi-Fi.

HUSA Oriente ★ With its wide, tiled hallways, high ceilings, and breakfast room in the glass-roofed courtyard, the Oriente is a nicely renovated example of a former grand hotel. All the plumbing is new, and the furnishings are sparely modern and comfortable. The location is prime and the prices are right. Double windows on Les Rambles keep the noise down as well. Note that this hotel is popular with tour packagers, so you can run into periods of limited availability.

Les Rambles, 45. ✆ **93-302-25-58.** www.hotelhusaoriente.com. 142 units. 61€–128€ double. Parking 30€. Metro: Liceu. **Amenities:** Restaurant; bar; concierge; free in-room Wi-Fi.

St Christopher's Inn ★ One of the newest (2012) in this European chain of deluxe backpacker hostels, the Barcelona version touts the city's late-night revelry, the nude beach (there is one, but it's not close), and the youthful vibe of the city. The four private rooms are as expensive as nearby hotels, but the dorm rooms are a pretty good deal. Male, female, and mixed dormitories are available, and they're clean and bright. All ages are welcome, but most guests are under 25. Location near Plaça de Catalunya means you can hop a subway or bus and get almost anywhere in minutes.

Carrer Bergara, 3. ✆ **93-667-45-88.** www.bookbeds.com. 11 rooms. 24€–30€ dorm bed; 110€–140€ private double. Metro: Plaça de Catalunya. **Amenities:** Kitchen facilities; bar-restaurant; towel rental; free Wi-Fi.

Barri Gòtic, La Ribera & El Born

If you are considering a visit of 3 nights or more in Barcelona, a good option is an apartment rental. It has advantages (your own cooking facilities, being embedded in a residential area) and disadvantages (cleaning deposits, no services). One of the better agencies is **apartmentsinbarcelona.net** (Carrer Jaume I, 30; ✆ **93-439-56-64**). You make arrangements online, then check in at the office, where someone will guide you to your apartment and hand over the keys. Selections are available all over the city and with varying numbers of bedrooms, but most are studios or one-bedroom apartments in the Barri Gòtic and El Born. Rates range from 50€ to 200€ per night depending on location, size, season, and length of stay.

EXPENSIVE

Hotel Neri ★★★ This delightful boutique hotel sits at the edge of the Call in the Barri Gòtic. Most of the hotel lies within a re-built medieval noble home, but the restaurant wing is a modern addition that harmonizes nicely with the ancient stone. Reception sits on the Call, while the restaurant terrace opens onto Plaça Sant Felip Neri, one of Barcelona's most storied old squares. The building skillfully combines 9 centuries of architecture while keeping the rooms open, airy, and timeless. Abstract Expressionist art hangs throughout the hotel, evoking a modern sensibility in a structure rooted in the very non-abstract materials of stone and exposed wood. The rooftop terrace (complete with hammocks as well as tables and chairs) functions as an auxiliary bar, weather permitting. The hotel restaurant, while open to the public, mainly services the guests with a contemporary Mediterranean menu. The Neri's location in the Call makes it a popular choice for travelers on Jewish heritage holidays.

Carrer Sant Severe, 5. ✆ **93-304-06-55.** www.hotelneri.com. 22 units. 200€–320€ double; 270€–350€ suite. Metro: Liceu or Jaume I. **Amenities:** Restaurant; bar-cafe; babysitting; free Wi-Fi.

MODERATE

Banys Orientals ★   Located in El Born at the doorway to the Barri Gòtic, this boutique hotel sits in the most historic part of Barcelona. It offers quality and comfort at an affordable price in a 19th-century private mansion turned modern hotel. The bathrooms gleam with marble, the floors are stained a dark walnut, and the crisp white linens stand out in high contrast. In addition to doubles, there are several suites, some with private patios. If you like the location, consider the upgrade to a suite, as doubles are beautiful but too tight to have more than one suitcase open at a time.

Carrer Argentería, 37. ⓒ **93-268-84-60.** www.hotelbanysorientals.com. 43 units. 90€–173€ double; 110€–185€ suite. Metro: Jaume I. **Amenities:** Restaurant; room service; free Wi-Fi.

Petit Palace Opera Garden Ramblas ★   This spiffy member of the Petit Palace high-tech hotel chain is more luxurious than most of its siblings, in part because it really does occupy a small palace that has been made over as a business hotel that would make Silicon Valley proud. All rooms have laptops and a very good work desk where the power outlets stay on after you remove the key card and go out for the day. Playing off the relative proximity to the Teatre Gran Liceu, rooms are nominally themed to classic operas.

Carrer La Boqueria, 10. ⓒ **93-302-00-92.** www.petitpalaceoperagardenhotel.com. 70 units. 120€–210€ double; suites from 215€. Metro: Liceu. **Amenities:** Bar-cafe; outdoor terrace; free Wi-Fi.

INEXPENSIVE

Barcelona Hotel Colonial ★★   Set in a handsome 19th-century building that once housed the Banco Hispano, this hotel is convenient for exploring Barcelona's waterfront as well as the old city. It's less than a 5-minute walk from the Moll de la Fusta and just a few hundred yards from the Museu Picasso. Perhaps because it's a former bank building, this lodging has a grander lobby than many old city hotels, especially those in Born. Rooms are rather less spacious than the lobby, though just as sumptuously appointed. Triple rooms with a sleeper couch are available.

Vía Laietana, 3. ⓒ **93-315-22-52.** www.hotelcolonialbarcelona.com. 81 rooms. 80€–165€ double; 108€–190€ triple. Metro: Jaume I or Barceloneta. **Amenities:** Cafeteria; free Wi-Fi.

Chic & Basic Born ★   By creating stylish budget lodging, the Chic & Basic chain has helped make cheap hotels fun. The proprietors know their clientele, and found a spot in the heart of the youthful bar scene for this Barcelona edition. There is a bit of dorm-room chic about it, with doorless closets, and a color scheme that is literally colorless. (It's like they painted the rooms by closing all the doors and windows and exploding a white paint bomb.) The result is either futuristic or hospital-like, depending on your sensibility. Echoing another "daring" design cliché, shower stalls are fully transparent. The hotel protests its design cred a little too much, and reception staff affect a maximum of attitude that can be childish and annoying. But much can be forgiven at prices like this, since most rooms are on the low end of the range, especially if booked directly on the Chic & Basic website.

Carrer Princesa, 50. ⓒ **93-295-45-62.** www.chicandbasic.com. 31 units. 65€–150€. Free parking. Metro: Jaume I. **Amenities:** Restaurant; bar; room service; free Wi-Fi.

Ciutat Barcelona Hotel ★★   A bargain-priced design hotel for grown-ups, the Ciutat Barcelona has soothing contemporary look to its rooms, including chairs and light fixtures that look they come straight from the showroom at Design Within Reach or some other such store. Spaces are compact but well-designed, and the rooftop terrace is like having a private oasis in the middle of the city. There is a side entrance for wheelchair users, and some of the rooms are fully accessible. The small but delightful pool is just big enough to make kids happy.

Carrer Princessa, 35. ✆ **93-269-7475.** www.ciutatbarcelona.com. 78 rooms. 80€–140€ double. Metro: Jaume I. **Amenities:** Internet corner; rooftop pool; free Wi-Fi and high-speed cable Internet.

Hotel Adagio ★   Barcelona hotels with an official two-star rating can be a pretty grim lot, but Adagio is a delightful exception following some substantial renovations in early 2013. Located about halfway between Plaça Reial and Plaça de Catalunya, Adagio fronts onto Carrer Ferran, one of the broader east-west streets of the Barri Gòtic. The reception area is tiny, as it was moved back to make room for the excellent tapas restaurant in the front. Rooms are small, as you'd expect in this price range, but very clean. Location is superb, but it's best to keep windows closed and use the air conditioning as the narrow stone streets can be noisy at night. Exceedingly friendly and eager-to-please staff helps compensate for the lack of luxury.

Carrer Ferran, 21. ✆ **93-318-90-61.** www.adagiohotel.com. 38 units. 49€–90€ double. Metro: Liceu or Jaume I. **Amenities:** Free Wi-Fi.

Hotel Gótico ★★   This hotel at the crossroads of Jaume I/Princesa and Via Laietana is our favorite among the cluster of Gargallo family hotels on the same block. The historic building from 1823 was transformed into a hotel in 1999 and completely renovated in 2012. Acres of marble cover the entry foyer (as well as the bathrooms) and golden accents glimmer against the wood inlay and exposed brick. The guest rooms are a little on the snug side, but are simply decorated with modern design furniture that reinterprets the Modernista aesthetic through the lens of Danish Modern. The location is terrific for walking swiftly to the cathedral in one direction, the Museu Picasso in the other. Friendly and solicitous staff make the experience of staying here all the more pleasant.

Carrer Jaume I, 14. ✆ **93-315-21-13.** www.hotelgotico.com. 81 units. 75€–120€ double. Metro: Jaume I. **Amenities:** Bar-cafe; room service; terrace; free Wi-Fi. Dogs permitted.

L'Eixample
EXPENSIVE

Casa Fuster ★★★   This stunning Modernista building was designed by Lluís Domènech i Montaner for the Fuster family in 1908, and it was reported at the time to be the most expensive home constructed in the city. Modernisme's heyday lives again in this deluxe hotel decked out in a palette of magenta, mauve, and taupe. Private balconies in many rooms open onto leafy Passeig de Gràcia. The hotel's Viennese cafe has become one of Barcelona's best jazz clubs, but soundproofing is so good that you won't hear a single saxophone honk in your room. The location is less convenient than most for exploring the city, but if you have your heart set on sleeping in a full-blown Modernista landmark, Casa Fuster is your place.

Passeig de Gràcia, 132. ✆ **93-255-30-00.** www.hotelcasafuster.com. 96 units. 173€–270€ double; 270€–322€ jr. suite; from 648€ suite. Parking 33€. Metro: Diagonal. **Amenities:** Restaurant; bar; babysitting; concierge; exercise room; Jacuzzi; outdoor heated pool; room service; sauna; free Wi-Fi.

Hotel Omm ★★★   It's almost worth staying at Omm just for the view from the rooftop bar and swimming pool of La Pedrera's fanciful chimneys across the street. Grupo Tragaluz, of Barcelona gourmet restaurant fame, set out to make this boutique property a 21st-century exemplar of style the way Gaudí's Casa Milà (La Pedrera) is the apex of Modernisme. The lobby, restaurant **Roca Moo** (p. 191), and other public areas are all high drama, while the rooms are breezy and relaxing. Guest rooms have parquet wood floors, handwoven rugs, and large windows with views of either the inner courtyard or Passeig de Gràcia.

Carrer Rosselló, 265. ✆ **93-445-40-00.** www.hotelomm.es. 91 units. 199€–360€ double; 440€–660€ suite. Parking 32€. Metro: Diagonal. **Amenities:** Restaurant; bar; babysitting; concierge; rooftop heated pool; room service; spa; free Wi-Fi and high-speed cable Internet.

MODERATE

Avenida Palace ★   Perhaps the biggest claim to fame for this very pleasant dowager hotel is that the Beatles stayed here when they played Barcelona in 1965. (Yes, you can book their suite.) The hotel stands behind an odd pair of pseudo-fortified towers, but once inside the strange architecture resolves into an old-world atmosphere of antiques, fresh flowers, and rather formally attired staff. Most rooms are doubles, and they are spacious by Spanish standards and filled with walnut and chestnut burl furniture. Beds are comfortable and each room has a workable desk. The neighborhood isn't loud, but the rooms are thoroughly soundproofed anyway.

Gran Vía de les Corts Catalanes, 605 (at Passeig de Gràcia). ✆ **93-301-96-00.** www.avenidapalace. com. 151 units. 110€–165€ double; 155€–280€ suite. Parking 20€. Metro: Passeig de Gràcia. **Amenities:** Restaurant; bar; babysitting; bikes; concierge; room service; sauna; free Wi-Fi.

Axel ★   Several gay travel publications have given Axel their imprimatur, and it's easy to see why. A huge mural of two men embracing adorns the lobby, there's gay erotic art in most of the guestrooms and the on-site boutique sells skimpy men's bathing trunks. As well, there's a strong flirting scene here at the rooftop pool, sun deck, and cocktail bar. Still, the hotel advertises itself as being hetero-friendly, and with its larger-than-usual rooms (with true king beds instead of two twins pushed together), rich linens, and a full menu of pillow choices, Axel should appeal to travelers of all orientations.

Carrer Aribau, 33. ✆ **93-323-93-93.** www.axelhotels.com. 105 units. 99€–149€ double; suites from 239€. Parking 25€. Metro: Universitat. **Amenities:** Restaurant; 2 bars; health club and spa; outdoor heated pool; room service; free Wi-Fi.

Europark Hotel ★   Designer Rosa Roselló finally brought some whimsy to the dark wood and chocolate fabrics design aesthetic so prominent in contemporary Barcelona business hotels. At the Europark, she outfitted the beds in spreads with broad stripes, almost like awning material, and followed through with the zebra pattern on the upholstered chairs, so though the rooms are boxy—she couldn't move walls!—they also provide an intriguing visual experience. The location—roughly a 10-minute stroll to the main Modernista monuments on Passeig de Gràcia or to La Sagrada Familia in the opposite direction—commands a lower price than you'd expect for the quality and comfort here.

Carrer Aragó, 323–325. ✆ **93-457-92-05.** www.hoteleuropark.com. 105 units. 100€–150€ double. Metro: Verdaguer or Girona. **Amenities:** Bar-cafe; room service; rooftop terrace and pool; fitness room; free Wi-Fi.

Hotel Balmes ★★   The bargain-priced member of the Derby group, the Balmes shares the serene modern style of the chain, which we'd call a cross between a small art museum and a well-appointed gentleman's club. (The owner of the hotel group is an indefatigable art collector.) In this case the art consists of an extensive collection of sub-Saharan African masks and small wooden sculptures in both the public areas and the individual guest rooms. Even the standard rooms are spacious, and several superior rooms feature small outdoor terraces.

Carrer de Mallorca, 216. ✆ **93-451-19-14.** www.derbyhotels.com. 105 units. 70€–140€ double. Metro: Diagonal. **Amenities:** Bar; restaurant; sauna; free Wi-Fi.

Hotel Granados 83 ★★   The stone and glass façade of this converted 19th-century hospital is accented with oxidized iron trim in an effort to give it what the designer thought was a "New York" Soho look. In truth, it couldn't be anywhere but Barcelona, and the enthusiasms of the architect fortunately do not continue into the hotel itself, which is quietly and confidently posh without being the least bit snooty. Like the Bagues and the Balmes (see above), it is a Derby Hotel, and maintains the company style of dark wood, polished glass, and artwork everywhere. In this case, the art is from south and southeast Asia. There are also a few Egyptian artifacts, and guests are given a free pass to the Museu Egipci of Barcelona a few blocks away. (The hotel's owner is on the board.)

Carrer Enric Granados, 83. ✆ **93-492-96-70.** www.derbyhotels.com. 77 units. 110€–430€ double. Metro: Diagonal. **Amenities:** Restaurant; bar; exercise room; outdoor pool; room service; free Wi-Fi.

Hotel Sixty-Two ★   It really is all about style on this stretch of Passeig de Gràcia between Gaudí's Casa Batlló and La Pedrera. The Sixty-Two maintains its Modernista façade from 1897, but taps into all the post-Modern masters of interior design once you step through the door. Furnishings are from the ateliers of Philippe Starck, Vitra, and Moooi; the televisions are from Bang + Olufsen; the phones from Jacob Jensen, and so on. Rooms even have Nespresso coffee machines. There's a certain pleasure in inhabiting a contemporary design catalog, and it's nice to have all those machines that actually work. The multiple design elements harmonize nicely in the rooms, creating visually dynamic but ultimately restful retreats.

Passeig de Gràcia, 62. ✆ **93-272-41-80.** www.sixtytwohotel.com. 45 units. 119€–219€ double. Parking 30€. Metro: Diagonal. **Amenities:** Bar; babysitting; bikes; concierge; exercise room; room service; free Wi-Fi.

Soho Hotel ★★   Barcelona-born designer Alfredo Arribas collaborated with Verner Panton's design company to create the organic minimalist look for this bargain-priced designer hotel. Certain contemporary clichés creep in, like the clear glass cube showers and beds so low that you're nearly sleeping on the floor. But those beds are super-comfortable and those showers have great showerheads. Lower-level rooms can be a little noisy with Gran Via traffic, so ask for a courtyard room. The most expensive rooms are seventh-floor suites that feature outdoor wood-decked terraces with terrific city views.

Gran Via de les Corts Catalanes, 543. ✆ **93-552-96-10.** www.hotelsohobarcelona.com. 51 units. 58€–165€ double; 108€–256€ terrace suite. Parking 28€. Metro: Plaça de Catalunya. **Amenities:** Bar; outdoor heated pool; free Wi-Fi and high-speed cable Internet.

INEXPENSIVE

Actahotels Antibes ★★   Modern and rather pretty with its spare black and white décor with pops of red, this pleasant and functional hotel, just a 7-minute walk from La Sagrada Familia, is a breath of fresh air in a neighborhood where most lodgings have grander pretensions. Rooms are compact, so don't plan on spreading out. But they're tidy and bright and the staff are cheerful. Lacking a restaurant or even a cafeteria (there is a breakfast room), the hotel only gets two stars from the official rating agency. That's okay—it guarantees a lower price for a quality lodging.

Carrer de la Diputació, 394. ✆ **93-232-62-11.** www.hotel-antibesbarcelona.com. 71 units. 46€–87€ double. Parking: 18€. Metro: Tetuan. **Amenities:** Internet corner; free Wi-Fi.

Hostal Girona ★   Early Modernista architect Ildefons Cerada designed this building in the 1860s, and it retains some significant traces of its design heyday. The hostal is located on an upper floor, and only some of the rooms show their history. All the units have private bathrooms, but the addition of plumbing has made some units quite small. Four units have balconies, but for the full Modernista effect, ask for one of the two large rooms with terraces.

Carrer Girona, 24 (piso 1, puerta 1). ℂ **93-265-02-59.** www.hostalgirona.com. 19 units. 50€–85€ double. Metro: Girona or Urquinaona. **Amenities:** Free Wi-Fi.

Hotel Constanza ★   The biggest problem with the Constanza is that the chocolate and honey decorating scheme could make you hungry all the time without knowing why. The location is a little removed from major attractions but the quite residential neighborhood makes for a serene stay and lower prices than you'd expect at a contemporary design hotel. Double superior rooms are very reasonable and include a small outdoor terrace (standard doubles only have a balcony). Family rooms that sleep four are also available at prices lower than you'd pay for a double in the thick of things.

Carrer Bruc, 33. ℂ **93-270-19-10.** www.hotelconstanza.com. 49 rooms. 40€–138€ double; family room 110€–181€. Metro: Tetuan or Urquinaona. **Amenities:** Restaurant; rooftop terrace; free Wi-Fi.

Waterfront
EXPENSIVE

Duquesa de Cardona Hotel ★   This 16th-century former noble home, heavily damaged during the occupation by Napoleon, was restored in 1850 as a private residence, and then was transformed into a boutique hotel in 2003. The developers' optimism that the strip between the Barri Gòtic and the harbor was about to gentrify was a little premature, as a low-rent backpacker hostel still operates two doors away. Still, it's hard to fault the fabulous views across the Moll de la Fusta to Port Vell, or the upper-level views back to the Columbus monument and up the coast to Port Olimpic. The rooms on the front (an extra charge for waterfront views) are larger and more romantic than some of the tighter quarters on the back that face into El Born.

Passeig Colom, 12. ℂ **93-268-90-90.** www.hduquesadecardona.com. 40 units. 165€–245€ double; 230€–280€ jr. suite. Parking 30€. Metro: Barceloneta or Jaume I. **Amenities:** Restaurant; babysitting; concierge; room service; free Wi-Fi.

Hotel Arts ★★★   This landmark hotel from the waterfront makeover for the Olympics occupies the lower 33 floors of a 44-story skyscraper and is known for its contemporary art collection. (Private condos take the upper floors.) The Ritz-Carlton-managed hotel is about 2.5km (1½ miles) southwest of Barcelona's old city, next to Port Olimpic. Contemporary, elegant décor has the class not to call attention to itself. The spacious, well-equipped guest rooms have built-in headboards, bedside tables, generously sized desks, and large, sumptuous beds. Pink marble dominates the bathrooms, and views from the windows take in the skyline and the Mediterranean. The hotel also possesses the city's only beachfront pool.

Carrer de la Marina 19–21. ℂ **800/241-3333** in the U.S., or 93-221-10-00. www.ritzcarlton.com. 483 units. 250€–370€ double; 475€–12,000€ suite. Parking 42€. Metro: Ciutadella or Vila Olimpica. **Amenities:** 5 restaurants; 2 bars; children's programs; concierge; exercise room; outdoor heated pool; room service; spa; free Wi-Fi.

MODERATE

Hotel 54 ★   If you can't score a room with a view at this pleasant hostelry in the former fishermen's association building, then console yourself by hanging out on the fifth floor terrace to enjoy a 270-degree view of the harbor and the city skyline. The location is terrific: You can cut through residential Barceloneta to walk to Platja San Sebastiá, and Les Rambles is a 15-minute walk up the Moll de la Fusta. A major renovation installed some nice decorative touches like the colored LED mood lights over the bed and the cast glass sinks in the bathroom.

Passeig Joan de Borbó, 54. ✆ **93-225-00-54.** www.hotel54barceloneta.com. 28 units. 90€–150€ double. Metro: Barceloneta. **Amenities:** Bar-cafe; room service; rooftop terrace; free Wi-Fi.

Medinacelli Hotel ★★   Built into the old palace of the Dukes of Medinacelli at the waterfront edge of the Barri Gòtic, the hotel expanded into an adjacent building and created 19 new rooms in spring 2013. Rooms are bright with ample windows that are double-glazed to seal out noise. Ceilings in some rooms are surprisingly low for a heritage building, and the pale modern furnishings are comfortable. Moreover, even the most modest rooms are fairly spacious, averaging around 250 square feet.

Plaça Duc de Medinacelli, 8. ✆ **93-481-77-25.** www.hotelmedinacelli.com. 78 units. 90€–200€ double. Metro: Drassanes. **Amenities:** Free Wi-Fi.

INEXPENSIVE

Hotel Ciutadella Barcelona ★★   Set between the Parc de Ciutadella and Barceloneta, this hotel opened in fall 2012 with bargain-priced contemporary design rooms. The location is surprisingly good for exploring the dining and nightlife of El Born—or spending the day at the beach. Most rooms are compact, but they're so well-designed that they seem more spacious. Views along the avenue are unremarkable, but windows are ample and double-glazed, ensuring that the light gets in and the traffic noise does not. Terrifically friendly and helpful staff make the Ciutadella a very pleasant choice.

Avinguda Marquès de L'Argentera, 4. ✆ **93-319-19-44.** www.hotelcitadellabarcelona.com. 59 units. 90€–110€. Metro: Barceloneta. **Amenities:** Free Wi-Fi.

Hotel del Mar ★   When the local Gargallo group created this hotel in 2006, they maintained the stately façade of the 19th-century neoclassical family palace known as Casa Carbonell while creating an airy contemporary hotel in the interior. The central courtyard provides light to interior rooms, but it is glassed over on the first floor to create a pleasant lounge. Rooms balance light wood furniture and hardwood floors with blue upholstery, blue drapes, and blue decorator accents—looking very much "del Mar," or "of the sea." Said ocean is visible from upper level rooms and the very pleasant rooftop terrace.

Plaça Palau, 19. ✆ **93-319-33-02.** www.hoteldelmarbarcelona.com. 72 units. 64€–94€ double; 86€–127€ triple. Metro: Barceloneta. **Amenities:** Rooftop terrace; free Wi-Fi. Dogs welcome.

WHERE TO EAT

One reason why Barcelona has evolved into one of the world's top gastronomic destinations is La Boqueria. The great market displays *everything* that is available in the city, from the catch of the day to the basket of still-warm-from-the-sun berries that the stall owner's wife brings in at midmorning. With no mystery about ingredients, the chefs and cooks have to work their magic to make a dish that is somehow even better than the pristine ingredients you saw in the market. Sometimes that's as simple as *pá amb tomate*—toasted or grilled bread rubbed with fresh tomato, drizzled with olive oil, and sprinkled with sea salt. During tomato season, it's what you get instead of a bread basket.

You can eat fabulously at some of most old-fashioned and casual spots in the city—places like Cal Pep, Can Ravell, La Gardunya, or even the ultimate comfort food restaurant, Los Caracoles. But Barcelona *is* one of the world's great eating cities, so it's worth splurging here if you can. It need not break the bank; some of the top chefs have opened tapas restaurants and other bargain venues to showcase their same culinary creativity using less expensive materials. Barcelona dining hours are closer to the European standard than in Madrid. Lunch is usually served 1-3pm (and can represent a great bargain), and dinner service starts around 8pm, although any time before 9pm is unfashionable.

Les Rambles & El Raval

MODERATE

Ca L'Isidre ★★ CATALAN   Isidre Gironés and his wife Montserrat have been serving market cuisine with a seafood emphasis at this El Raval restaurant since 1970. Although the neighborhood was fairly rough until recently, gastronomes have always sought them out for hard-to-find old-fashioned dishes like fried salt cod with white beans. At the same time, you can also order contemporary preparations like a tartare of bream and *cigalas* (the local saltwater crawfish) with parsley oil, or roast kid with baby onions. In summer and early fall, the best available starter—hands down—is the gazpacho with assorted seafood.

Carrer Les Flors, 12. 🕭 **93-441-11-39.** www.calisidre.com. Reservations required. Main courses 10€–40€; weekday lunch menu 40€. Mon–Sat 1:30–4pm and 8:30–11pm. Closed 1st 2 weeks in Aug. Metro: Paral.lel.

Fonda España ★★ BASQUE   The value for price ratio is very, very high at this superb restaurant in the Hotel España in El Raval. That's partially because the menu is created by star chef Martín Berasategui (he's based in Basque country but visits often). Because he's focusing on traditional fare here, rather than the more inventive food he serves at his other restaurants, he's charging less (and using fewer organ meats, which may be a blessing for squeamish American diners). That said, dishes are impeccably prepared. Look for grilled kid chops (like lamb chops), baked monkfish, or fried mullet. The most Basque of the desserts is a glass of slightly sparkling txacolí wine with strawberries with a side scoop of lemon peel ice cream. The hotel management recently restored Lluís Domènech i Montaner's designs and decorations of the main dining room, which is a highlight on the hotel's Modernista tour, and the Art Nouveau mosaics positively gleam.

Hotel España, Carrer Sant Pau, 9. 🕭 **93-550-00-10.** www.hotelespanya.com. Reservations suggested. Main courses 12€–24€; weekday lunch menu 26€; dinner tasting menu 50€. Mon–Sat 1–4pm and 8–11pm. Metro: Liceu.

INEXPENSIVE

Bar Lobo ★ SPANISH   Literally around the corner from Les Rambles in El Raval, this casual dining spot attracts a largely local clientele. They come for the fresh-market dinner dishes (duck breast with glazed onions, steak tartare) and the extensive list of salads, soups, and tapas. In keeping with Barcelona's passion for Italian pasta, Bar Lobo offers several dishes inspired by "the Boot", like rigatoni with pesto and chopped tomatoes or penne carbonara. It also offers a long list of desserts and many customers pop in for coffee and a sweet after an evening at one of the neighborhood theaters.

Carrer Pinto Fortuny, 3. 🕭 **93-481-53-46.** www.grupotragaluz.com. Main courses 11€–18€; tapas 4.50€–15€; midday menu 12€. Sun–Wed 9am–midnight; Thurs–Sat 9am–2:30am. Metro: Liceu or Plaça de Catalunya.

7 Portes **28**
Adagiotapas **16**
Agua **25**
Alkimia **61**
Ávalon **41**
Bar del Pi **9**
Bar Lobo **6**
Botafumeiro **62**
Brunells Pastisseria
i Saló de Te **37**
bubó Pastisseria **30**
Ca L'Isidre **2**
Cafè de l'
Acadèmia **36**
Cafè de l'Opera **12**
Cafe Viena **4**
Café Zurich **3**

Cal Pep **27**
Can Costa **19**
Can Culleretes **15**
Can Majó **22**
Can Ravell **48**
Can Solé **23**
Casa Calvet **44**
Cata 1.81 **53**
Cinc Sentits **51**
Comerç 24 **39**
Cuines Santa
Caterina **40**
Dos Palillos
Barcelona **5**
El Caballito
Blanco **52**
El Xampanyet **34**

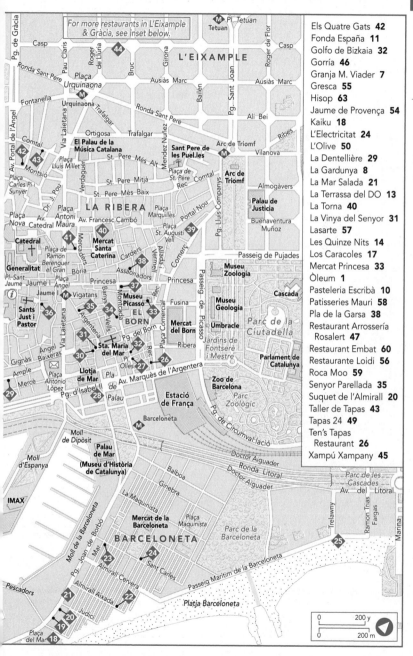

Els Quatre Gats **42**
Fonda España **11**
Golfo de Bizkaia **32**
Gorría **46**
Granja M. Viader **7**
Gresca **55**
Hisop **63**
Jaume de Provença **54**
Kaiku **18**
L'Electricitat **24**
L'Olive **50**
La Dentellière **29**
La Gardunya **8**
La Mar Salada **21**
La Terrassa del DO **13**
La Torna **40**
La Vinya del Senyor **31**
Lasarte **57**
Les Quinze Nits **14**
Los Caracoles **17**
Mercat Princesa **33**
Òleum **1**
Pasteleria Escribà **10**
Patisseries Mauri **58**
Pla de la Garsa **38**
Restaurant Arrossería
  Rosalert **47**
Restaurant Embat **60**
Restaurante Loidi **56**
Roca Moo **59**
Senyor Parellada **35**
Suquet de l'Almirall **20**
Taller de Tapas **43**
Tapas 24 **49**
Ten's Tapas
  Restaurant **26**
Xampú Xampany **45**

cafe society **ALONG LES RAMBLES**

Many of the cafes of Les Rambles have been keeping Barcelona bohemians caffeinated since Picasso was in art school. They go in and out of style—Italian coffee bars and Starbucks have them in a slight eclipse right now—but they're likely to be around to greet your grandchildren when they visit Barcelona. Here are four of the best:

Cafè de L'Òpera ★ Barcelona's most famous cafe, across from the Gran Teatre Liceu, was originally a 19th-century hot chocolate shop, but by 1929 had switched to coffee. The styling is Modernista without putting too fine a point on it, and the cafe frankly shows its age. But it remains a popular stopover for operagoers as well as strollers on Les Rambles. The establishment opens at 8:30am, making it a good bet for a traditional breakfast, with or without the semi-traditional shot of brandy in the coffee. On a hot summer afternoon, it's great to duck into the dark, air-conditioned recesses for a granizado of either coffee or lemon (like an American slushie, but not as sweet). Les Rambles, 74. ✆ **93-317-75-85.** www.cafeoperabcn.com. Metro: Liceu.

Cafe Viena ★ The cafes of the Viena baking company are ubiquitous in Catalunya—there are six alone in Barcelona. But this is the one where everyone stops for a draft beer and one of the best ham sandwiches you will ever eat, the "flauta d'ibéric jabugo." It's a crisp, slender baguette sliced in half and filled with paper-thin slices of the air-dried ham from Jabugo in Andalucía. The ham comes from the Iberian black-footed pig that spends its life gorging on acorns in the cork oak forests near the Portuguese border and is considered Spain's finest mountain ham. This version of a ham sandwich is almost twice as expensive as others (6.75€), and worth every cent. Les Rambles, 115. ✆ **93-317-14-92.** www.viena.es. Metro: Liceu or Catalunya.

Pastelería Escribà ★★ The 1902 Art Nouveau exterior, created by Modernista stage designer Ros i Güell, makes an appropriately ornate box for the chocolates crafted here. The shop is decorated with mosaics, wrought iron, and stained-glass lattice windows. The bakery is equally revered for its orange cake and *lenguas de gats* (cats' tongues) of pure chocolate. But Escribà makes more than candy and pastry. There are a handful of tables inside and more in a shady nook outside to enjoy a croissant and coffee in the morning, a light lunch of shrimp and pear, smoked salmon, or goat cheese and spinach quiche, or an afternoon snack of sacher torte or a strawberry tart. Les Rambles, 83. ✆ **93-301-60-27.** www.escriba.es. Metro: Liceu.

Café Zurich ★ Looking for one of your friends or family members? Have you checked Café Zurich? Located at the top of Les Rambles, Zurich is the still point in the swirl of passing humanity, making it a favorite meeting place. French style breakfast pastries (croissants, pain au chocolate) are available in the morning, but by noon most patrons order *bocadillos*, small sandwiches on finger rolls. The cafe interior has a marvelously formal feel with lots of dark wood and mirrors, but whenever the weather permits, most customers are willing to pay a little more for service at one of the Plaça de Catalunya tables. Plaça de Catalunya, 1. ✆ **93-317-91-53.** Metro: Catalunya.

Dos Palillos Barcelona ★★ ASIAN/SPANISH Albert Raurich heads this oddball tapas restaurant, and given that he spent 11 years at el Bulli (the last six as head chef under Ferran Adrià), the restaurant had to have a twist. When he and Adrià ate their way through New York's Chinatown on a research visit, Raurich became enamored of the idea of a dim sum tapas restaurant. Casa Camper thought it was great idea, and the "two sticks" launched in their hotel in December 2008 as homage to the chopsticks of Asian cuisine and the toothpicks of Spanish bar food. Dishes run the gamut from Chinese dumplings filled with Spanish prawns and Iberico pork belly to Japanese-style burgers with ginger, cucumber, and miso. Regulars swear by the combination of tempura vegetables with glasses of sherry.

Carrer Elisabets, 11. *C* **93-304-05-13.** www.dospalillos.com. Tapas 4€–15€. Thurs–Sat 1:30–3:30pm; Tues–Sat 7:30–11:30pm. Closed 2 weeks in Aug. Metro: Liceu or Catalunya.

La Gardunya ★★ CATALAN   Tony Magaña Huertas is the boss behind this unexpected little restaurant tucked in the back of Barcelona's covered food market, La Boqueria, and he clearly loves good, simple food. Somewhat fancier table settings are available upstairs but most diners opt for the downstairs bar. There are also a few tables by the back door, if you like to watch the market workers coming and going. The food is "market cuisine" in the most direct sense of the term—the cooks don't have to go far for their ingredients—but the preparations show real imagination. Fresh cod, for example, might be roasted with quince and served with a dab of aioli and wilted spinach. A grilled steak could come with a confit of piquillo peppers. Fixed price menus at lunch and dinner are real bargains.

Carrer Jerusalem, 18. *C* **93-302-43-23.** Reservations recommended. Main courses 13€–30€; fixed-price lunch 14€, dinner 16€. Bar Mon–Sat 7am–midnight. Restaurant Mon–Sat noon–3pm and 8pm–midnight. Metro: Liceu.

Granja M. Viader ★ CATALAN   One of Barcelona's original "milk bars," M. Viader invented the drink you see next to the sodas in every cooler: Cacaolat. It's exactly what you might think from the name—chocolate milk—and Catalans of a certain age gush with nostalgia over it. The founder was instrumental in getting pasteurized milk products out to the public, and this wonderfully old-fashioned cafe, founded in 1870, still serves coffee, pastries, sandwiches, hot chocolate, and (of course!) chocolate milk. In the morning, you can also get hot churros to go with the hot chocolate.

Carrer Xucla, 4–6. *C* **93-318-34-86.** www.granjaviader.cat. Sandwiches 3–5€; pastries 1.80€–4€. Mon–Sat 9am–1:15pm and 5–8:15pm. Metro: Liceu or Catalunya.

Barri Gòtic, La Ribera & Born

Moderate

Cal Pep ★★★ CATALAN   The only bad thing to be said about Cal Pep—the only thing—is that it closes after lunch on Saturday and doesn't reopen until Monday dinner. Folks in Barcelona for the weekend miss out joining the swarm of happy people dining on Pep's small dishes during the week, which is a tragedy. So plan your time wisely, so that you can try what other places call *media raciones*, that is, bigger than a tapa and smaller than a racion. There are a number of Catalan classics among the 70 or so dishes available here on a given day, but most are the restaurant's own invention—the "atomic" omelet with crumbled sausage, chewy beans and potent garlic sauce, for example, or the baked artichokes stuffed with onions and black olives. Pep himself plays host, making sure everyone is having a good time and recommending what they should try next. There's a small dining room inside, but most patrons try to pin down one of the counter seats up front.

Plaça des les Olles, 8. *C* **93-310-79-61.** www.calpep.com. Reservations for groups of 4–20 only. Main courses 14€–28€. Mon–Fri 7:30–11:30pm; Tues–Sat 1–3:45pm. Closed Aug. Metro: Barceloneta or Jaume I.

Comerç 24 ★★★ CATALAN   Chef-owner Carles Abellan re-invents classic Catalan dishes through the lens of world cuisine. An elBulli alumnus, he's not afraid to experiment with techniques and flavors, but the results are inevitably harmonious—as in "what a great idea!" The rabbit paella offers the rabbit cooked on a spit. He perfumes fresh salmon with vanilla and serves it with a yogurt cheese instead of crème fraîche. His roast suckling pig is done Hanoi style, gorgeously glazed and scented with astringent herbs. This is vibrant, earthy, real food—not a speck of foam in sight. Abellan also makes one of the great Catalan classics, arròs de pato (duck paella) with dabs of foie gras along with the duck confit. The dining room is a bit out of the way, up the street from the Museu de Xocolata at the east end of La Ribera. In addition to a la carte service, Abellan offers two tasting menus with tapas-sized portions: One is 7 courses, and the other is 12.

Carrer Comerç 24. ✆ **93-319-21-02.** www.carlesabellan.es. Reservations required. Main courses 18€–38€; tasting menus 92€ or 116€. Tues–Sat 1:30–3:30pm and 8:30–11:30pm. Closed 10 days in Dec. Metro: Arc de Triomf or Estació de Franca.

Cuines Santa Caterina ★★ ASIAN/MEDITERRANEAN   This soaring adjunct to the Mercat Santa Caterina (p. 206) is one of the classiest eating halls in Barcelona. A simple tapas bar stands at the entrance but the main action is the dining room of chunky wooden tables surrounded on two sides by open kitchens. That's right, "kitchens" in the plural. Order a *paella* and it comes from the Spanish kitchen; order fried rice and it comes from the Asian kitchen. The restaurant prides itself on total integration with the market, and many of the dishes are suitable for vegetarians, if not always for vegans. Light vegetable tempuras are offered, as are vegetable sushi rolls and excellent sashimi cut to order. Spanish and Catalan market food—roast duck, monkfish and clams with romesco sauce—is just as plentiful and just as good. You can't make reservations, so show up early or be prepared to wait.

Mercat de Santa Caterina, Avinguda Francesc Cambó, 17. ✆ **93-268-99-18.** www.cuinessantacaterina.com. Main courses 9€–24€. Daily 1–4pm; Sun–Wed 8–11:30pm; Thurs–Sat 8pm–12:30am. Metro: Jaume I.

Els Quatre Gats ★ CATALAN   Founded in 1897 as Barcelona's bohemian hangout—modeled on Le Chat Noir in Paris—the "four cats" (Catalan slang for "just a few people") hit its mark early on, thanks to backing by artists Santiago Rusiñol and Ramón Casas. The Modernista crowd hung out here, and the owner gave Picasso one of his first paying art jobs by commissioning the illustration still used on the menu cover. In fact, the young Picasso had his first exhibition at El Quatre Gats in 1900. Even the building, designed by Puig i Cadalfach, is a period piece of art. Every tourist in Barcelona comes here at least once; unfortunately, many of them dress poorly and wear flip-flops, which the management bans as in bad taste. (We suspect many of the restaurant's nay-sayers on crowd-sourced websites were bounced for disrespectful attire.) The food is hardly revolutionary—cod cooked in ratatouille, roast shoulder of lamb, duck confit with mushrooms—but the midday menu is a good bargain for the neighborhood and the memorabilia on the walls can be engrossing.

Carrer Montsió, 3. ✆ **93-302-41-40.** www.4gats.com. Reservations required Sat–Sun. Main courses 12€–28€. Daily 10am–2am. Metro: Plaça de Catalunya.

Senyor Parellada ★ CATALAN   This elegant set of dining rooms in the Banys Orientals hotel looks ready for a closeup with its glittering chandeliers and vaguely Art Nouveau décor. But it's a lot more than just a pretty face. The kitchen of this stylish restaurant produces authentic Catalan fare—roasted lamb stuffed with heads of garlic and grilled asparagus with Idiazabel cheese—at very good prices.

Carrer Argentería, 37. ✆ **93-310-50-94.** www.senyorparellada.com. Reservations recommended. Main courses 8€–21€. Metro: Jaume I.

La Terrassa del DO ★ CATALAN   The casual dining space of the grandly named DO Plaça Reial Boutique Hotel Gastronomic is only marginally more expensive than its less accomplished neighbors on the Plaça Reial. The forte here is drinks with tapas, but even the tapas are a welcome respite from most bar food. Imagine a glass of cava with a salad of escarole, mango, and grilled fresh Atlantic bonito, or a glass of Priorat red with griddled calamari and garlic. The DO kitchen also prepares solid comfort food like charcoal-grilled octopus with mashed potatoes, roasted catch of the day with vegetables of the season, or a burger made with Galician veal (the closest thing to real beef you'll find in Spain). There are many tables inside, and (weather permitting) many more outdoors on the Plaça, so reservations are rarely an issue.

Plaça Reial, 1. ✆ **93-481-36-66.** www.hoteldoreial.com. Tapas 1.50€–10€, main courses 9€–25€. Daily 9–11am, noon–4pm, and 7pm–2am. Metro: Liceu.

INEXPENSIVE

Adagiotapas ★★ CATALAN   The chef/owner Jordi Herrera—a former revered teacher of cuisine at Barcelona's hotel school—is a master of tradition and innovation alike. His capacity for giving old dishes new legs won him a Michelin star at his fine-dining restaurant, but in July 2013 he decided to have some fun by opening a creative tapas operation in a modest hotel in the Barri Gòtic. Some of the dishes are straightforward, like the briny oyster with a ginger mignonette, while others are clever reinventions of classics. Most places that serve tortilla (potato omelet) as a tapa, serve a wedge. Herrera makes a super intense tortilla with caramelized onion that he finishes in the oven as a small tart cooked in a cupcake paper—a perfect two bites. Instead of the conventional ham croquettes, he serves delicious rabbit croquettes encrusted with shredded phyllo and accompanied by a few dabs of ratatouille. The wine list is short and inexpensive.

Carrer Ferran, 21. ✆ **93-318-90-61.** Tapas 4€–10€. Daily 1–4pm and 7–11pm. Metro: Liceu or Jaume I.

Ávalon ★ CATALAN   One of the salutary effects of Spain's wrenching fiscal crisis has been the proliferation of inexpensive restaurants with menus designed by decorated, upmarket chefs. This welcoming, breezy spot in the Grand Hotel Central is one, the brainchild of rockstar chef Ramón Freixa. In contrast to his fine-dining restaurants (where he has four Michelin stars), Ávalon feels like a casual American spot with Catalan food. It's warm and bright and unfussy and offers free Wi-Fi (many customers are solo business travelers staying at the hotel). The dishes are unfussy as well—a dozen little plates ranging from mini-pizzas to green salads and small rice plates, and then nine larger plates: three different burgers topped with fried egg, three different roasted sausage casseroles, three different cannelloni. (Cannelloni have been part of casual Catalan cuisine since at least the 19th c.) It's playful and very affordable.

Carrer Pare Gallifa, 3. ✆ **93-295-79-05.** www.avalonrestaurant.es. Reservations recommended. Main dishes 12€–17€. Daily 1:30–4pm and 8–11pm. Metro: Jaume I.

Bar del Pi ★ SPANISH   Just because it's a popular spot deson't mean you should skip this bar that sprawls across two of the three plazas surrounding Santa María del Pi. The location is prime and the limited food choices tend to be well-executed. Mainly a drinking establishment—coffee as well as wine and beer—its food offerings are limited to bar classics like small sandwiches, slices of tortilla, cod-stuffed peppers, and patatas bravas. When the weather is nice, no one stands at the bar—everyone wants one of the tables on the plaza. The menu also includes an unusually long list of pastries and cakes, which tend to be popular with the North Americans and Brits who often frequent the bar.

Plaça Sant Josep Oriol, 1. © **93-302-21-23.** www.bardelpi.com. Tapas 2€–8€. Tues–Fri 9am–11pm; Sat 9:30am–11pm; Sun 10am–10pm (closed Sun July–Aug). Closed mid-Jan to mid-Feb. Metro: Liceu.

Cafè de L'Acadèmia ★★ CATALAN

Set into a 15th-century building opposite the church on the tiny plaza of Sant Just, Cafè de L'Acadèmia is both more inventive and less expensive than it looks. Chef-owner Jordí Casteldi prepares Catalan market cuisine, offering, for example, a delicious cold carrot soup with a dollop of pesto in warm weather. (It comes paired with a second bowl of gazpacho.) Fish dishes—roasted salt cod gratinée with artichoke mousse, for example—are always a little more involved than the usual fare. Like many modern Catalan chefs, he also prepares a number of nominally Italian dishes that can range from lasagna with blood pudding sausage to risotto finished with thin slices of foie gras on top. Caramelized grapes underneath the rice are a foil to the foie. Casteldi owns his own vineyards, so the house wine is truly the wine of the house.

Carrer Lledó, 1. © **93-319-82-53.** Reservations required. Main courses 10€–14€; midday menu 16€. Mon–Fri 1:30–4pm and 8:30pm–1am. Closed last 2 weeks of Aug. Metro: Jaume I.

Can Culleretes ★ CATALAN

Tucked onto a tiny side street near the Plaça Reial, Culleretes has been serving traditional Catalan fare since 1786—dishes like spinach cannoli with salt cod brandade, stewed wild boar, or partridge casserole. The priciest meal (36€ for two) is the assorted fish and shellfish, a three-course spread that starts with garlic shrimp and steamed mussels and clams, moves on to assorted fried fish (usually monkfish and squid), and concludes with grilled prawns, scampi, and baby calamari.

Carrer Quintana, 5. © **93-317-30-20.** http://culleretes.com. Reservations recommended. Main courses 8€–18€. Tues–Sun 9am–4pm and Tues–Sat 9–11pm. Closed mid-July to mid-Aug.

Los Caracoles ★ SPANISH

It is a rite of passage, at least for American tourists, to dine at "The Snails," where the Bofarull family has been welcoming hungry travelers ever since 1835. You may even smell it before you see it, as no one else that we know of spit-roasts whole chicken in an open window. The snails, for which the restaurant was renamed sometime in the mid–20th century, are very good and garlicky, but most diners come for the comfort food: chicken and ham croquettes, roast chicken, roast suckling pig, and the pricey lobster paella. The menu has basically remained unchanged since Los Caracoles was featured in the inaugural edition of "Spain on $5 a Day," and that's okay with us. Honest food without subtext is always welcome.

Carrer Escudellers, 14. © **93-301-20-41.** www.loscaracoles.es. Reservations recommended. Main courses 8€–27€. Daily 1:15pm–midnight. Metro: Liceu or Drassanes.

La Dentellière ★ MEDITERRANEAN

This charming little bar-restaurant is a reminder of how close Barcelona is to southern France, as this atmospherically dark Barri Gòtic watering hole is really a provincial boîte—a bar with good if unchallenging food. The menu hopscotches around the Mediterranean with a sidetrip to Switzerland for three fondues. But even nominally Italian dishes like tagliatelle with duck

ON THE sweeter SIDE

Barcelona restaurants may serve more (and more elaborate) desserts than any other city in Spain. These two shops represent real artisanry in pastry and confections.

Brunells Pastisseria i Saló de Te ★

The menu here is so modest it barely warrants mention—nice little "entrepans" (sandwiches on thin baguettelike rolls)—except that Brunells makes its own croissants and breads. More importantly, Brunells makes its own chocolate. On the pastry shop side that translates into some elegant bars. In the snack bar (saló de te), it means a terrific cup of hot chocolate (Xuix de Crema for Swiss-style with whipped cream) with a warm-from-the-oven croissant or a plate of hot churros. The breakfast will fortify you to stand in line at the nearby Museu Picasso if you neglected to buy your ticket ahead of time. If you did plan ahead, you get to linger over the hot chocolate.

Carrer Montcada, 7. ✆ **93-319-68-25.** www.brunells.es.tl. Pastries and chocolate 1.50€– 3.10€. Tues–Sat 8:30am–8pm, Sun 8:30am–3pm. Metro: Jaume I.

bubó ★★

Pastry chef Carles Mampel has shelves full of trophies and medals, including one from Lyon in 2005 for his world champion chocolate cake. With bubó, he brings great pastry to the masses. This shop, in an alley near Santa María del Mar, in the heart of El Born, was his base for further expansion into other neighborhoods—and to Kuwait. If you don't like chocolate, you can sample his carrot jelly swirled with coconut mousse and served with litchi ice cream topped with a hazelnut crunch. Of course, there are glittering macarons and chocolate confections, even sugar-encrusted marshmallow bonbons.

Carrer Caputxes, 10. ✆ **93-268-72-24.** www.bubo.es. Pastries 3.50€–7€. Daily 10am–6pm, bar Sun–Thurs 10am–10pm, Fri–Sat 10am–midnight. Metro: Jaume I.

---

come out tasting Spanish (maybe because the sauce includes bits of serrano ham). By mining some of the lesser-known Spanish wine regions, the wine list offers some excellent drinking bargains to go with the inexpensive meals.

Carrer Ample, 165. ✆ **93-319-68-21.** www.ladentellierebcn.com. Main courses 9€–16€; fixed-price dinner 17€. Daily 7:30pm–midnight. Metro: Drassanes or Jaume I.

Golfo de Bizkaia ★ BASQUE   Named for the Bay of Biscay, this smart little *pintxos* bar and restaurant specializes in Basque cooking in small format dishes. More than 80 *pintxos* are laid out on the bar at mealtime—everything from Getaria white anchovies to montaditos (toasts) of spicy green peppers or perfect cubes of fresh tuna. The restaurant portion expands the choices to plates of Basque cheeses and homemade croquettes as starters and to larger plates like bonito cooked with chopped fresh tomato or roast beef sirloin with baked potatoes. (In Basque parlance, "beef" is often called "old cow," because veal is more common.) The wine list leans heavily on Navarre reds but also offers the prickly acidic Txocolí whites of the Basque region.

Carrer Vidreria, 12. ✆ **93-268-48-88.** www.golfodebizkaia.com. Dishes 4€–11€. Daily 10am–12:30am. Metro: Jaume I or Barceloneta.

Pla de la Garsa ★★ CATALAN   Although a new generation is in charge, this venerable family restaurant retains its terrific collection of Modernista graphic art, its 18th-century tiles and wrought iron, and its commitment to the dark and savory side of

THE food court TO END ALL FOOD COURTS

Tucked into an out-of-the-way corner of El Born, **Mercat Princesa ★★★** is a welcoming space where 16 small vendors offer great food at bargain prices. The building dates from the 14th century, and its central courtyard has been glassed over to create the main dining space. Just 16 seats ring the area, though plans are afoot to expand into the basement for another 40. The Bravas Mercat stall sells fried potatoes with eight sauce variants (bravas, aioli, wasabi, and so forth). A Nespresso coffee bar prepares coffee, hot chocolate and churros. An oyster bar also cooks mussels and prawns. The charcuterie specialist serves plates of cheese or plates of Iberian ham. Right next to him a sushi chef prepares sashimi to order. A noodle bar has everything from Vietnamese soups to Catalan fideùs—a paella made with noodles. One bar just does different rice dishes. Pepe Fritz specializes in deep-fried Andalucían fish dishes. The Vins & Cocktails stall sells beer and wine. There's even a pastry and ice cream case in case you find room for dessert.

Carrer Flassaders, 21. ⓒ **93-268-15-18.** www.mercatprincesa.com. Main dishes 4€-22€. Sun-Wed 9am-midnight, Thurs-Sat 9am–1am. Metro: Jaume I.

traditional Catalan cookery. The kitchen makes its own pâtés and terrines—the anchovy-black olive terrine *(garum)* is especially good—and offers a wide array of traditional sausages and cured meats, including the air-dried beef usually only found in mountainous western Catalunya. When it's available, ask for the sturgeon carpaccio with cava vinaigrette as a starter. (Sturgeon cooked in cider is also usually on the menu as a main dish.) Duck is a staple here; one of the restaurant's most popular dishes is duck three ways (gizzards, liver, and thighs). The short and powerful wine list is strong on Priorat, and for dessert you can't go wrong with any of the Catalan cheeses.

Carrer Assaonadors, 13. ⓒ **93-315-24-13.** www.pladelagarsa.com. Reservations recommended Fri–Sat. Main courses 9€–14€. Daily 8pm–1am. Metro: Jaume I.

Les Quinze Nits ★ SPANISH   The proprietors of this large restaurant with lots of outdoor tables on Plaça Reial know how to whip up a crowd: Offer the least expensive meals on the scenic plaza. The food is pretty good, especially if you stick to simple preparations like grilled tuna with squash and olives, roast lamb with potatoes, or *arròc negre* (paella-like black rice with squid in its own ink). Be careful with the drink orders, though, as wine, beer, and soft drinks are actually more expensive than at otherwise higher-priced restaurants.

Plaça Reial, 6. ⓒ **93-317-30-75.** www.lesquinzenits.com. No reservations. Main dishes 7€–13€. Daily 12:30–11:30pm. Metro: Liceu.

Taller de Tapas ★ SPANISH   Taller de Tapas offers more than four dozen small plates from all over Spain—everything from grilled razor clams with lemon and olive oil to scrambled eggs with prawns and asparagus. The wine list looks pricey (most around 15€) until you realize that those prices are for the bottle, not the glass. The sheer variety of plates means that there is literally something for every taste. In an unusual departure, Taller de Tapas also offers a dozen dessert plates that range from homemade chocolate truffles to an almond tart.

Plaça Sant Josep Oriol, 9. ⓒ **93-301-80-20.** www.tallerdetapas.com. Tapas 4€–12€. Daily 10am–1am. Metro: Liceu.

La Torna ★★ SPANISH Holding down one corner of the Santa Caterina market, La Torna is a bakery (great breads, by the way) with a dining counter circling a bar/ kitchen. The two dozen people who score seats get a certain amount of theater (two waitresses and two cooks operating in an area the size of a large closet) and terrific market food. Given the restrictions, the food tends to be simple—almost everything is cooked on a griddle or seared under a broiler. But the ingredients are super-fresh, since the vendors are only steps away. During the summer, sautéed zucchini flowers stuffed with salt cod brandade are a specialty, as are grilled or sautéed mixed wild mushrooms. The pork and veal meatballs with mushrooms are a dependable standby in any season, as are the sweet and tender squid grilled and dressed with Catalan olive oil. The bakery does breakfast pastry as well as bread, so many market workers come here for coffee, a croissant, and a big glass of freshly squeezed juice from Spain's blood oranges.

Mercat Santa Caterina, stall 182, Avinguda de Francesc Cambó, 16. ✆ **93-319-58-21.** Plates 7€–15€. Mon–Sat 7am–5pm. Metro: Jaume I.

Ten's Tapas Restaurant ★★ CATALAN When culinary magician Jordi Cruz decided to move his two-star Michelin restaurant aBaC out to Tibidabo, he repaid the foodies of El Born by establishing this refreshingly unpretentious tapas restaurant in its space. The pale natural wood of the tables and chairs is intended to strike a fresh, informal tone. At its simplest, the tapas menu has a great version of fried potatoes with aioli mousse and spicy bravas sauce, but you'll also find more ambitious plates like foie gras with figs, sweet and salted breadcrumbs, and Sichuan pepper ice cream. One of the most inspired dishes might be the oysters on the half shell with a dollop of cucumber ice cream, finely minced lemon peel, and a drizzle of arbequina olive oil. Roughly 15 dishes are offered at a time, including one special from the aBaC menu.

Carrer del Rec 79. ✆ **93-319-22-22.** www.tensbarcelona.com. Reservations suggested. Tapas 5€–15€. Sun and Tues–Thurs 1–3:30pm and 8–11:30pm, Fri–Sat 1–3:30pm and 8pm–midnight. Metro: Barceloneta or Jaume I.

La Vinya del Senyor ★ VINOTECA/TAPAS It doesn't get much better than spending an afternoon on the terrace of La Vinya del Senyor taking in the glorious Gothic facade of the church of Santa María del Mar—especially if there's a wedding taking place. Ostensibly a wine shop, the vinoteca serves glasses of wine with a modest tapas menu. It's not uncommon to find a half dozen Priorats, another half dozen Riojas, and several Ruedas and Albariños by the glass. If you're drinking a bottle, you can choose from more than 300 still wines and cavas, sherries, and Moscatels. Tapas include some of the usual suspects—Manchego cheese, air-dried Iberian ham—and some Catalan surprises like walnut rolls drizzled with a suave Catalan olive oil. La Vinya also serves the sweet, crisp version of "coca," a Catalan flatbread scented with anisette and rolled in sugar and pine nuts. Because it absorbs the tannins in your mouth, it's a great complement to a powerful red wine.

Plaça Santa María, 5. ✆ **93-310-33-79.** www.lavinyadelsenyor.com. Tapas 3€–11€. Sun–Thur noon–1:30am, Fri–Sat noon–2am. Metro: Jaume I or Barceloneta.

El Xampanyet ★ One of the city's best-loved "champagne bars" since it opened in 1929, El Xampanyet knows that no bar ever went broke by selling inexpensive drinks. By day it keeps a low profile on the street just across from the Museu Picasso; the corrugated steel garage door doesn't roll up until after the museum closes. Within minutes that establishment is jammed, as drinkers take their places standing next to wine barrels, marble-topped tables, or the long zinc bar as if someone were about to start shooting a party commercial. The tapas are simple and salty (olives, ham, croquettes), and the house cava (white or pink) is a great deal.

Carrer Montcada, 22. ℰ **93-319-70-03.** Tapas 2€–6€. Mon–Sat 8pm–2am. Metro: Jaume I. Closed in Aug.

L'Eixample
EXPENSIVE

Alkimia ★★ CATALAN   As the name suggests, chef Jordi Vila fashions himself as an alchemist, transmuting some of the base materials of Catalan cuisine into a kind of gastronomic gold. Some of the signature dishes—like a "fried egg" of cauliflower cream—are almost impossibly labor-intensive (and priced accordingly), while others like the roast chicken cannelloni, the veal kidneys with coffee crumbs, or the pickled oyster with glazed pork are surprising in their tastes but more straightforward to prepare. He can elevate some of the simplest ingredients, poaching red mullet in olive oil and gracing the plate with an apple-cucumber chutney.

Carrer Industria, 79. ℰ **93-207-61-15.** www.alkimia.cat. Reservations required. Main dishes 11€–28€; fixed-price menus 39€–94€. Mon–Fri 1:30–3:30pm and 8:30–10:30pm. Closed 3 weeks in Aug. Metro: Sagrada Família.

Botafumeiro ★★ SEAFOOD   Owner Moncho Neira hails from Galicia and holds the opinion (shared by much of Spain) that Galicians know more about fish than anyone. Neira sources his fish directly from the auctions on both the Catalan and Galician coasts and presents them in a glamorous, old-world fine-dining setting where the waiters wear white jackets and diners are expected to dress accordingly. You can begin with a selection of clams and oysters from the raw bar, or take Neira's advice and start with his spider crab pie. Because he has access to the Galician catch, he always has live lobsters, "Norway lobster" (scampi), two or three species of crab, clams, mussels, and percebes (goose barnacles) on hand in enormous tanks at the restaurant entrance. Diners who prefer meat can choose from a few steaks, some veal dishes, and a traditional Galician stewed pork with turnips. The wine list is as Galician as many of the fish, with several bracing albariño whites from the Rias Baixas along with a nice selection of Catalan cavas.

Carrer Gran de Gràcia, 81. ℰ **93-218-42-30.** www.botafumeiro.es. Reservations recommended. Main courses 18€–44€; tasting menu 80€. Daily 1pm–1am. Metro: Fontana.

Casa Calvet ★★ CATALAN   Antoni Gaudí designed this Modernista building in 1899 for a textile manufacturer, who lived here with his family and ran the business from the downstairs offices now occupied by the restaurant. Casa Calvet has lovingly preserved the stained glass and wood-trimmed Gaudí design, matching it with a cuisine that is equally ornamented, essentially Catalan, and tempered by some French nouveau. Sherry-roasted lamb chops, for example, are paired with ratatouille-filled ravioli and a beet-garlic sauce, while bonito tuna is seared and served with fresh green melon, spiced yogurt, and green beans. Even vegetarians can find a dedicated dish—a ragout of vegetables with tofu and porcini mushrooms.

Carrer Casp, 48. ℰ **93-412-40-12.** www.casacalvet.es. Reservations recommended. Main courses 18€–28€; tasting menus 44€–68€. Mon–Sat 1–3:30pm and 8:30–11pm. Metro: Passeig de Gràcia.

Cinc Sentits ★★ MEDITERRANEAN   The name of the restaurant is Catalan for "Five Senses," and a sense of restraint is not one of them. Only tasting menus are served here, although you can limit yourself to just four courses by going for lunch on a weekday. Otherwise the choices are 5, 7, or 10 courses. Chef Jordi Artal is keen to appeal to all five senses, so the orchestration of the meal will include sight, smell, touch, and sound, as well as taste. Like most Michelin-starred chefs, Artal adores serving foie gras and must have a dozen different ways to prepare it. During the summer cherry season, for example, he barely sears the foie so it comes out rich and creamy on top of a crisp pastry base that makes a perfect foil. The pastry has bits of tart cherry worked into it, along with enough butter that the bottom caramelizes in the oven. The idea is to eat foie and crust together for the custardlike meat against the crisp, slightly sour crust—all of it finishing with a complex salty flavor.

Carrer Aribau, 58. © **93-323-94-90.** www.cincsentits.com. Reservations required. Tasting menus 49€–109€. Tues–Sat 1:30–3:30pm and 8:30–11pm. Closed last 3 weeks of Aug. Metro: Passeig de Gràcia.

Gorría ★★ BASQUE/NAVARRESE   Javier Gorría continues where his father, the famous Basque chef Fermin Gorría, left off: presenting the best cooking from the mountains of Navarre and the Basque coast. In the grand Basque tradition, many of the raw materials are presented on display tables that look like altars, and diners are invited to select their fish and cuts of meat from the refrigerated case. The wood-fired grill and oven are the keys to the cooking, and though Gorría is not, strictly speaking, a Basque asador, some of the greatest dishes are the roasted Roncal valley lamb, redolent of mountain herbs, and the slowly braised suckling pig. The kitchen is equally adept with fish, including the all-time classic cod a pil-pil—a sauce where the cook's technique must be perfect to emulsify the olive oil and the juices of the fish. The wine list is a delightful mix of classic Riojas, a number of bright txocolís from the Basque coast, and the rich garnatxas and cabernet sauvignons from Navarre.

Carrer Diputación, 421. © **93-245-11-64.** www.restaurantegorria.com. Reservations recommended. Main courses 14€–33€. Mon 11am–3:30pm; Tues–Sat 1–3:30pm and 9–11:30pm. Closed Easter and Aug. Metro: Monumental.

Hisop ★ CATALAN   Oriol Ivern Bondia and Guillem Pla wowed their fellow chefs when they opened Hisop in 2001 to serve radically reinvented Catalan cuisine at bargain prices. Pla has moved on, but Ivern keeps Hisop percolating in a more streamlined style, constantly reimagining the flavors of the region in pure, unmuddled form. This results in some marvelously stripped-down dishes—whole grilled red mullet with a zucchini flower, or a john dory with cockles steamed in a vanilla broth. There is, of course, suckling pig, but it's made all the more unctuous by an accompaniment of roasted plums. The menu changes four times a year, with weekly adjustments. (What chef can resist the tomato harvest or a seasonal fish spawn?) Hisop's desserts are equally brilliant combinations of flavors—peach with ginger and coffee, chocolate with basil and almonds, pistachio with kaffir lime.

Pasatje Marimon, 9. © **93-241-32-33.** www.hisop.com. Reservations required. Main courses 24€–28€; 10-course tasting menu 67€, with wine tasting 90€. Mon–Fri 1:30–3:30pm and 9–11pm; Sat 9–11pm. Closed first 3 weeks in Aug. Metro: Hospital Clínic.

Lasarte ★★★ BASQUE   If you consider yourself a foodie and have plans for one big splurge in Barcelona, Lasarte might be your best bet. It's the elegant Barcelona outpost of much-decorated Basque chef Martín Berasategui, and since 2009 has held two Michelin stars of its own. Berasategui is known for his innovations, but also for mentoring young chefs, so chef de cuisine Paolo Casagrande interprets some of the classics of the master and adds some dishes of his own in the same spirit. This is world-class dining, and it doesn't come cheap. Many dishes are no more than four bites, which translates to more than 10€ per bite. But they are dishes that form part of your

diy: COOKING CLASSES

If you want to recreate some of your favorite meals at home, several workshops will introduce you to the ingredients and basic techniques of Spanish and Catalan cuisine.

BCN Kitchen ★ A kitchen and dining room in the El Born neighborhood is the base for this organization that offers a number of hands-on classes. A tapas workshop, for example, usually includes such classics as tortilla española, gazpacho, and fried calamari with squid ink aioli. If you also want to gain more familiarity with Spanish food products, you can combine the tapas workshop with a visit to a local market to shop for the ingredients.

Carrer de la Fusina, 15. ℂ **93-268-12-53.** www.bcnkitchen.com. Tapas workshop 50€, with market visit 65€.

Cook & Taste ★ Students in the half-day cooking classes in a kitchen in the old city have the option of taking a guided tour of La Boqueria before the class begins. It's a great way to get a real feel for Spanish foodstuffs and for the discerning way that Spanish cooks select their ingredients. Classes usually prepare two tapas, often tortilla española and pa amb tomate (bread rubbed with tomato), followed by a Catalan dessert like crema Catalana.

Carrer Paradis, 3. ℂ **93-302-13-20.** www.cookandtaste.net. Cooking class 65€, market tour 13€.

---

sensory memory bank—the plates against which all others are measured. Red prawns, for example, come into the restaurant live from the boat. The kitchen prepares them in a sea urchin flan topped with a sheep's milk "caviar" (thanks to the miracles of spherification) and sends them to the dining room on a wet black slate to evoke the dark ocean where they swam only hours before. Tuna belly might be flash-grilled over charcoal and served with mango and capers in soy sauce and a tiny bowl of raw celery minestrone for an orgy of sweet, salt, and umami. If this is all just too breathtaking (especially the price), consider the more casual sister restaurant across the street, Loidi.

Carrer Mallorca, 259 (in Hotel Condes de Barcelona). ℂ **93-445-00-00.** www.restaurantlasarte.com. Smart dress and reservations required. Main dishes 43€–52€; 7-course luncheon tasting menu 115€, 10-course dinner tasting menu 135€. Tues–Sat 1:30–3:30pm and 8:30–11pm. Closed Aug. Metro: Provença.

Restaurante Loidi ★★ BASQUE Also part of the Hotel Condes de Barcelona, Loidi serves a conventional buffet breakfast to hotel guests and then turns into Berasategui's gastro bistro for lunch and dinner. Dishes are less elaborate than at Lasarte, but are available only as set menus, of which the whole table must order the same number of courses. The six-course "Martín Selection" gives you more or less the whole menu for about the cost of a main dish at Lasarte. A three-course version is also available. Dishes might include a large veal ravioli candied in carrot juice and served with meat broth, and fish with cauliflower purée and beet couscous. In keeping with the food, Loidi is much more casual, though many diners dress smartly for dinner anyway.

Carrer Mallorca, 248–250. ℂ **93-492-92-92.** www.loidi.com. Martín Selection menu 48€, 64€ with matching wines; 3-course menu 28€. Daily 1–3:30pm, Mon–Sat 8–11pm. Metro: Provença.

L'Olive ★ CATALAN Celebrating his 30th anniversary at this eponymous restaurant in 2014, chef Josep Olive continues to serve traditional home cooking dressed up for a night out. You can start with batter-fried baby onions, cod fritters, grilled cockles, or a cold dish like a bright Provençal salad or Olive's signature salt cod "carpaccio." He serves duck breast with strawberry sauce and offers whole bream cooked on a bed of salt. In season, Olive even offers a main dish of nothing more than the local Rossinyols mushrooms sautéed with garlic and parsley. Desserts tend to feature fresh fruit or local fresh cheeses, although you can also get a crema catalana or a chocolate mousse.

Carrer Balmes, 47. ⓒ **93-452-19-90**. www.rte-olive.com. Reservations recommended. Main courses 18€–24€. Daily 1–4pm; Mon–Sat 8:30pm–midnight. Metro: Passeig de Gràcia.

Roca Moo ★★★ CATALAN   If you're not planning a gastronomic pilgrimage to Girona to eat at **El Celler de Can Roca** (p. 242), you might want to book a dinner here. Chef de cuisine Felip Llufriu executes Joan Roca's inspired dishes perfectly and the design-centric decadence of Hotel Omm pumps the otherworldliness up a notch. You might start with *cigalas* (salt water crayfish) with curry, rose petals, and licorice—a brilliant combination of flavors to give a fairly bland crustacean some real taste. The kitchen also does a *bogavente* (Atlantic lobster) version of the dish with a licorice curry sauce. Kid is slowly braised and finished with a rosemary-honey glaze and served on a "cloud" of goat's milk foam. Jordi Roca designs the desserts, which must be ordered at the start of the meal. His classic "Trip to Havana" features rum sponge cake, lime soup, peppermint granita, and a frozen ice cream cigar with a spice ash. Roca Moo now boasts its own Michelin star (the Roca brothers' establishment in Girona has three) and has become more exclusive, trimming back the size of the dining room to expand the adjacent Roca Bar, where the same kitchen serves innovative tapas.

Carrer Rosselló, 265 (in Hotel Omm). ⓒ **93-445-40-00**. www.hotelomm.es. Reservations required. Main courses 20€–27€; 7-course Classics Menu 79€, matching wines 35€; 8-course Joan Roca Menu 100€, matching wines 40€. Mon–Sat 1:30–4pm and 8:30–11pm. Metro: Diagonal.

Restaurant Arrosseria Rosalert ★ CATALAN/SEAFOOD   Just a few blocks from La Sagrada Família, Jordi Alert has been serving great grilled seafood and baked rice dishes since the late 1970s. What you order depends on how much of a hurry you're in. Alert offers a "menu express" of a choice of shellfish grilled or steamed, a choice of grilled finfish, and a pastry for dessert. The *arròs* menu (minimum of two people) is designed for lingering. You get a selection of fish bites and shellfish *para pica,* that is, to pick up with your fingers and nibble on, and then a paella or similar arròs, and a pastry. Best order a bottle of wine, as you'll be halfway through it before the rice is ready. If you have a voracious appetite, order the *parrillada* of assorted grilled fish and shellfish and it will just keep coming, plate after plate.

Avinguda Diagonal, 301. ⓒ **93-207-10-19**. Reservations recommended. Main courses 22€–50€. Tues–Sat noon–5pm and 8pm–2am; Sun noon–5pm. Closed 10 days in Jan and Aug. Metro: Verdaguer/Sagrada Família.

MODERATE

El Caballito Blanco ★ SEAFOOD   Romantic it's not (no one looks good under fluorescent lights), but the simply prepared seafood is a bargain by L'Eixample standards. The menu usually includes shrimp, sole, sea bass, hake, and tuna, then lists three or four possible preparations that range from oven roasted to grilled to baked in a casserole with a sauce. Diners who prefer meat should consider either grilled lamb chops or pork sirloin steak.

Carrer Mallorca, 196. ⓒ **93-453-10-33**. Main courses 18€–29€. Tues–Sat 1–3:45pm and 9–10:45pm; Sun 1–3:45pm. Closed Aug. Metro: Hospital Clínic or Diagonal.

Can Ravell ★★★ CATALAN Ignasi Ravell founded this gourmet shop in 1929, and kept it running through the Franco years by having faith that even in the worst of times, there will be people who are willing to pay for the best of things. Ignasi's son Josep runs the place now, and it's a monument to the Catalan table. There's always been a small area in the back where Can Ravell served a few small plates (pork with snails, tortilla with sautéed green peppers) with drinks. But only regular deli customers know that there's a full restaurant on the upper level. You have to go through the kitchen and climb a very narrow circular stair to reach the airy room filled with solid wooden tables with marble slab tops. The menu is brief, consisting of four starters and four main dishes selected by the chef that day after a visit to the market. In the summer the chef goes wild featuring one vegetable after another—a feast of green beans one week, of tomatoes the next. In the fall, you might find lentils stewed with pig's ear and jowls, a roast quarter lamb (for two or three diners), and the popualr side dish of mashed potatoes with foie gras. The cellar here is very extensive, and includes literally dozens of cava choices in addition to still wines.

Carrer Aragó, 313. ✆ **93-457-51-14.** www.ravell.com. Reservations required. Main courses 13€–32€. Tues–Sat 10am–9pm; Sun 10am–3pm. Metro: Girona.

Cata 1.81 ★★ CATALAN/TAPAS Calling itself a "wine restaurant," Cata 1.81 serves only tapas, but they're hardly run-of-the-mill small plates. Here you'll find steak tartare with a Dijon mustard gelato, a "bikini" (the ubiquitous grilled ham and cheese sandwich) with black truffle, or even grilled foie gras with orange marmalade and "caviar" of chocolate grains. The inventions go on and on, even extending to a ground pork burger with curry ketchup and a fried egg. You can order a la carte, or opt for a tasting menu that is cheaper than ordering the dishes separately. The wine list is deep and broad, covering most areas of Spain and some of France, Italy, Australia, and California.

Carrer Valencia, 181. ✆ **93-323-68-18.** www.cata181.com. Reservations required. Tasting menu 30€ for 7 savory dishes and 2 desserts, 45€ with 4 glasses of wine; individual tapas 4.75€–8€. Sun–Fri 1pm–midnight; Sat 8pm–12:30am. Closed 3 weeks in Aug. Metro: Passeig de Gràcia or Hospital Clínic.

Gresca ★★ CATALAN Rafa Penya may have trained at elBulli, but he prefers well-priced innovative cooking over gastronomic theater. (Okay, you may be moved to applaud when you break through the shell of his soufflé and find a whole, just-cooked yolk inside.) Diners with more taste than money come here to enjoy Penya's penchant for tickling the palate with novel combinations, such as tuna tartare graced with white garlic flowers or lichi and apple pie with blue cheese. Other dishes seem to have been created from Penya's memories of his grandmother's cooking: veal tongue with sage, pig's feet with mushrooms, and braised beef cheeks. Barcelonans call a restaurant like this "bistronomic." We call it a bargain worth seeking out.

Carrer Provenca, 230. ✆ **93-451-61-93.** www.gresca.net. Reservations required. Main courses 15€–23€; 5-course menu 38€, 9-course 52€, 12-course 70€. Mon–Fri 1:30–3:30pm and 8:30–11pm; Sat 8:30–11pm. Metro: Plaça de Catalunya or Hospital Clínic.

Jaume de Provença ★ CATALAN Chef-owner Jaume Bargués goes in and out of style. He held a Michelin star here for 2 decades when Michelin stars were rare in Spain, and he's done just fine without it since 2001. Bargués has always cooked straightforward but luxe Catalan market cuisine—dishes like truffle and mushroom ravioli in a mushroom bechamel, sole stuffed with crab and herbs, veal filet in a Madeira sauce. He may use more truffles than any other chef in town. The beef tartare, for example, is served in two small towers—one topped with foie gras, the other with sliced black truffle. The restaurant is small, intimate, and surprisingly casual. That doesn't keep members of the royal family and pop music stars from sneaking in occasionally for a quiet dinner out of the public eye.

Carrer Provença, 88. ℰ **93-430-00-29.** www.jaumeprovenza.com. Reservations recommended. Main courses 13€–33€; fixed-price menu 60€. Tues–Sat 1–3:45pm and 9–11:15pm; Sun 1–3:45pm. Closed Easter week and Aug. Metro: Entença.

Restaurant Embat ★★ CATALAN Another stalwart of Barcelona's bargain-priced "bistronomic" restaurants, Embat has just 10 tables in a modest little space with white stucco walls. It bustles at lunch, when the menu usually has but three main dishes, none over 12€, and often requires reservations at night, when the prices go up but the choices expand dramatically. The dishes are not radical—just re-thought. Gazpacho comes with a few shrimp and a small ball of burrata (cream-filled mozzarella) with a flurry of basil. The classic of monkfish with spinach and creamy potato is complemented by a thin sheet of crackly almond praline. Desserts are a specialty—the chef has a pastry background. One favorite is the hot chocolate pudding with walnut ice cream.

Carrer Mallorca, 304. ℰ **93-458-08-55.** www.restaurantembat.es. Main courses lunch 10€–12€, dinner 18€–22€; dinner 5-course tasting menu 42€. Tue–Fri 1–3:30pm, Sat 2–3:30pm, Thur–Sat 9–10:45pm. Metro: Girona or Diagonal.

INEXPENSIVE

Patisseries Mauri ★ PASTRY This marvelously old-fashioned pastry shop and tea salon has been around since 1929, and while it's not exactly Modernista in style, it fits right into L'Eixample's aristocratic style. Ladies of the neighborhood line up here for the Viennese style pastries by the box, but it also makes a good spot to take a break while exploring. You can select pastry or deli salads and the clerk will ring each item onto a magnetically striped card. Then take a seat and order drinks or sandwiches, which the waiter will also ring onto the card. When you're done, the checkout clerk reads the card and tells you the damages.

Rambla de Catalunya, 102–103. ℰ **93-215-10-20.** www.pasteleriasmauri.com. Pastries and sandwiches 2.25€–5€. Mon–Sat 8am–9pm, Sun 9am–4pm. Metro: Diagonal.

Tapas 24 ★★ TAPAS Tapas in the morning, tapas in the evening, tapas at suppertime. Carles Abellan of **Comerç 24** (p. 182) set up this basement restaurant in L'Eixample as his personal homage to the tapas lifestyle, and it is, quite simply, a treat. Come for breakfast and you can order *estrellitas*—fried potatoes with a broken fried egg stirred in on top, with or without extra sausage, ham, or foie gras. (Catalan chefs love foie gras, which is local and inexpensive.) Service is nonstop from morning through evening, but the menu keeps changing as the day progresses. Count on always being able to order a bowl of lentils stewed with chorizo, the "McFoie" burger (a hamburger topped with foie gras), or *cap i pota,* which is a gelatinous stew of calf's head and feet beloved by Catalan bar patrons. (It's said to prevent a hangover.) Abellan is also famous for his "bikini" grilled ham and cheese sandwich with black truffle.

Carrer de la Diputació, 269. ℰ **93-488-09-77.** www.carlesabellan.es. Tapas 4€–15€. Mon–Sat 9am–midnight. Metro: Passeig de Gràcia.

Xampú Xampany ★ One of the last of Barcelona's old-fashioned *xampanyerías,* this spot on the corner of Carrer Bailèn at Plaça de Tetuan functions as a wine store that specializes in cavas, the Catalan sparkling wines that used to be called "champagne" before E.U. rules kicked in. It also functions as a bar that usually has at least a half dozen cavas in the ice bucket. On top of that, it is also a casual restaurant that serves breakfast food, sandwiches, and small plates of sausages and grilled fish. The omelet sandwich (French omelet—just eggs) makes a very good breakfast for only a few euros. This being Spain, many breakfast customers also have a glass of cava. Like most things involving inexpensive sparkling wine, it looks a lot more romantic after dark.

Gran Vía de les Corts Catalanes, 702. ✆ **93-265-04-83.** http://xampuxampany.com. Mon–Sat 8pm–1:30am. Metro: Girona or Tetuan

Waterfront & La Barceloneta
EXPENSIVE

La Mar Salada ★ CATALAN/SEAFOOD   One of the more prominent members of Barceloneta Cuina, a restaurant organization that aims to promote the seafood gastronomic traditions of the fishermen's neighborhood, La Mar Salada serves some very old-fashioned dishes like *bombas* (potato balls with a bit of blood sausage in the middle) and heavily breaded and deep-fried squid. Both dishes are usually bathed in the garlicky Catalan eggless mayonnaise called "allioli." But this inventive restaurant is also known for its lobster fritters and a dynamite version of rape *suquet*, a seafood soup made with monkfish, clams, onions, tomato, saffron, and sweet paprika.

Passeig Juan de Borbo, 58–59. ✆ **93-221-21-27.** www.lamarsalada.cat. Reservations recommended. Main dishes 17€–29€. Mon and Wed–Fri 12:30–4:40pm and 8–11:30pm, Sat–Sun 12:30–11:30pm. Metro: Barceloneta.

7 Portes ★ CATALAN/SEAFOOD   Located under the arches on elegant Isabel II, 7 Portes has the quintessential look of a grand Old World restaurant. Its waitstaff wear either long black aprons or short white jackets and hustle from table to table with solicitous service. Many tourists take exception to the relative formality of the place, but that's part of its charm. To enjoy the restaurant, skip the paella. They make a different one each day and some can be good, but it's not their strong suit. One of the most famous dishes is the chicken roasted with mushrooms and Moscatel wine—sort of a Catalan coq au vin. Light eaters and bargain hunters will be glad to know that the menu encourages sharing larger dishes like the Dover sole, which typically weighs in at more than 2 pounds, or the large steamed or grilled medleys of seafood. The smaller fried fish plate is also very good—all the fish are pan-fried in butter. The restaurant's name means "Seven Doors," and it really does have seven doors.

Passeig Isabel II, 14. ✆ **93-319-30-33.** www.7portes.com. Reservations required. Main courses 14€–30€. Daily 1pm–1am. Metro: Barceloneta.

Suquet de l'Almirall ★★ CATALAN/SEAFOOD   Quim Marqués worked at some of the leading restaurants in Spain (including elBulli) before taking over this Barceloneta gem from his parents in 1997. He has since become a champion of the local, buying all his fish from the fish auction less than 100 yards away, and supplementing the fish with local milk, cheese, eggs, and organically grown vegetables. He's also the author of two Catalan cookbooks focusing on Barceloneta cuisine, including a new one with his son, Manel Marqués, who works alongside him in the family business. All the fish dishes here are terrific, but the *suquet* (a traditional Catalan seafood stew) is a classic. Best of all, this is one place on the street where you can eat the seafood paella and know it's the real thing.

Passeig Joan Borbo, 65. ✆ **93-221-62-33.** www.suquetdelalmirall.com. Main dishes 19€–28€. Tues–Sat 1:30–4:30pm and 9–11:30pm, Sun 1:30–4:30pm. Metro: Barceloneta.

MODERATE

Agua ★ MEDITERRANEAN   This ultramodern seafood restaurant at the Port Olímpic really is about the sparkling water of the harbor, and it's named accordingly. It's also about sitting out on the terrace with wraparound sunglasses and an Audrey Hepburn scarf (for the women) and looking like you're Someone going incognito. Even the menu has a bit of the Hollywood-goes-the-Cinque-Terre feel, with starters like cantaloupe soup, tomato salad with onions and capers, or fried egg and calamari with potatoes. The house specialties, though, are rice dishes cooked in paella pans over open charcoal fires. (To Agua's credit, not one of them is called a "paella.") Meat and fish simply grilled over charcoal are also popular, and you will see a number of the headscarf set just eating salad and drinking cosmopolitans from the bar. Check for risotto specials featuring fresh shellfish. Agua also makes a good hamburger, with or without cheese.

Passeig Marítim de la Barceloneta, 30 (Port Olímpic). ✆ **93-225-12-72.** www.grupotragaluz.com. Reservations recommended. Main courses 9€–22€. Mon–Fri 1–4pm and 8:30–11:30pm; Sat–Sun 1–4:30pm and 8pm–12:30am. Metro: Ciutadella or Vila Olímpic.

Can Costa ★ CATALAN/SEAFOOD   The first seafront fish shack to actually put up a masonry building, Can Costa has been around since the 1920s when this stretch of Barceloneta was a much saltier locale. With two indoor dining rooms (a warehouse blocks the harbor view anyway), Can Costa seats a lot of diners. This can be a drawback if you mind waiting while your food is cooked, but the seafood is fresh and the kitchen cooks it as simply as possible. The fried baby squid are some of the best in Barceloneta as they're very quickly sautéed so they remain tender. The "fideuà de peix," a dish baked in a shallow paella pan with noodles instead of rice, is a house specialty. Can Costa also makes a black version flavored and colored with squid ink and featuring more calamari than shellfish.

Passeig Don Joan de Borbò, 70. ✆ **93-221-59-03.** www.cancosta.com. Reservations recommended. Main courses 12€–32€. Sun–Tues and Thurs–Sat 12:30–4pm; Mon–Tues and Thurs–Sat 8–11:30pm. Metro: Barceloneta.

Can Majó ★ CATALAN/SEAFOOD   Literally steps from the beach, this family restaurant dates from 1968 and is now run by two generations of the Majó family. The dining room resembles a country tavern, but as long as the weather is good, everyone wants to eat outdoors at the white-linen-clad tables beneath umbrellas. Not all the seafood is local—they fly in amazing oysters from Galicia and France for the raw bar. Many of the shellfish are cooked over a wood-fired grill, which gives them a smoky tang. The restaurant is known, however, for fish soups—both the simple fish and shellfish in a fish broth, and the more elaborate *zarzuela,* a Catalan dish where the mixed fish are more important than the broth. On request, the kitchen will prepare the very similar French dish, bouillabaisse.

Almirall Aixada 23, Barceloneta. ✆ **93-221-54-55.** www.canmajo.es. Reservations recommended. Main courses 12€–32€. Tues–Sat 1–3:30pm and 8–11:30pm; Sun 1–3:30pm. Metro: Barceloneta.

Can Solé ★★ CATALAN/SEAFOOD   Proprietor Josep Maria Garcia believes fervently in tradition. While many surrounding restaurants offer suspiciously orange rice studded with mussels and call it paella, Can Solé adheres to the traditional plates of La Barceloneta. That could mean starting with a briny bowl of tiny sweet clams or cabbage hearts stuffed with tuna. Some vanishing dishes make their last stand here, like the fried cod and onions with sweet currants that hint at its North African roots. And then there's the *zarzuela,* the most expensive dish on the Can Solé menu because it is an encyclopedia of the Barceloneta catch, jammed with everything from whiting to shrimp, cigalas, bream, mackerel, clams, mussels, and even lobster.

Carrer Sant Carles, 4. ✆ **93-221-50-12.** www.restaurantcansole.com. Reservations suggested. Main courses 12€–28€. Tues–Sat 1:30–4pm and 8:30–11pm; Sun 1:30–4pm. Closed 2 weeks Aug. Metro: Barceloneta.

Kaiku ★★ CATALAN/SEAFOOD   Owner Rafa Alberdi held out as long as he could just serving lunch, but the clamor of customers for dinner at Kaiku finally won out. Diners never really know what's on the menu until they arrive, as Alberdi and his chef are always looking for unusual items at the fish market. There will be some kind of shrimp, some form of finfish, cockles, oysters, sea anemones, smoked rice dishes, and grilled zaburinyes—seared scallops with ginger and lime. A few plates are standards, like the sautéed mushrooms with shrimp and egg, and the seared tuna with green apple and mango.

Plaça del Mar, 1. ✆ **93-221-90-82.** www.restaurantkaiku.cat. Main dishes 15€–20€. Tues–Sun 1–3:30pm and Tues–Sat 7–10:30pm. Metro: Barceloneta.

INEXPENSIVE
L'Electricitat ★★ TAPAS   Possibly the favorite neighborhood bar in all of Barceloneta, the atmosphere here at midday matches the name—it's positively electric. Tapas are a steal, and it's a great place to have steamed mussels or clams, maybe a bite of fried fish, some anchovies, a finger sandwich with smoked trout, and then perhaps a small crab salad. There's beer on tap and a lot of inexpensive Catalan wines. In cold weather, they also tap the big barrels of house vermouth that are more or less ornamental the rest of the year.

Carrer Sant Carles, 15. ✆ **93-221-50-17.** Tapas 1.50€–12€. Mon–Sat 8am–3pm and 7–10:30pm, Sun 8–3:45pm. Metro: Barceloneta.

Montjuïc
MODERATE
Òleum ★★ CATALAN   Montjuïc is known for its views of the city, and there's no place more serene to lord it over the metropolis than from the dining room of this exquisite restaurant at the Museu Nacional d'Art de Catalunya. Usually there's a reverse correlation between the quality of the food and the quality of the view, but not here. Òleum presents a fairly light menu at midday and evening. All dishes have a little twist, whether it's the nut bread and sliced grilled foie on the venison burger, or the pumpkin with the mushroom and truffle risotto. Prices are reasonable for such an exquisite venue—you may wish you hadn't worn sneakers to the museum. There's a fair bit of wit (and local food references as well) afoot on the menu. For example, one desserts is a modern interpretation of Escoffier's peach melba as served at **7 Portes** (p. 194) in the 1960s. At Òleum, they call it the Barcelona "pijama" cup because it is as casual as the 7 Portes version was formal and composed. It includes crème caramel, creamy yogurt with peach and pineapple, raspberry coulis, vanilla ice cream, and a crispy rolled wafer.

Palau Nacional, Parc de Montjuïc, s/n. ✆ **93-289-06-79.** www.laierestaurants.es. Main dishes 16€–27€. Tues–Sat 12:30–4pm and 7:30–11pm, Sun 12:30–4pm. Metro: Plaça d'Espanya.

EXPLORING BARCELONA

Barcelona is a pretty compact city, and you can explore it easily if you take public transit to a starting point and then set out on foot. In broad strokes, there are four areas of interest: **the medieval old city, the post-1880 new city, the waterfront,** and **Montjuïc.**

All the neighborhoods of the old city (Ciutat Vell) combined are much smaller in area than the new city, but you'll probably want to spend at least as much time exploring the old than the new. We've broken it down into historic neighborhoods for convenience, but as you wander, you'll find that one neighborhood flows into the next. The central, largely pedestrian, artery of the old city is **Les Rambles.** To the west lies **El Raval;** to the east is the medieval **Barri Gòtic.** Keep going east past the cathedral and you'll enter **La Ribera** and **El Born.** The old city has beautiful Gothic churches (including the cathedral), the most atmospheric medieval streets, and the biggest crowds. It also has the **Museu Picasso,** the **Palau de la Música Catalana,** the **Museu d'Art Contemporani de Barcelona,** and the two greatest of the city's 35 markets.

The new city begins north of Plaça de Catalunya and includes the districts of **L'Eixample** and **Gràcia,** which are more residential than most of the old city. You'll go here to shop in upscale international boutiques and to visit most of the masterpieces of Modernista architecture, including **La Pedrera, Casa Batlló,** and the **Basilica de la Sagrada Familia.** L'Eixample also has several small art museums, including the **Fundació Antoni Tapiès.**

From a practical standpoint, the **Waterfront** begins at the base of Les Rambles. It includes the modern cruise ship port, **Port Vell** (Old Port) yacht basin, the long sandy spit of barrier beach known as **La Barceloneta,** and the more recently developed **Port Olimpic,** east of the older part of the city. The main attractions include boat cruises, **L'Aquàrium de Barcelona,** and the **seafood restaurants and beaches** of Barceloneta.

Last but hardly least is **Montjuïc.** The mountain at the edge of town has been used over the last century for major expositions and events, including the 1929 International Exposition and the 1992 Olympics. It's covered with parkland, and you'll visit for the views, both indoors and out. Several overlooks have great vistas of the city and harbor, but some of the most interesting sights lie within the **Museu Nacional d'Art de Catalunya** and the **Fundació Joan Miró.**

BARCELONA'S TOP SIGHTS

OTHER ATTRACTIONS

Les Rambles & El Raval

If you're not jazzed walking up and down **Les Rambles ★★★**, you'd better check to make sure you still have a pulse. You can spend a whole day here just exploring the street life, cafes, and shops. But you'll want to take some of that time to turn into El Raval on streets named Nou de la Rambla, Sant Pau, Hospital, Carme, and Elisabets. You'll find both the wonderfully récherché world of old Raval, and the modern, hip neighborhood of the arts. Get to Les Rambles by one of three Metro stops: Drassanes at the waterfront, Liceu halfway up, and Plaça de Catalunya at the top.

La Boqueria ★★★ MARKET   Foodies visiting Spain consider the Mercat de Sant Josep de la Boqueria (its official name) a temple deserving a reverential pilgrimage. The spot has been a marketplace since the medieval period when Raval farmers sold their produce to the inhabitants of the walled city. The current market is the largest of Barcelona's 35 public markets. It has a wonderful sidewalk mosaic in front created by Joan Miró in the 1970s, and the metal-roofed structure is an amalgam of building styles erected between 1840 and 1914. From the outside, it resembles a train station. Inside, it is jammed with stalls selling every imaginable type of fresh produce, fish (segregated to one side), and meat (toward the back). There are bakeries and sandwich stalls and juice bars and cafes all tucked into the mix. Even if you're not someone normally intoxicated by food, it's an important spot to visit. By paying attention to what the stalls are selling, you'll quickly learn what's fresh and in season and can order accordingly at the restaurants.

Les Rambles, 91. No phone. Mon–Sat 8am–8pm. Metro: Liceu.

Gran Teatre del Liceu ★★ THEATER   Despite its plain exterior, this 2,700-seat Belle Epoque opera house is opulent and extravagant inside. One of the world's grand theaters, it was designed in 1861 to replace an earlier theater destroyed by fire. Flames gutted the opera house again in 1994, but it was restored to its 19th-century glory and resumed its role as the most important place to be seen if you're a member of Barcelona high society. It's also a great place to take in opera, dance, or a concert. The building has a modest cafe on the lower level where you can get an 11€ menu (appetizer, main course, and drink) from 1:30-4pm before one of the matinee performances at 3pm, 5pm, or 6pm. The Liceu also offers **guided** and **self-guided tours** of the public areas, and a limited number of guided tours of the stage and service areas.

Les Rambles, 51–59. ✆ **93-485-99-13** or 93-485-99-00. www.liceubarcelona.com. 80-min. guided tour of public areas daily at 10am, 12€; nonguided tours daily 11:30am–1pm every 30 min., 5.50€; stage and service area tours selected weekdays at 9:15am, 13€. Metro: Liceu.

SAVINGS ON exploring

There are four discount programs that may or may not work for you, depending on what you want to see and how you're planning to get around.

A ticket on the **Barcelona Bus Turistic** (p. 162) gets you a coupon book for discounts good for the rest of the calendar year. Most sightseeing discounts are modest, and the Museu Picasso is not included, but if you decide to ride the bus as transportation or for orientation, be sure to use the coupons.

The **Barcelona Card** features several free museum admissions (not Picasso) and allows you to skip the lines. It also provides discounts on other admissions and tours, including 15-20 percent on admissions to major Modernista buildings. Unlimited use of Metro, buses, and commuter rail can be a plus. Available at all Barcelona Turisme offices and El Corte Inglés department stores, the BCN Card costs 37€ for 2 days, 47€ for 3 days, 56€ for 4 days and 62€ for 5 days. The corresponding prices for children ages 4-12 are 26€, 31€, 33€, and 40€.

The **Articket BCN** is geared to the major art museums, providing priority entry to six museums for 30€: Museu Picasso, Museu Nacional d'Art de Catalunya, Fundació Joan Miró, Fundació Antoni Tàpies, the Centre de Cultura Contemporània de Barcelona (CCCB), and the Museu d'Art Contemporani de Barcelona (MACBA). Tickets to the first three alone will cost more than the pass. The pass also allows you to skip the line—a huge timesaver at the Museu Picasso.

Purchasing the **Ruta de Modernisme guide** (12€) at any bookstore or tourist office supplies you with a coupon book of discounts of up to 50 percent on entrance fees to the Modernista buildings. The guide itself and its accompanying map make invaluable, if highly detailed references to 116 Modernista sites around the city.

When weighing the options, keep in mind that on the first Sunday of each month, **admission is free** at the Museu Picasso, the Museu Nacional d'Art de Catalunya (MNAC), and the Museu d'Història de Catalunya. Museu Picasso is also free every Sunday after 3pm, while MNAC is free every Saturday after 3pm.

Hotel España ★ HISTORIC SITE   This mid-19th-century hotel got its most important facelift in 1903-04 under the direction of the great Modernista architect Lluís Domènech i Montaner. He worked with two of the greatest artisans of the era to execute the design: sculptor Eusebi Arnau, who created a striking alabaster chimney in one of the dining rooms, and painter Ramon Casas, who did a lot of the decorative painting and sgraffito work. Domènech i Montaner completed the look with wooden wainscoting and decorative blue and white tiles. The hotel restored some of the Modernista features when it renovated in 2010 and now offers architectural tours.

Carrer Sant Pau, 9–11. ✆ **93-550-00-00.** www.hotelespanya.com. Guided tours Mon–Fri 12:15pm and 4:30pm, 5[e], 2.50€ hotel guests and restaurant diners.

Museu d'Art Contemporani de Barcelona ★ MUSEUM   This soaring white structure at the north end of El Raval (just a short distance west of Plaça de Catalunya) has played a key role in the neighborhood's revival. It brings a youth and vibrancy to the area—even the ramps around the building have become a key gathering spot for Barcelona skateboard athletes. Designed by American architect Richard Meier, the building applies the lessons of Josep Sert's building for the **Fundació Miró** (p. 216)

6 | Barcelona Attractions

Barcelona Beaches **45**
Basilica de la
  Sagrada Família **13**
Call **29**
Casa Amatller **18**
Casa Batlló **17**
Casa Lleó Morera **19**
Castell de Montjuïc **6**
Catedral de
  Barcelona **30**
Fundació Antoni
  Tàpies **16**
Fundació Francisco
  Godia **21**
Fundació Joan Miró **4**
Gran Teatre
  del Liceu **26**

Hospital de la Santa
  Creu i Sant Pau **12**
Hotel España **25**
Jardí Botànic **5**
La Boqueria **24**
La Pedrera **15**
L'Aquarium de
  Barcelona **43**
Mercat Santa
  Caterina **34**
Mirador de Colom **42**
Museu d'Arqueologia
  de Catalunya **3**
Museu d'Art Contem-
  porani de Barcelona **9**
Museu de la
  Xocolata **35**

Museu del Modern-
  isme Català **20**
Museu d'Història
  de Catalunya **44**
Museu Frederic
  Marès **33**
Museu Maritim **7**
Museu Nacional d'Art
  de Catalunya **2**
Museu Picasso **37**
Palau de la Música
  Catalana **23**
Palau del Baró
  de Quadras **14**
Palau Güell **41**
Parc d'Atraccions **10**

Parc de la
  Ciutadella **36**
Parc Güell **11**
Plaça de
  Catalunya **22**
Plaça de San Felip
  Neri **28**
Plaça de Sant Just **39**
Plaça del Pi **27**
Plaça del Rei **32**
Plaça Reial **40**
Poble Espanyol **1**
Sant Pau del Camp **8**
Santa Maria
  del Mar **38**
Temple d'August **31**

To Tibidabo Mountain ⑩ ⑪

GRÀCIA

Pg. de Gràcia

Indústria

Còrsega

Rosselló

L'EIXAMPLE

Av. Gaudí

Lepant

Marina

Sardenya

Padilla

Castillejos

Plaça Joan Carles I ⑭

Casa de les Punxes

Diagonal

Enric Granados

Balmes

Rambla Catalunya

Ⓜ ⑮ Casa Milà (La Pedrera)

Av. Diagonal

Casa Thomas

Ⓜ Verdaguer

Provença

La Sagrada Família

La Sagrada Família ⑬

Ⓜ Sagrada Família

Passeig de Gràcia

Pau Claris

Roger de Llúria

Bruc

Girona

Bailèn

Pg. Sant Joan

Roger de Flor

Mallorca

València

Aragó

Av. Diagonal

Enamorats

⑯

⑰

⑱

⑲

Passeig de Gràcia

Ⓜ Girona

Diputació

Consell de Cent

Plaça Dr. Letamendi

⑳

㉑

Universitat de Barcelona

Gran Via Corts Catalanes

Plaça Tetuan

Gran Via Corts Catalanes

Plaça Toros Monumental

Ⓜ Monumental

Ronda Universitat

L'EIXAMPLE

Casp

Tetuan

Pg. Sant Joan

Nàpols

Sicília

Ribes

Teatre Nacional de Catalunya

L'Auditori

Meridiana

Marina

Ⓜ Catalunya

Plaça Catalunya

㉒ Ⓜ

Plaça Urquinaona

Ausiàs Marc

Ronda Sant Pere

Arc de Triomf

Estació del Nord

Parc Estació del Nord

Marina

Ⓜ Almogàvers

Pallars

La Rambla

Av. Portal de l'Angel

Via Laietana

Ⓜ Urquinaona

㉓

LA RIBERA

Ⓜ Arc de Triomf

Palau de Justícia

Carme

La Boqueria

㉔

㉗

㉘ ㉝

Pl. Antoni Maura

Mercat Sta. Caterina

㉞

Comerç

㉟

Pg. de Pujades

Pujades

Av.

Wellington

Sardenya

Marina

Joan d'Àustria

Zamora

Pamplona

Pere IV

Ⓜ Bogatell

Llull

Ⓜ Liceu

BARRI

㉙ ㉚ ㉜ ㉛

Ferran

㉖

㉕

㉑ ㊵

La Rambla

GÒTIC

Ⓜ Jaume I

Jaume I

Princesa

㊲

Mercat del Born

㊳

Parc de la Ciutadella

㊱

Parlament de Catalunya

Sta. Maria del Mar

Ⓜ Drassanes

Via Laietana

Plaça Antonio López

Pla de Palau

Estació de França

Passeig de Circumval·lació

Parc Zoològic

Ⓜ Barceloneta

Passeig de Colom

Moll d'Espanya

㊹ Palau de Mar

Doctor Aiguader

Ronda Litoral

Doctor Aiguader

Ⓜ Ciutadella-Vila Olímpica

Salvador Espriu

Av. del Litoral

Rambla de Mar

IMAX

㊸

Maremàgnum

L'Aquàrium de Barcelona

Pg. Joan de Borbó

BARCELONETA

Pg. Marítim Barceloneta

Port Olímpic

Platja Barceloneta

㊺

by manipulating angles of exterior walls to allow natural diffused light to enter the galleries. Many of the the galleries are often given over to highly conceptual temporary exhibitions, but they do draw on the permanent collection, which is strong in Antoni Tàpies and younger Spanish artists. Guided tours in English are available. The museum is also experimenting with a downloadable app to enable users to access additional audio and video about selected works of art—and to share responses to the work on Facebook and Twitter.

Plaça dels Angels 1. ✆ **93-412-08-10.** www.macba.cat. Admission 9€ adults, 7€ students, free for children 14 and under and seniors 65 and over. Late June to late Sept Mon and Wed–Fri 11am–8pm; Sat 10am–8pm, Sun 10am–3pm; late Sept to late June Mon and Wed–Fri 11am–7:30pm, Sat 10am–8pm, Sun 10am–3pm. Free guided tours in English Mon 4pm and 6pm, Wed–Sat 4pm. Metro: Plaça de Catalunya.

Museu Maritim ★ MUSEUM Massive renovations and reconstruction of the historic facility have closed the museum until at least late 2014.In its previous incarnation, the museum's exhibits chronicled Barcelona's maritime history from the time when Rome established the trading port of Barcino up to the 20th century. New exhibits are expected to bring state of the art exhibition technologies to telling that same story. The museum is housed inside medieval royal shipyards, the Drassanes Reiales. So vast were these shipyards, built between 1255 and 1378, that it was possible to construct 30 galleys at a time. As a result, the crown of Aragón became one of the most powerful naval forces in the Mediterranean.

Avinguda de les Drassanes, s/n. ✆ **93-342-99-20.** www.mmb.cat. Hours and admission prices to be announced. Metro: Drassanes.

Palau Güell ★★ HISTORIC SITE Much of this second commission by young architect Antoni Gaudí looks almost as if it were grown rather than built. Constructed 1886-90 for aristocrat and industrialist Eusebi Güell, the home shows Gaudí's budding originality. The family quarters are rather conventional—["]a normal Venetian palace," a guide once sniffed on one of our tours—but the architect's imagination ran wild both above and below. The underground forest of brick columns and vaults in 10 musty cellars creates a honeycomb of stables and servants' quarters, and function as much as the building's root system as its foundation. The rooftop is even more startling. Gaudí wrapped the chimneys with swirling abstract sculptures. Not only are they embedded with mosaics of broken pottery, they also employ artistic symbols from ancient Catalan tradition. After the restraint of the main residence, the rooftop is an exultation of the spirit.

Carrer Nou de la Rambla, 3–5. ✆ **93-472-57-75.** www.palauguell.cat. Admission 12€ adults, 8€ students and seniors. Apr–Oct Tues–Sun 10am–7pm, Nov–Mar Tues–Sun 10am–5:30pm. Metro: Liceu.

Plaça de Catalunya ★ PLAZA Considered the heart of the city, this large circular plaza marks the spot where the old city and the 19th-century extension meet. Since its last renovation in 1929, it has also been the crossroads of the Metro system. It is known for its fountains. Legend says that anyone who drinks from the Font de Canaletes will inevitably return to Barcelona. Surrounding the plaza are many hotels and the city's largest outlet of the Spanish department store, **El Corte Inglés** (p. 220).

Sant Pau del Camp ★★ RELIGIOUS SITE The antithesis of Gaudí's La Sagrada Familia, the modest ancient church and monastery of Sant Pau del Camp (St. Paul of the Fields) is one of the most serene and most moving religious spaces in Barcelona. According to his gravestone, which was unearthed in 1596, the monastery was founded between 897 and 911 by Guifré Borrell, then count of Barcelona (and son of Wilfred the Hairy). The church was sacked by Al-Mansur's Moorish troops in 985, but the whole complex was rebuilt during the 13th century, which seems to be the period of the charming cloister and its stone capitals carved with Biblical tales. Centuries of erosion have not dimmed Eve's sudden embarrassment about her nakedness or the ferocity of the reptilian devil being skewered by archangel Michael. The intimate piety of the church and its small altar are striking. A side chapel holds a beautiful polychrome Gothic statue of María del Deu, as well as the founder's gravestone.

Carrer Sant Pau, 101. ✆ **93-441-00-01.** Admission 3€, Sun morning free. Daily 10am–12:30pm and 4–6:30pm. Masses Sat 8pm in Castilian Spanish, Sun noon in Catalan. Metro: Paral.lel.

Barri Gòtic

Barcelona came into its own as a Mediterranean power in the 12th century when the Aragonese King Jaume I erected a defensive wall around the city. This area—roughly from Les Rambles east to Via Laietana and from the waterfront north to Plaça de Catalunya—is the **Barri Gòtic (Gothic Quarter)** ★★★, which retains much of its medieval street pattern. It's a fascinating neighborhood of narrow streets and pocket squares, most fronting on Gothic churches. Plan on spending at least a half day exploring, knowing that you will get a little lost, no matter how good your map. (That's part of the charm of the quarter.) It assumes a special magic on Sunday mornings, when you can emerge from a warren of small streets onto a square where a musician may be playing for change. Metro stops for the Barri Gòtic are Liceu and Jaume I.

Call ★ NEIGHBORHOOD   Barcelona had one of the most robust Jewish communities in Iberia from the 12th century until 1391, when the community in the heart of the Barri Gòtic came under siege. Six centuries of absence have wiped away most evidence of Jewish presence, but since the 1990s, a concerted effort by scholars and community activists has helped establish the old limits of the Call and has begun to restore the remains of the principal synagogue. The main street of the Call (a Jewish word meaning "small street" and closely related to the modern Spanish "calle" and Catalan "carrer") was Carrer de Sant Domènc, where the great synagogue, the kosher butcher's shop, and the homes of the leading Jewish citizens were located. An information center and display of artifacts recovered through excavations is operated by the Associació Call de Barcelona in a shop above the remains of the **Sinagoga Mayor.**

Carrer Marlet, 5. Admission 2.50€. Mon–Fri 10:30am–6pm, Sat–Sun 10:30am–3pm. Metro: Jaume I.

Catedral de Barcelona ★★ RELIGIOUS SITE   A celebrated example of Catalan Gothic architecture, Barcelona's cathedral was begun at the end of the 13th century and more or less completed by the mid–15th century. One notable exception, the western facade, dates from the 19th century when church-goers felt that the unadorned Gothic surface was somehow inadequate. If you really want to get a feel for the cathedral, skip the "tourist visit" completely and go to Mass, or at least sit silently and reflect. The high naves, which have been cleaned and lit in recent years, are filled with terrific Gothic architectural details, including the elongated and tapered columns that blossom into arches in their upper reaches. The separate **cloister** has vaulted galleries that surround a garden of magnolias, medlars, and palm trees and the so called "well of the geese." (Thirteen geese live in the cloister as a symbol of Barcelona co-patron Santa Eulalia.) The cloister also contains the cathedral's museum, of which the most notable piece is a 15th-century *pieta* by Bartolomé Bermejo. You can also take an elevator to the roof, which has a number of fanciful gargoyles and terrific views of the rest of the Barri Gòtic. At noon on Sundays (and sometimes on Sat), folk dancers gather below the cathedral steps to dance the traditional circular dance, the *sardana*. On the feast of Corpus Christi, the cathedral maintains the Catalan tradition of a dancing egg—a decorated hollow egg that "dances" atop a water jet in one of the fountains.

Plaça de la Seu s/n. ℂ **93-315-15-54.** www.catedralbcn.org. Admission to cathedral free; ticket to museum, choir, rooftop terraces, and towers 6€. Cathedral Mon–Fri 8am–12:45pm and 5:15–7:30pm, Sat–Sun 8am–12:45pm and 5:15–7:30pm; cloister museum daily 10am–12:30pm and 5:15–7pm. Metro: Jaume I.

Museu Frederic Marès ★ MUSEUM Situated behind the cathedral in part of the old royal palace of the Counts of Barcelona, this striking collection of Iberian sculpture is not for everyone—although its quiet courtyard and hidden plaza are. (It's a great spot to escape the hubbub of crowds around the cathedral.) Marès (1893–1991) was himself a sculptor, but his greatest legacy is the collection that he amassed that covers sculptural styles from the ancient world to the 19th century. The vast majority of the works are Gothic polychrome statues from around Spain, with special emphasis on Castilla and Catalunya. The galleries begin with serene and all-knowing representations of Maria del Deu (Madonna and Child), but Marès seems to have been taken with particularly vivid depictions, especially of gruesome martyrdoms. Crucifixions run the gamut from the sagging flesh of a resigned Christ to more vigorous images of Christ literally writhing on the cross. Some small children might find the imagery disturbing. Upper levels of the museum contain some of Marès's peculiar personal collections (locks, especially) that may not appeal to many viewers who nonetheless appreciate the sculptures.

Plaça de San Iu, 5. ℂ **93-256-35-00.** www.museumares.bcn.cat. Admission 4.20€, 2.40€ seniors and students. Mon and Wed–Sat 10am–7pm, Sun 11am–8pm. Metro: Jaume I.

Plaça de Sant Just ★ PLAZA Most people find this tranquil little plaza because they want to dine at **Cafè de L'Acadèmia** (p. 184), but in Roman times, Jews and Christians came here to trade. The 13th-century church on the plaza, the Basilica dels Sants Just i Pastor, stands on the site of the original 4th-century Christian basilica in Barcino, and the predecessor to this Gothic church functioned as the seat of the archbishop until the city's cathedral was constructed. The plaza's fountain is said to be the oldest water source in the city. Made of Montjuïc stone, it was carved in 1367. Above the three pipes are an image of one-handed Sant Just, another of the royal shield, and a third of a shield showing a hawk catching a partridge.

Plaça Sant Just. ℂ **93-301-74-33.** http://basilicasantjust.cat. Free admission. Church open Mon–Sat 11am–2pm and 5–9pm, Sun 10am–1pm. Metro: Jaume I.

Plaça del Pi ★ RELIGIOUS SITE Three pretty, contiguous plazas surround the 15th-century church of **Santa María del Pi ★**, which is acclaimed for its rose window. At 10m (33 ft.) in diameter, it is considered one of the world's largest. Destroyed at the beginning of the Civil War in 1936, it was slowly restored in the 1950s and is the only window in the basilica to retain its original 14th-century design. It shows the 24 Elders of the Apocalypse with the coats of arms of the church and the Counts of Barcelona. The pews of the church sit on the stones marking graves in the floor. Don't let the skull and crossbones motifs disturb your prayer. During the summer, the church also operates a series of concerts in the basilica's so-called "Secret Garden," with programs that can range from pop music to Vivaldi and include a tour of the church museum. The main square out front is the official Plaça del Pi, but **Plaça de Sant Josep Oriol** adjoins it and flows behind the church to tiny **Placeta del Pi.** The squares are known for the unusual *sgraffito* decorative technique on the plaster facades of several buildings, an 18th-century style imported from Italy. But the leafy squares are also popular for the weekend artisans' market and open-air cafe-bars.

Santa María del Pi, Carrer del Cardenal Casañas, 16. © **93-318-47-43.** http://basilicadelpi.com. Free. "Secret Garden" concerts 14€. Daily 9am–1pm and 4–9pm.

Plaça del Rei ★ ARCHEOLOGICAL SITE   Seemingly wedged in between the cathedral and the remains of Barcino's Roman walls, this stately old square serves as the front porch of the 11th-century Palau Reial Major, palace of the kings of Aragon and Catalunya, and its related complex of buildings, including the **Museu Frederic Marès** (above). The chief attraction here is the guided tour of underground walkways over the excavations of Barcino, the city founded by the Romans in the 1st century B.C. and ruled by the Visigoths until the Moors leveled it in the 8th century A.D. The tour is offered by the **Museu d'Història de la Ciutat.** Although they are partially visible from Plaça del Rei, the last remaining Roman walls and defensive towers of Barcino— a section from the A.D. 4th-century second enclosure—are easier to make out from the opposite side, on **Plaça Ramon Berenguer** on Via Laietana. Embedded within the wall are the royal chapel of Santa Ágata and a 14th-century segment of the Palau Reial.

Plaça del Rei, s/n. © **93-315-11-11.** www.museuhistoria.bcn.es. 7€ adults, 5€ students and seniors, free under age 16. June–Sept Tues–Sat 10am–8pm; Oct–Mar Tues–Sat 10am–2pm and 4–7pm; year-round Sun 10am–3pm. Metro: Jaume I.

Plaça Reial ★ PLAZA   Barcelona's first big urban renewal project in the 19th century, this large and harmonious square occupies the former site of the Santa Madrona Capuchin monastery, which had been demolished at mid-century. Inspired by the renewal projects of Paris, architect Francesc Daniel Molina conceived the Plaça Reial as a residential square formed by buildings with two stories and a partial upper floor. These days it's surrounded largely by cafes, and although it attracts many more tourists than locals, it is still a great place to sit beneath an arcade, drink beer, and observe the passing scene. The fountain of the three graces in the center is flanked by handsome Art Nouveau lampposts that were Antoni Gaudí's first commission (1878). He decorated them with a caduceus (a messenger's wand with two snakes entwined around it) and winged helmets—attributes of Hermes, patron of shopkeepers.

Metro: Liceu.

Plaça de Sant Felip Neri ★ HISTORIC SITE   This quiet little plaza at the north end of the Call is one of the few spots in the city to bear witness to Barcelona's suffering during the Civil War. Pockmarks on the façade of the San Felipe Neri church recall the Nationalist bombs that fell in the plaza on January 30, 1938. Twenty children and 22 adults who were taking refuge in the church cellars were killed. The fall of Barcelona took place 10 weeks later, when Franco and his forces dropped 44 tons of bombs on the civilian population. Franco saw himself as uniting the country. Many Catalans still see it as genocide.

Metro: Liceu.

Temple d'August ★ ARCHEOLOGICAL SITE   One of the four columns of this A.D. 1st-century temple discovered during late-19th-century excavations is incorporated into the display of the Roman wall on Plaça Ramon Berenguer. The other three remain where they were originally erected, now inside the 19th-century building that now houses the Centre Excursionista de Catalunya. The temple once formed part of the Roman Forum dedicated to Emperor Caesar Augustus. The ruins are part of the city-wide collection of the Museu d'Història de la Ciutat (see Plaça Reial, above) and can be visited free of charge.

Carrer Paradis, 10. ✆ **93-315-23-11.** www.museuhistoria.bcn.es. Free admission. June–Sept Tues–Sat 10am–8pm, Sun 10am–2pm; Oct–May Tues–Sat 10am–2pm and 4–8pm, Sun 10am–2pm. Metro: Jaume 1.

La Ribera & El Born

With streets a little wider, buildings a little newer, and street patterns that at least approach a grid, **La Ribera and El Born** ★★ push the Barri Gòtic eastward. They are still very obviously part of the old city, and can be combined with the Barri Gòtic for a long day or even two of touring. Both La Ribera and El Born combine commercial and residential uses, and both have been extensively gentrified in the last quarter century. There's little or no laundry hanging from the balconies in Born these days. In most cases, flower planters have taken its place. Both neighborhoods seem to have sprouted a gelateria on every block, along with a large number of tapas bars. Metro stops for these neighborhoods include Jaume I, Arc de Triomf, and Urquinaona.

Mercat Santa Caterina ★★ ARCHEOLOGICAL SITE/MARKET   La Boqueria's rival in La Ribera, this fresh food market is possibly a little easier to navigate, if only because it is smaller. It is certainly no less thorough, though prices might be marginally lower. On one side of the market is an archaeological site, another in the collection of the Museu d'Història de la Ciutat (see Plaça Reial, above). The excavations trace Barcelona culture from the Bronze Age to present. Chief among the ruins are the Dominican monastery of Santa Caterina, established here in 1219 and torn down in the anti-clerical fervor in 1835. In 1845, the site was used to erect the city's second enclosed market (after La Boqueria). The interpretive site, enclosed in a glass cube on one side of the food market, is open Mondya through Friday 10am to 2pm and Tuesday and Thursday 4 to 8pm. Admission is free.

Avinguda de Francesc Cambó, 16. ✆ **93-319-57-40.** www.mercatsantacaterina.net. Daily 8am–11:30pm. Metro: Jaume I.

Museu de la Xocolata ★ MUSEUM   Barcelona claims to have been the entry port of chocolate into Europe, based on the arrival of a 1520 shipment of cacao from Mexico. A Cistercian monk in the New World sent it to the Monasterio de Piedra in Aragón complete with a recipe for a chocolate drink. This little museum is chock full of such historical and quasi-historical tidbits, but it's really designed to make you crave chocolate. The first thing you see is a chocolate fountain, and even your ticket is a chocolate bar. Some of the chocolate sculptures are truly amazing—a Komodo dragon, a bullfight, soccer players, the Barcelona Zoo's late and lamented albino gorilla (in white chocolate), and even a tableau of Sancho Panza and Don Quijote.

Carrer Comerç, 36. ✆ **93-368-78-78.** www.museuxocolata.cat. Admission [5€ adults, 4.25€ students and seniors, free under age 7. Mid-Sept to mid-June Mon–Sat 10am–7pm, mid-June to mid-Sept Mon–Sat 10am–8pm.

Museu Picasso ★★★ MUSEUM   This terrific museum celebrated its 50th anniversary in 2013 by rehanging many of the works. So even if you've visited before, a return will likely feel fresh.

The first pieces in the collection came mostly from Jaume Sabartés, a childhood friend who became Picasso's personal secretary in 1935. They include a number of works made when Picasso was a student in Barcelona or when he retreated back here to gather himself for another assault on the art world of Paris. As such, they provide a

ONLINE INSTEAD OF in line

On many summer days, the line to get into the **Museu Picasso** stretches from La Ribera back into the Barri Gòtic. Get there late and you could wait 2 hours or more to buy your ticket and enter the museum. If you do, you have no one to blame but yourself. Purchase a ticket on the museum website (or purchase the ArtTicket BCN elsewhere) and you enter via a different door—no line, no hassle. Just proceed to the person scanning entry tickets. There's a 1€ fee—a small price to pay to save hours out of your day.

Two other long (but faster moving) lines are at the **Basílica de la Sagrada Família** (p. 209), and at Gaudí's amazing apartment building, **Casa Milà, or La Pedrera** (p. 213). In both cases, entry tickets available on their websites for a small service fee will allow you to skip ahead of the lines.

striking portrait of Barcelona at the end of the 19th century as well as an intriguing look at an evolving artistic genius. Picasso also donated generously to the museum, including 2,400 works in memory of his friend Sabartés. His most significant donation was his entire "Las Meninas" series, which he painted as a tribute to and exploration of the art of Velázquez. The large canvas and dozens of smaller studies are the center-piece of the rehung collection, which fills five adjoining historic townhouses. Allow plenty of time to study "Las Meninas." It's a rare opportunity to follow Picasso's thought process and artistic instincts at the height of his mature power. It may be true that Picasso's greatest masterpieces are elsewhere, but you will leave this museum wondering how there could possibly be more.

Carrer Montcada, 15–19. ⏲ **93-256-30-00.** www.museupicasso.bcn.cat. Admission 11€ adults, 6€ students and ages 16–25; free for children 15 and under and seniors over 65; free Sun after 3pm and all day first Sun of the month. Tues–Sun 10am–8pm. Metro: Jaume I

Palau de la Música Catalana ★★★ LANDMARK   One of the most extreme and most exciting of the Modernista buildings, this structure may be the greatest by Lluís Domènech i Montaner. Commissioned by the Orfeó Català choral music society, the architect saw to it that the first stone was laid on St. George's Day (May 5, the feast of Catalunya's patron saint) in 1905. It finally opened in 1908—a marvel of stained glass, ceramics, statuary, ornate wrought iron, and carved stone. In keeping with the architect's signature style, the façade features exposed brick combined with colorful ceramic mosaics. The sculptures are symbolic and, frankly, nationalistic. The stone prow, a work by Miquel Blay, is an allegory of popular music with two boys and two old men embracing a nymph while St. George protects them with the Catalan flag. Inside, the vaults of the foyer are lined with Valencian tiles. The concert hall itself is topped with an enormous stained glass skylight representing a circle of female angels surrounding the sun as a choir—quite appropriate for a choral society. If you want a detailed explanation of all the imagery, plan to take a guided tour. We find that the best way to enjoy the hall is to attend a concert. Arrive early and you can study the rich details from your seat.

Carrer Sant Francesc de Paula, 2. ⏲ **93-295-72-00.** www.palaumusica.org. Guided tours in several languages 17€. Open daily from 10am–3:30pm. Box office open daily 9:30am–3:30pm. Metro: Urquinaona.

ruta del MODERNISME

You could easily spend days visiting Modernista landmarks in Barcelona and the **Ruta del Modernisme de Barcelona** promoted by the city (www.rutadelmodernisme.com; ✆ **93-317-76-52**) will point the way. You can plan a self-guided tour of some of the 116 sites by using the detailed text on the website and the free route map. Or you can purchase the guide (12€), complete with full text and photos. It's accompanied by a booklet of discount coupons that offer admission discounts of 20-30 percent at many major as well as lesser-known buildings—everything from palaces to pharmacies. For 18€, you can purchase the guide and its companion volume on Modernista hotels and restaurants. You can find them at department stores, book stores, and at the Ruta del Modernisme desk inside the Plaça de Catalunya tourist information office. The desk is open Monday through Saturday 10am to 7pm and Sunday 10am to 2pm.

Parc de la Ciutadella ★ PARK   When Barcelona picked the losing side in the War of the Spanish Succession (1701–14), the victorious Felipe V repaid the city by leveling a neighborhood to erect a citadel. As it turned out, the fortification was of little use against Napoleon, and the fort was torn down in the mid–19th century. Lakes, gardens, and promenades fill most of the park that took its place, and admission to the park itself is free. The large green patch is also the site of the **Zoo de Barcelona** ★, which covers 13 hectares (32 acres) and is home to more than 300 species. The animals run the gamut from lumbering hippos to jumpy Saharan gazelles, from western lowland gorillas to Komodo dragons.

Parc de la Ciutadella. ✆ **90-245-75-45.** www.zoobarcelona.com. Admission 20€ adults, 12€ ages 3–12, 9.95€ ages 65 and older. Summer daily 10am–7pm; off season daily 10am–5:30pm. Metro: Ciutadella.

Santa Maria del Mar ★★ RELIGIOUS SITE   Built by the trade guilds rather than the nobility, this church is the city's most harmonious example of the Catalan Gothic style. Construction began in 1329 and was more or less finished in 1383 (the bell towers were added in 1496 and 1902). Three soaring naves are supported by wide-spaced columns that bloom like thick stalks as they reach the ceiling. Stained glass windows throughout fill the church with light during the day. Guided views of the roof and towers are available daily, weather permitting.

Plaça de Santa María. ✆ **93-215-74-11.** www.stamariadelmar.org. Free. Mon–Sat 9am–1:30pm and 4:30–8pm; Sun 9am–2pm and 5–8:30pm. Tours: ✆ 93-343-56-33. www.itineraplus.com. Admission 5€. Tours on the hour Mon–Fri noon–7pm, Sat–Sun 11am–7pm. Metro: Jaume I.

L'Eixample & Gràcia

Where Les Rambles meets Plaça de Catalunya, the tangled streets of the old city give way to the orderly gridiron of **L'Eixample** ★★★, and strolling the wide boulevards can seem like a breath of fresh air. Largely built 1890-1910, L'Eixample contains no less than three dozen Modernista landmarks. You'll want a least a day, perhaps two to visit the major sites and enjoy some of the shops and cafes. Don't overlook the small details like the Modernista light posts designed by Gaudí, and the hexagonal paving tiles he designed in 1904 that still cover the sidewalks on parts of Passeig de Gràcia. Take a break on the Modernista tile benches on the street corners. Modernisme was one of the first movements that emphasized "design for living," and those designs still bring delight more than a century later. Major Metro stops for the neighborhood include Passeig de Gràcia, Diagonal, Provença, Universitat, Girona, and Sagrada Familia.

Basilica de la Sagrada Familia ★★★ RELIGIOUS SITE Antoni Gaudí (1852–1926) was a profoundly religious man, and from 1912 forward he made the design of this soaring basilica his life's work. If it is not the grandest church in all of Spain, it is certainly the grandest constructed within living memory. Gaudí originally planned to base the church on all the stories of the Bible, but, as a guide once told us, "he decided that was too long, so he settled on the New Testament." The "church of the Holy Family" is, to say the least, a strange and wonderful building that represents the intersection of the imaginative style of Modernisme with the medieval faith that drove construction of the great Gothic cathedrals. The façades are particularly ornate. Every projection, ledge, window, corner, step or other surface is encrusted with carvings. Fruits of the seasons surround one set of spires, dragons and gargoyles hang off corners, an entire Noah's ark of preposterous animals (rhinos! elephants!) are carved in stone. One façade tells the stories of the birth and childhood of Jesus, another (completed by modern sculptor Josep Maria Subirachs in 1987) the passion and crucifixion. And that's just the exterior. Once inside, the light streaming through high stained glass windows seems to tint the air with colored light. Gaudí conceived the interior as a vast forest, and the columns seem to grow from the floor like powerful trees holding the roof aloft. Construction of the church came to a near halt at the outbreak of the Civil War and languished until the late 1980s. Yet new construction techniques (and more tourist admissions) have sped up the process. The church was consecrated in 2010 by Pope Benedict XVI, and builders hope to complete construction by the 2026 centenary of Gaudí's death. (He is buried in the Chapel of Carmel, one level down from the main church.) Buy tickets online in advance to avoid the wait of an hour or more during high season.

Entrance from Carrer de Sardenya or Carrer de la Marina. (C) **93-207-30-31.** www.sagradafamilia. cat. Admission 15€ adults, 8.80€ under 18 or retired; elevator for tower tour (about 60m/200 ft.) 4.50€; audio guide additional 4€. Online ticket sales at http://ow.ly/lqdwr. Oct–Mar daily 9am–6pm; Apr–Sept daily 9am–8pm. Closed Christmas Day, Dec 26, New Year's Day, and Jan 6. Metro: Sagrada Família.

Casa Amatller ★ LANDMARK Three of the greatest residential Modernista buildings in Barcelona stand along the single block of Passeig de Gràcia between Carrer del Consell de Cent and Carrer d' Aragó. Architecture critics call it the Mançana de la Discòrdia (Block of Discord), an allusion to the mythical Judgment of Paris over which of three goddesses is the most beautiful. Tourism promoters call the same group the Quadrat d'Or, or "Golden Quarter," which at least points out that they are all wonderful. Casa Amatller is the masterpiece by Josep Puig i Cadalfach. Closed for restoration until sometime in 2015, this Modernista home designed in 1900 reflects the architect's attachment to northern European Gothic decoration. That makes it a striking contrast to the Gaudí-designed Casa Batlló (see below) next door. Puig i Cadafalch made extensive use of ceramics, wrought iron, and fanciful sculptures. The original Gothic Revival interior is now the headquarters of the Institut Amatller d'Art Hispanic, but the library is normally the only part of the building open to the public.

Passeig de Gràcia, 41. (C) **93-487-72-17.** www.amatller.org. Free admission. Mon–Sun 10am–8pm. Metro: Passeig de Gràcia.

Casa Batlló ★★ LANDMARK Next door to Casa Amatller, Casa Batlló was designed by Gaudí in 1905. The façade's sinuous curves in iron and stone give the structure a very lush appeal and the balconies, like those at La Pedrera, seem to be sculpted ocean waves. Floral references in the ornament turn more faunalike as the building rises. The roof evokes the scaly skin of a dragon. Touring means climbing the spiral staircase around the central light shaft and starting with the Batlló family quarters, where Gaudí's architectural flourishes and his furniture designs vie for your attention. Sr. Batlló's office has a little nook with two benches and a stove for warmth—perfect for a courting couple to sit on one side and their chaperone on the other. Even this smallest of the rooms has a skylight to let in some natural light. The living room overlooks Passeig de Gràcia. All the décor, including the eddies of water in the swirling ceiling, allude to the marine world. The sewing room, which overlooks an interior courtyard, has an ingenious ventilation system of sliding slats that seem inspired by fish gills. The roof terrace has chimneys designed to evoke the backbone of the dragon slain by Sant Jordi (St. George), patron saint of Catalunya. The outdoor terrace has live music with cocktails from late June through September. An audiotour is included with admission, which has the effect of creating bottlenecks at each spot the tour highlights. Lines for admission can get quite long here; buy your ticket online in advance.

Passeig de Gràcia, 43. ☎ **93-216-03-06.** www.casabatllo.cat. Admission 20€ adults; 16€ children 7–18, students, seniors, and Catalunya residents; free for children 7 and under. Music and cocktails mid-June to Sept Tues–Sun from 9pm, 29€. Tours daily 9am–8pm. Metro: Passeig de Gràcia.

Casa Lleó Morera ★ LANDMARK The third member of the Golden Quarter, Casa Lleó Morera was designed by the remaining member of the Modernista triumvirate, Lluís Domènech i Montaner. The 1905 home was revolutionary in its day for its extensive use of different forms of artisanry on the interior (alas, closed to the public) to realize the architect's distinctly floral design. Because it occupies a corner, the house has two beautiful facades that mirror each other with a tower of sorts dividing them. Domènech i Montaner's signature floral capitals appear in several variants, and he created a gallery of columns on the top floor that evokes the rhythm of a convent cloister. The one part of the ground level that can be visited—the shop of Loewe, purveyor of fine leather goods—does not retain the architect's designs.

Passeig de Gràcia, 35. No phone. Metro: Passeig de Gràcia.

Fundació Antoni Tàpies ★★ MUSEUM This museum is dedicated to Antoni Tàpies (1923–2012), Catalunya's leading artist of the late 20th century. Major holdings consist of gifts from the artist and his wife and, as such, tend to emphasize late works and large-scale pieces. Nonetheless, changing exhibitions show the artist's evolving viewpoints and leave no doubt about his role in bringing non-artistic materials (gravel, broken sticks, chunks of cement) into high art. One of the most striking things about seeing so many works by Tàpies in one place is to see how, like so many Spanish artists, he returned repeatedly to the motif of the cross for works both secular and, in his own abstract way, sacred. This being L'Eixample, it's not really a surprise that the museum occupies a Modernista landmark. The former home of publishing company Editorial Montaner i Simon was built by Lluís Domènech i Montaner from 1880 to 1882 (the company belonged to his mother's family). The pioneering structure has a jaunty Moorish cast to it.

Carrer Aragó, 255. ☎ **93-487-03-15.** www.fundaciotapies.org. Admission 7€ adults, 4.90€ students, free over age 65. Tues–Sun 10am–7pm. Metro: Passeig de Gràcia.

HALLMARKS OF modernisme

Architecture blossomed with creativity throughout Europe at the end of the 19th century. Barcelona spearheaded the movement in Spain as architects such as **Lluís Domènech i Montaner** (1850–1923) and the great master **Antoni Gaudí** (1852–1926) developed the radical Catalan cousin of Art Nouveau called Modernisme. This Catalan variant, which truly set Barcelona on the path to becoming an international capital of design, jettisoned the stacked boxes of traditional architectural to embrace undulating lines and colorful, broken-tile mosaics.

As you stroll through the city, you will soon recognize some of Modernisme's most characteristic features:

o **Emphasis on the uniqueness of craft.** Like Art Nouveau practitioners in other countries, Catalan artists and architects rebelled against the era of mass production.

o **Use of organic motifs.** Asymmetrical, curvilinear designs were often based on plants and flowers.

o **Variety of media.** Wrought iron, stained glass, tile, and hand-painted wallpaper were some of the most popular materials.

Fundació Francisco Godia ★ MUSEUM With its gorgeous terrazzo floors, grand marble staircase, high ceilings, and beautifully proportioned rooms, Casa Garriga Nogués runs the risk of overshadowing the art it contains. It was designed by Enric Sagnier and built between 1899 and 1905 and has been impeccably restored. The museum showcases the art collected by entrepreneur and race car driver Francisco Godia Sales (1921–90). He was particularly close to a number of Catalan painters, and collected major canvases by Santiago Rusiñol and Ramon Casas, among others. But his heart belonged to the past. The best works in the museum draw from the seemingly inexhaustible well of Catalan Gothic polychrome sculpture.

Carrer de la Diputació, 250.(93-272-31-80. www.fundacionfgodia.org. Admission 5.50€ adults, 3.25€ children 5–16 and students, free for children 4 and under. Mon and Wed–Sat 10am–8pm, Sun 10am–3pm. Metro: Passeig de Gràcia.

Hospital de la Santa Creu i Sant Pau ★★★ LANDMARK This UNESCO World Heritage complex was designed by Lluis Domènech i Montaner as a hospital village that looked after all the lifestyle needs of its patients, providing parks and gardens for the healing powers of pleasant reflection, a freestanding library, and personal services such as a barber shop in the cluster of independent pavilions. The buildings represent the architect at the height of his powers, and his use of graceful sculpture, stained glass, and exquisite mosaic tiles makes the group of buildings perhaps the most beautiful and largest Modernisme/Art Nouveau campus in the world. It covers the equivalent of 9 city blocks, although the architect set it at a 45-degree angle to the grid of the L'Eixample streets to make it an architectural island in the city. The site includes 19 Modernista pavilions, some of which were completed by Domènech i Montaner's son Pere Domènec i Roura after the older architect's death. Declared a UNESCO World Heritage Site in 1997, the hospital complex is only a 10-minute stroll up Avinguda Gaudí from La Sagrada Familia—stop halfway and you can gaze up and down the street for a view of each masterpiece. Renovation and restoration work is ongoing at the site, making much of the area a construction zone. The campus is really only accessible by guided hardhat tour.

Carrer Sant Antoni Maria Claret, 167. ℰ **93-317-76-52.** visitsantpau.com. Tour 10€ adults, 5€ students and seniors. English tours daily at 10am, 11am, noon, and 1pm. Metro: Hospital de Sant Pau or Guinardó.

Museu del Modernisme Català ★ MUSEUM

The first museum dedicated exclusively to Catalan Modernisme opened in 2010 on two floors of a Modernist former textile factory designed by Enric Sagnier and built 1902-04. The ground level is dominated by a mix of graphic art—wonderful posters, in many cases—and furniture designed by Antoni Gaudí, Joan Busquets, and Gaspar Homar. The Gaudí displays include some seminal pieces from his collaborations with Josep Maria Jujol. (They worked together on most of the furniture for Casa Batlló and Jujol assisted with the ornamentation of Casa Mila.) You can't touch the works, let alone sit in the chairs, but nowhere else can you get so close to pieces and study their design lines and construction techniques. The basement exhibitions include a lot of Modernisme painting and sculpture, including the impassioned marbles of Eusebi Arnau, who did some of the major sculpture for the **Palau de la Música Catalana** (p. 207).

Carrer Balmes, 48. ℰ **93-273-28-96.** www.mmcat.cat. Admission 10€ adults, 5.50€ ages 5–15. Mon–Sat 10am–8pm, Sun 10am–2pm. Metro: Passeig de Gràcia or Universitat.

Palau del Baró de Quadras ★ HISTORIC SITE

Fans of graphic novels and Gothic gargoyles should not miss seeing this extraordinary building that appears to be clad in a nightmare of stone. In 1900, Josep Puig i Cadalfach was commissioned by the Baron of Quadras to refurbish this residential block. Over the next 3 years, he completely transformed the structure. The façade is carved in an intricate style that nods to the Plateresque tradition of Castilla, while employing imagery and iconography of French and German medieval stone carving. The long, ornate balcony is covered with busts of eminent medieval and Renaissance figures, floral motifs, and heraldic shields. The carved cornices on columns at the entrance show an archer on one side of the main door firing at arrow at a dragon on the other side. The gargoyles, especially at the lower levels, have unusually expressive faces. Alas, the interior has been closed since 2013, but it's worth a detour to see the exterior.

Avinguda Diagonal, 373. Metro: Diagonal.

Parc Güell ★ PARK

Gaudí began this idiosyncratic park in Gràcia as a real-estate venture for his friend and patron, the well-known Catalan industrialist Count Eusebi Güell. Although it never came to fruition, Gaudí did complete several of the public areas, which today look like a surrealist Disneyland, complete with a mosaic-encrusted pagoda and lizard fountain spitting water. (Adults smile and move on, but kids tend to find the fountain fascinating.) The original plans called for a model community of 60 dwellings. He did construct a grand central plaza with a market below it, and lined the plaza with a long, undulating bench decorated with ceramic fragments. The oddly Doric columns of the would-be market are hollow, part of Gaudí's drainage system. Despite all this effort, only two houses were ever completed. One of them (designed by Ramón Berenguer, not Gaudí) serves as the **Casa-Museu Gaudí ★**. The architect lived here from 1906 to 1925, the period during which he worked on La Pedrera and La Sagrada Familia. The museum contains Gaudí models, furniture, drawings, and other memorabilia.

Calle de Olot for park, Carrer del Carmel, 23 for Casa-Museu Gaudí. ℰ **93-219-38-11.** www.casamuseugaudi.org. Free admission to park. Casa-Museu Gaudí: 5.50€ adults, 4.50€ students and seniors. Park open May–Sept daily 9am–9pm; Oct–Apr daily 9am–7pm; Casa-Museu Gaudí open Apr–Sept 10am–8pm, Oct–Mar 10am–6pm. Metro: Lesseps.

6

BARCELONA

Exploring La Barceloneta & the Waterfront

La Pedrera (Casa Milà) ★★★ LANDMARK   It took the neighbors a long time to warm up to Modernisme. When Gaudí's last secular commission, Casa Milà, was finished in 1912, they took one look at the undulating lines of seemingly wind-eroded rock and dubbed the building La Pedrera ("the stone quarry"). The shock of its novelty has faded, but the nickname has stuck as a term of endearment. With a sinuous, rippling facade, it is one of the most beloved of Gaudí's works, and is another spot where purchasing an advance ticket online will save you precious time. The tour includes the patios and the Espai Gaudí (loft and roof). But the best part is visiting the Pedrera Apartment, complete with Gaudí furniture. Substitute a modern music system for the Edison phonograph, and most visitors would be ready to sign a lease on the spot. The Espai Gaudí holds period photographs, drawings, and models that elucidate Gaudí's design techniques. Gaudí may have been a genius, but he was no math whiz. To calculate the loads an arch could bear, he hung weights on knotted cord to get the shapes he wanted, then extrapolated to life size. Gaudí saved his grandest gestures for the rooftop, transforming functional chimneys into a sculpture garden of swirling mosaic forms and ominous hooded warriors. Gaudí intended that the roof be used as an open-air terrace, and during the summer, jazz musicians hold forth several evenings each week. Amid the chimneys Gaudí built a lovely parabolic arch to frame what would become the towering steeples of his masterpiece, La Sagrada Familia. Starting in 2013, La Pedrera began offering special night visits called "The Secret Pedrera" with a very limited number of admissions.

Carrer Provença, 261–265. (*€*) **90-220-21-38.** www.lapedrera.com. Admission 17€ adults, 15€ seniors and students, 8.25€ ages 7–12, free ages 6 and younger; audioguide 4€. Nov–Feb daily 9am–6:30pm; Mar–Oct daily 9am–8pm. Jazz on Rooftop June–Sept Thur–Sat 27€. Secret Pedrera night visits Mar–Oct daily 9:30pm–midnight, Nov–Feb Wed–Sat 8–10:30pm. Metro: Diagonal.

La Barceloneta & the Waterfront

Barcelona has always lived by the water, and fishing boats, trade vessels, and ferries continue to come and go in its harbor. But the **waterfront ★★** has become much more than the working docks. From the Mirador de Colom east to Port Olimpic along the motorized Passeig de Colom and the pedestrian **Moll de la Fusta ★**, there's new vitality along the water's edge. Starting in the late 1980s and accelerating around the 1992 Olympics, Barcelona built new quays and waterfront paths and even constructed new islands to house a world-class aquarium and a shopping and entertainment complex. At the same time, it carefully preserved the barrier-beach sand-spit of **La Barceloneta ★★**, the former fishermen's village that also boasts the city's finest recreational beaches.

You'll want to spend some time exploring the back streets of La Barceloneta, where the residents still hang their laundry on the balconies. As you tromp the length of Moll de la Fusta, you'll find two playful pieces of public art: the giant fiberglass lobster that Xavier Mariscal created for the restaurant "Gambrinus," and pop artist Roy Lichtenstein's "Barcelona Head" at the foot of Via Laietana. Continue east up the beach to Port Olimpic and you'll encounter Frank O. Gehry's abstract sculpture called "Peix" (Fish), which has become the de facto symbol of Barcelona's rejuvenated waterfront. This district is the place to enjoy a casual seafood lunch and catch some rays at the beach. Plan on spending a full day and you'll still have time to take a boat tour and to see some of the sights. Three Metro stops provide access to the sites below. From west to east, they are Drassanes, Barceloneta, and Ciutadella/Vila Olimpica.

WATER views

Barcelona is such a visually rich city that you can discover something new every time you look at it. For a view from the water, that takes in the beaches and the city skyline, you can choose from several excursion boats that dock below the Mirador de Colom. All can be reached by the Drassanes Metro stop.

Las Golondrinas ★ Operating since 1888, when construction was finished on the Mirador de Colom, this tour company has seen the city grow up around it. For a quick overview, Las Golondrinas offers a 40-minute tour of the port, although the 1½-hour tour of the port and the coastline is more relaxing. It covers an 18-mile stretch and takes in the Barceloneta beaches, with views of the spires of La Sagrada Familia and the much newer landmark of Frank Gehry's giant fish. If you can bear to go below, the two catamarans Trimar and Omnibus have hull windows for underwater views.

Moll de Drassanes, s/n. ⓒ **93-442-31-06.** www. lasgolondrinas.com. 40-minute tour 7€ adults,

2.75€ ages 4-10; 90-minute tour 15€ adults, 11€ students and seniors, 4.25€ ages 4-10.

Barcelona Naval Tours ★ Operated by two electric motors that run (in part) on photovoltaic cells, the Eco Slim is billed as the largest ecological passenger catamaran in Europe. It offers 40-minute tours of the port. Another ship with "submarine vision" offers a 75-minute round-trip tour of the port and beaches.

Moll de Drassanes, s/n. ⓒ **93-795-85-68.** www. barcelonanavaltours.com. 40-minute tour 7.5€, 75-minute tour 12€ adults, free under age 6.

Orsom Barcelona ★ The sail-powered catamaran Orsom offers a graceful way to get out on the water. In addition to 90-minute sightseeing cruises, she makes jazz cruises timed so that passengers can enjoy sunset.

Moll de Drassanes, s/n. ⓒ **93-441-05-37.** www. barcelona-orsom.com. Sightseeing cruise 15€ adults, 12€ ages 11-18, 8.50€ ages 4-10; sunset jazz cruise 19€ adults, 17€ ages 11-18, 15€ ages 4-10.

L'Aquarium de Barcelona ★★ AQUARIUM This contemporary aquarium dedicated to Mediterranean species and habitats does its best to make you feel like you're underwater interacting with the fish. The centerpiece of the facility is the giant ocean tank that wraps around an 80m (262-ft.) corridor with a moving walkway on one side. On the other is a strip where you can step off the path to take photos or simply marvel at the flow of creatures swimming by. Another 21 smaller tanks, which ring the ocean tank, focus on different habitats within the Mediterranean. Each is populated with characteristic fish and flora. Some resemble home aquariums full of brightly colored fish, while others are deepwater habitats where bottom-dwelling eels and anglerfish lie in wait for their prey. The dead-eyed sharks are an enduring attraction, and SCUBA-certified visitors with their own gear can arrange to swim with the sharks in the giant tank for a 300€ fee.

Moll d'Espanya, Port Vell. ⓒ **93-221-74-74.** www.aquariumbcn.com. Admission 20€ adults, 15€ ages 5–10 and 65 and older, 5€ ages 3–4, free under age 3. July–Aug Mon–Fri 9:30am–9pm, Sat–Sun 9:30am–11pm; June and Sept Mon–Fri 9:30am–9pm, Sat–Sun 9:30am–9:30pm; Oct–May daily 9:30am–9pm. Metro: Drassanes or Barceloneta.

Barcelona Beaches ★★ NATURE SITE You don't have to leave the city to hit the beach. European blue flags (indicators of the highest water quality) fly on all 10 of Barcelona's beaches. Four of the best lie along the strand from the tip of La

Barceloneta eastward to Port Olimpic. Each has showers, bathrooms, snack bars, umbrella and hammock rentals, and lifeguards. Moreover, they are all free. Platja de Barceloneta and adjacent Platja del Somorrostro (near Port Olimpic) also have changing rooms and lockers. (Carmen Amaya, perhaps the most famous flamenco dancer of all time, was born in the shanty town that once stood on Platja del Somorrostro.) These two beaches and the more westerly Platja de Sant Sebastià and Platja de Sant Miquel can be reached from Metro stops Barceloneta or Ciutadella/La Vila Olimpica. A little farther east at Metro stop Poblenou, you'll find the most popular beach with college-age Barcelonans and visitors alike, Platja de Mar Bella. It too has all the facilities, including lockers, and is the only beach in Barcelona with a section set off for nude sunbathing and swimming.

Mirador de Colom ★ MONUMENT   Les Rambles meets the waterfront at this monument to Christopher Columbus that was erected for the Universal Exposition of 1888. Bas-reliefs on the plinth recount the feats of the great navigator, and various symbolic sculptures in florid Victorian style surround the base. At the top of a 50m (174-ft.) column stands a bronze of Columbus pointing to the New World from beneath a white wig of bird droppings that deflate the pomposity of it all. Inside the iron column, a small elevator ascends to the lookout just below Columbus's feet. It provides a panoramic view of Barcelona and the harbor and a chance to play "name that spire," as every church in the city pokes up just above its surrounding buildings.

Portal de la Pau. ⓒ **93-285-38-32.** Admission 4€ adults, 3€ children 4–12 and seniors, free for children 3 and under. June–Sept daily 9am–1:30pm and 4:30–8:30pm; Oct–May daily 9am–2pm and 3:30–7:30pm. Closed Jan 1, Oct 12, and Dec 25–26. Metro: Drassanes.

Museu d'Història de Catalunya ★★ MUSEUM   This museum uses "the memory of a country" as its tagline and makes no bones about promoting a Catalan national identity. But it's anything but a radical separatist organization. In fact, it's one of the best cultural history museums that we've seen anywhere in the world. Signage in Catalan, Castilian, and English allows the museum to make its points to the widest possible audience. The coverage begins in the Lower Paleolithic era and works its way up to the present—quickly. Historic exhibits linger at some of the high points of the Catalan experience, such as the reigns of Jaume I and II when Catalunya was a major power on the Mediterranean, and the 19th-century industrial revolution that made Catalunya in general and Barcelona in particular rich and powerful. The 20th-century coverage is almost giddy with its depictions of a vibrant Barcelona in the first few decades—and almost numbing in its accounting of the horrors of the Civil War and the 4 decades the region spent as Franco's whipping boy. The era since the death of the dictator seems less well digested, but history museums always have trouble with periods where they lack hindsight. It's worth visiting just to appreciate the building, the Palau de Mar, the last survivor among the 19th-century Barcelona warehouses. The fourth-floor restaurant, 1881, has a spectacular outdoor terrace with great views of the port and waterfront. It's not necessary to book a meal—most people come just for a drink and the view.

Plaça de Pau Vila, 3. ⓒ **93-225-47-00.** www.mhcat.cat. Admission 4€ adults, 3€ students and seniors. Tues and Thur–Sat 10am–7pm, Wed 10am–8pm, Sun 10am–2:30pm. Metro: Barceloneta.

Montjuïc

Residents of Barcelona used to quarry stone, harvest firewood, and graze livestock on this flat-topped hill southwest of the old city. **Montjuic** ★ began to assume its current shape in the early 20th century, when parks were planted and the 1929 International

Exposition was held here. Many of the park's structures, including the Palau Nacional, and the Font Màgica date from this period. The 1992 Olympics brought even more structures to Montjuïc, including world-class pools that are still used for international swimming meets. The biggest attractions on the mountain are two stunning art museums, one dedicated exclusively to Joan Miró, the other to the sweep of Catalan art. It takes some effort—and walking—to reach them but it's worth the effort. The most useful bus lines are Route 55 from Plaça d'Espanya and Route 150 for circling the Montjuïc roads. You can also take the funicular (mostly underground) from the Paral.lel Metro station, which delivers you to the Telefèric de Montjuic station. Many visitors prefer the **Bus Turistic** (p. 162) for visiting Montjuïc, since it makes stops at all the attractions. If you're up for a moderately steep climb, you can also walk from Plaça d'Espanya through the Font Màgica and up the ceremonial staircase of the Palau Nacional, now home of the Museu Nacional d'Art de Catalunya (MNAC), where you can start your explorations.

Castell de Montjuïc ★ HISTORIC SITE   In sharp contrast to its often grim history, this mass of military stone is now surrounded by serene gardens. Barcelonans come here for Sunday picnics and to literally get above it all. The fort last saw action in the Civil War when it kept changing hands and was used by both sides for political and military executions. In 1940, the Franco government prevailed on Germany to hand over the refugee president of Catalunya and summarily executed him here. The fort then served as a prison for political prisoners until Franco's death. The city assumed control of the property in 2007 and launched a development program to create a memorial to Catalan political martyrs, but the economic crisis halted those plans. Today the fortress is just a place to enjoy the views and the gardens. The best way to get here is on the 8-passenger cable cars of the **Telefèric de Montjuïc.**

Castell: free admission. Telefèric: Avinguda Miramar (opposite Montjuic Municipal Swimming Pool at funicular station). No phone. 10€ roundtrip adults, 7.40€ ages 4–12. Mar–May and Oct 10am–7pm, June–Sept 10am–9pm, Jan–Feb and Nov–Dec 10am–6pm. Closed last Mon of Jan to third Fri of Feb. Montjuïc funicular; Bus 55 or 150.

Fundació Joan Miró ★★ MUSEUM   Revered as the embodiment of the artistic genius of the Catalan people, Joan Miró (1893–1983) was born in Barcelona in the Barri Gòtic and trained locally. This marvelous museum (it opened in 1975) assembles 10,000 of his works, including paintings, graphic art, sculpture, and even tapestries.

Like many artists of the early 20th century, Miró gravitated to Paris and ultimately fell in with Andre Breton and the Surrealist movement. But his surrealism was radically different from his slightly younger countryman, Salvador Dalí, and evolved into a personal vocabulary of abstract forms and brilliant colors. His strong sense of line and tendency to lay in patches of color like a cloissonné jeweler (his father was a goldsmith) gave him a style all his own.

The original museum building was designed by Miró's close friend, Catalan architect Josep Lluís Sert. Its simple, smooth lines are a perfect counterpoint to Miró's often complex tangle of vectors and complicated abstract compositions. A recent extension by Jaume Freixa has made it possible to display a number of pieces donated by Miró and others since the museum opened. Many of those works came from his grandson, Emil Fernandez Miró, who died in an accident in 2012. Among them are a number of works on paper. The dimly lit **Octagonal Room** contains many of Miró's drawings on paper—the medium where he generally worked out his personal visual language that informed his paintings. Don't miss the amusing sculptures on the rooftop terrace, or the unusually good gift shop.

Plaça de Neptú, Parc de Montjuïc. ✆ **93-443-94-70.** http://fundaciomiro-bcn.org. Admission 11€ adults, 7€ seniors and students, free ages 14 and under. July–Sept Tues–Wed and Fri–Sat 10am–8pm, Thurs 10am–9:30pm, Sun 10am–2:30pm; Oct–June Tues–Wed and Fri–Sat 10am–7pm, Thurs 10am–9:30pm, Sun 10am–2:30pm. Bus: 50 (at Plaça d'Espanya) or 150.

Jardi Botànic ★ GARDEN   The Botanic Gardens of Barcelona, originally established in 1930, were completely overhauled in the 1990s. They are now a beautifully landscaped, green space that showcases Mediterranean-climate plants from all over the globe, including Africa, Australia, California, the Canary Islands, and Chile. The collection continues to evolve. New species are grown in greenhouses every year and planted in the gardens. Those that fail to flourish in Montjuïc's climate and soils are pruned from the collection. The 71 planting zones are connected by walking paths, many of them crossing small bridges and walkways over ponds.

Carrer Dr. Font i Quer, 2, Parc de Montjuïc. ✆ **93-256-41-60.** www.jardibotanic.bcn.es. Admission 3.50€ adults, 1.70€ seniors, free under age 16. Nov–Jan, Apr–May, and Sept daily 10am–5pm; Feb–Mar and Oct daily 10am–6pm; June–Aug daily 10am–8pm.

Museu d'Arqueologia de Catalunya ★   Housed in the former Palace of Graphic Arts built for the 1929 International Exposition, this museum plumbs the history and pre-history of Catalunya with extensive permanent exhibitions of artifacts recovered in archaeological excavations around the region and on the Balearic Islands. The first seven galleries all deal with pre-history, and feature some imaginative if speculative dioramas that strive mightily to make the rather limited artifacts more interesting. Unless you're enamored of the "Clan of the Cave Bear" books, we recommend moving quickly to the five galleries dealing with the Phoenicians and Greeks ("The Great Blue Sea") where artifacts from early Mediterranean trade show how Catalunya related to the rest of the Mediterranean basin. The Roman era is well-documented. Gallery areas devoted to the native Iberian Celtic culture and the Visigothic period are being substantially re-ordered and should be finished sometime in 2014. Until then, a few emblematic artifacts are on display.

Passeig Santa Madrona, 39–41. ✆ **93-423-21-48.** www.mac.cat. Admission 3€ adults, 2.10€ seniors and students, free under age 16. Tues–Sat 9:30am–7pm, Sun 10am–2:30pm.

Museu Nacional d'Art de Catalunya (MNAC) ★★★ MUSEUM   Some of the greatest Romanesque and early Gothic art in Europe is collected in this stunning museum housed in the grand Palau Nacional. The museum's collection of Romanesque murals, in particular, is unmatched. Most of them were discovered at the beginning of the 20th century in crumbling ancient churches in the Pyrenees. When one such church was sold to Boston's Museum of Fine Arts, it set off a storm of outrage over losing Catalunya's cultural patrimony. So church after church was purchased by public institutions. The mural paintings were detached from the walls and ultimately moved to this museum. MNAC displays more than 100 pieces from the churches, including wall painting panels, polychrome wood carvings, and other items. They date from the 11th- to 13th centuries, a fundamental period in Catalan art. The museum does chronicle other eras, but the collections are a little thin until they reach the Modernisme era. As part of the Europeana Partage-Plus project on Art Nouveau, MNAC has been digitizing images of more than 2,000 Modernista objects in its collection. The images will be available at www.partage-plus.eu beginning in March 2014. The Modernista gallery exhibits have such treasures as the Gaudí-designed furniture from **Casa Lleó Morera** (p. 210), a 1907 fireplace by Lluís Domènech i Montaner, and paintings by second-generation Modernista artist Joaquim Mir and by Catalunya's only noted Impressionist painter, Marià Pidelaserra.

Palau Nacional, Parc de Montjuïc. ℂ **93-622-03-76.** www.mnac.es. Admission 10€ adults, 7€ ages 15–20, free for children 16 and under and seniors 65 and older. Tues–Sat 10am–7pm; Sun 10am–2:30pm. Metro: Espanya.

Poble Espanyol ★ HISTORIC PARK   It's not real Spain, but it was probably as close as many people could get in 1929, when this faux Spanish village that Josep Puig i Cadalfach designed for the International Exposition opened. Each little plaza or street in the village simulates the architecture of some other place in Spain from Galicia to Valencia. Buildings are full-scale, and after more than 8 decades of patina, some portions are so authentic that they make us do a double-take. Appropriately, the main plaza is ringed with restaurants and cafes, and there are plenty of places to buy provincial crafts and souvenir items. In an attempt to make the whole site less hokey, management has invited real contemporary craft artists to use the workshops, so you might see someone like jewelry designer and leather worker Diana Cristo at work. Other artists might be printing fabric or blowing glass. Since 2001, the village has also housed the Fundació Fran Daurel contemporary Spanish art collection, a small museum that shows about 200 works that range from prints by Eduardo Chillida to ceramics by Pablo Picasso. Note that if you decide to buy tickets for the **Tablao de Carmen flamenco show** (p. 222) you get free admission to Poble Espanyol any time after 4pm, giving you plenty of time to look around and have dinner before the show.

Avinguda Marqués de Comillas, 13, Parc de Montjuïc. ℂ **93-508-63-00.** www.poble-espanyol. com. Admission 11€ adults, 7.40€ seniors and students, 6.25€ ages 4–12, free for children 3 and younger. Mon 9am–8pm; Tues–Thurs and Sun 9am–midnight; Fri 9am–3am; Sat 9am–4am. Metro: Espanya. Bus: 55 or 150.

Barcelona for Families

Many central Barcelona attractions are good for families, including **L'Aquarium Barcelona** (p. 214), the **Zoo de Barcelona** (p. 208), and, of course, the **beaches** (p. 214). Parents who want to see **La Sagrada Familia** (p. 209) can reward the youngsters with the tower tour, and at **La Pedrera** (p. 213), the whole family can go out on the roof to come face to face with Gaudí's mosaic-covered chimneys with shapes that evoke the hooded Darth Vader of "Star Wars." In similar fashion, if the kids accompany you to the Fundació Miró and the Museu d'Art Nacional de Catalunya on Montjuïc, treat them to the Telefèric de Montjuïc cable car ride to the **Castell** (p. 216).

But the big family excursion is the trip up **Tibidabo Mountain,** which offers spectacular city views and a century-old amusement park. The kids will also enjoy the ride up the mountain on the **Funicular de Tibidabo** (7.10€, or 4.10€ if you're also buying amusement park entries). To reach the funicular, take Metro Line 7 to Avinguda Tibidabo, exit onto Plaça Kennedy, and take either the 1901 tram called **Tramvía Blau** (Blue Streetcar; 4.70€) or **Bus 196** (2€) to the funicular.

Parc d'Atraccions ★ AMUSEMENT PARK   As fans of Woody Allen's film "Vicky Cristina Barcelona" might recall, this amusement park has some charming retro rides—a carousel, an "airplane" that spins around a pole, whirling teacups, various train rides, water slides—along with more modern attractions like a roller coaster, a pirate ship, and a haunted castle. A family visit can be a fairly expensive proposition, but depending on how many adults and how many children are involved, you can limit costs by focusing on the Sky Walk section of the park and the adjacent 255m (837-ft.) communications tower, **Torre de Collserola,** with its observation deck.

Plaça Tibidabo 3–4, Cumbre del Tibidabo. © **93-211-79-42.** www.tibidabo.cat. Ticket for all rides: 29€ adults, 10€ ages 60 and over, 10€ children up to 1.2m (4 ft.) in height, free for children under 90cm (3 ft.); Sky Walk: 13€ adults, 7.80€ under 1.2m tall, 6.70€ ages 60 and up; Torre de Collserola: 5.60€ adults, 3.30€ ages 4–12 and 60 and older, free age 3 and younger. May–June Sat–Sun noon–9pm; July–Sept Wed–Sun noon–10pm; off season Sat–Sun and holidays noon–6pm.

Organized Tours

Barcelona is a city best appreciated on foot, and the Barcelona tourist office has developed a number of **Barcelona Walking Tours** that are offered in English and hit the highlights. Tours of the Barri Gòtic depart from the Plaça de Sant Jaume (Metro: Jaume I) daily at 9:30am (15€ adults, 5€ ages 4–12). A visit to the Museu Picasso is included in the walking tour of Picasso's Barcelona (21€ adults, 7€ ages 4–12) which is offered at 3pm on Tuesday, Thursday, and Saturday. A walking tour of the Modernisme masterpieces in L'Eixample is offered on Friday and Saturday at 4pm (15€ adults, 5€ ages 4–12). A gourmet tour (21€ adults, 7€ ages 4–12) is based in the old city and includes visits to noteworthy shops and food outlets and a few tastings. The last three tour options depart from Plaça de Catalunya (Metro: Plaça de Catalunya). For more information, call © **93-285-38-32,** or visit http://bcnshop.barcelonaturisme.cat.

Surprisingly good free tours are offered daily by **Runner Bean Tours** (www.runnerbeantours.com) on two itineraries: the Gothic Quarter and a tour of Gaudi's greatest hits. At the end, the guide asks participants for a tip, and most give generously as the tours are both informative and entertaining. Hit the website for into on meeting places and times.

For a more specialized point of view, **Architours** (www.shopatarchitours.com; 40€) takes architects out of the studio to lead walking tours of L'Eixample, El Born and La Ribera, and Raval on Monday, Friday, and Saturday. Check specific availability and make bookings on the website. **Discover Walks** (www.discoverwalks.com; © **93-181-68-10**) are led by Barcelonans eager to share their enthusiasm for their city with visitors. These personal and often quirky walks are held daily from spring through fall and require no advance booking. The Gaudí tour departs from the front of **Casa Batlló** (p. 210) at 10:30am, the Picasso tour departs from Plaça de l'Angel (Metro: Jaume I) at 5pm, and the Ramblas and Barri Gòtic walk departs from in front of the **Teatre del Liceu** (p. 198) at 3pm. The walks are free, but tips are expected.

If you are comfortable riding a bicycle in big-city traffic, several firms offer guided bike tours. **Barcelona by Bicycle** (www.bicicletabarcelona.com; © **93-268-21-05**) offers a daily 3-hour tour with English speaking guide at 11am. It hits most of the city highlights. A 4:30pm tour is offered Friday-Monday from July through mid-September. The 22€ fee includes bike rental. Tours depart from the Plaça de Sant Jaume (Metro: Jaume I). **Barcelona Ciclo Tour** (www.barcelonaciclotour.com; © **93-317-19-70**) offers a similar overview tour at the same price. It departs from the Plaça de Catalunya (Metro: Plaça de Catalunya) daily at 11am and also at 4:30pm from mid-April through October. A "night tour" for the same price is also offered Thursday-Sunday from June through September and on Friday and Saturday in October at 7:30pm.

If you'd rather enjoy the city lights and cooler evening air in a more leisurely fashion, the **Barcelona Bus Turistic** (p. 162) offers a 2½-hour tour starting at 9:30pm from June through mid-September. It costs 19€ for adults and 10€ for children and departs from Plaça de Catalunya (Metro: Plaça de Catalunya).

If you seek the convenience of a tour that picks you up in your hotel lobby, consider the 4-hour city tour (59€) offered by **Barcelona Day Tours** (www.barcelonadaytours.com; © **93-181-52-87**). Vans hold up to 12 people. The same company offers a

half-day tour to Montserrat (p. 223) for 69€ or full-day options that combine Montserrat with a city tour (99€) or with a **visit to the sparkling wine region** (89€).

The **Barcelona Guide Bureau** (www.barcelonaguidebureau.com; ✆ **93-268-24-22**) offers English language tours aboard deluxe motorcoaches. A 5-hour highlights tour is 59€ for adults and 30€ for children and includes admission to **La Sagrada Familia** (p. 209) and **Poble Espanyol** (p. 218). Other offerings include a tour focused on Gaudí and **Parc Güell** (p. 212; 25€ adults, 15€ children) or a tour that concentrates on great city views, including Montjuïc (33€ adults, 15€ children). A 4-hour tour to **Montserrat** is 47€ for adults and 23€ for children.

For boat tours of the Barcelona port and beaches, see p. 214.

SHOPPING IN BARCELONA

If you don't want to spend a lot of time shopping, but do want to bring home a few unusual souvenirs and gifts, museum shops are your best bet. Since the merchandise is coordinated to the museum collection, you'll often find unique offerings not available elsewhere. Our favorites in Barcelona are the **Museu Picasso** (p. 206) and the **Fundació Joan Miró** (p. 216). They have broad selections of jewelry, scarves and other accessories, books, posters, and interesting objects for the home at reasonable prices. If, by some chance, you are in the market for an original piece of graphic art by a Spanish master, check out the shop at the **Fundació Antoni Tàpies** (p. 210).

The shops at **La Pedrera** (p. 213) and **Casa Batlló** (p. 210) have merchandise inspired by the Modernisme movement that gave Barcelona its unique architectural style. At Casa Batlló, you can even find nail polish in an Antoni Gaudí-inspired color palette. The gift shop at the **Museu del Modernisme Català** (p. 212) is more limited, but it does stock beautiful door hardware from an original design by Gaudí.

If you, or your friends and family members, are sports fans, check out the merchandise at **FC Botiga,** the official shops of Barcelona's wildly popular football club. (The most convenient locations are Carrer Jaume 1, 18, ✆ **93-269-15-32,** Metro: Jaume I; and Ronda Universitat at the corner of Plaça de Catalunya, no phone, Metro: Catalunya. For last-minute shopping, there are outlets at terminals T1 and T2 at the airport and at the Sants train station.) The handsome red, blue, and gold gear will definitely stand out at home.

The football club also has shops in two of Barcelona's big shopping centers. **Centre Comercial Maremagnum** (Moll d' Espanya s/n; www.maremagnum.es; ✆ **93-225-81-00;** Metro: Drassanes or Barceloneta) opened in the early 1990s on the waterfront and is as much a destination for its movie theaters, restaurants, and pubs, as it is for its shops. More interesting is **Arenas de Barcelona** (Gran Via, 373–385; www.arenasde-barcelona.com; ✆ **93-289-02-44**), originally Barcelona's bullring, built between 1889 and 1900. It closed in 1977 and stood vacant for many years until developers hired British architect Richard Rogers to transform the historic complex into a shopping center, which opened in March 2011. In addition to six floors of shops and a movie theater, it also has an excellent food court on the lowest level.

As in the United States, the merchants in the shopping centers are fairly predictable. A better option for one-stop shopping is **El Corte Inglés.** Barcelona's largest branch of Spain's major department store chain is at Plaça de Catalunya, 14 (www.elcorteingles.es; ✆ **93-493-48-00;** Metro: Plaça de Catalunya). You'll find handcrafts and other souvenir items, along with clothing and accessories for men, women, and children, and a good selection of food (keep in mind that Spanish saffron, paprika, and olive oil—in tin, not glass containers—make great gifts).

But shoppers and window shoppers alike will probably find neighborhood streets more interesting. For a peek at how the other half lives, check out the boutiques along **Passeig de Gracia,** Barcelona's most prestigious shopping promenade. Spain's famous leather goods chain **Loewe** has staked out a Modernista masterpiece as its showroom (Passeig de Gracia, 35; www.loewe.com; ✆ **93-216-04-00;** Metro: Passeig de Gracia).

For our (more limited) money, the streets of the Barri Gòtic and adjacent Born and La Ribera are more interesting to explore and the shops more fun and unpredictable. For an overview of the handcrafts traditions of the region, check out **Artesania Catalunya** (Carrer dels Banys Nous, 11; ✆ **93-467-46-60;** Metro: Liceu or Jaume I). Craft and fashion merge in the humble espadrille. **La Manual Alpargatara** (Carrer Avinyo, 7; www.lamanual.net; ✆ **93-301-01-72;** Metro: Jaume I or Barceloneta) has been making the iconic shoes since the 1940s and claims that Salvador Dalí was an aficionado. Dalí is also one of the inspirations for the jewelry designers at **BCN Art Design** (Carrer Argenteria, 76, Metro: Jaume I; and Carrer Princesa, 24, Metro: Jaume I, www.bcnartdesign.es, ✆ **93-268-13-08**), but you'll find an even broader selection of rings, bracelets, necklaces, and earrings inspired by the works of Gaudí and Picasso. **Krappa** (Carrer Freneria, 1; www.krappa-bcn.com; ✆ **93-442-51-00;** Metro: Jaume I) makes engravings based on historic woodcuts. Many of the maps, cards, bookplates, and larger prints suitable for framing, are colored by hand.

Hagglers will want to check out some of Barcelona's better street markets. **El Encants** antiques market is held 9am to 5pm (although some dealers start leaving around 3pm) on Monday, Wednesday, Friday, and Saturday in the Plaça de les Glòries Catalanes (www.encantsbcn.com; Metro: Glòries). One form or another of market has operated here since the 14th century, but El Encants moved into a soaring new pavilion in September 2013.

One of the best flea markets in Catalunya is held 9am to 8pm on Thursday at **Plaça Nova** at the base of the Cathedral of Barcelona (Metro: Jaume 1). If you miss it, there is a smaller flea market 10am to 5pm Friday through Sunday near the **Mirador de Colom** (Metro: Drassanes). **Plaça Reial** (Metro: Liceu) is the site of a stamp and coin market 10am to 8pm on Sunday. **Plaça del Pi** (Metro: Liceu) hosts an art fair (www.pintorspibarcelona.com) featuring dozens on artists on Saturday 11am to 8pm and Sunday 11am to 2pm while contemporary artisans line **Carrer Argentería,** from Santa María del Pi to Via Laietana on weekends from 10am to 5pm.

La Boqueria (p. 198) and **Mercat Santa Caterina** (p. 206) are the best of Barcelona's fresh food markets. These colorful food extravaganzas are perfect for buying the ingredients to prepare meals (if you are renting an apartment) or to assemble a picnic. But you can also purchase spices and other packaged goods to bring home. If you are in the market for chocolate, check out **Cacao Sampaka** (Carrer Consell de Cent, 292; www.cacaosampaka.com; ✆ **92-272-08-33;** Metro: Passeig de Gràcia), which was co-founded by Albert Adrià, the brother of famed chef Ferran. The best gifts are bars of chocolate molded in the forms of Modernista architectural ornaments. **Brunells Pastisseria** (p. 185) offers beautifully wrapped bars of Xocolata a La Pedra, scented with cinnamon. If your taste runs more to nuts or the traditional "torron" (nougat made with honey and almonds), be sure to check out the ancient (since 1851) nut roaster **E & A Gispert** (Carrer dels Sombrerers, 23; www.casagispert.com; ✆ **93-319-75-75;** Metro: Jaume I). For a huge selection of gourmet olive oils from around Spain, specialty dried beans and pulses, and canned fish and shellfish from Galicia, check the floor-to-ceiling shelves of upscale caterer **Colmado Quilez** (La Rambla de Catalunya, 63; www.lafuente.es; ✆ **93-215-23-56;** Metro: Passeig de Gràcia).

ENTERTAINMENT & NIGHTLIFE

Barcelona is as vibrant by night as it is by day. To get into the rhythm of the city, enjoy an early evening promenade along Les Rambles, and a stop in a tapas bar or two, followed by a late dinner. If you don't want to dine in a nearly deserted restaurant—or among other tourists only—plan to arrive in your chosen restaurant sometime after 9pm. Most nights, that will probably be all the entertainment you need.

But Barcelona also has a rich cultural scene, and the landmark venues of **Palau de la Música Catalana** (p. 207) and **Gran Teatre del Liceu** (p. 198) come alive when performers take the stage. As the name suggests, the Palau de la Musica specializes in musical performances which present no language barriers. Although the Liceu is known for its opera and theatrical productions, it also schedules an interesting mix of dance and music.

There are also several notable theater venues on Montjuïc, including **Teatre Grec** (Passeig de Santa Madrona, 36; www.bcn.cat/grec; ✆ **93-316-10-00;** Metro: Espanya), an atmospheric open-air amphitheater on the site of a former quarry; and **Mercat de Les Flors** (Carrer Lleida, 59; www.bcn.cat/grec; ✆ **93-426-18-75;** Metro: Espanya or Poble Sec), which occupies a building from the 1929 International Exposition and is known for championing innovative drama, dance, and music. These two venues, along with **Teatre Lliure** (Passeig Santa Madrona, 40–46; www.bcn.cat/grec; ✆ **93-289-27-70;** Metro: Espanya), host Barcelona's acclaimed Grec Festival in July—an extravaganza of dance, theater, music, and even circus arts.

During the summer, one of the best places to enjoy jazz is on the rooftop of **La Pedrera** (p. 213). Otherwise, check out the schedule of jazz, blues, and world music at **Sala Jamboree** in the Barri Gòtic (Plaça Reial, 17; www.masimas.com/jamboree; ✆ 93-319-17-89; Metro: Liceu), which features both up-and-coming and established artists. **Santa María del Pi** (p. 204) also has a summer concert series in the church's "Secret Garden."

The concentration of bars at the **Maremagnum shopping complex** (p. 220) is very popular with the college crowd and, surprisingly, the somewhat old-fashioned **Poble Espanyol** (p. 218) has a number of popular venues, including the open-air disco La Terrazza (www.laterrazza.com; ✆ 93-272-49-80) with its great city views, and The One (www.poble-espanyol.com/en/night), a trendy club with a lively DJ scene.

Barcelona is not in the forefront of the flamenco revival, but several venues present colorful and enjoyable performances with dancers, singers, and musicians. Flamenco Tablao Cordobes (Les Rambles, 35; www.tablaocordobes.com; ✆ 93-317-57-11; 42€; Metro: Liceu) occupies a lovely Moorish-style performance space with tilework and arched ceilings. Flamenco Tablao Patio Andaluz (Carrer Aribau, 242; www.jesus-cortes.net; ✆ 93-209-35-24; 33€; Metro: Gràcia) features dancer Jesús Cortés, a member of an accomplished family of flamenco artists. At Poble Espanyol, El Tablao de Carmen (www.tablaodecarmen.com; ✆ 93-325-68-95; 39€) is named for the Barcelona-born dance legend Carmen Amaya. Note that prices quoted here are for the performance and one drink. Most clubs offer dinner as well, but you are better off eating elsewhere.

Wherever you begin, end your evening with a glass of cava, as Catalunya's sparkling wine is called, at one of the city's classic xampanyerias, such as **El Xampanyet** (p. 187) or **Xampú Xampany** (p. 193).

If you are looking for overnight excursions from Barcelona, see the Side Trips from Barcelona chapter (p. 227). But you don't need to pack a suitcase for these 3 day trips into the countryside. And the three destinations could not be more different. The monastery at **Montserrat** is one of the most important religious pilgrimage sites in Spain. **Sant Sadurní d'Anoia** is for oenephiles; more than 40 winemakers in the village of open their cellars for tastings of cava, the Catalan sparkling wine. Finally, the **Teatre-Museu Dalí** in Figueres, designed by madcap artist Salvador Dalì, offers an alternately disturbing and hilarious look into the mind of its creator.

Montserrat ★★

Thousands flock to this mountainside monastery each year to see and touch the medieval statue of **La Moreneta** (the Black Virgin). She figures so large in Catalan faith that many newly married couples come here for her blessing on their honeymoon, and many name their daughters "Montserrat" ("Montse" for short). If you want to meet Catalans, visit on Sunday, especially when the weather is nice; for smaller crowds, visit on a weekday. The winds blow cold on the mountain, even during summer, so bring a sweater or jacket.

ESSENTIALS

GETTING THERE   The best way to get to Montserrat is via the Catalunyan railway, **Ferrocarrils de la Generalitat de Catalunya** (FGC; R5-Manresa; www.fgc.es; ✆ 93-237-71-56), with 12 trains a day leaving from the Plaça d'Espanya in Barcelona. The R5 line connects with an aerial cableway (Aeri de Montserrat), which is included in the fare of 27€ round-trip. An excellent alternative to the Aeri (especially when windy weather grounds the cable car) is the **Cremallera de Montserrat,** a 15-minute funicular ride from the village below the mountain. You get off the train one stop sooner at Olesa de Montserrat, and transfer to the funicular. The fare is also 27€ roundtrip. Either combination ticket can be purchased at any FGC train station. Alternatively, a package that includes the train and choice of cable car or funicular, admission to the museum and the new interactive audiovisual gallery, and a self-service lunch is sold online (http://barcelonaturisme.cat) and in the brick-and-mortar stores of **Turisme de Barcelona** (p. 159). Called "Tot Montserrat," it costs 43€.

VISITOR INFORMATION   The **tourist office,** at Plaça de la Creu (www.montserratvisita.com; ✆ 93-877-77-01), is open daily from 9am to 5:30pm.

EXPLORING MONTSERRAT

You can see Montserrat's jagged peaks from all over eastern Catalunya, and the almost otherworldly serrated ridgeline is a symbol of Catalan identity. As a buffer state between Christian France and often Islamic Spain, medieval Catalunya espoused a particularly fierce and intense Christian faith that reached its apogee in the cult of the **Virgin of Montserrat,** one of the legendary "dark" virgins of Iberian Catholicism. A polychrome carving of the Virgin and Child (a form known in Catalan as Maria del Deu) was discovered in a grotto on the mountainside in the 12th century, and many miracles have been ascribed to the figure.

The **Basilica de Montserrat** and a Benedictine monastery have grown up on the site. But most believers are less interested in the impressive glories of the basilica than they are in getting close to the statue. To view **La Moreneta,** enter the church through a side door to the right. The meter-high carving is mounted in a silver altar in a chapel high above the main altar. You will be in a long line of people who parade past the statue, which is mostly encased in bulletproof acrylic to protect it from vandalism. The casing has a cutout that lets the faithful kiss her extended hand. If you are around at 1pm daily, you can hear the **Escolanía,** a renowned boys' choir established in the 13th century, singing "Salve Regina" and the "Virolai" (hymn of Montserrat). The basilica is open daily from 8 to 10:30am and noon to 6:30pm. Admission is free.

At the Plaça de Santa María, you can also visit the **Museu de Montserrat** (✆ **93-877-77-77**), a repository of art donated by the faithful over the years. While many of the works are religious subjects, some by major artists like Caravaggio and El Greco, others are purely secular pieces, including an early Picasso ("El Viejo Pescador" from 1895) and some lovely Impressionist works by Monet, Sisley, and Degas. The museum is open daily from 10am to 5:45pm, charging 7€ adults, 6€ seniors and students, 4€ ages 8-16.

You can also make an excursion to **Santa Cova (Holy Grotto),** the purported site of the discovery of La Moreneta. The natural grotto was reworked in the 17th century and a small church in the shape of a cross was built here. You go halfway by funicular, but must complete the trip on foot. The monastery and the Catalunya government began a collaboration in late 2013 to transform the church into a gallery with a permanent exhibition of religious art. The grotto is open daily from 10am to 1pm and 4 to 7pm. The round-trip fare is 4€.

Sant Sadurní d'Anoia ★

Plenty of terrific wine is made in the countryside around Barcelona, but only Sant Sadurnì d'Anoia is easily visited on public transportation—a must if you're planning to taste a number of the sparkling wines (cava) for which the village is famous.

ESSENTIALS
GETTING THERE The easiest way to get to Sant Sadurní is to take an R4 train from Plaça de Catalunya or Barcelona-Sants station in the direction of Sant Vicenç de Calders. Trains run about every half-hour from 5:30am until 11:15pm and the journey take 45-50 minutes. The fare is 3.80€ each way.

VISITOR INFORMATION The tourist office at Carrer de l'Hosital, 26 (www.turismesantsadurni.cat; ✆ 93-891-31-88), is open Tuesday through Sunday 10am to 2pm.

EXPLORING SANT SADURNÍ D'ANOIA
Thick-walled 19th-century cava cellars fill the town, but you should make your first stop the new **Centre d'Interpretació del Cava ★** (Carrer de l'Hospital, 23; www.turismesantsadurni.cat; ✆ 93-891-31-88). Located inside an old distillery, it mixes old-fashioned and high-tech exhibits to introduce visitors to the history of cava, the grapes used to make it, and the entire production process. You can even hold a (dead) phylloxera louse—just to drive home the history of cava. (When phylloxera struck the vineyards of champagne, the makers there desperately sought new territory, thus giving birth to the Catalan cava industry.) The interpretation center charges 6€.

The tourist office inside the center is free and can help you plan your excursion in Sant Sadurní, including making calls to cava operations that require reservations. The cellars that are open for visits and tastes, usually for a token fee or no charge, are listed on the interpretation center's website. Sometimes a paper printout is available, but don't count on it. Some small cellars make a few hundred cases of cava; some are bigger—much bigger. Note that many cellars close on Friday and Saturday afternoons and all day Sunday. Just walking around the village and stopping at some of the tiny operations with open doors by their loading docks can be a lot of fun. Two of the larger producers that put the town on the map offer excellent overviews of the traditional champagne process.

Located at the edge of town, the massive **Freixenet ★★** operation (Carrer Joan Sala, 2; www.freixenet.es; ⓒ **93-891-70-96**) pioneered U.S. distribution of cava as a less expensive alternative to champagne. Since the winery gets large groups, much of the tour is via video and includes a heavy dose of marketing, complemented by a quick trip into the deep cellars to see aging bottles and—finally—a tasting. The entire tour takes about 90 minutes and should be reserved in advance. The basic tour costs 6.50€ for adults, 3.90€ for children 9 to 17, and is free for children 8 and younger. Tours are offered Monday through Saturday 9:30am to 4pm and Sunday 10am to 1pm. Reserve by phone or email at enotourism@freixenet.es. It's closed the last 2 weeks of December and the first week of January.

The other giant of Sant Sadurní cava production, **Codorníu ★★** (Avinguda Jaume Codorníu, s/n; www.codorniu.es; ⓒ **93-891-33-42**) is worth visiting to see the so-called "Cathedral of Cava," the winemaking and storage facility built 1895–1915 and designed by Modernista architect Josep Puig i Cadalfach. If you know Codorníu from its entry-level cava, the tasting will open your eyes (and palate) to some extraordinary high-end selections. Several options are offered, from a standard tour and tasting to extended tastings or even a tapas lunch. The basic tour costs 7€ and is offered Monday through Friday 9am to 5pm and Saturday and Sunday 9am to 1pm. Reserve by phone or email at reserves@codorniu.es.

Teatre-Museu Dalí ★★

The clown prince of modern Spanish art, Salvador Dalí, was born in Figueres, a small city in northern Catalunya where the dry foothills look a lot like the parched landscape of his famous melting clocks. Seeking to capitalize on the artist's fame, in 1961 the mayor of Figueres invited him to create a museum there. Dalí chose the ruins of the old municipal theater because his first childhood art show had been hung there. Asked why the old theater, he replied, "Because I am a theatrical painter." In fact, he considered the entire project as a surreal object—his last and greatest work. With no disrespect to the community, the chief reason to visit Figueres is to tour the strange world of the Teatre-Museu Dalí.

ESSENTIALS

GETTING THERE RENFE (www.renfe.com; ⓒ **90-232-03-20**) has hourly **train** service between Barcelona-Sants and Figueres. The trip takes around 2 hours, give or take 15 minutes, and costs 11€-15€, depending on type of train. Be sure to book for the Figueres station, not Figueres Vilafant, which is in a neighboring town.

VISITOR INFORMATION The Figueres **tourist office** is at the Plaça del Sol (www.figueresciutat.com; ⓒ **97-250-31-55**). The office is open July through September Monday through Saturday 9am to 8pm and Sunday 10am to 3pm; from November to Easter, hours are Monday through Friday 9am to 3pm; and from Easter through June and October, hours are Monday through Friday 9am to 3pm and 4 to 7pm, and Saturday 10am to 2pm and 3:30 to 6:30pm.

EXPLORING THE TEATRE-MUSEU DALÍ

This thoroughly bizarre museum is less a monument to Salvador Felipe Jacinto Dalí i Domènech (to use his full name) than a series of snapshots of corners of his psyche all collaged together inside a carnival funhouse. It helps to know a little bit about the artist. He began his career in the 1920s as one of Spain's three *enfants terribles* (the others were Federico García Lorca and Luis Buñuel). Seeing Lorca persecuted for his homosexuality, Dalí vigorously embraced heterosexuality and entered into an obsessive and dependent relationship with Elena Ivanova Diakonova, known as Gala. Ten years his senior, Gala was the wife of Paul Eluard when Dalí met her in 1929. She became Dalí's muse and they married in 1934. He remained tenaciously loyal to her until her death in 1982 (although the same can't be said of Gaia toward Dalí).

Many of the works in the Teatre-Museu relate to this relationship and Dalí's complicated feelings about sexual intimacy. It took the artist a long time to assemble the museum, since he made all the initial placements of objects. It finally opened in 1974. When the artist died in 1989, thousands of artifacts and artworks from throughout his life passed to the Gala-Salvador Dalí Fundació, which maintains the museum, and the exhibits have been moved around—but not so much to jeopardize Dali's claim that it is the largest surreal object in the world. Dalí spent his final 4 years living adjacent to the museum in the Torre Galatea, named for Gala. He was buried beneath the theater's great dome, which he had painted as the eye of a fly as seen through a microscope. Also painted on the ceiling are portraits of himself and Gala as seen from below the ground. (You're looking at them feet first.) Don't miss the artist's first Cadillac in the courtyard, where it rains **inside** the car.

Plaça de Gala-Dalí 5. ℰ **97-267-75-00.** www.salvador-dali.org. Admission 12€ adults, 9€ students and seniors, free ages 9 and under. Mar–June and Oct daily 9:30am–6pm; Nov–Feb daily 10:30am–6pm; July–Sept daily 9am–8pm.

SIDE TRIPS FROM BARCELONA

Barcelona may be the center of Catalunya's galaxy, but three bright stars shine nearby, each reflecting and supplying a deeply Catalan experience. **Tarragona** to the south was the Roman capital of eastern Iberia, and its ruins have been respectfully assimilated into the modern city, creating a sense of timelessness that, in its own provincial way, rivals eternal Rome. **Sitges,** also to the south, is a beach resort that has grown up into a genuine city that offers art and culture to round out your stay when you've had enough sea, sand, and sun. **Girona** is perhaps the most intriguing of all—a Roman, Moorish, and medieval Catalan city of multi-layered cultural complexity accompanied by good hotels and a few great restaurants. Each is just a short train ride from Barcelona, but don't be tempted to relegate them to day trips. Each of these cities is compelling enough to seduce you into overnight stays, and you might find any one of them so simpatico that you will want to stretch your visit longer.

TARRAGONA ★★★

For sheer historic sites, the Roman port city of **Tarragona** is one of the grandest, yet most overlooked cities in Spain. A natural fortress, the city perches on a rocky bluff 82m (269 ft.) above its deep and sheltered harbor. Although the Romans landed farther north at Empúries in 218 B.C. to savage the Carthaginians during the Second Punic War, they made their military and administrative headquarters at Tarraco, now Tarragona. At its Roman apogee, Tarraco boasted a population of nearly 1 million people and launched the legions on the conquest of the peninsula, bringing the western reaches of Europe under Roman control.

The most famous of the Roman roads in Iberia, the Via Augusta, connected Rome to Tarraco, and pieces of it remain in the plazas of the city. In fact, the extensive Roman ruins that survive in Tarragona were declared a UNESCO World Heritage Site in 2000. But not all the architectural elements remain where the Romans placed them. Just as the Catalans absorbed Roman culture, they also appropriated the Roman architecture, mining the monuments for building blocks that show up in the medieval city that clusters around the cathedral.

Essentials

GETTING THERE   There's a train from Barcelona-Sants station to Tarragona about every 15 minutes. They take from 31 minutes to 1¼ hours and cost 7.50€-32€; AVANT trains have the best combination of speed and value: 31 minutes for 17€. In Tarragona, the RENFE office is in the train station, Plaza Pedrera s/n (www.renfe.com; ✆ **90-232-03-20**). There are also about 10 **buses** per day from Barcelona to Tarragona (trip time: 1½ hr.), but the bus is slower, less convenient, and often more expensive than the train. Call ✆ **97-722-91-26** in Tarragona for more information. To drive, take the A-2 south-west from Barcelona to the A-7, and then take the N-340. It is a fast and costly toll road, with one-way tolls of 15€.

VISITOR INFORMATION   The main **tourist office,** at Calle Major, 39 (www.tarragonaturisme.es; ✆ **97-725-07-95**), is open July through September Monday through Saturday 10am to 8pm and Sunday 10am to 2pm; October through June Monday through Saturday 10am to 2pm and 4 to 6pm and Sunday 10am to 2pm.

Where to Stay

Ciutat de Tarragona ★★★
Set right on the main city park (a good spot for joggers), this sleekly modern hostelry offers downtown Tarragona's fanciest digs. It's convenient for sightseeing, as everything (except the beaches) is within close walking distance. The rooftop deck around the pool is especially popular for families, as are the special family rooms with extra beds and a layout designed to give parents and kids both a little privacy. Triple and quad rooms are also available for adults traveling together. Free parking is provided if booked through the hotel web site.

Plaça Imperial Tarraco, 5. ✆ **97-725-09-99.** www.hotelciutatdetarragona.com. 58 units. 72€–136€ double; from 101€ junior suite. **Amenities:** Restaurant; bar; exercise room; outdoor pool; room service; sauna; free Wi-Fi.

HUSA Imperial Tarraco ★★
You can often get a very good deal at business hotels when no conference has been booked. The public rooms here have the usual hallmarks of a HUSA business hotel: lots of polished white marble and furniture upholstered in brown leather. But, the Imperial Tarraco was originally built for leisure, and the crescent shape with rooms angling out toward the sea gives most guests a pretty striking view of the sea and the Roman ruins from their small balconies.

Passeig Palmeras/Rambla Vella. ✆ **97-723-30-40.** www.hotelhusaimperialtarraco.com. 170 units. 64€–140€ double; 127€-170€ suite. **Amenities:** Restaurant; bar; babysitting; children's center; concierge; outdoor pool; room service; outdoor tennis court; free Wi-Fi.

Hotel Lauria ★
If you want a view of the ocean, ask for a room at the back. But all guests can enjoy the large outdoor pool and the close proximity to the Balcony of Europe promenade. In fact, the hotel is well-situated for sightseeing in general. The rooms range from small to medium and have comfortable, but spare, modern furnishings brightened with bold pops of color.

Rambla Nova, 20. ✆ **97-723-67-12.** www.hotel-lauria.com. 72 units. 60€–80€ double. Parking 19€ but worth trying to negotiate. Amenities: Bar; outdoor freshwater pool; room service; free Wi-Fi.

Hotel Plaça de la Font ★
Photo murals behind the beds bring images of Tarragona's stately architecture and rocky coast into the guest rooms. But if you like to turn in early, take note the hotel sits on a lively old city plaza and you may find that

Tarragona

ATTRACTIONS ●
Amfiteatre Romà **11**
Catedral de Santa María
  de Tarragona **2**
Museu d'Art Modern
  de Tarragona **4**

Museu Nacional
  Arqueològic de
  Tarragona **10**
Passeig Arqueològic **1**
Pretori i Circ Romà **9**

HOTELS ■
Hotel Lauria **13**
Hotel Plaça de
  la Font **7**
Hotel SB Ciutat
  de Tarragona **15**
HUSA Imperial
  Tarraco **12**

RESTAURANTS ◆
Barquet **14**
La Taula Rodona
  Brasserie **6**
Les Coques **3**
Les Voltes **8**
Restaurante
  El Llagut **5**

you can't escape the cafe noise at night. Many consider it a minor inconvenience for the charming and convenient location and the good price for simple, modern rooms.

Plaça de la Font, 26. ℂ **97-724-61-34.** www.hotelpdelafont.com. 20 rooms. 55€–70€. **Amenities:** Bar; restaurant; free Wi-Fi.

Where to Eat

Cooking in Tarragona is rather Janus-like, looking out to the sea for all the bounty of the Mediterranean and glancing over its shoulder to the mountainous country that begins a short distance from the coast. As a result, its menus are always brimming with both coastal fish like sea bream and bass, and deep-water predators like yellowfin tuna. At the same time, the local lamb and kid are as good as any in Spain since the herds feed on the rosemary scrub of the nearby hillsides.

Barquet ★★ CATALAN/SEAFOOD One of Tarragona's most established seafood restaurants (since 1950), Barquet's nautically themed dining rooms may look a bit old-fashioned, but the food is fresh and the kitchen really knows how to cook and present both fish and shellfish. Look for the local specialty of fried fish with toasted noodles called *fideos rossejat*. Local oysters are available on the half shell as well as roasted, and the garlicky steamed mussels are the equal of any on the coast. One of the best bets is often the grilled catch of the day (usually sea bream or bass), and diners who don't care for fish have a few grilled options of veal and chicken. The house selections of **D.O. Terra Alta** wines are good, economical complements to most dishes. Once one of Tarragona's more expensive options, Barquet has introduced several less expensive set menus to help diners cope with the ongoing financial crisis.

Carrer Gasometro, 16. ℂ **97-724-00-23.** www.restaurantbarquet.com. Reservations recommended. Main courses 15€–28€; daily menus from 20€, tasting menus 23€–43€. Mon–Sat 1–3:30pm; Tues–Sat 9–10:30pm. Closed Aug 15–Sept 15.

El Llagut Taverna Marinera ★★ CATALAN/SEAFOOD El Llagut considers itself a Slow Food restaurant, and does indeed use local meat, fish, fruits, and vegetables. But it is blessedly free of foodie pretensions. The rough stone walls and checked tablecloths give diners the message that they can relax and enjoy their meal and staff take the time to fully explain unfamiliar dishes. Rice dishes with seafood are the sure winners here. Some are a veritable encyclopedia of the local catch, while the arròs negre focuses on just one species, gaining its flavor and color from the squid and squid ink.

Carrer Natzaret, 10. ℂ **97-722-89-38.** Main dishes 11€–20€, Slow Food menu 21-24€. Tue–Sun 1–3:30pm and 9–10:30pm.

La Taula Rodona Brasserie ★★ CATALAN The most casual of the restaurants we recommend in Tarragona, it's also our favorite because it offers great value in an atmospheric tavern dominated by the towering chimney. Tarragona may be a city on the sea, but this establishment showcases the excellent veal, pork, lamb, and kid from the nearby mountains. Everything is grilled over an open wood fire, and the place is inevitably packed with local students, courting couples, and even entire large families.

Calle La Nau, 4. ℂ **97-724-25-92.** www.braseriatarragona.com. Main dishes 9€–17€. Tue–Sun 1–3:30pm; Tue–Sat 9–10:30pm.

Les Coques ★★ CATALAN If you are looking for a meal with a sense of occasion, Les Coques is a good choice. The restaurant is set within thick stone walls and features arched entrances and wood-beamed ceilings. As befitting the setting, many of the dishes, such as lamb glazed with red wine, can be rather pricey. But you can enjoy the setting and fine service equally well even if you stick with the less expensive and more homey dishes such as whole fish baked in salt or meatballs made with chopped octopus.

Carrer San Llorenç, 15. © **97-722-83-00.** www.les-coques.com. Main dishes 13€–30€. Daily menu 18€. Mon–Sat 1–3pm and 9–11pm.

Les Voltes ★★ CATALAN   Thick plate glass and stainless surfaces harmonize surprisingly well with the ancient stone to create a very upscale look for this modern restaurant in the vaults of the Roman circus. It's a bit of a circus itself, as it seats 250 people and is popular with tour groups as well as individual travelers. Despite an almost all-tourist clientele, Les Voltes has very good prices for expertly grilled and roasted meats, including lamb shoulder and a spicy casserole of pork trotters. The springtime shellfish assortment is a rather spectacular presentation of shrimp, lobster, and Dublin prawns, but it is expensive (40€ and up, depending on market prices) and requires that at least two people at a table order it.

Carrer Trinquet Vell, 12. © **97-723-06-51.** www.restaurantlesvoltes.cat. Main courses 9€–21€. Tues–Sun 1–3:30pm (July–Aug closed Sun at lunch); Tues–Sat 8:30–11:30pm. Closed first half of Jan and last 2 weeks in July.

Exploring Tarragona

Central Tarragona consists of a new city organized around the broad avenues of the Rambles on fairly flat terrain, and a partially walled old city that huddles around the cathedral on high rocky ground. Traces of Roman Tarroco are found in the upper and lower cities, as are a few gems of Modernisme architecture and design. In the new city, the **Balcó del Mediterráni (Balcony of the Mediterranean)** seaside belvedere connects the old and new Rambles. Be sure to stroll the main artery, **Rambla Nova,** a fashionable wide boulevard that is also the site of a flea market Fridays and Saturdays 10am–4pm. Running parallel with Rambla Nova to the east is the **Rambla Vella,** which marks the beginning of the old town and was once part of the Roman Via Augusta. Just off Rambla Vella, the **Plaça de La Font** functions as the go-between from old to new cities. It has a lively cafe scene as well as the offices of city government.

Catedral ★ RELIGIOUS SITE   Begun in the mid–12th century and finally consecrated in 1331, the cathedral spans the transition from Romanesque to Gothic architecture. It has a fortresslike quality, if for no other reason than it stands at the highest point of the city. The immense rose window of the main façade is balanced by the Gothic upper tier of the octagonal bell tower, where windows flood the interior with light. The most striking work of art in the church is the altarpiece dedicated to Santa Tecla, patron of Tarragona, carved by Père Joan in 1430. Two flamboyant Gothic doors open into the east end of the church, where you'll find the **Museu Diocesà,** with a collection of Catalan religious art.

Plaça de la Seu. © **97-723-86-85.** Cathedral and museum 3.50€. Mar 16–May 31 Mon–Sat 10am–1pm and 4–7pm; June 1–Oct 15 Mon–Sat 10am–7pm; Oct 16–Nov 15 Mon–Sat 10am–5pm; Nov 16–Mar 15 Mon–Sat 10am–2pm. Bus: 1.

Museu d'Art Modern de Tarragona ★ MUSEUM   "Modern" at this museum is more a statement of era than style, as the paintings ignore all the avant-garde movements of the 20th century. It was founded by the donation of several sculptures by Julio Antonio that had been in the possession of his family. Additional bequests have expanded the collection, which includes many more Catalan artists, especially the painter Josep Sancho i Piqué and sculptors Santiago Costa i Vaqué and Salvador

modernisme AMID THE ROMANS

Just as Tarroco was a provincial reflection of the glories of Rome, modern Tarragona can boast some glimmers of the Modernista masterpieces of Barcelona. When you're making your promenade on Rambla Nova in the new city, stop in to see the Modernista interior of the **Teatre Metropol** (Rambla Nove, 46; © **97-724-47-95**), built in 1908 and still used for live theater, dance, and concerts. At the edge of the old city, **L'Església de Sant Francesc** (Rambla Vella, 28) has a striking Modernista chapel well worth the time to visit (Mon–Sat 11am–1pm and 5–8pm; free admission). If you're continuing uphill to the old city through Plaça de la Font, pop into the **Ayuntament** (City Hall) to see the Modernista ship-shaped tomb of Jaume I of Aragón (1208–76), the conqueror who brought together the political fates of Aragón and Catalunya and stands today as a rallying symbol for Catalan autonomy, if not outright independence from Spain. The Ayuntament is open daily 8am–10pm and admission is free.

Martorell i Ollé. Along the way, curators also acquired an extensive collection of late-20th-century Catalan photography.

Carrer Santa Anna, 8. © **97-723-50-32.** www.altanet.org/MAMT. Free admission. Tues–Fri 10am–8pm; Sat 10am–3pm and 5–8pm; Sun 11am–2pm.

Museu Nacional Arqueològic de Tarragona ★★ MUSEUM   Catalunya's oldest archeology museum was established in the first half of the 19th century and continued to add to its collection as urban expansion and building projects unearthed more evidence of the city's early history. This is a good place to get an overview of Tarragona's Roman era before you explore the ancient sites that still dot the city. The museum's displays of household objects such as jewelry, cups and plates, cooking utensils, and children's toys bring a human touch to history. They are balanced by works of great artistry, such as a carved head of Medusa, and intricate mosaic murals of peacocks and marine life.

Plaça del Rei 5. © **97-723-62-09.** www.mnat.es. Admission 2.40€. June–Sept Tues–Sat 9:30am–8:30pm; Sun 10am–2pm; Oct–May Tues–Sat 10am–6pm; Sun 10am–2pm. Bus: 8.

Roman Tarragona

Since the Roman ruins are distributed throughout the city, we have drawn them together here for travelers who want to immerse themselves in the remains of Tarroco. Apart from the sections of the Roman aqueduct still standing on the northern fringe of the city proper, most of the Roman ruins are grouped together under the umbrella of the **Museu d'História de Tarragona** (**Tarragona History Museum;** Calle Cavallers, 14; www.museutgn.com; © **97-724-22-20**). The museum itself is distributed among a few historic houses owned by the city (included in the combined admission pass), but visitors will find the Roman sites themselves of greater interest. To see the best Roman artifacts, visit the the Museu Nacional Arqueològic de Tarragona (above).

Single site admissions to the Roman monuments are 3.15€ adults, 1.50€ seniors and students, free ages 16 and younger. Combined admission to all the museum's sites (available at any one) is 11€ adults, 5.25€ seniors and students. Oct–Mar Tues–Sat 9am–6:30pm, Sun and holidays 10am–3pm; Apr–Sept Tues–Sat 9am–9pm, Sun and holidays 9am–3pm. Closed Dec 25-26, Jan 1, and Jan 6. They can all be reached by city bus 2 (1€).

Amfiteatre Romà ★★★ HISTORIC SITE   This A.D. 2nd-century theater was carved from the cliff that rises above the crashing ocean. Contrasted against the vast spread of seaside sky and the abrupt and rugged cliff, the amphitheater must have been one of the most dramatic in the ancient world. Even in ruins, it is not a sight that you will soon forget. In its day, up to 14,000 spectators would gather here for bloody gladiator battles, other games, and executions. The tiered seats that they sat upon are the same ones you'll see today. Lest the beauty of the site entrance you, a monument declares that "Many innocent lives were taken in this amphitheater."

Parc del Milagro. ✆ **97-724-25-79.**

Passeig Arqueològic ★★ HISTORIC SITE   When the Romans decided to enclose their city of Tarraco in the A.D. 2nd century, they built their walls on top of huge boulders. Only about a third of the original 3,500-meter construction still stands and you can follow a gardenlike path for about 0.8km (½ mile) of that length. There are a number of historic markers along the way, as well as opportunities to climb up onto the ramparts for views of the sea and country. As a reminder of the progression of history, you'll find cannon placed in battlements by the Spanish in the early 18th century.

El Portal del Roser. ✆ **97-724-57-96.**

Pretorì i Circ Romà ★★ HISTORIC SITE   In the A.D. 1st century, the Romans selected a hillside location to build this three-level complex that dedicated a floor each to worship (the top level), government (the middle level) and the circus (the lower level). The well-preserved circus, with a capacity of 30,000 spectators, is the most visited and evocative part of the site. It was used for horse and chariot races and it's still possible to imagine the winners exiting through the grand, arched Porta Triumphalis.

Plaça del Rei, s/n. ✆ **97-723-01-71.**

SITGES ★★

Sitges is one of the most popular vacation resorts in southern Europe. Long a beach escape for Barcelonans, it became a resort town in the late 19th century, as artists, authors, and industrialists transformed fishermen's houses into summer villas. The Modernisme movement took hold in Sitges by the late 1870s, and the town remained the scene of artistic encounters and demonstrations long after the movement waned, attracting such giants as Salvador Dalí and poet Federico García Lorca. The bohemian exuberance and intellectual and artistic ferment came to an abrupt halt with the Spanish Civil War. Although other artists and writers arrived in the decades after World War II, none had the fame or the impact of those who had gone before.

But the beach remains as great as ever, and Sitges is the brightest light on Catalunya's Costa Daurada. It becomes especially crowded in the summer with affluent and young northern Europeans, many of them gay, and there's a lively art and gallery scene, mostly featuring bright, loosely representational but expressive painting. A new contemporary art museum has re-introduced a more challenging edginess. Sitges is also famous for its raucous celebration of Carnestoltes, or Carnival, in the days leading up to Lent.

Essentials

GETTING THERE   There are commuter rail (cercanias) **trains** to Sitges every 15-30 minutes between 6am and midnight from Barcelona-Sants station. Travel time is about 30 minutes and the fare is 3.80€. In Barcelona, call ✆ **90-232-03-20** or click the cercanias tab at www.renfe.com for details on schedules. Sitges is a 45-minute drive from Barcelona along the C-246, a coastal road. An express highway, the A-7, is less scenic but usually faster on weekends when the free coastal road is clogged with traffic.

VISITOR INFORMATION The **tourist office** is at Plaza Eduard Maristany, 2 (www.sitgestur.cat; ℂ **93-894-42-51**). Year-round hours are Mon-Fri 10am-2pm and 4-6:30pm, Sat 10am-2pm and 4-7pm, and Sun 10am-2pm.

Where to Stay

Book far ahead if you're planning a visit in July or August, as every room in Sitges will be full. If you decide to visit between mid-October and Easter, you might find most lodgings closed.

Galeón Hotel ★ Part of a three-hotel group all located a 2-minute walk from the beach near the Plaça d'Espanya, the Galeón offers the best balance between price and comfort. Nicely maintained, it has been updated to place streamlined furniture in the wood-paneled rooms and to provide a pillow menu for the firm and comfortable beds. The public areas are small, but if you're not in your room at Sitges, you're likely at the beach. The hotel provides guests with beach towels and umbrellas—a nice touch.

Carrer Sant Francesc 44. ℂ **93-894-13-79**. www.hotelsitges.com. 74 units. 77€–113€ double. Parking 15€. **Amenities:** Restaurant; bar; outdoor freshwater pool; free Wi-Fi in public areas.

Hotel Calipolis ★ The graceful curve of this beachfront hotel is echoed in the shape of the outdoor pool. This somewhat conventional resort is under private ownership and management with all the local pride that entails. Mountain view rooms tend to be a little larger, quieter, and less expensive. But opt for a sea view room with a balcony if you can afford it. It's a great place to sit outside and enjoy a glass of wine while listening to the surf. The hotel is a 5-10 minute stroll from the center of the town and beachside restaurants. This means that it is quiet at night, despite the basement nightclub.

Carrer Sofia, 2-6. ℂ **93-894-15-00**. www.hotelcalipolis.com. 170 rooms. 98€–200€. **Amenities:** Bar; restaurant; swimming pool; solarium; nightclub; gym; limited parking.

Hotel El Xalet and Hotel Noucentista ★★★ Everyone who sees these adjoining hotels falls in love with them. Set in the city center a good 10-minute walk from the beach, they occupy two adjoining Modernisme landmark buildings constructed by architects Gaietà Buigas i Monravà in 1882 and Gaietà Miret i Raventos in 1881, respectively. The ornate stonework, carved trim, fanciful spires, and stained glass in floral motifs reflect the neo-medieval side of Modernisme design. The lobbies and reception areas are filled with period tile mosaics and marble, while the fairly small guest rooms are more simply furnished and are painted in summery pastels. (Each building also has a few larger suites.) The nicely maintained gardens surround a small pool at El Xalet. Breakfast is served (weather permitting) on the roof terrace, and there is a summer-only restaurant in El Xalet.

Carrer Illa de Cuba, 21 and 35. ℂ **93-811-00-70**. www.elxalet.com. 17 units in Hotel El Xalet, 12 units in Hotel Noucentista. 60€–100€ double; 80€–125€ suite. **Amenities:** Restaurant; outdoor pool; free Wi-Fi.

Hotel Romàntic ★★ Created by combining three 19th-century townhouse villas, the Romantic has a kind of casual sprawl that's part of its charm. The hotel makes the most of the art-colony history of Sitges, practically plastering the walls with bright,

Sitges

HOTELS ■
El Xalet **4**
Hotel Calipolis **1**
Hotel Romàntic
de Sitges **5**

RESTAURANTS ◆
El Velero **2**
Fragata **7**
Xaimar Res-
taurant SL **6**

ATTRACTIONS ●
Fundaciò Stämpfli–
Art Contemporani **8**
Museu Cau Ferrat **10**

Museu Maricel **9**
Museu Romàntic
("Can Llopis") **3**

often whimsical canvases that make up in enthusiasm what they might lack in execution. The paintings continue into the guest rooms, but they certainly beat the generic posters of other hotels striving for an arty, romantic atmosphere. In fact, the name is justified—both gay and straight travelers from all over Europe congregate here and get the day off to a grand start with breakfast in the lovely garden. Note, however, that few of the rooms have en suite bathrooms, and many of the rooms are quite small and furnished with single beds. Companion property, Hotel de la Renaixenca, is used for overflow guests, who have full use of the grounds. Beach and train station are nearby.

Carrer de Sant Isidre, 33. ℰ **93-894-83-75.** www.hotelromantic.com. 60 units (57 with shared bathroom). 83€–108€ double with shared bathroom; 83€–126€ double with private bathroom. **Amenities:** Bar; babysitting.

Where to Eat

Seafood always seems best at the beach, and Sitges restaurants serve a wide variety of Catalan rice plates or stews with fish and shellfish. But hilly pastoral country is literally just a few miles inland on the other side of the coastal mountains, and meat dishes are also popular.

L'Estrella de Xaimar ★ CATALAN   One of the best bargains in Sitges, this tavern has the florid panache of Modernisme décor combined with the casual atmosphere of a *cerveseria* (as the Catalans spell "beer hall"). The menu emphasizes fish and shellfish, often in casserole, as well as lamb, kid, and veal grilled with fresh herbs from the nearby mountainside. Beer is usually the drink of choice. Wine selections are limited but local, featuring reds, whites, and rosés from the nearby Penedes region and cava from Sant Sadurní d'Anoia.

Calle Major, 52. ✆ **93-894-70-54.** Main dishes 11€–26€, menus from 13€. Daily 1:30–4pm and 8:30–11:30pm (in winter, dinner Fri–Sat only).

Fragata ★★ SEAFOOD   Located on the beach at the edge of Plaça Baluarte, Fragata is a contemporary jewel box of a restaurant: all glass, with taupe and nutmeg upholstery and table linens. Even the impressive wine cellar is a frosted glass cube. There's a bit of an international air to parts of the menu—lollypop baby lamb chops, for example—but beautifully presented Catalan seafood carries the day, whether as a *suquet* (the Catalan answer to bouillabaisse), a tossed salad of salt cod and oranges on lettuce, or grilled baby squid in a sauce of their own ink. The mixed grill of fresh fish is always a good bet—except on Sunday, when the fishermen stay ashore.

Passeig de la Ribera, 1. ✆ **93-894-10-86.** www.restaurantefragata.com. Reservations recommended. Main dishes 15€–32€. Daily 1:30–4:30pm and 8:30–11:30pm.

El Velero ★★ SEAFOOD   Florencio Martínez is the big starfish among Sitges chefs, and his venerable El Velero ranks among the city's leading seafood establishments. It sits right on the promenade at the beach; the elegant scene is indoors, but when the weather is balmy, ask for a table on the glassed-in terrace that opens onto the esplanade. The workhorse fish here is daurada (gilthead bream), a member of the bass family, and the size of the catch will determine the preparation. Small bream are often baked in salt or pan-fried like Dover sole, while larger fish are cut into steaks rather than filets and roasted with fresh herbs and a garlicky aioli. If you're in the mood for beef, the chateaubriand for two with a Spanish brandy sauce is both spectacular and a good deal. David Martínez, the chef's son, is the expert sommelier who is equally happy recommending a brisk Empordà white for the fish or a dignified Poblet red for the meat.

Passeig de la Ribera, 38. ✆ **93-894-20-51.** www.restaurantevelero.com. Reservations required. Main courses 14€–31€; fixed-price menu 45€. Wed–Sun 8:30–11:30pm.

Exploring Sitges

Sitges was once a fortified medieval town on the hillside above the beach, and bits and pieces of that fortress persist. The modest former castle, for example, is now the seat of the town government. The oceanfront **Passeig de la Ribera** is much more emblematic of modern Sitges. A favorite spot to promenade in the early evening, it is defined by two landmarks of different eras and sensibilities. A sign on **Chinguito** ★ (Paseo de la Ribera; ✆ **98-894-75-96**), a beachside restaurant/bar founded in 1913, identifies it as the probable source of the name now used by all similar casual spots along the Spanish coast.

At the east end of the promenade, booming surf soaks the stone steps leading to Plaça del Baluart, where the 17th-century baroque **Església de Sant Bartomeu i Santa Tecla** ★ overlooks the harbor. So does a single cannon, the last of six that drove off English warships in 1797. Behind the landmark church are the Museu Cau Ferrat and the Museu Maricel (see below).

Most people come here to hit the beach, which comes equipped with showers, bathing cabins, and stalls; kiosks rent motorboats and water sports equipment. Beaches on

SITGES after dark

In true Spanish fashion, nightclubs and bars with live entertainment rarely open much before 11pm, and in Sitges, most cater to a gay clientele. The greatest concentration is on **Carrer Sant Bonaventura** in the center of town, a short walk from the beach (near the Museu Romàntic). A map detailing gay bars and their style—from leather to black rubber to disco-ball dancing—is available at the bars themselves and online at www.gaysitgesguide.com.

the eastern end and inside the town center, such as **Aiguadoiç** and **Els Balomins** are the most peaceful. **Playa San Sebastián, Fragata Beach,** and the **"Beach of the Boats"** (below the church and next to the yacht club) are the area's family beaches. A somewhat hipper, more youthful crowd congregates at **Playa de la Ribera** to the west.

All along the coast, women can and certainly do go topless. Farther west are the most solitary beaches, where the attire grows skimpier, especially along the **Playas del Muerto,** where two tiny nude beaches lie between Sitges and Vilanova i la Geltrú. A shuttle bus runs between the cathedral and Golf Terramar. From Golf Terramar, go along the road to the club L'Atlántida, and then walk along the railway. The first beach draws nudists of every sexual orientation, while the second is principally if not quite exclusively gay.

Fundació Stämpfli-Art Contemporani ★ MUSEUM This new organization rounds out the artistic reputation of Sitges by bringing it up to date—the oldest works are from the 1960s—and by injecting an international perspective to the seaside art colony. Small but growing, the permanent collection includes more than 80 works by 55 different artists from 22 countries. Changing temporary exhibitions explore aspects of contemporary art from op art of the 20th century to video art of the 21st. The clean, modern space inside a historic building frequently serves as a venue for arts events and receptions.

Plaça de l'Ajuntament, 13. ✆ **93-894-03-64.** www.fundacio-stampfli.org. Admission 3.50€, or 6.50€ combined with Museu Romàntic. Oct–June Fri 3:30-7pm, Sat 10am-2pm and 3:30-7pm, Sun 11am-3pm; July–Sept Thurs-Fri 4-8pm, Sat-Sun 11am-8pm.

Museu Cau Ferrat ★★ MUSEUM Nearing completion of a several-year restoration project, this museum captures the life, lifestyle, and art of the early years of Sitges as an art colony. In the late 19th century, modern artist Santiago Rusiñol (1861-1931) created his combined studio, home, and art gallery by joining two 16th-century fishermen's cottages. His unique property soon attracted Catalan bohemians whose presence helped spur the transformation of the town into a popular seaside resort. Upon his death in 1931, Rusiñol willed the house and his collection to the city and visitors can see examples of his work as well as work by his contemporaries. The collection includes a few notable pieces by Picasso and El Greco. But the appeal of the museum lies less in any individual work of art than in the way that it captures the excitement, allure, and tensions of an avant-garde artistic salon in the years before the Spanish Civil War. **Note:** Re-opening of the museum has been delayed by the economic crisis, but renovations are expected to be complete in 2014.

Carrer Fonollar. ✆ **93-894-03-64.** www.museusdesitges.com. Anticipated admission 3.50€ adults, 2€ seniors and students, free for children 5 and under. Combined ticket with Museu Maricel 6.50€ adults, 4€ seniors and students. June 15–Sept Tues–Sat 9:30am–2pm and 4–7pm, Sun 10am–3pm; Oct–June 14 Tues–Sat 9:30am–2pm and 3:30–6:30pm, Sun 10am–3pm.

Museu Maricel ★ MUSEUM   One of the people attracted to the Sitges art scene was American industrialist Charles Deering (heir to the company that would become International Harvester), who had this charming palace built right after World War I. Today it displays the collection of Dr. Jésus Pérez Rosales, which ranges from Gothic and Renaissance altarpieces to Catalan ceramics. The town's own art collection is of more local interest as it features work created by Sitges artists in the 19th and 20th centuries, including the members of the Sitges "Luminist School," a movement that preceded Catalan Modernisme. As part of the museum restoration program that included the Museu Cau Ferrat, the Museu Maricel is expected to re-open in 2014.

Carrer Fonallar. ✆ **93-894-03-64.** www.museusdesitges.com. Anticipated admission 3.50€ adults, 2€ seniors and students, free for children 5 and under. Combined ticket with Museu Cau Ferrat 6.50€ adults, 4€ seniors and students. June 15–Sept Tues–Sat 9:30am–2pm and 4–7pm, Sun 10am–3pm; Oct–June 14 Tues–Sat 9:30am–2pm and 3:30–6:30pm, Sun 10am–3pm.

Museu Romàntic (Can Llopis) ★ MUSEUM   Using furniture and household objects to recreate family rooms in the downstairs section of the building, this museum conjures the daily life of a landed Sitges family in the 18th and 19th centuries. The wine cellars are a reminder that the Llopis family, while nominally involved in farming and statecraft, reserved their true passions for making sophisticated wines from the Malvasia grape. The upper level, formerly the servants' quarters, contains a collection of more than 400 dolls donated by writer and illustrator Lola Anglada Barcelona. Made of wood, papier-mâché and porcelain, they date from the 17th through the 19th centuries. Some feature mechanical or musical movements.

Carrer Sant Gaudenci, 1. ✆ **93-894-29-69.** www.museusdesitges.com. Admission 3.50€ adults, 2€ seniors and students, free for children 5 and under; combination ticket with Fundació Stämpfli 6.50€ adults, 4€ students and seniors. Mon–Sat 10am–1pm and 3–6:30pm; Sun 10am–1pm.

GIRONA ★★★

Girona is Barcelona's country cousin—slower-paced and more compact, yet strikingly sophisticated and cosmopolitan. It is the perfect escape valve when the pressure of the Barcelona crowds begins to get to you. Girona is simply a charming, disarming Catalan city with lots to look at and some delicious things to eat. It was founded by the Romans on a hill crouching above the Ríu Onyar, and the shape of the city remains as Roman as it was 2,000 years ago. As those Romans realized, the river crossing here was so strategically important that Girona has been besieged 25 times over the centuries, beginning with Charlemagne in 785. The most devastating siege was by Napoleon in 1809, when he starved the city into submission.

Fortunately, Napoleon did not destroy Girona, and the elegant and graceful city retains traces of the Roman era along with medieval buildings on the Roman street structure. Gorgeous 19th-century pastel houses line the riverfront. As a citadel city, Girona is blessedly compact and, while steep, walkable. You'll be glad to work up an appetite because, like Barcelona, Girona is a city with a passionate local food culture.

Essentials

GETTING THERE   More than 25 **trains** per day run between Girona and Barcelona from 6:10am to 9:30pm. Trip time ranges from 37 minutes on AVANT and AVE trains to 1 ¾ hours on the slow regional. Tickets range from 8€ to 28€ one-way, with the best combination of time and price being the AVANT trains at 37 minutes and 15-18€.

Girona

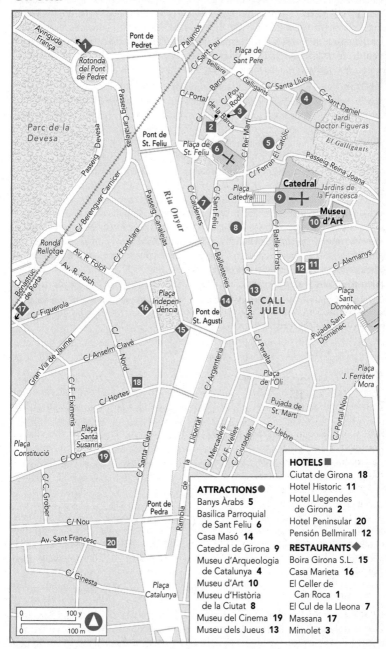

ATTRACTIONS●
Banys Àrabs **5**
Basilica Parroquial
  de Sant Feliu **6**
Casa Masó **14**
Catedral de Girona **9**
Museu d'Arqueologia
  de Catalunya **4**
Museu d'Art **10**
Museu d'Història
  de la Ciutat **8**
Museu del Cinema **19**
Museu dels Jueus **13**

HOTELS■
Ciutat de Girona **18**
Hotel Historic **11**
Hotel Llegendes
  de Girona **2**
Hotel Peninsular **20**
Pensión Bellmirall **12**

RESTAURANTS◆
Boira Girona S.L. **15**
Casa Marieta **16**
El Celler de
  Can Roca **1**
El Cul de la Lleona **7**
Massana **17**
Mimolet **3**

Trains arrive in Girona at the Plaça Espanya (www.renfe.com; ✆ **90-232-03-20**). If you really prefer taking a bus and don't mind paying more than you would for a train ride, Barcelona Bus (www.barcelonabus.com; ✆ **97-220-24-32** in Girona) operates express buses between Girona and Barcelona at the rate of 6 to 13 runs per day, depending on the season and demand. Fare is 21€. From Barcelona or the French border, drivers connect with the main north-south route (A-7), taking the turnoff to Girona. From Barcelona, take the A-2 north to reach the A-7.

VISITOR INFORMATION The **tourist office,** at Rambla de la Llibertat, 1 (www.girona.cat/turisme; ✆ **97-201-00-01**), is open Monday through Friday 9am to 8pm, Saturday 9am to 2pm and 4 to 8pm, and Sunday 9am to 2pm. The **Welcome Point** at Carrer Berenguer Carnicer, 3 (✆ **97-221-16-78**), is open July through mid-September Monday through Saturday 9am to 8pm and Sunday 9am to 2pm. The rest of the year it is open Monday through Saturday 9am to 2pm. In addition to providing information on lodging, dining, attractions, and transport, the Welcome Center offers guided tours.

Where to Stay

Most visitors to Girona come to see the medieval old city on the east bank of the river. In the last decade, several small boutique hotels have opened in ancient buildings here and offer lots of character and great location. The downside, of course, is that they are not inexpensive. For more options, we have also included two lodgings in the modern commercial city that retain a local character.

Bellmirall ★★ At least one rough stone wall in each room reminds visitors that this building in the center of the old Call dates from the 14th century. If you want to immerse yourself in the atmospheric old city, this lodging is a good choice at a good price. The rooms are small to midsize and feature simple furnishings, but you can also take advantage of the small courtyard. You'll find a TV in the common living space, but the bedrooms are TV- and phone-free. There is a garage for bicycles or motorcycles.

Carrer Bellmirall, 3. ✆**97-220-40-09.** www.bellmirall.eu. 7 units. 65€–85€ double. Closed Jan–Feb.

Ciutat de Girona ★★ This modern hotel is located on the west side of the river between the San Feliu footbridge and Parque de la Devesa, a popular evening gathering spot in the summer. The generously sized bedrooms feature contemporary furnishings and up-to-date technology. When you're ready to see the sites, the cathedral is only about a 10-minute walk away, and when you return, the indoor swimming pool is a plus.

Carrer Nord, 2. ✆ **97-248-30-38.** www.hotel-ciutatdegirona.com. 44 units. 85€–130€ double. **Amenities:** Restaurant; bar; parking; room service; pool; free Wi-Fi in public areas.

Hotel Historic ★★★ Architecture buffs should not miss this lodging that seems to almost recapitulate Girona history. The 9th-century building, now hotel, includes a portion of a Roman wall and a 3rd-century aqueduct. Lodging choices include both guestrooms and apartments that can accommodate three or four people. Most of the guest rooms have beautiful stone walls, balconies, and stylish modern furniture. The apartments tend toward more rustic, but comfortable, decor and are a good option for families.

Carrer Bellmirall, 4A. ✆ **97-222-35-83.** www.hotelhistoric.com. 15 units. 115€ double; 200€ junior suite. Apartments 90€ up to 3 people, 120€ up to 4. **Amenities:** Restaurant; room service; free Wi-Fi and cable high-speed Internet.

Hotel Llegendes de Girona ★★   This hotel has gotten a bit carried away with the romance of Girona. Three "Eros" rooms have two levels and feature romantic décor. The Suite Margarita Bonita goes farther with rather explicit artwork, a bed mounted on a stage, liberal use of mirrors, and a sofa designed for tantric exercise. But, this hotel in a 9th- to 10th-century building adjacent to Sant Feliu also has lovely rooms for those who just want a comfortable, stylish, and convenient base for exploring the old city.

Portal de la Barca, 4. ✆ **97-222-09-05.** www.llegendeshotel.com. 15 rooms. 109€–150€ double, 170€-190€ Eros room, 270€ suite. **Amenities:** Restaurant; room service; free Wi-Fi.

Where to Eat

The residents of Girona takes Catalan gastronomy very seriously, making it one of the best cities its size for contemporary fine dining. The gourmet emphasis trickles down to more casual and less pricey venues as well, and it's easy to make a meal of tapas. One good area for tapas-hopping is the Plaça Independencia, just across the Pont Sant Augusti from the Call. Some of the bars lining the plaza also have good full restaurants, usually located upstairs.

Boira Restaurant ★ CATALAN   Boira has some seating outdoors on the square, but we prefer a romantic table overlooking the river in the tranquil upstairs dining room. In contrast to the more traditional menus of surrounding restaurants on Plaça Independencia, Boira emphasizes seasonal, local food. Creamy goat cheeses from the Catalan countryside could show up in a small tart or in a salad with toasted nuts and figs. In the spring, local asparagus often graces fish plates, and in the fall, mushrooms abound. Part of Boira's appeal is the daily menu of starter, main dish, dessert, and wine for less than the cost of a main dish in many restaurants. Accordingly, portions are modest. Some of the trimmest and most fit people in Girona—professional bicycle racers who train here—eat regularly at Boiras.

Plaça Independencia, 17. ✆ **97-221-96-05.** Main dishes 12€–14€, daily menu 14€–17€. Daily 1-3:30pm and 8-10:30pm.

El Cul de la Lleona ★ MOROCCAN   Named for the well-kissed hindquarters of the lion statue in Plaça San Feliu, this modest Moroccan restaurant on a quiet street in the Call is a good bet for vegetarians. Whether you opt for the chickpea couscous or a tagine, your dish will be graced with such warm spices as saffron, cumin, and coriander. The spicy roast chicken is topped with a roasted preserved lemon. Simple desserts range from honey pastries to cold mango soup. The inexpensive daily menu includes house wine.

Carrer Calderera, 8. ✆ **97-220-31-58.** Main dishes 8€–13€, daily menu 12€–14€. Mon-Sat 1-3:30pm and 8-10:30pm.

Casa Marieta ★★ CATALAN   Fans of quirky local foods might want to try the trinxat, a casserole of rice, ham, cabbage, and potatoes. It's the sort of regional dish you would expect to find in the oldest restaurant in town. Casa Marieta is also a reliable place to enjoy suquet, the seafood stew served throughout Catalunya. For an old-fashioned place, Casa Marieta also offers a good seasonal menu that might include roast duck with pears in the fall or beef steak with porcini mushrooms in the fall. Art Nouveau style stained glass and banquette seating enhance the dining experience.

Plaça Independencia, 5-6. ✆ **97-220-10-16.** www.casamarieta.com. Reservations recommended. Main courses 13€–22€. Tues–Sun 1-3:30pm and 8-10:30pm. Closed Feb.

El Celler de Can Roca ★★★ CATALAN/INTERNATIONAL   Named the best restaurant in the world in 2013 by the readers of "Restaurant" magazine in the United Kingdom, El Celler de Can Roca picked up the avant-garde baton when Ferran Adriá closed the famous elBulli. With Roca brothers Joan (head chef), Jordi (head pastry chef), and Josep (sommelier) in charge, the restaurant belies the old trope about too many chefs and spoiled broth. The cuisine is firmly rooted in classic Catalan home cooking but with sometimes surreal twists, as if the ghost of Salvador Dalí were in the kitchen. For example, the simple appetizer of local olives is served as caramelized olives. On a bonsai tree. (Be careful with the branches—they need the tree for the next customer.) The meal begins with small bites from the El Mundo section of the kitchen (a spicy ball of frozen fish broth coated in cocoa butter, for example), followed by inventive main dishes of the moment. Rarely are they repeated, although the veal tartare with mustard ice cream, spicy ketchup, and fruit compotes is one of the stalwarts. Not surprisingly, the Roca brothers describe the establishment as a "freestyle restaurant committed to the avant garde." Jordi is famous for inventing desserts that re-create the aromas of classic perfumes. For a once-in-a-lifetime experience, it's worth the splurge and the cost of a cab ride, as the restaurant sits about 2km (1¼ miles) from the center of town.

Carrer Can Sunyer, 48. www.cellercanroca.com. ℗ **97-222-21-57.** Reservations essential. Main courses 22€–50€; fixed-price menus 95€–145€. Tues-Sat 1-4pm and 9-11pm.

Massana ★★★ CATALAN   We love the advice that Pere Massana gives to diners who hesitate to try the sea cucumbers that he offers as a starter. After the description on the menu he adds, "Do not ask. Taste them." That's good advice overall, and diners would be wise to simply trust Massana's instincts and his sure hand at combining flavors and textures into winning dishes. Massana started his culinary journey by opening an *asador,* or roast meat restaurant, more than 25 years ago. Even though he is now the proprietor of one of Catalunya's best restaurants and the recipient of a Michelin star, he has not forgotten the great Catalan culinary traditions. One section of the menu is devoted to "The Pure Product, barely touched" and includes such plates as Palamós prawns from the Costa Brava roasted in coarse sea salt.

Bonastruch de Porta 10. ℗ **97-221-38-20.** www.restaurantmassana.com. Reservations recommended. Main courses 24€-30€. Mon-Sat 1:15-3:45pm; Mon and Wed-Sat 8:45-10:45pm.

Mimolet Restaurant ★ CATALAN/FRENCH   French food still has a certain cachet in Catalunya, and Mimolet specializes in French bistro comfort food: cassoulet, duck, roasted daurada with root vegetables, and even steak-frites. Some of the most tasty dishes are found among the starters, including tempura-fried small fish, salmon tartare with basil oil, mussel salad with a creamy wasabi dressing, and Iberian ham croquettes with a red wine reduction. For a set price, you can chooses a starter and a main dish and the chef will surprise you with dessert (usually some combination of genoise, fresh fruit, cream, and chocolate). The menu may be bistro food, but the room is bright and sleekly designed, something of a surprise given its location in the old city.

Carrer Pou Rodó, 12. ℗ **97-220-21-24.** www.mimolet.net. Main dishes 13€–22€. Daily menu 22€, 3-course a la carte 30€, tasting menu 40€. Tues–Sat 1-3:30pm and 8-10:30pm, Sun 1-3:30pm.

Exploring Girona

Crossing the **Ríu Onyar** is much easier than it was in Roman times. From the vast city parking lot and train station, simply walk east over the pedestrian footbridge to the 14th-century Romanesque hulk of **Sant Feliu,** one of the oldest churches outside the

Roman walls. The **Plaça de Sant Feliu** is a central meeting point for Gironans and visitors alike. Take note of the statue of a lioness mounted on a stone column. In a city rife with legends, tradition holds that a Gironan returning from a journey must kiss the statue's hindquarters to prove his good citizenship (tourists do it, too).

If you walk around behind the church and uphill, staying outside the walls, you will find the medieval baths (erroneously attributed to the Moors) and the handsome Benedictine monastery of Sant Pere de Galligants (St. Peter of the Cock Crows), which houses the **Museu d'Arqueologia de Catalunya.**

Alternatively, you can pass through the walls at the towering Roman gate on Plaça de San Feliu to the plaza in front of the **Catedral de Girona,** centerpiece of the medieval old city. Crane your neck upward for a good look at the decorative carvings. According to another Gironan legend, the witch gargoyle on the cathedral was once a human witch, magically transformed into stone in the midst of curses and rants. Ever since, rainwater has washed blasphemy from her mouth.

Girona's medieval prosperity came in large part from its flourishing Jewish community, which concentrated in the **Call,** or Jewish Quarter, the narrow streets near the cathedral. You can wander for hours through the labyrinthine medieval quarter with its narrow, steep alleyways and lanes and its ancient stone houses, which form a rampart chain along the Onyar. **Carrer de la Força** is the Call's main street, but photographers will want to explore the atmospheric side streets.

The new city is on the west bank of the Ríu Onyar. Its main shopping street is **Carrer Santa Clara.** The new city also has a number of tapas bars, especially on Les Rambles and **Plaça de Independencia,** just across the Pont de Sant Agusti from the Call. One of the most appealing things to do in Girona after dark, at least between June and September, is to walk into the new city's **Parque de la Devesa,** an artfully landscaped terrain of stately trees, flowering shrubs, refreshment kiosks, and open-air bars.

Els Banys Àrabs ★ HISTORIC SITE   Despite their name, these baths were built in the 1194, almost 2 centuries after the Moors were driven from Girona in 1015. They are a terrific exemplar of Romanesque civic architecture, but they represent the Roman, not the Arabic bath design. The public baths closed in the 15th century when they were given to a Capuchin convent. By the 17th century, the nuns were using the cold bath as a pantry and the hot bath as a laundry. Following the dissolution of the convent, the baths fell into disrepair. When they became state property and were restored in 1929, historic accuracy played second fiddle to romantic ideas about the Middle Ages. You can visit the **caldarium** (hot bath), with its paved floor, and the **frigidarium** (cold bath), with its central octagonal pool surrounded by pillars that support a prismlike structure in the overhead window. Current interpretation emphasizes the engineering ingenuity of medieval hygiene.

Carrer Ferran el Católic. ℰ **97-221-32-62.** www.banysarabs.org. Admission 2€ adults, 1€ students and seniors. Apr–Sept Mon–Sat 10am–7pm, Sun 10am–2pm; Oct–Mar Mon–Sat 10am–2pm.

Casa Masó ★ HISTORIC SITE   No visitor leaves Girona without a photograph of the picturesque pastel houses along the Riú Onyar. But with a little advance planning, you can also visit one of these iconic homes. Casa Masó, which consists of four houses combined in the late 19th and early 20th centuries, was the birthplace of Catalan architect Rafael Masó (1880–1935). He studied in Barcelona as a disciple of Antoni Gaudí before joining the Noucentisme movement. His work was heavily influenced by the British Arts & Crafts movement and the furnishings and decorations in the home show an interesting blend of Catalan Modernisme, British Arts & Crafts, and French Art Nouveau. Admission is by guided tour only and requires an advance reservation.

Carrer Ballesteries, 29. *Ⓒ* **97-241-39-89.** www.rafaelmaso.org. Admission 5€ adults, 2.50€ students and seniors. Tues-Sat 10am-6pm.

Catedral de Girona ★★★ RELIGIOUS SITE   The magnificent cathedral is Girona's leading attraction, but visiting is not for the faint of heart or weak of limb. To enter, you must climb a 17th-century baroque staircase of 89 steep steps. (Fitness enthusiasts race up and down the steps in the early morning.) The cathedral dates from the 14th century, so the basic structure bridges Romanesque and Gothic. What is most evident, though, is the surface decoration that is pure Catalan baroque. As you climb the stairs, you'll be staring at a facade added in the late 17th and early 18th centuries. The bell tower, which rises from a cornice, is crowned by a dome capped with a bronze angel weather vane. Go through the cathedral's main door and enter the nave, which at 23m (75 ft.) is the broadest Gothic nave in the world.

Most of the cathedral's extensive art collection is displayed in its treasury. The prize exhibit is the **Tapestry of the Creation ★★★**, a unique piece of 11th- or 12th-century Romanesque embroidery that depicts humans and animals in the Garden of Eden along with portraits of Girona citizens, including members of the city's prominent Jewish population. The other major work is a 10th-century manuscript, the **Códex del Beatus,** which contains an illustrated commentary on the Book of the Apocalypse. From the cathedral's **Chapel of Hope,** a door leads to a **Romanesque cloister** from the 12th and 13th centuries, with an unusual trapezoidal layout. The cloister gallery, with a double colonnade, has a series of friezes that narrate scenes from the New Testament. Guides tout them as the prize jewel of Catalan Romanesque art, but even more fantastic are the carved capitals of the cloister, which vividly narrate moral tales in intricate twists of stone. From the cloister you can view the 12th-century **Torre de Carlemany (Charlemagne's Tower),** the only surviving section of the 12th-century church that the cathedral displaced.

Plaça de la Catedral. *Ⓒ* **97-221-58-14.** www.catedraldegirona.org. Admission to cathedral free; cloister and museum with audioguide 7€ adults, 5€ students and children 16 and under. (Nave, treasury, and cloister are free Sun, audioguide 1€.) Cathedral daily 9am–1pm and during cloister and museum visiting hours. Cloister and museum Apr–Oct daily 10am–8pm; Nov–Mar daily 10am–7pm.

Església de Sant Feliu ★ RELIGIOUS SITE   Eight Roman and early Christian sepulchres are the main attractions of this Romanesque church with Gothic flourishes. In fact, the two oldest date from the A.D. 2nd century and one shows Pluto carrying Persephone to the underworld. Inside, a chapel contains the remains of city patron Sant Narcís. According to legend, flies escaping from his tomb drove away the French armies during the 1285 siege of Girona. The church itself was built slowly over the 14th to 17th centuries on the spot held by tradition to be the tomb of the 4th-century martyr, Feliu of Africa. The structure is significant in Catalan architectural history because its pillars and arches are Romanesque while the nave is Gothic. The bell tower, prominent on the Girona skyline, has eight pinnacles and one central tower, each supported on a solid octagonal base. Some exceptional works within the church include a 16th-century altarpiece and a 14th-century alabaster statue of a Reclining Christ.

Pujada de San Feliu. *Ⓒ* **97-220-14-07.** Free admission. Mon–Sat 7am–12:30pm and 4–6:30pm; Sun and holidays 4–6:30pm.

Museu d'Arqueologia ★ MUSEUM   Everyone from Celtic Iberians to Greeks to Carthaginians to Romans, Moors, and Visigoths passed through Girona and the surrounding countryside at one point, and the very thorough collections of this regional branch of the **Museu d'Arqueologia de Catalunya** (p. 217) headquartered in Barcelona chronicle them all. The museum occupies the Catalan Romanesque building that once housed the Benedictine monastery of Sant Pere de Gallignants (St. Peter of the Cock Crows). The cloister contains some Hebrew inscriptions from gravestones of the old Jewish cemetery on nearby Montjuïc. Most of the artifacts represent the Roman period and the quality overall is very high. In 2014, the museum is mounting a special exhibition on medicine as practiced in Roman times.

Plaça Santa Llúcia, s/n. ⓒ **97-220-26-32.** www.mac.cat. Admission 2.30€ adults, 1.50€ students, free for seniors and children 15 and under. Oct–May Tues–Sat 10am–2pm and 4–6pm, Sun 10am–2pm; June–Sept Tues–Sat 10:30am–1:30pm and 4–7pm, Sun 10am–2pm.

Museu d'Art ★★ MUSEUM   As you have probably already gathered, the people of Girona love a good legend. So it is only fitting that the 10th- to 11th-century altar stone of Sant Pere de Roda is one of the most prized objects in the museum. Made of wood and stone, it depicts both religious stories and Catalan legends. It's just one piece in a collection that brings together Catalan art from the 12th to the 20th centuries. The Gothic wood carvings and altar pieces seem particularly at home in the erstwhile Episcopal Palace's Romanesque vaults. But the museum is also the main repository worldwide of 20th-century Noucentisme, a reactionary Catalan art movement that rejected Modernisme in favor of a more ordered and refined classicism. The museum has introduced a "touch" curriculum that permits visually impaired visitors to handle works of art. Do not miss the shaded gardens behind the museum, the Jardins de la Francesa. A staircase in the gardens lets you ascend to the ancient city walls, where you can walk for a considerable distance to gain a unique perspective on the medieval city. The walls are a favorite with children.

Pujada de la Catedral, 12. ⓒ **97-220-38-34.** www.museuart.com. Admission 2€ adults; 1.50€ students and seniors. May–Sept Tues–Sat 10am–7pm, Sun 10am–2pm; Oct–Apr Tues–Sat 10am–6pm, Sun 10am–2pm.

Museu del Cinema ★ MUSEUM   If you're a film buff, you probably see the development of cinema as the inevitable result of human fascination with moving images. Film buff and historian Tomàs Mallol certainly took that view, and he assembled more than 25,000 artifacts from early crude camera obscura devices and Chinese shadow puppets to attempts to animate photography when that technology was still in its infancy. The collection dates from early history (including the original camera of the Lumière brothers) up to about 1970. On Mallol's death, it was donated to the city and formed the basis for this museum that opened in 1998. Cinema aficionados from around the globe come here to study the origins of their artform. Many of the displays, of course, are still images—photographs, posters, engravings, drawings, and paintings—but about 800 films of various styles and periods are also available for screening. The museum played an instrumental role in launching the annual Festival de Cinema de Girona in September, which dedicated the 2013 ceremonies to Tomàs Mallol.

Carrer Sèquia, 1. ⓒ **97-241-27-77.** www.girona.cat/cinema. Admission 5€ adults, 2.50€ students, free for children 16 and under. Oct–Apr Tues–Fri 10am–6pm, Sat 10am–8pm, Sun 11am–3pm; May–June and Sept Tues–Sat 10am–8pm, Sun 11am–3pm; July–Aug daily 10am–8pm.

Museu dels Jueus ★★ MUSEUM   The Jewish population of Girona flourished in the 12th century, when scholars, including the great rabbi Nahmanides, established one of Europe's most important philosophical centers of Kabbalistic mysticism. In keeping with European tradition, the Jewish Quarter or "Call" grew up in the protective shadow of the cathedral—until Isabel and Fernando expelled all the Jews from Spain in 1492. As part of the 1992 nationwide reassessment of Spain's gains and losses from the events of 1492, the Girona government established a non-profit organization to recover the Jewish history and culture of the city. One part of that effort was to establish this museum. In the decades since it opened, it has grown to an extensive warren of 11 galleries that examine community life, festivals and traditions, synagogues and forms of worship, and even the disapora and the tricky matter of conversions during the Spanish Inquisition. Some of the most striking exhibitions deal with Jewish artistic and cultural traditions specific to Catalunya, while some of the most poignant include carved sepulchers unearthed during excavations at the old Jewish cemetery on Montjuïc. On summer nights in July and August, the museum and the related Patronat Call de Girona have instituted a cultural series of Jewish films, live theater, puppet shows, story-telling, and Sephardic klezmer music.

Carrer Força Vella 8. ℰ **97-221-67-61.** www.ajuntament.gi/call. Admission 2€ adults,1.50€ seniors and students. May–Oct Mon–Sat 10am–8pm and Sun 10am–3pm; Nov–Apr Mon–Sat 10am–6pm.

Museu d'Història de la Ciutat ★ MUSEUM   This collection covers the sweep of local history and prehistory from the flint and iron tools of the first Neolithic peoples through the glories of medieval Girona to the dark days of the Spanish Civil War, when the city built an underground shelter to protect its children from the relentless bombardment by Franco's forces. One of the more interesting themed exhibits deals with the traditional sardana circle dance and the cobla band that accompanies the dancers. Although the 18th-century Capuchin Convent de Sant Antoni has been transformed into a modern museum, one room does retain the macabre vision of the 18 niches where dead friars were propped up in a seated position until their bodies became naturally mummified. In 2013, the museum initiated a series of guided tours that begin at the museum and visit various parts of the city; at present, they are offered only in Catalan. A new summer program also combines gastronomic dinners and dancing to live music in the cellars of the museum during July and Aug.

Carrer de la Força 27. ℰ **97-222-22-29.** www.ajuntament.gi/museuciutat. Admission 4€ adults, 2€ students and seniors, free for children 16 and under. Tues–Sat 10am–2pm and 5–7pm; Sun 10am–2pm.

PLANNING YOUR TRIP TO SPAIN

G etting to Spain is relatively easy, especially for those who live in western Europe or in eastern North America. If all your documents are in order, you should clear Customs and Immigration smoothly. The staffs of entry ports into Spain often speak English, and they'll usually speed you on your way.

GETTING THERE

By Plane

FROM THE U.S.   See "Essentials" in Madrid (p. 44) and Barcelona (p. 157) chapters.

FROM CANADA   Air Canada (www.aircanada.com; ✆ 888/247-2262) flies from Vancouver, Toronto, and Montreal to gateway cities in Europe, where code-share connections with Lufthansa continue to Madrid and Barcelona.

FROM THE U.K.   **British Airways** (www.britishairways.com; ✆ 0844-493-0787) and **Iberia** (www.iberia.com; ✆ 0870-609-0500 in London) are the two major carriers flying between London and Spain. The Midlands is served by flights from Manchester and Birmingham. British newspapers are filled with classified advertisements touting "slashed" fares to Spain. A travel agent can advise you on the best values at the intended time of your departure.

FROM AUSTRALIA   The most popular option is **Qantas/British Airways** (www.qantas.com.au; ✆ 612/13-13-13), which flies daily via Asia and London. Other popular and cheaper options are Qantas/Lufthansa via Asia and Frankfurt; Qantas/Air France via Asia and Paris; and Alitalia via Bangkok and Rome. The most direct option is offered by Singapore Airlines, with just one stop in Singapore.

By Car

If you're touring the rest of Europe in a rented car, you might, for an added cost, be allowed to drop off your vehicle in Madrid or Barcelona.

Highway approaches to Spain are across France on expressways. The most popular border crossing is near Biarritz, but there are 17 other border stations between Spain and France. Driving time from Paris to Barcelona takes about 9½ hours without stops, to Madrid about 12 hours without stops.

By Train

If you're already in Europe, you might want to reach Spain by train, especially if you have a Eurailpass. Even without a pass, you'll find that the cost of a train ticket is relatively moderate. With the widespread use of high-speed rail in Spain, all Spanish tracks are compatible with the rest of Europe except the narrow-gauge tracks used in Basque Country. For long journeys, seat and sleeper reservations are mandatory. For more information, visit www.renfe.com or call ✆ **91-631-38-00.**

The most comfortable and fastest trains in Spain are the AVE, Alvia, and Alaris. However, you pay a supplement to ride on these fast trains. Both first- and second-class fares are available. Tickets can be purchased in the United States or Canada from Rail Europe (see below) or from any reputable travel agent. Confirmation of your reservation takes about a week.

To go from London to Spain by rail, you'll need to transfer not only from the train but also from the rail terminus in Paris. A TGV from Paris to Barcelona takes less than 7 hours. Paris directly to Madrid takes 14-15 hours.

By Bus

Bus travel to Spain is possible but usually a waste of precious time. (Service from London will take 24 hr. or more.) But coach services do operate regularly from major capitals of western Europe and, once they're in Spain, usually head for Madrid or Barcelona. The major bus line running from London to Spain is **Eurolines Limited** (www.nationalexpress.com; ✆ **0871-781-8181**).

GETTING AROUND

By Plane

By European standards, domestic flights within Spain are relatively inexpensive, and make sense for travel to the islands. Otherwise, train travel is as fast and cheaper. For reservations on the national airline, **Iberia,** call ✆ **800/772-4642** or visit www.iberia.com. **Iberia, Vueling** (www.vueling.com; ✆ **906-754-75-41** in Spain) and **Air Europa** (www.aireuropa.com; ✆ **90-240-15-01** in Spain) offer 12 to 19 flights a day each way between Madrid and Barcelona.

By Car

A car offers the greatest flexibility while you're touring, but public transit is almost always nearly as convenient and less expensive. That's especially true for daytrips from Madrid and Barcelona.

RENTALS See "Getting Around" in the Madrid and Barcelona chapters for details on car rentals. For best mileage and least-expensive touring, rent a hybrid vehicle or one that runs on clean diesel fuel.

DRIVING RULES Spaniards drive on the right-hand side of the road. Drivers should pass on the left; local drivers sound their horns when passing another car and flash their lights at you if you're driving slowly (slowly for high-speed Spain) in the left lane. Autos coming from the right have the right of way.

Spain's express highways are known as autopistas, which charge a toll, and autovías, which don't. To exit in Spain, follow the SALIDA (exit) sign, except in Catalunya, where the exit sign in Catalan says SORTIDA. On most express highways, the speed limit is 120kmph (75 mph). On other roads, speed limits range from 90kmph to 100kmph (56–62 mph). You will see many drivers far exceeding these limits.

If you must drive through a Spanish city, try to avoid morning and evening rush hours. Never park your car facing oncoming traffic, which is against the law. If you are fined by the Guardia Civil de Tráfico (highway patrol), you must pay on the spot. Penalties for drinking and driving are very stiff.

BREAKDOWNS   On a major motorway you'll find strategically placed emergency phone boxes. On secondary roads, call for help by asking the operator to locate the nearest Guardia Civil, which will put you in touch with a garage that can tow you to a repair shop.

The Spanish affiliate of AAA and the British AA, **Real Automóvil Club de España** (**RACE;** www.race.es; ✆ **90-240-45-45**), can provide limited assistance in the event of a breakdown and also provides helpful information about road conditions.

GASOLINE (PETROL)   Most service stations in Madrid and Barcelona are open 24 hours a day and are self-service. All gas is unleaded—gasolina sin plomo. Many vehicles run on clean diesel fuel called Gasoleo A or on Biodiesel. Most stations will accept credit cards.

By Train

The best way to get around Spain is by train, even for a relatively long-distance connection like that between Madrid and Barcelona. In practice, it's faster and less expensive to take the train between the two cities than to fly. High-speed rail lines using the AVE and Alvia trains have reduced travel time between Madrid and Barcelona to only 2½ hours. If you are only visiting the cities outlined in this book, you will save the most money by purchasing each ticket a la carte at a RENFE office in Spain (www.renfe.com; ✆ **91-631-38-00**).

You should, however, investigate whether you are eligible for one of RENFE's discount programs. The **Carné Joven** is available to anyone between ages 14 and 26 who holds a GO 25 (IYTC) Card, available through local travel agencies. It provides a 20 percent discount on all train fares. The **Tarjeta Dorada** card provides discounts of 25-40 percent. It is available to anyone 60 years or older but must be purchased at a RENFE station with proof of identity. The card costs 5.15€ and is valid for 1 year.

If you're planning more extensive train travel, consider a **Eurail Spain Pass.** It entitles you to unlimited rail travel in Spain. It is available for 3 to 10 days of travel within 2 months in either first or second class. For 3 days within 2 months, the cost is $301 in first class or $242 in second class; for 10 days within 2 months, the charge is $613 in first class or $491 in second class. Children 4 to 11 pay half fare on any of these discount passes. For more information, consult a travel agent or **Rail Europe** (www.raileurope.com; ✆ **877/272-RAIL** [272-7245]).

By Bus

Bus service in Spain is extensive, low priced, and comfortable enough for short distances. Generally, commuter rail is faster and more convenient. A bus ride between two major cities in Spain, such as from Madrid to Barcelona, is about two-thirds the price of a train ride and takes about three times longer. Almost every bus schedule in Spain is available on the **Movelia** website (www.movelia.es), which also provides a means for purchasing tickets through the Internet if you have access to a printer.

[FastFACTS] SPAIN

ATMs/Banks See "Fast Facts" in Madrid (p. 51) and Barcelona (p. 163) chapters.

Business Hours See "Fast Facts" in Madrid (p. 51) and Barcelona (p. 163) chapters.

Customs In practice, you can bring your usual personal effects with you into Spain. In theory, you are permitted the following items duty-free: one portable typewriter, and one video camera or two still cameras with 10 rolls of film each; one portable radio, one tape recorder, and one laptop per person, provided they show signs of use; 400 cigarettes, or 50 cigars, or 250 grams of tobacco; and 2 liters of wine or 1 liter of liquor per person ages 18 and over. For sports equipment you are allowed fishing gear, one bicycle, skis, tennis or squash racquets, and golf clubs.

Disabled Travelers Because of Spain's many hills and endless flights of stairs, visitors with disabilities may have difficulty getting around the country, but conditions are slowly improving. Newer hotels are more sensitive to the needs of those with disabilities, and the more expensive restaurants, in general, are wheelchair accessible. To ease planning, you might consider taking an organized tour specifically designed to accommodate travelers with disabilities. Check **Flying Wheels Travel** (www.flyingwheelstravel.com; ☎ **877/451-5006** or 507/451-5005) or **Accessible Journeys** (www.disabilitytravel.com; ☎ **800/846-4537** or 610/521-0339).

Organizations that offer a vast range of resources and assistance to travelers with disabilities include **MossRehab** (www.mossresourcenet.org; ☎ **800/CALL-MOSS** [225-5667]); the **American Foundation for the Blind** (**AFB;** www.afb.org; ☎ **800/232-5463**); and **SATH** (Society for Accessible Travel & Hospitality; www.sath.org; ☎ **212/447-7284**). **AirAmbulanceCard.com** (☎ **877/424-7633**) is now partnered with SATH and allows you to preselect top-notch hospitals in case of an emergency.

Access-Able Travel Source (www.access-able.com) offers a comprehensive database on travel agents from around the world with experience in accessible travel; destination-specific access information; and links to such resources as service animals, equipment rentals, and access guides.

Flying with Disability (www.flying-with-disability.org) is a comprehensive information source on airplane travel. The "Accessible Travel" link at Mobility-Advisor.com (www.mobility-advisor.com) offers a variety of travel resources to persons with disabilities. British travelers should contact Tourism for All (www.tourismforall.org.uk; ☎ 0845/124-9971 in the U.K. only) to access travel information and resources for seniors and those with disabilities.

Doctors & Dentists See "Fast Facts" in Madrid (p. 51) and Barcelona (p. 163) chapters.

Drinking Laws The legal drinking age is 18. Bars, taverns, and cafeterias usually open at 8am, and many serve alcohol to 1:30am or later. Generally, you can purchase alcoholic beverages at almost any market.

Drugstores See "Fast Facts" in Madrid (p. 51) and Barcelona (p. 163) chapters.

Electricity The U.S. and Canada use 110-volt electricity, Spain 220-volt. Most low-voltage electronics, such as laptops, iPods, and cellphone chargers, will do fine with 220-volt. It's still smart to check with the manufacturer to determine if your appliance will handle a voltage switch. If it can't, a voltage converter can be used. Small adapters change a plug from a North American flat prong to a Spanish round prong so that you can fit it into a local socket, but they don't work as electrical converters. Adapters are sold at most ferreterías (hardware stores) in Spain, but converters are hard to come by. It's better to purchase one before flying off to Spain.

Embassies & Consulates See "Fast Facts" in Madrid (p. 51) and Barcelona (p. 163) chapters.

Emergencies The national emergency number for Spain is 🕿 112. For other emergency numbers call: 🕿 091 for the national police, 🕿 092 for the local police, 🕿 080 to report a fire, or 🕿 061 for an ambulance.

Health Tap water is safe to drink but many travelers prefer bottled or mineral water. Fish and shellfish from the Mediterranean should only be eaten cooked; sushi and sashimi from Atlantic fish are safe to be eaten raw.

If a medical emergency arises, your hotel staff can usually put you in touch with a reliable doctor. If not, contact the American embassy or a consulate; each maintains a list of English-speaking doctors. For medical and hospital services, be sure that you have appropriate insurance before you travel. We list hospital and emergency numbers in the "Fast Facts" sections for Madrid and Barcelona.

Insurance For information on traveler's insurance, trip cancellation insurance, and medical insurance, please visit www.frommers.com/tips.

Internet See "Fast Facts" in Madrid (p. 51) and Barcelona (p. 163).

LGBT Travelers In 1978, Spain legalized homosexuality among consenting adults. In April 1995, the parliament of Spain banned discrimination based on sexual orientation. And in 2005, gay marriage was legalized across Spain. Madrid and Barcelona are the major centers of gay life in Spain. Sitges (south of Barcelona) is a popular gay resort.

Legal Aid In case of trouble with the authorities, contact your local embassy or consulate, which will recommend an English-speaking lawyer.

Mail See "Fast Facts" in Madrid (p. 51) and Barcelona (p. 163) chapters.

Mobile Phones You can probably use your North American cellphone in Spain if it is GSM/GPRS compatible and uses a SIM card. Virtually all cellphones in Spain operate with this system, as do AT&T and T-Mobile cellphones from North America. Most mobile phones from the U.K. are compatible. Even if your phone is compatible with the system that operates in Spain, you'll probably need to have it unlocked, which means taking it to one of the small shops in Spain that offer this service (look for a SE LIBRAN MÓVILES sign; expect to pay 20€). Roaming charges for U.S.-based phones, even after you successfully convert them, are

more expensive than using a Spanish cellphone plan.

Many travelers opt to simply buy a prepaid cellphone on location. **Vodafone** (www.vodafone.com), **Movistar** (aka Telefónica; www.movistar.com), **Orange** (www.orange.es), and **Yoigo** (www.yoigo.com) are the four largest and most reliable mobile phone service providers in Spain. Movistar is the oldest and most established.

You can buy a mobile phone in Spain through either the providers' specific dealer networks or at independent electronics stores or department stores like El Corte Inglés. Generally, the prices for new mobile phones in Spain start at 25€ for the cheapest models.

In Spain, whoever makes the cellphone call pays the charges, whether it's to or from either a landline or mobile phone. (Unlike what generally happens in the U.S., the receiving phone is not charged.) Whoever makes the call pays for the call connection and for the usage, which is charged per second. Also, most rates don't include IVA (VAT tax), which is charged at 22%.

You can recharge your prepaid phone with additional saldo (credit) at grocery stores, tobacco shops, phone stores, bank machines, and even with online banking.

Money & Costs The ongoing economic crisis has cut demand in Spain, resulting in very slow inflation of meal and room costs. Paying in anything but euros will cost you dearly. Either use credit cards or withdraw euros from ATMs. The official exchange rate is published daily by the European Central Bank: www.ecb. europa.eu.

In Spain, many prices for children—ages 6 to 17—are lower than for adults. Admissions for seniors (60, 62, or 65, depending on venue) are also reduced.

Bring a mix of cash and credit cards. Exchange enough petty cash to cover airport incidentals, tipping, and transportation to your hotel before you leave home, or withdraw money upon arrival at an airport ATM, which often offers the best exchange rates. Avoid exchanging money at commercial exchange bureaus and hotels.

Newspapers & Magazines See "Fast Facts" in Madrid (p. 51) and Barcelona (p. 163) chapters.

Packing For helpful information on packing, go to Frommers.com and follow the links to the "Packing Tips" section of the website.

Safety See "Fast Facts" in Madrid (p. 51) and Barcelona (p. 163) chapters for city tips on safety. Report loss or theft of a passport immediately to the police and nearest embassy or consulate.

Senior Travel Major discounts are available to seniors in Spain, including reduced rates on most admissions, and reduced fares on public conveyances. Special room rates are also available at the national parador network.

Smoking In 2006, Spain banned smoking in the workplace, and on January 1, 2011, included restaurants, bars, and nightclubs in the ban. Smoking is also banned on public transportation and in other areas such as cultural centers.

Student Travel Obtain an International Student Identity Card (ISIC) for savings on rail passes, air travel, and entrance fees. The card is available from STA Travel (www.sta.com; ✆ 800/781-4040 in North America) If you're not a student but under 26, get an International Youth Travel Card (IYTC) from the same source for some discounts, but not reduced museum admission. Travel CUTS (www.travelcuts.com; ✆ 800/667-2887) offers the services for Canadian and U.S. residents.

Taxes The internal sales tax (known in Spain as IVA) ranges 8-33 percent, depending on the commodity being sold. Tax refunds for non-E.U. visitors are no longer available.

Tipping Restaurant and hotel bills include their service charges—usually 15 percent of the bill. However, that doesn't mean you should skip out of a place without dispensing an extra euro or two. Some guidelines:

Your **hotel porter** should get 1€ per bag. **Chambermaids** should be given at least 1€ per day. Tip **doormen** 1€ for assisting with baggage or calling a cab. If you've used **concierge** services a lot, 20€ would be an appropriate tip. In less expensive hotels, you generally tip much less, perhaps 1€ or 2€ for some minor service rendered.

In restaurants, it is customary to tip extra—in fact, the **waiter** will expect a tip. Some Spanish diners leave nothing if the service was bad. More generous diners tip 5-10 percent for good service.

Barbers and hairdressers expect a 10-15 percent tip. Tour guides expect 2€, although a tip is not mandatory. For cabdrivers, add about 10 percent to the fare as shown on the meter.

Toilets In Spain they're called aseos, servicios, or lavabos and are labeled caballeros for men and damas or señoras for women. Museums are the most reliable locations for public facilities. Otherwise, order a drink in a bar or cafe in order to use their servicios.